THE LITERARY MIND AND THE
CARVING OF DRAGONS

by Liu Hsieh

NUMBER LVIII OF THE

RECORDS OF CIVILIZATION: SOURCES AND STUDIES

The Literary Mind and the Carving of Dragons

BY LIU HSIEH

A STUDY OF THOUGHT AND PATTERN

IN CHINESE LITERATURE

Translated

WITH AN INTRODUCTION AND NOTES

by Vincent Yu-chung Shih

IN LITTERIS
LIBERTAS ∴

1754·1893

New York Columbia University Press 1959

The addition to the "Records of Civilization: Sources and Studies" of a group of translations of Oriental historical materials, of which this volume is one, was made possible by funds granted by Carnegie Corporation of New York. That Corporation is not, however, the author, owner, publisher, or proprietor of this publication, and is not to be understood as approving by virtue of its grant any of the statements made or views expressed therein.

RECORDS OF CIVILIZATION
SOURCES AND STUDIES

*EDITED UNDER THE AUSPICES OF THE
DEPARTMENT OF HISTORY, COLUMBIA UNIVERSITY*

GENERAL EDITOR

JACQUES BARZUN, *Professor of History*

EDITORS EMERITI

JAMES T. SHOTWELL, *Bryce Professor Emeritus of the History of International Relations*

AUSTIN P. EVANS, *Professor Emeritus of History*

EDITOR: EUROPEAN RECORDS

JOHN H. MUNDY, *Associate Professor of History*

EDITORS: ORIENTAL RECORDS

C. MARTIN WILBUR, *Professor of Chinese History*

WM. THEODORE DE BARY, *Associate Professor of Chinese and Japanese*

CONSULTING EDITORS

SALO W. BARON, *Professor of Jewish History, Literature, and Institutions on the Miller Foundation; Director of the Center of Israeli Studies*

GILBERT HIGHET, *Anthon Professor of the Latin Language and Literature*

DONALD KEENE, *Associate Professor of Japanese*

PAUL O. KRISTELLER, *Professor of Philosophy*

GARRETT MATTINGLY, *Professor of History*

ACKNOWLEDGMENTS

I am greatly indebted to the Graduate School of the University of Washington for giving me grants from both the Graduate School Research Fund and the Agnes Anderson Research Fund which made it possible for me to devote two summers to my study of Chinese literary criticism; I am also grateful to Columbia University for including my translation of the *Wen-hsin tiao-lung* in the Records of Civilization Series. I wish also to thank Mrs. Beverly Plank for editing and typing a part of the manuscript, and Mrs. Mercedes MacDonald and Mrs. Margaret T. Myers for typing and proofreading the other part of it. Above all, I owe much to Mrs. Julia Lin for her assistance in collecting material for the introduction, and to the selfless help Mrs. Jacqueline Garnett has given me in reading over the whole manuscript, suggesting appropriate terms, polishing the English, and improving the style. Without Mrs. Garnett's generous assistance, the translation would not have the form it now has. But I alone am responsible for both the translation itself and the final form in which it appears.

VINCENT YU-CHUNG SHIH

University of Washington
September 3, 1957

CONTENTS

INTRODUCTION

Liu Hsieh (c. A.D. 465-522), in his *Wen-hsin tiao-lung*, or *The Literary Mind and the Carving of Dragons*, gives a comprehensive treatment of literary theories and critical opinions from the earliest period to his own time. As a critic, his genius is demonstrated by the exhaustive and penetrating manner in which he deals with literary and rhetorical problems. For a better understanding of his insight, a brief survey of the development of literary criticism in ancient China will be of great help, for here we shall find the main sources of his inspiration.

Literary opinions in ancient China developed and expanded as literary writing advanced. The first traces of such opinions are found in the *Book of History*. "Poetry is the expression of sentiments, and songs are these expressions set to music. Tones are prolonged according to rules of prosody and intervals chosen according to rules of harmony."[1] This theory of poetry as the expression of sentiments was to exert a tremendous influence upon subsequent critics. The idea was first elaborated in the "Great Preface" to the *Book of Poetry*, believed to be the work of Wei Hung of the Later Han (flourishing about A.D. 25). Since then it has appeared in one form or another in the works of the most important critics, including Lu Chi of the Chin (261-303), and Liu Hsieh and Chung Hung of the Liang (flourishing during the latter part of the fifth and the first part of the sixth centuries). Poetry was conceived to be predominantly lyrical in nature, and intimately linked to music. The songs and odes in the *Book of Poetry* conform very well to this pattern—a pattern which may be considered purely literary.

The philosophical period in ancient China was in many ways analogous to the golden era of classical Greece. Many incidental remarks on literature were made by philosophers, whose primary interest was not in literature as such, but rather in philosophical truth. Thus their

[1] *Shang-shu t'ung-chien* (Peking, 1936), 02/0681-0692.

critical judgment was basically ethical rather than esthetic. In China, Confucius and others after him valued art chiefly for its moral effect on the conduct of the people, frequently mixing moral with literary and poetic issues. In Greece Plato, alarmed by the unhealthy effect of poetry, banished poets from his city state. Of the two, Confucius was perhaps the more enlightened. He not only included poetry as one of his main texts for instruction but also told his son and disciples to study and imitate its disciplined artistry in order to improve their ability to express themselves.[2] He also reminded his students of the importance of literary ornament, without which truth will not travel far.[3]

This apparent love of beauty of form on the part of Confucius, however, is completely overbalanced by his underlying utilitarian motive. This utilitarian attitude is most clearly indicated by his remarks on the *Book of Poetry*. He said:

The odes can stimulate the mind, train the observation, encourage social intercourse, and enable one to give vent to his complaint. From them one may learn how to fulfil the immediate duty to one's father, and the remote duty to one's ruler. And in them one may become widely acquainted with the names of birds, beasts, plants, and trees.[4]

Once he characterized the whole *Book of Poetry* by one single line: "It has no undisciplined thought."[5] The virtues of the *Poetry* being such, no Aristotelian defense of the poetic art is necessary.

However, it would be unjust to say that Confucius lacked esthetic appreciation and sensitivity. We are told that at one time he was so enthralled by the beauty of the *Shao*[6] that for three months he did not know the taste of meat.[7] This subjective experience, however, did not influence his attitude toward art. Because of his authority elsewhere, his didacticism was also firmly established as one of the chief traditions in the field of literary criticism.

---

[2] *Li-chi yin-te*, 32/26.
[3] *Ch'un-ch'iu ching-chuan yin-te*, 307/Hsiang 25, fu 2.
[4] *Lun-yü yin-te*, 36/17/8.   [5] *Ibid.*, 2/2/2.
[6] A musical score attributed to Shun, one of the legendary rulers.
[7] *Lun-yü yin-te*, 12/7/14.

After Confucius came Mencius and Hsüntzu, who continued to perpetuate and develop this tradition. Both Mencius and Hsüntzu were classical scholars, quoting the Six Classics extensively in their works. In their discourse on the *Poetry*, both emphasized the ethical and cultural values as did the Master. Mencius, however, with his idealism and mystical leanings, was able to adopt a freer approach to literary problems. Maintaining that the *Poetry* should be elucidated in an enlightened manner, he said:

Therefore, those who comment upon the *Book of Poetry* should not because of one term misconstrue the meaning of a sentence, and should not because of a sentence misconstrue the original idea. They must try with their thoughts to meet that idea, and then they will apprehend it.[8]

This plan for a freer interpretation of creative literature displays an insight unique in antiquity.

It is true that a purely intuitive or subjective judgment is extremely hazardous and in many instances nothing more than a wild guess, too farfetched to be valid. Very often it is the personal impression of the critic, expressive of his emotional approval or disapproval. However, a subjective judgment is not entirely without merit. At a time when criticism was still in its infancy, sincere opinion was a contribution in itself.[9]

The evil of Mencius' subjective approach is mitigated somewhat by another theory of his that a work should not be considered in isolation, but in the total context of the life and time of the author.[10] Unfortunately, not many critics who believe in subjective criticism and intuitive evaluation are able to balance their view by a historical consideration as Mencius advocated.[11]

An even more important contribution is contained in the famous theory of *yang-ch'i*, the fostering of the vital spirit or breath. The nature

---

[8] *Meng-tzu yin-te*, 36/5A/4.

[9] The evil effect of this subjective criticism will be clearly seen when we come to deal with the "Prefaces" to the *Book of Poetry*.

[10] *Meng-tzu yin-te*, 42/5B/8.

[11] Cheng Hsüan of the Later Han wrote his *Shih-p'u* on the basis of historical criticism.

of this breath or spirit (*ch'i*), as conceived by Mencius, is clearly ethical. Mencius said,

> Such is the breath (*ch'i*): it is most great and most strong. Being fostered by uprightness and sustaining no injury, it fills up all between heaven and earth.
>
> Such is the breath: it is the correlate of righteousness (*i*) and moral principle (*tao*). Without it man is starved. It is produced by the accumulation of righteous deeds, and not to be obtained by incidental acts of righteousness.[12]

It is clear that the term *ch'i* (breath, or vital life or spirit) stands for that moral quality which is attained through a moral life. Yet in a later development, it seems to have undergone a shift in meaning, a shift from the moralistic pure and simple to a sense which is at once moral and esthetic. It is in this latter sense that the term *ch'i* achieved prominence in literary and critical nomenclature, for it became a criterion by which both the talent of a writer and the quality of his work were judged and appraised.

Hsüntzu held a more practical view of literature than did Mencius. To him, the only validity of literature lies in its usefulness, an opinion originally found in Confucius and further strengthened by the utilitarian Mohists. However, being concerned with the principle of social conduct and the ways and means of producing social harmony, Hsüntzu was able to see some value in *wen-hsüeh*, i.e., literature, in its beautifying effect upon man's character.[13] The problem here is the sense in which he used the term *wen-hsüeh*, generally translated "literature." From the context it seems clear that Hsüntzu meant by it learning in general. The concept of literature as we understand it today was not clearly delineated until the Han period. Prior to the Han, the concept of pure literature did not seem to have emerged except when poetry was specifically referred to. This lack of a clear distinction between literature and learning may have been one of the reasons why poetry, which had a glorious start as pure literature, gradually came to assume

---

[12] *Meng-tzu yin-te*, 11/2A/2.
[13] *Hsüntzu* (Chu-tzu chi-ch'eng ed.), chüan 19, Chapter 27, p. 334.

the function of moral didacticism. This is nowhere better illustrated than in the case of Hsüntzu who, more than anybody else, quoted the *Book of Poetry* at every turn to demonstrate his moral points.

As a philosopher, Hsüntzu was naturalistic. Despite this tendency, he seems to have probed deep into the origin and nature of creative activities, and to have emerged in the end with a reasonable explanation of the psychology of creative processes. Observe his penetrating insight in his discussion of the principle of music:

Music is the expression of joy. This is something which human feelings made unavoidable. For man cannot be without joy. And when there is joy, it must be expressed in sound and given embodiment through movement and repose. This is the way with man. In sounds, movements, and pauses are expressed all the changes in his mood. Hence man cannot be without joy, and when there is joy, it must have a physical embodiment. When this embodiment does not conform to right principles, there will be disorder. The early kings hated disorder, and so they established the music of the *Ya* and *Sung* to guide it. They caused its music to be joyful and not to degenerate, and its beauty to be distinct and not limited. They caused it in its indirect and direct appeals, its completeness and simplicity, its frugality and richness, its rests and notes to stir up the goodness in men's minds and to prevent evil feelings from gaining any foothold. This is the manner in which the early kings established music.[14]

The function of music, accordingly, is to regulate and harmonize human emotions, and this inner harmony serves as the basis for the achievement of social harmony through *li*, the principle of social conduct which is the outer counterpart of the inner principle of *yüeh*, or music. In view of the intimate relation between music and poetry, Hsüntzu's theory could not but exercise great influence on subsequent poetics.

Not all philosophers shared this didactic view of poetry with the Confucians. Taoism, with its principle of *Tao* in the realm of meta-

---

[14] *Ibid.*, chüan 14, Chapter 20, p. 252. Bodde's translation of Fung Yu-lan's *History of Chinese Philosophy* (Princeton University Press, 1952), I, 342. The first four lines are also found in the *Li-chi* with minor modification, suggesting a different reading, which seems to make better sense. On this basis I have taken the liberty of making some changes in the translation.

physics and the principle of nonaction on the plane of experience, would have nothing to do with either institution or words. Therefore, in the Taoist system of thought, there is no room for literature, because for the Taoists language oftener obstructs than assists the communication of ideas; it is to be tolerated only as a suggestive aid to the attainment of truth, and to be discarded the moment truth is obtained. The inability of language to convey truth is imbedded in the very nature of language itself. Language is a system of symbols designed for the communication of ideas born of common experience. But truth, according to the Taoists, is a mystical state which, being unique, cannot be expressed in language devised for the conveyance of experience common to all who use the same language. But paradoxically, it was Chuangtzu, the most noted Taoist, who wrote some of the most imaginative literature of his time, and provided the literary world with vivid descriptions of his mystical insight into the inner process of creation. His philosophical writings, essentially mystical in nature and allegorical in form, are characterized with distinct originality and unique spontaneity. They are further marked by a keen poetic sensitivity and an acute esthetic awareness, qualities extremely rare in an age suffering from stifling dogmatism and paucity of imagination.

The transcendental mysticism which permeates all of Chuangtzu's works finally crystallizes in the concept of *shen* (the spiritual or divine), which has since become the most important word in our critical terminology. The supreme state of *shen* is sometimes described as the "realm of pure experience." It is true that both Mencius and Chuangtzu held mystical experience as the highest aim of self-cultivation, but their means of reaching this ultimate goal are different. In the case of Mencius, it was through "an accumulation of righteous deeds," or to be more specific, through acting "with a vigorous effort at altruism." But Chuangtzu, instead of following the conventional ethical approach, which he openly condemned, took an intuitive and mystical approach. The life of "pure experience" is a state which transcends both the human senses and the intellect, a state in which one forgets the entire world, including his own existence. In such a state, one attains that sudden enlightenment in which one experiences union with the universe. Such is Chuangtzu's mysticism, and such is his vision of the Supreme State.

His concept of *shen*, when applied to the process of creation, led him to another vision which is equally mystical and equally transcendental, that is, the vision of an effortless creativity born of perfect understanding and comprehension. This creativity is illustrated in parables of the Master Butcher, the Wheelwright, and many others.[15] It is a process which the artist intuits but is unable either to describe or to impart.

Chuangtzu, in his outspoken condemnation of all established institutions, including language itself, challenged the very standards which provided the primary tests of literary values of his time. In so doing, he foreshadowed a fresh outlook in art and a new esthetic interest in later generations. If Confucius contributed the essential ethical basis for traditional criticism in China, Chuangtzu awakened an esthetic sensitivity which is even more essential to literary criticism. Moreover, the term *shen* is responsible for a highly mystical and impressionistic interpretation of literature which has assumed an equally important role in the history of Chinese literary criticism.

The Former Han period is relatively barren as far as literary theory is concerned. The supremacy of Han Confucianism, which was brought about during the reign of Emperor Wu (141-87 B.C.) through the influence of Tung Chung-shu (flourishing 179-93 B.C.), may be considered the crowning stage of an effort at the unification of thought initiated during the time of the first emperor of the preceding Ch'in dynasty. Such a unification may have stifled individual initiative during that time, for Confucius, from being honored simply as a great teacher, was finally canonized as a deity, and his words became sacred utterances to be reverentially followed with unquestioning faith.

However, the dearth of critical speculations does not imply paucity of literary creation. There were writers in plenty who, under the influence of the Ch'u poets, wrote a type of melodic and highly adorned

[15] *Chuangtzu yin-te*, 7-8/3/2-12; 36/13/68-74.

prose known as the *fu*. This outburst of literary activity brought about a clear conception of literature as distinct from learning in general. From now on we can speak of literature without a feeling of uncertainty as to what is meant by the term.

Rich experience in writing is often a *sine qua non* to a profound understanding of the nature of literature. The conception of "the mind of *fu*" held by Ssu-ma Hsiang-ju (c. 179-117 B.C.) seems to confirm this. When people questioned Ssu-ma as to the nature of *fu*, he is reported to have said:

The form which we create by means of weaving and the substance which we cause to body forth in brocade are the results of the interlacing of the warp and the woof and the organizing of *kung* and *shang* [i.e., musical tones]. These are the external traces of the *fu*. But the mind of a *fu* writer encompasses the whole universe, and holds in its view everything from human beings to the inanimate world. This encompassing vision is born within, and is not to be transmitted.[16]

Later, Yang Hsiung (53 B.C.-A.D. 18) spoke of Ssu-ma Hsiang-ju's *fu* as "not from the human world." For to Yang, it was divine: "It is the product of one who has attained the state of spiritual transformation."[17] Here we see a community of spirit between Ssu-ma Hsiang-ju and Chuangtzu in the conception of *shen*, which was later expressed by Wei-wen (Ts'ao P'ei, 187-226) in his conception of *ch'i*.

The years between the Former and the Later Han are important years in the annals of Chinese literary criticism. We have mentioned Wei Hung's elaboration of the classical definition of poetry, and Cheng Hsüan's application of Mencius's historical method to his own consideration and arrangement of poems in the *Book of Poetry*. Let us dwell a little more fully on Wei Hung.

Wei Hung's elaboration of the classical definition of poetry as the expression of the sentiments led to another important theory of literary development, which Wei treated in his "Great Preface,"[18] a most

16 *Hsi-ching cha-chi* (Han-wei ts'ung-shu ed.), chüan 2, pp. 4b-5a.
17 *Ibid.*, chüan 3, p. 6a.
18 Shen Chung of the Northern Chou (500-583) attributed the "Great Preface" to Tzu-hsia, a disciple of Confucius; Fan Yeh of Liu Sung (398-445), in his *Hou-han-shu*,

important document in the annals of literary criticism. He believed that the nature of poetry was determined by the nature of government. The intimate relationship between poetry and government was thought to be derived from the fact that, since the function of poetry is to express the sentiments, and since we must assume the sentiments to be genuine and the expression spontaneous, poetry becomes the most concrete and articulate manifestation of the people's attitude toward the government. If the government is good, poetry will reflect joy and satisfaction; and if the government is bad, poetry will reflect the people's resentment and complaint. We must give the ancient rulers credit for being shrewd enough to go to poetry for information about the quality of local government and the feelings of the people, if the tradition concerning the collection of poetry for political purposes can be trusted.

As a descriptive principle, there is nothing wrong with this theory. It is just a special application of the general theory that art, however fortuitously, reflects life—a meaningful statement even in modern times. In ancient China, this theory had a wider application. When Prince Chi-cha of Wu visited the state of Lu, he is reported to have been able to pass perfect judgment on the government of different states by listening to their music.[19] But when a critic follows this theory in his interpretation or a poet attempts to conform to it, the theory exerts a harmful influence. Since the writing of the "Great and Lesser Prefaces," beautiful poems in the *Book of Poetry* have been so burdened with allegorical and moral lessons that the genuine feelings expressed in them are completely overlooked.

As a corollary, poetry was assigned a new function utterly extraneous to itself: it was made to remonstrate with and admonish the superior. For it was believed that to admonish by means of poetic devices, such as metaphors, allegories, and parables, was both effective and safe. As late as the T'ang dynasty, we still find Po Chü-i (772-846) obsessed

---

"Ju-lin chuan," and Cheng Ch'iao of Sung (1104-1162), in his *Shih-hsü pien*, both attributed it to Wei Hung, and their opinion has been accepted by scholars.

[19] *Ch'un-ch'iu ching-chuan yin-te*, 326-327/Hsiang 29/8 Tso.

with the desire to be remembered as a poet who has given the world moral insight to serve as a guide to life.

The theory that art reflects the conditions of the time presupposes extreme sensitivity on the part of the artist or poet to the ever-changing situations and needs of the time. Faced with such a fluid world, he naturally varies his moods in response to it, producing quite spontaneously different literary and artistic forms. All this is either well described or implied in Wei Hung's "Preface." This principle has been known as the principle of flexible adaptability. But strangely enough, he failed to take the one step more which would have awakened him to the truth that any effort on the part of the artist or poet, in the face of the changing need, to hold on to the ancient truths will inevitably result in failure.

It was also in these years that classicism was reaffirmed and new paths were indicated. Yang Hsiung (53 B.C.-A.D. 18) may be said to be responsible for the former and Wang Ch'ung for the latter.

A Confucian scholar, a poet, and an academician turned "critic," Yang Hsiung seemed promising as a critic in his earlier career when he enthusiastically applauded the beautiful *fu* composed by Ssu-ma Hsiang-ju, the supreme architect of *fu* of an earlier generation. We have seen how once he was so moved by Ssu-ma's creative talent that he believed Ssu-ma Hsiang-ju's *fu* not to have come from this human world of ours. He was not only an admirer of Hsiang-ju's *fu*, but also an ardent imitator of his style. At this time he seemed capable of enjoying what is of sheer beauty and pure delight, revealing thus his unmistakable awareness of that undefinable act of intuition or vision out of which all art originates. His description of the works of Ssu-ma Hsiang-ju as *shen-hua* (spiritual or divine transformation) marks him as a believer in the theory that a genius is born and not taught. But with this pronouncement came the end of the early phase of his critical position.

In his biography, Yang Hsiung was described as a "lover of antiquity," a phrase which reveals his final allegiance and also his final critical standpoint. In the chapter "Wu-tzu" in his *Fa-yen*, he expressed deep regret for having wasted his youth in the writing of *fu,* and represented Ssu-ma Hsiang-ju's *fu,* which once elicited from him so great an admiration, as beautiful but useless.[20] He wrote the *T'ai-hsüan* (The great mystery) in imitation of the *Book of Changes* and the *Tao-te ching,* and the *Fa-yen* (Model sayings) in imitation of the *Analects,* indulging in the use of archaic expressions and obsolete words. This love of pedantic display invoked the ire both of his contemporaries and of later writers. Liu Hsin (c. 53 B.C.-A.D. 23), a contemporary and friend, described his works as fit only to cover pickle jars, and Su Shih of the Sung (1036-1101) believed that Yang Hsiung was trying to conceal his shallow scholarship behind the façade of pedantry.

The influence of Yang Hsiung's classicism on his criticism is clear. First of all, Yang Hsiung returned to Confucius as the source of all inspiration. He said,

Books, however excellent, are just bookstores if they are not based on the principle advocated by Confucius; and talks, however eloquent, are just the sound of petty bells when not based on the principle advocated by Confucius.[21]

And again,

Mountain paths are too numerous all to be walked over, and doors in walls are too numerous all to be entered. So it may be asked, "By what is one to walk or enter?" I reply, "By Confucius. Confucius is the door."[22]

Secondly, he returned to the Classics as the source of all wisdom. He said,

For discussing heaven, there is nothing more discerning than the *Book of Changes.* For discussing human affairs, there is nothing more discerning than the *Book of History.* For discussing the essential, there is nothing more discerning than the *Book of Rites.* For discussing sentiments, there is nothing more discerning than the *Book of Poetry.* For discussing principles, there is nothing more discerning than the *Annals of Spring and Autumn.*[23] As a result, Yang Hsiung adopted the simple and unadorned style of

---

[20] Yang Hsiung, *Fa-yen* (Chu-tzu chi-ch'eng ed.), chüan 2, p. 4.
[21] *Ibid.,* p. 6. [22] *Ibid.,* p. 5. [23] *Ibid.,* chüan 7, p. 19.

the Classics, the style advocated first in the *Book of History*: "In the choice of language one should emphasize the essential and should not indulge in the extraordinary.[24] In pronouncing that books which did not follow the style of the Classics were no books and words which did not conform to the style of the Classics were no words, for these were useless,[25] he had definitely reduced criticism to a set of dogmas which were to become infallible rules among writers and critics for a long time to come. He may be compared to the Scaligers, the Johnsons, and the Popes of the West. But like them, Yang Hsiung also succeeded in imparting to later generations a sense of perspective, a consciousness of traditions and a literary taste strengthened through an assimilation of the Classics.

Slightly later than Yang Hsiung, another Confucian scholar was also occupied with the ethical content and utilitarian function of literature. Wang Ch'ung (A.D. 27-c. 100) was, however, more concerned with history and philosophy. This preoccupation caused him to blur the distinction between pure literature and other forms of scholarly writings, reverting thus to the pre-Han conception of "literature." Hence it was philosophy and history that he had in mind when he asserted that all literature should be good and true, and should aim to instruct. This, however, did not blind him to the beauty of literature. To him all that is good and true was beautiful, requiring no additional labor to perfect it. And yet he would not go the whole way with Keats and chant that truth is beauty and beauty is truth. Wang's concern with historical truth committed him to a type of realism which condemned all kinds of literary exaggeration and embellishment that did not correspond to truth.[26] It is apparent that, despite his esthetic interest, he still considered truth the essence of literature, and this essence deter-mined for him both the quality and the form of literature.

By nature and interest, Wang Ch'ung was an excellent historian. His daring theory of history displays a liberalism unique in an age of

[24] *Shang-shu t'ung-chien*, 44/0218-0225.

[25] Yang Hsiung, *Fa-yen*, chüan 5, p. 14.

[26] For his criticism of exaggeration, see the following three chapters in his *Lun-heng*: "Yü-tseng," "I-tseng," and Ju-tseng."

dogmatism. When most of the writers were idealizing antiquity and slavishly imitating the Classics, he alone set out to attack that attitude. He said,

Those who in ancient times gave good government were sages, and those who in later times have given good government are likewise sages.[27]

Again,

Narrators of events like to exalt antiquity and disparage the present; they esteem what they know through hearsay and slight what they themselves see. Debaters discourse on what is long ago, and men of letters write on what is far away. The wonderful things near at hand the debaters do not mention, and the extraordinary events of our own time the writers do not record.[28]

In these words he broke away from the orthodox view of history that had hitherto dominated and still continued to dominate the minds of the writers in ancient China. Not only did he single out this traditional attitude for attack, but he even went so far as to assert that the present is better than the past. He said,

As far as the actual transformation effected by virtues are concerned, the Chou dynasty (1100 B.C.-256 B.C.) cannot exceed the Han (206 B.C.-A.D. 220), whereas if we speak about auspicious omens and prognostications, the Han excels the Chou. And if we measure their extent of territory, that of Chou was more limited than that of Han. How then is the Han not equal to the Chou? It may only be claimed that the Chou had many sages, whose government brought about universal peace. But the literati, in acclaiming the sages, go too far, placing them on such pedestals that their actual traces are lost. In acclaiming their government they are also too fulsome, treating of universal peace as something that has been cut off and has had no continuation.[29]

In short, history is progressive. To be realistic, literature has to be progressive too. Here we have an inkling of the principle of flexible adaptability to the varying needs of a changing world. We shall see this tendency to change reappear in Ke Hung of the Chin (c. 250-330).

[27] *Lun-heng*, "Ch'i-shih p'ien," p. 185.   [28] *Ibid.*, p. 187.
[29] *Ibid.*, "Hsüan-han p'ien," p. 191. Translations from the *Lun-heng* are adapted from Bodde's. See Fung Yu-lan, *History of Chinese Philosophy*, II, 158-59.

During the subsequent four centuries—the Three Kingdoms, the Wei and Chin, the Southern and Northern dynasties after the collapse of the Han Empire (220-589)—China was divided into many small states and dynasties, each in power for a short period and then giving way to others equally ephemeral. The land was constantly engulfed in warfare and political chaos; social upheaval and economic disruption were the order of the day. Yet, paradoxically, out of these chaotic conditions and destructive forces a most constructive phase of critical and creative vitality emerged. Among the various stages in the history of Chinese criticism, this period of disunity may be considered the most creative period.

At a time when all standards seemed to have collapsed, Confucianism likewise lost the prominent position which it enjoyed during the Han times. It is true that people still paid lip service to it, but many scholars and creative artists, disillusioned and embittered, turned more and more to Taoism and Buddhism. Literature, with a new emphasis on linguistic, tonal and formal structures, seemed to have come into its own, and its function became more esthetic in nature than morally didactic. An increasing interest in esthetic experience is shown in the writers' attempt to penetrate further into the nature of the creative process.

This esthetic awareness brought about the distinction between pure literature (*wen*) and useful literature (*pi*). And this distinction, once achieved, deepened the awareness which gave birth to it. The vivified consciousness was then able to lead creative literature and critical analysis to a new height of productivity. Many poets now found their primary occupation in verse writing; others, more scholarly, gave their attention to literary anthologies. Due to this sudden expansion of literary output, an increasing demand for critical judgment was felt. With the growing complexities of literature, which brought with them new problems, a re-examination of the basic principle of criticism became urgent, and it is not at all surprising that a movement of intensified critical analysis arose.

In both the West and in China, emperors and princes often played a prominent role as patrons of art. It was under the patronage of the great Medicis that Renaissance art flourished in Europe. And in China, there emerged during the dark age of political disunity a number of emperors and princes who were not only great patrons of art and literature but accomplished writers themselves. The real founder of the Wei dynasty, Ts'ao Ts'ao (155-220) was a competent poet; his younger son Ts'ao Chih (192-232) a poet of the highest calibre. Another son, Ts'ao P'ei (187-226), who usurped the throne from the Han and founded the Wei, also proved himself a talented poet and an astute critic, as well as a great patron of literature. He wrote the famous critical essay, the *Tien-lun lun-wen*.

The ruling house of the Liang dynasty was equally known for its artistic ability and interest in literature. Hsiao T'ung (501-531), who died an heir apparent and the patron of our author Liu Hsieh, compiled the famous *Wen-hsüan* (An anthology of literature), in the preface of which he accounted for excluding the Classics and historical works from his anthology, the reason being that they were not pure literature. Although the ethical considerations still prevailed, they were linked to esthetic considerations. Hsiao T'ung's younger brother, Hsiao Kang (503-551), who succeeded to the throne in 550 and met a tragic death at the hands of a traitor in the following year, displayed a pronounced antitraditional attitude when he commissioned Hsü Ling (507-583) to compile a collection of contemporary poems under the title *Yü-t'ai hsin-yung* (Jade terrace new songs). These exceedingly ornate lyrical poems, marked with sensual imagery, are anything but proper and instructive.

What has been said may be insufficient to explain why the period of disunity became an important period in literary criticism, but it serves to show the atmosphere in which the critical spirit was fostered.

The first important critic who is to engage our attention has already been mentioned. Ts'ao P'ei, in his *Tien-lun lun-wen* (Essay on literature), made the first attempt to define the specific nature of some dominant literary genres.[30] He says:

[30] Ts'ao P'ei: "Tien-lun-wen," in *Wen-hsüan, chüan* 52.

Literary compositions are all derived from a common source, but they develop into different forms. The *tsou* and *i* [memorial and discussion] should be graceful; the *shu* and *lun* [epistle and essay] should be logical; the *ming* and *lei* [inscription and elegy] should be factual; and *shih* and *fu* [poetry and poetic prose] should be beautiful.[31]

While strictly classical in his definition of poetry, he had gone beyond the scope of any previous work.

The essay also marks the beginning of a systematic evaluation of the works of seven distinguished poets of his time, known collectively in the history of Chinese literature as "Chien-an ch'i-tzu" (the Seven Masters of the chien-an period, 196-220). Ts'ao's chief contribution to literary theory is his concept of *ch'i* (breath or spirit), a term he borrowed from Mencius. Elevating the term to a new level of meaning, signifying individual talent, he further classified it into two categories, the clear and the muddy. Then he asserted that a man is born with his talent, which cannot be handed down through instruction. The influence of Chuangtzu is evident, for the nontransferable quality of talent reminds us of the master wheelwright's grief at having to keep at making wheels at the age of seventy because he was unable to impart his knowledge to anyone else, not even his own son and younger brother. In Ts'ao P'ei's words, "Even a father or an elder brother cannot teach his son or younger brother."[32]

With the application of the term *ch'i* to literary work itself, its meaning seems to have shifted, for it now denotes a literary style. Here Ts'ao P'ei perceived that talent for one style need not imply talent for any other style, and that few men have an all-round talent for all the styles. Therefore, he concluded, every poet should seek the style which best suits his special talent. And then, in a passage as incongruous as a dog's tail at the end of a fox fur, he spoke of literary composition as a means of acquiring eternal fame. It is unfortunate that this became for many a writer, including Liu Hsieh, a dominant motive for writing at all.

[31] *Ibid.*   [32] *Ibid.*

In the Chin dynasty, the most important work on criticism and rhetoric is Lu Chi's (261-303) *Wen-fu* (Essay on literature in the form of a *fu*). Scintillating with poetic beauty and critical insight, the *Wen-fu* is a landmark in the history of Chinese literary criticism. A poet of great talent himself, Lu Chi revealed the subtle and mysterious nature of esthetic experience and the creative process with a clarity and beauty of expression that are seldom excelled. Convinced that the *Wen-fu* must be read to be appreciated, I shall quote a few passages from the remarkable translation by Ch'en Shih-hsiang[33] to show the poet's penetrating insight into the state of creativity.

In regard to creative impulse he says,

> In the beginning,
> All external vision and sound are suspended,
> Perpetual thought itself gropes in time and space;
> Then, the spirit at full gallop reaches the eight limits of
>   the cosmos,
> And the mind, self-buoyant, will ever soar to new unsur-
>   mountable heights.
>   When the search succeeds,
> Feeling, at first but a glimmer, will gradually gather into
>   full luminosity,
> Whence all objects thus lit up glow as if each the other's
>   light reflects.

On the arduous process of preparation, when words, expressions, images and metaphors are wrung out of the subconsciousness, he says:

> Hence,
> Arduously sought expressions, hitherto evasive, hidden,
> Will be like stray fishes out of the ocean bottom to emerge
>   on the angler's hook;
> And quick-winged metaphors, fleeting, far-fetched
> Feathered tribes, while sky-faring are brought down from
>   the curl-clouds by the fowler's bow.

---

[33] All quotations are taken from Ch'en Shih-hsiang's translation of Lu Ch'i's *Wen-fu*, entitled *Essay on Literature* (The Anthoensen Press, Portland, Maine, 1953). See note 13, "Preface," for the other English translations of this work.

On composition he says:

> A composition comes into being as the incarnation of
>   many living gestures.
> It is (like the act of Tao) the embodiment of endless
>   change.
> To attain Meaning, it depends on a grasp of the subtle,
> While such words are employed as best serve beauty's
>   sake.

One of the most penetrating passages in the *fu* is the one on inspiration:

> Such moments when Mind and Matter hold perfect
>   communion,
> And wide vistas open to regions hitherto entirely barred,
> Will come with irresistible force,
> And go, their departure none can hinder.
> Hiding, they vanish like a flash of light;
> Manifest, they are like sounds arising in mid-air.
> So acute is the mind in such instants of divine compre-
>   hension,
> What chaos is there that it cannot marshal in miraculous
>   order?
> While winged thoughts, like quick breezes, soar from
>   depths of the heart,
> Eloquent words, like a gushing spring, flow between lips
>   and teeth.
> No flower, or plant, or animal is too prodigal of splendour
> To recreate under the writer's pen,
> Hence the most wondrous spectacle that ever whelmed
>   the eye,
> And notes of the loftiest music that rejoiced the ear.

But of all the lines I must choose the following as a superb expression
of the mysterious source of an artistic impulse:

> For it is Being, created by tasking the Great Void.[34]
> And 'tis sound rung out of Profound Silence.

[34] The Chinese character here rendered as "tasking" literally means "to try" or "to tax." A more literal translation of the line would be: "Tax the Void or nonbeing to yield Being" (a Taoist conception).

Lu Chi was evidently deeply influenced by Chuangtzu's concept of nonbeing, the Great Void, the supreme state which is not only the source of an artistic impulse, but also the ultimate state of pure experience which transcends all logic and words. Lu Chi spoke of this state as "a force which even the Master Wheelwright Pien could not express in words."

Another contribution to literary history made by Lu Chi is his definitions of a number of literary genres, definitions which are much more adequate than those attempted by Ts'ao P'ei in his *Tien-lun lun-wen*. He says:

> The Lyric (*Shih*), born of pure emotion, is gossamer fibre woven into the finest fabric;
>
> The exhibitory Essay (*Fu*), being true to the objects, is vividness incarnate;
>
> In Monumental Inscriptions (*Pei*) rhetoric must be a foil to facts;
>
> The Elegy (*Lai, lei*) tenderly spins out ceaseless heartfelt grief.
>
> The Mnemonic (*Ming*) is a smooth flow of genial phrases, succinct but pregnant;
>
> The staccato cadences of the Epigram (*Chen*) are all transparent force.
>
> While Eulogy (*Sung*) enjoys the full abandon of grand style,
>
> The Expository (*Lun*) must in exactitude and clarity excel.
>
> The Memorial (*Tsou*), balanced and lucid, must be worthy of the dignity of its royal audience,
>
> The Argument (*Shuo*) with glowing words and cunning parables persuades.
>
> Meticulous as these classifications are,
>
> Lest passion and thought, given free rein, may wantonly go astray,
>
> The maxim holds: Let Truth in terms most felicitous be spoken,
>
> While of verbiage beware.

At the same time we find Tso Ssu (?-c. 306) developing the Classical definition of poetry into a kind of realism. In the preface to his *Three Capital Fu* he said that in poetry we express our sentiments and in *fu* we describe what we see. If we deviate from these fundamental facts, that is, our feelings and the objective world, to indulge in ornate expressions and fabrications, such as the *fu* of Ssu-ma Hsiangju, Yang Hsiung, Pan Ku, Chang Heng, and their group, in which are mentioned many things contrary to known facts, we commit a crime against truth. This attitude explains why it took him ten years to complete his *Three Capital Fu*, for he needed that long to collect and verify his facts. It would seem that he did not countenance the use of imagination, the very soul of any work of art, including literary art. Fortunately, he did not follow his own advice, for how else could his *fu* have caused the price of paper in Lo-Yang to go up?[35]

Chih Yü (?-312), following the lead of Ts'ao P'ei and Lu Chi, made another attempt to classify literary works but, like Prince Hsiao T'ung later, he did it by compiling anthologies. From the fragments of his work, we find him advocating the function of literature as the depicting of natural scenes, the clarifying of human relations, the extensive study of reason and human nature, and ultimately, the determining of the proper station of all things.[36] It is clear that his view of literature is not a pure one. It includes in its province all that is written, in much the same spirit as that in which literature was later conceived by Liu Hsieh, the author of *Wen-hsin tiao-lung*. It is also clear that his view is a utilitarian one, as may be seen from his conception of literary development as a concomitant to the changing process of historical needs.[37]

At approximately the same time, Ke Hung (250-330) applied Wang

---

[35] See his biography in the *Chin-shu*.   [36] *Ch'üan-chin-wen*, chüan 77.

[37] Many other attempts at literary classification were made at this time, one of which was the *Han-lin lun* of Li Ch'ung (c. 323). The work has not come down to us, but from Liu Hsieh's evaluation, it is "shallow and of little consequence." At Liu Hsieh's own time, Hsiao T'ung, reportedly a patron of Liu Hsieh, introduced a clear-cut definition of literature by including in his anthology, the *Wen-hsüan*, only works of imagination and art, and excluding the Classics, philosophical, and historical works. He might have been one source of inspiration to Chung Hung, who restricted his scope still further to that of the five-word-line poetry. But he exercised little or no influence on Liu Hsieh, who took all written records to be within the scope of literature.

Ch'ung's progressive theory of history to literary criticism. But he displayed a liberalism seldom found in the other critics of the time. He did not attack literary embellishment as superfluous and useless, nor did he prize the Classics above contemporary literature. On the contrary, he asserted unequivocally that current compositions were more beautiful than the ancient, unadorned or simple Classics, and that to evolve from simplicity to beauty of form was a natural tendency.[38]

On the question of which is more important, talent or discipline, he entertained a balanced view. He believed that natural talent and literary discipline complement each other. The importance of talent was recognized by Ts'ao P'ei, and that of discipline by Lu Chi. To Ke Hung, one was as indispensable as the other. To separate them was to rob each of its vital complement.

Due to certain characteristics of the Chinese language, tonal pattern has always occupied the attention of great literary writers. Ssu-ma Hsiang-ju considered it an element in the embellishment of the *fu*, and Lu Chi spoke of it in the following lines:

> The interactions of sounds and tones are like
> The five colours that each the others enhances.[39]

Even Chung Hung, who wrote scathingly against Shen Yüeh's arbitrary rules for the sound pattern, acknowledged the natural musical quality of the language, which he felt should be spontaneously applied by the poet.[40] But it was Shen Yüeh (441-513) and his group who, dissatisfied with the looseness with which tones and sounds had hitherto been employed in the field of versification, succeeded in formulating rules governing poetic language. These rules formed a body of intricately technical prosodic laws. Nevertheless they were accepted by many men of the period, including Liu Hsieh, who devoted a chapter in his *Wen-hsin* (Chapter XXXIII) to their discussion.

Since Shen Yüeh and his group flourished during the Yung-ming period (483-493), the style, in accordance with their tonal laws, is

[38] Ke Hung, *Pao-p'u tzu*, chüan 30, pp. 155-156.

[39] Ch'en, *Essay on Literature*, p. xxiv.

[40] Chung Hung, *Shih-p'in chu* (notation by Ch'en Yen-chieh), K'ai-ming shu-chü (Shanghai, 1930), pp. 8-9.

known as *Yung-ming ti*, or the style of the Yung-ming period. In spite
of some opposition from writers like Chung Hung, these tonal laws,
while never followed to the letter, not even by Shen Yüeh himself,
were destined to exercise tremendous influence upon the prosody of
subsequent ages, particularly the T'ang period.

Chung Hung (c. 500) and Liu Hsieh were contemporaries but, since
they apparently did not know each other, Chung had no direct influence
on Liu Hsieh. However, since his *Shih-p'ing* is one of the most important critical works of the time, it deserves a short account here.

The main purpose of the work was to evaluate the poets of the
five-word-line pattern. Adopting the political system of selecting officials by classifying all nominees into three groups and nine categories,
Chung likewise classified the poets into three groups, arranging them
in order of excellence from the highest through the middle to the
lowest. "The lowest" does not mean poor, since it is a relative term,
and to be included at all in any of the groups, a poet had to possess
unusual talent. Although later generations have not agreed with all
of his judgments—the one concerning T'ao Ch'ien of the Chin having
been the most hotly contested—they are generally sound. The classification is prefaced by a short historical introduction, tracing the development of the five-word-line pattern poetry from earliest times to the
time of the Chin. But in the classification Chung included poets of
his own day. In judging each poet, he usually began by linking him
to an earlier source; then he gave the poet's specific quality.

This practice of classification, the sterility of which is quite obvious
to us today, was nevertheless a popular and legitimate method in Chung
Hung's time, and it was also used in much ancient Greek and Latin
criticism. Aristophanes, perhaps the first serious critic in the West,
made exactly such an attempt to classify poets into various ranks of
excellence. Chung Hung's judgment may have been subjective and
impressionistic, but he seems to have raised some of the basic critical
problems which we still encounter today. Like Aristophanes, he asked
implicitly: In what order of merit should poets be ranked and on
what ground should they be judged? If he did not give us clear answers

to these questions, he at least offered his contemporaries and students of later ages some suggestive guides for their evaluation of literature.

To sum up: Throughout the early periods, the classical definition of poetry as the expression of the sentiments ruled supreme. However, the conception of the sentiments as moral ideas as well as emotion prevented poetry and, for that matter, literature in general, from developing into pure lyricism, but destined it to be a vehicle of moral principles, and its function to be primarily didactic. Such being the case, it is easy to see why the Classics were always held as the criteria of literary excellence, in spite of the recognized need of the principle of flexible adaptability to historical changes. One refreshing view is the conception of the creative process, a view which grew, in nearly every case, out of the personal esthetic experience of the creative artist. In accounting for this creativity, it is interesting to note that nearly all writers, or poet-critics, emphasized both natural gifts and hard-earned erudition. This sense of balance is particularly marked in Liu Hsieh.

Liu Hsieh,[41] alias Yen-ho (c. A.D. 465-522) was a native of Tung-kuan, the present Lü-hsien in Shangtung province. His father died when he was a child and he was reared in poverty by his mother. When he was about twenty years of age, his mother died. He never married, partly because of his poverty, and partly, no doubt, because of his interest in Buddhism. He is said to have assisted Seng-yu in editing Buddhist sutras in Ting-lin Monastery, and to have taken part in the preparation of the *Hung-ming chi.* His own contribution to this collection is "Mieh-huo lun," which is found in chüan 8. We are told that both Hsiao T'ung, the author of the famous anthology entitled *Wen hsüan,* and Shen Yüeh, the great exponent of musical patterns in literature, spoke well of his literary talents. But no mention of Liu occurs in the biography of either writer. Liu wrote *Wen-hsin tiao-lung (The Literary Mind and the Carving of Dragons)* in the Southern Ch'i period; but as he lived into the Liang dynasty, he is generally regarded as belonging to the Liang period, and his biography is

---

[41] The section on Liu Hsieh first appeared as an article in the *Asiatische Studien/Etudes Asiatiques,* 3/4 (1953), 123-34.

included in the *History of Liang*. Late in life, he was commissioned by Emperor Wu of Liang to re-edit Buddhist sutras in Ting-lin Monastery, this time in cooperation with a monk by the name of Hui-chen. With the completion of this task, he petitioned the emperor for permission to take Buddhist vows. The permission was granted, and he became a monk in the same monastery where he twice had edited Buddhist sutras. There he received the Buddhist name of Hui-ti. Shortly afterwards he died.

Some modern writers believe that Liu Hsieh's classicism was motivated by a desire to lend authority to his own views,[42] a version of "reform in the name of antiquity." But many others[43] think that Liu was sincere in preferring classicism to the growing tendency in current literary circles to deviate from the classical pattern. Here I shall first give a brief account of Liu's classicism, then turn to a study of his literary criticism and, finally, try to ascertain what role classicism does play in his system and to what degree he may be considered a classicist.

Liu's classicism is revealed in his "Preface," where he tells us that he, ceremonial vessels in his hands, followed Confucius in a dream. He also indicates that had there been no Ma Yung and Cheng Hsüan before him, he would have used his talent to make commentaries on the Classics.[44] Even his decision to devote himself to literary criticism was influenced by the fact that for him the functions of literature have their source in the Classics.[45] In view of the prevalent indulgence in an exceedingly florid style in literature, he considered it his duty to try, by writing critically on literature, to check this divergent tendency. Thus he says, "The writing of *Wen-hsin* has its source in the *Tao*, its model in the Sage, and its pattern in the Classics."[46] His book opens with the chapter "On Tao, the Source," followed by "On the Evidence from the Sages" and "On the Classics as Literary Sources."

[42] Liang Sheng-wei, "Wen-hsüeh p'i-p'ing-chia Liu Yen-ho p'ing-chuan," *Hsiao-shuo yüeh-pao*, Vol. XVII, Supplement.

[43] Lo Ken-tse, *Wei-chin liu-ch'ao wen-hsüeh p'i-p'ing shih* (Chungking, 1944).

[44] *Wen-hsin tiao-lung chu*, ed. by Fan Wen-lan, K'ai-ming shu-tien, 1947 (henceforth abbreviated as *Wen-hsin*), chüan 10, pp. 20b-21a.

[45] *Ibid.*

[46] *Ibid.*, p. 21b.

In the first chapter, while tracing the origin of literature to nature, he seems to envisage an orthodox principle taken from nature, a principle which was handed down from one sage to another until Confucius completed it by writing the "wings."[47] The other Classics were developed in the hands of sages and it was again Confucius who, excelling all others before him, brought the six Classics to their final form.[48]

In the second chapter, Liu seeks to establish Confucius as the authority for the various functions of literary forms by reference to his utterances, as recorded in the Classics and their commentaries. The functions of these literary forms are political and moral in nature.[49] As for the literary styles exemplified in the Classics, they are: simplicity in conveying thought, linguistic richness in embodying emotions, logical clarity in establishing fundamental principles, and allegorical and figurative speech as a means of suggestive remonstration.[50]

In Chapter Three, "On the Classics as Literary Sources," Liu defines the Classics as the essence of literature, embodying eternal principles.[51] According to him, the general characteristics of the Classics are that they contain ideas which are completely adequate for expressing one's emotions, and that their language is of such a quality that it follows perfectly the literary principles.[52] If one is versed in them, one's utterance would naturally be profound, for, he says, "a bell of ten thousand weights will not ring out petty sounds."[53] Liu traces all literary genres back to the Classics. If one always took the Classics as his sources, there would be no danger of his becoming withered up and fading away. If a writer relied on the Classics, his work would be distinguished by one of the following characteristics: deep emotions untainted by artificiality, unmixed purity of form, empirical truth untarnished by falsehood, moral ideas uninvolved in perversity, simple style free from verbosity, and literary beauty unmarred by excess.[54]

---

[47] Commentaries in the *Book of Changes*. Liu Hsieh apparently adopted the belief that these were written by Confucius, a belief which has been generally discredited.

[48] *Ibid.*, chüan 1, pp. 1a-1b. [49] *Ibid.*, p. 9b. [50] *Ibid.*, p. 10a.

[51] *Ibid.*, p. 13a. [52] *Ibid.* [53] *Ibid.*, pp. 13a-13b.

[54] *Ibid.*, p. 14a.

Apart from these first three chapters, there are many other references to the Classics. In the chapter entitled "An Analysis of *Sao* or *Ch'u-tz'u*," Liu considers the rise of *Sao* as a consequence of the decline of *feng* and *ya*.[55] In considering different views concerning the conformity of *Li-sao* to the Classics, Liu recognizes two divergent tendencies in *Li-sao*, one of which is in harmony with the Classics and the other contrary to them. In *Li-sao* Liu finds four ways in which *Li-sao* is in harmony with *feng* and *ya*. These are: The *Li-sao* contains a style of *tien* and *kao*, it employs the style of satirical suggestion, it adopts the use of metaphor and allegory, and it expresses the sentiments of loyalty and lament. There are also four things which mark *Li-sao* as unclassical. These are: the inclusion of strange tales, and of fantastic stories, and evidence of an eccentric and narrow mind, and of an indecent desire for a loose life.[56]

In the chapter on "An Exegesis of Poetry," a province in which classical and literary elements coincide, Liu quotes the description of poetry from the *Shu-ching*: "Poetry is the expression of sentiments, and songs are these expressions set to music."[57] He also repeats Confucius' statement that in the *Shih-ching* there is no undisciplined thought.[58] He cites with approval Confucius' utilitarian view of poetry,[59] and endorses the general theory enunciated in Mao's "Preface" that poetry reflects the political conditions of the times, and that poetry declines as time passes and departs from the age of the Sage. In line with this view, he condemns the poetry of the Cheng-shih period (240-248) and of the Eastern Chin for being adulterated by Taoism and having a metaphysical flavor.[60]

He believes that musical poetry (*yüeh-fu*) rose after the decline of the *ya* odes,[61] and refers to the *fu* as one of the six elements of the

[55] *Ibid.*, p. 28b.   [56] *Ibid.*, pp. 29a-29b.

[57] *Ibid.*, chüan 2, p. 1a; *Shu-ching*, "Shun-tien" (Shih-san-ching chu-shu ed.), chüan 3, p. 26a.

[58] *Lun-yü yin-te* (Harvard Yenching Institute, Peiping, 1940), 2/2/2.

[59] *Wen-hsin*, chüan 2, p. 1a; *Lun-yü yin-te*, 2/1/15; 4/3/8.

[60] *Wen-hsin*, chüan 2, p. 2a.

[61] *Ibid.*, p. 24b.

Shih-ching.[62] Liu claims that the *fu* receives its life from the poets of the Odes,[63] and therefore may be traced back to them.

Liu makes many allusions to the Classics, particularly the *Shih-ching.* The chapter entitled "Metaphor and Allegory" is completely dominated by the spirit of traditional interpretation. But what has been said is enough to indicate Liu's classical tendency. We shall pass on to the discussion of his literary criticism.

The term "literary criticism" is used here in its broadest possible sense. It includes literary history, literary theory, and literary appreciation and evaluation. In the case of Liu Hsieh, these three are closely interwoven and give his work an underlying unity in the midst of apparent chaos.

Liu's desire to write the *Wen-hsin tiao-lung* arises from his dissatisfaction with the general state of literary production of the times, and with the fragmentary manner in which literary criticism has been dealt with. As a prelude to his work, he reviews existing critical works and gives to each an epigrammatic verdict which implies some general criteria of his own. Of Wei-wen, Lu Chi, Chih Yü, and others, he says, "Each reflects a particular corner, and few have envisioned the open vista."[64] And he further comments, "They are all unable to trace back from the leaves to the roots, or back from the tide to its source."[65] These verdicts indicate a discerning mind equipped with a penetrating critical spirit. He is truly a critic of critics. In the chapter called "A General Consideration of the Art of Writing," he says of Lu Chi, "His *Wen-fu* has been known for its penetrating and exhaustive discussion of the art of writing, but, in its superficial attention to details, it has not adequately dealt with the substance."[66] Thus Liu apparently feels that it is up to him to offer a comprehensive account of the principles of literary criticism.

Liu has an interesting idea of a competent critic. In his opinion a competent critic is one who, to begin with, is widely acquainted with literature and highly sensitive to its intrinsic values. Then there are

---

[62] *Ibid.*, p. 46a.   [63] *Ibid.*, p. 46b.   [64] *Ibid.*, chüan 10, p. 21a.
[65] *Ibid.*, p. 21b.   [66] *Ibid.*, chüan 9, p. 12a.

other prerequisites to the understanding of a piece of literature: the ability to recognize the genre and style, the ability to determine if the work complies with the principle of adaptability to change, and the ability to distinguish between the extraordinary and the orthodox in subject matter and to pass judgment on the appropriateness of historical allusions and musical patterns. Above all, the critic should be able to trace back from the words to the feeling of the author,[67] a criterion that vaguely indicates a belief in the oneness of the creative genius and appreciative taste. Through these abilities, a critic is enabled to grasp the meaning or the esthetic beauty of a literary work.[68] But an understanding critic is rare, because most people depreciate their contemporaries and worship only the Ancients.[69] However, an appreciative critic is essential to the realization of the value of a literary work. For a literary work loses much of its richness if it is not appreciated.[70]

Liu traces the origin of literature to nature. For him, just as it was for Horace, literature is both sweet and useful. His verbal emphasis is on the useful and his real interest in the sweet.[71] In his "Preface" he says, "Time is fleeting and life itself is transitory. If a man really wants to achieve fame, his only chance is to devote himself to writing." This utilitarian view is more than balanced by his deep interest in aspects which are *purely* literary. This interest is revealed in the title of his book: *The Literary Mind and the Carving of Dragons*. His own explanation is: "The literary mind is that mind which strives after literary forms."[72] And the term "the carving of dragons" stands specifically for literary embellishment. For, he says, "since from time immemorial literature has always been characterized by certain embellishments."[73] His view of the scope of literature is broad. From the types of writing he includes in his discussion of literature, it is apparent that he holds nothing in writing to be beyond the province of literature.

Literary development is treated by Liu Hsieh in a number of ways. Development of general trends, Liu believes, follows the principle of

[67] *Ibid.*, chüan 10, p. 14a.   [68] *Ibid.*, p. 13b.   [69] *Ibid.*, p. 13b.
[70] *Ibid.*, p. 14b.   [71] *Ibid.*, p. 21b.   [72] *Ibid.*, p. 20b.
[73] *Ibid.*

the flexible adaptability to change. He says, "As time has passed and as dynasties have risen and fallen, literature has developed from the simple to the more ornate in form as well as in content."[74] And again he says, "It is the law of literature both to move along and to come to full circle; the merit of literature renews itself from day to day. If it changes, it will endure; if it adapts itself to the changing tide, it will lack nothing."[75] Thus, the literary forms of each generation conform to the spirit of that generation and, when changes take place in the spirit of the age, literary forms modify themselves accordingly. This explains the rise of different genres in different ages. Occasionally Liu emphasizes the moral and political influence of an age on the character of literature.

When Liu moves from the discussion of general trends in literature to a discussion of literary genres, he holds that the form of each genre is characterized by certain norms, and his classification of literary genres is based on these norms. His distinctions between literary genres are, at times, very strict. This indicates that he does not seem to see the possibility that changes might have taken place across the ages in the conception of these genres. But, on the other hand, the arbitrariness of his classification cannot escape the attention of even the most casual reader when it is noted that his genres are not mutually exclusive but are overlapping.

Liu's book abounds in critical evaluation of individual authors and their works. All that can be attempted here is to ferret out the criteria he seems to have used in making these evaluations. These criteria seem to fall into the following categories: (1) natural talents, (2) fullness of feelings and emotions, (3) style as expressed in terms of artisitc quality of language, (4) moral convictions and philosophy of life, (5) scholarship and learning, (6) the nature of the subject matter treated, and (7) the musical patterns. Liu himself, on two occasions, reduces these categories to neat formulas. On one occasion he offers three main patterns: the pattern of colors, the pattern of sounds, and the pattern of emotions.[76] On another occasion he gives four categories: emotions

---

[74] *Ibid.*, chüan 9, p. 22.   [75] *Ibid.*, chüan 6, p. 18a.   [76] *Ibid.*, chüan 7, p. 1a.

and sentiments, which are the spirit of literature; facts and principles, which are the bone and marrow; linguistic patterns, which are the flesh; and musical patterns, which are the voice and the breath.[77] He devotes most of the second portion of his work to the elaboration of these elements, and the discussion of the relationship between them. In view of the fact that Liu never discusses any element in isolation, it may be wise to begin our analysis with the relationship between the elements.

In considering the relative importance of these literary elements, Liu shows a remarkable sense of balance. He is a critic in whom emotion and intellect, beauty of linguistic form and fullness of emotional content are balanced. He says,

Literary beauty means adorning the language; but language's appropriateness and beauty is conditioned by inner feelings. Therefore, feelings are the warp of literary patterns and linguistic forms are the woof of ideas. Only when the warp is straight, can the woof be formed; and only when ideas are definite, can linguistic forms be expressive.[78]

His respect for the ancient poets lies in the fact that they built their literary forms on emotions, while later poets fabricated emotions to fit literary forms.[79] But literary forms are not fallacious in themselves; the fallacy lies in having the forms alone without emotions. Emotions are tuned to changes of external scene. Spring, summer, autumn, and winter—each affects us in a specific way and arouses in us certain specific emotions.[80] Since stock phrases are inadequate for the depicting of varying emotions, Liu demands freshness in linguistic pattern as a condition of good literature.[81] Thus the importance of emotion is matched by that of literary expression. In defense of linguistic beauty he says, "What is written by the sages and worthy men is summed up under the phrase *wen-chang*. What is it, if not beauty of form?"[82] Liu is apparently expressing a new appreciation of the literary qualities of the Classics. For him, substance depends on literary pattern for expression, just as expressions depend on emotions for their content.

---

[77] *Ibid.*, chüan 9, p. 9b.   [78] *Ibid.*, chüan 7, p. 1b.   [79] *Ibid.*
[80] *Ibid.*, chüan 10, p. 1a.   [81] *Ibid.*   [82] *Ibid.*, chüan 7, p. 1a.

Liu not only defends rhetoric; he also endorses literary exaggeration and embellishment. For his justification, he paraphrases Mencius, "Though the language be exaggerated, it harms not the ideas."[83] Here Liu sees the real function of literature as consisting in the creation of beautiful linguistic forms for the purpose of moving the heart of the reader.

In his discussion of musical poetry he discloses the intimate relationship between music and poetry. He says, "Poetry is the heart of music, and sound is the body of music. Since the body of music lies in sound, musicians must tune their instruments; since the heart of music lies in poetry, superior men should make right their literary forms."[84] From this it is only a short step to the view that music is the reflection of the age, and that by listening to the music of any age one is able to discern the character of that age. Poetry and music are thus intimately bound together by their identical function.

The ability to weave these literary elements into beautiful rhythmic and musical expressions of real emotion and feeling, incorporating into the texture true moral convictions and principles, is, of course, a gift of nature. But effort and learning contribute much to the richness in materials and the resourcefulness and ease with which one adapts his style to the nature of the subject under treatment.[85] As natural talents vary with individuals, Liu conceives of eight different styles: first, elegant and graceful, or in the style of *tien* and *ya*; second, far-ranging and profound; third, polished and concise; fourth, lucid and logical; fifth, profuse and flowery; sixth, vigorous and beautiful; seventh, fresh and extraordinary; and eighth, light and trivial. Few have the genius to command all these styles, but many can adapt some style to fit their talents.[86]

In the discussion of talents, there is a chapter on "The Wind and the Bone," "wind" meaning lyrical, or in the manner of *feng*, and "bone" meaning vigor and strength. Liu says, "He who would express mournful emotions must begin with the wind, and to organize his

[83] *Ibid.*, chüan 8, p. 5b.
[84] *Ibid.*, chüan 2, p. 25a.
[85] *Ibid.*, chüan 6. p. 1b.
[86] *Ibid.*, pp. 8a-8b.

linguistic elements, he must above all emphasize the bone."[87] The wind gives wings to words and the bone gives them vigor and strength.[88] By the wind and the bone, Liu is talking about what Wei-wen had called the breath. His quotation from Wei-wen convinces us that he shares with Wei-wen the feeling that genius is born and not made.[89] But important as genius is, it is only half the story; the other half depends on experience and scholarship. It is by means of wide acquaintance with literary works and extensive experience that one can hope to avoid poverty of expression.[90]

Genius operates through imagination, the power of association of ideas, and the ability to forge metaphors. The manner in which genius operates is such that it cannot be transmitted by instruction. Like I Chih who could not inform people how he cooked, and the wheelwright Pien who could not tell people how he wielded his ax, so a writer is unable to transmit his manner of operation to others.[91]

Liu, in his treatment of metaphor and of the couplet, displays remarkable analytical power. His analysis of metaphor includes what is now described as onomatopoeia,[92] and his analytical categorization of the couplet seems to be the first attempt of its kind.[93]

With his insistence on the importance of real emotions and feelings as the foundation of literature, Liu inclines toward spontaneity and naturalness.[94] It is not accidental that in the first chapter he traces literature to natural patterns and forms. By nature we have seven emotions, and these emotions are naturally aroused when affected by

[87] *Ibid.*, pp. 13a-13b.   [88] *Ibid.*, pp. 13b-14a.

[89] *Ibid.*, p. 13b. Wei-wen-ti, "Tien-lun lun-wen," *Wei-wen-ti chi* (Han Wei liu-ch'ao pai-san ming-chia chi ed., 1892), chüan 1, p. 70a.

[90] *Wen-hsin*, chüan 6, p. 1b.

[91] *Wen-hsin*, chüan 6, p. 2a. "I Chih" is another name for I Yin. The reference is to a passage in *Lü-shih ch'un-ch'iu* where I Yin, in answer to T'ang's question, says: ". . . The changes which take place in a cauldron are subtle and delicate, neither expressible in words by the mouth nor conceivable by the mind." *Lü-shih ch'un-ch'iu* (Chu-tzu chi-ch'eng ed., Shanghai, 1935), chapter on "Pen-wei," chüan 14, pp. 140-1. (Cf. *Frühling und Herbst des Lü Bu We*, translated by R. Wilhelm [Jena, 1928], p. 182.) For the Wheelwright Pien, see *Chuangtzu*, Book XIII, Chapter 10.

[92] *Wen-hsin*, chüan 8, pp. 1a-1b; chüan 10, p. 1a.

[93] *Ibid.*, chüan 7, p. 33b.

[94] *Ibid.*, chüan 1, p. 1a; chüan 7, 1a-10b.

external circumstances.[95] When thus affected, it is only natural for us to try to express our sentiments in winged words. If we follow our spontaneous tendency, it will be internal emotions which determine the literary forms and styles, and not the external forms which force themselves upon our inner feelings. In this spontaneity we shall find the unlimited resourcefulness of our spirit. Liu holds that if we should in any way work against our nature, in the end we would be exhausted and withered up.[96] His chapter on "The Nourishing of Vitality" is a lesson in spontaneity, which is apparently based on Chuangtzu. Liu shares Chuangtzu's view that to keep one's mind empty and quiet is the only way to keep one's vigor forever fresh and sharp as a newly honed blade.[97]

Now, in evaluating Liu's position as a classicist, let us see what his attitude really is when he talks about the Classics. He eulogizes the Classics as the source of all literary genres and maintains a properly reverent attitude for the orthodox ideas in them. It is in his evaluation of the Classics as literature, however, that he discards all platitudes, and waxes warm in true praise. Moreover, in pronouncing *Li-sao* to be a "hero" of poetry, but only a "ruffian" in the realm of *ya* and *sung*,[98] he definitely conceives of poetry as independent of the *Shih-ching*. In reiterating the traditional theory of poetic function and development, Liu seems to have done so as a matter of habit rather than as a result of conviction. His belief that literature develops in accordance with the needs of the times, and that each new age gives literature a new emphasis and a fresh point of view is in violent contradiction to traditionalism. Poetry must change according to the principle of flexible adaptability to new needs of new ages. This principle of adaptability to change is enunciated in the same breath with which he advises people to go back to the Classics. At the very moment when he exhorts men to worship the Classics, he condemns the popular view of depreci-

---

[95] *Ibid.*, chüan 2, p. 1a.   [96] *Ibid.*, chüan 9, pp. 8b-9a.

[97] *Ibid.*, pp. 6b-7b. Cf. Wang Hsien-ch'ien, *Chuang-tzu chi-chieh* (Chu-tzu chi-ch'eng ed.), chüan I, Chapter 3, "Yang-sheng-chu," 18-9. (Cf. translations of *Chuangtzu*, Book III, Chapter 2.)

[98] *Wen-hsin*, chüan 1, p. 29b.

ating the contemporaries and worshipping the Ancients.[99] From the
general tenor of his writing, we must conclude that his conservatism
is a matter of habit, while his progressive ideas rise from convictions.
He pays lip service to the Classics, but gives his heart to the study of
elements which are purely literary. And even in treating the Classics,
he gives them more of a literary appreciation than a moralistic interpretation. For him, it seems, the Classics are important because they
possess literary value; he does not believe that literary value depends
upon conformity to the Classics.

When he discusses literary elements in the second portion of his
book, his freedom from classicism is even more surprising. He occupies
himself almost exclusively with what is purely literary. In the eight
styles he formulates, only the first style, *tien ya*, refers to the *Shu-ching*
and the *Shih-ching*. But as used in his critical judgments on individual
authors and their works, these terms mean merely "elegant" and
"graceful." It is, therefore, abundantly clear that whatever he conceives to be the value of a classical element, this value is only one
among many other literary values. He brings the Classics down to
earth for us to admire as works of literature. Such being Liu's literary
outlook, it would not be far wrong to conclude that in his system
classicism plays the same role as any other literary element, and thus
it is not possible to call Liu Hsieh a classicist without doing him
a grave injustice.

Liu Hsieh seems to have gathered up in his *Wen-hsin tiao-lung* all
the strands of literary and critical thought which we have discussed
in the preceding pages. He has apparently read widely, weighing the
ideas of earlier authors and then formulating his own. Being a great
writer himself, a past master of the beautiful style of the Six Dynasties
period, which is characterized by balance in structure, parallelism of
expressions, and consonance of language, he inspires the reader not
only by the content of his work, but also by his incomparable style.

In the chapter on "An Understanding Critic," Liu Hsieh made the

99 *Ibid.*, chüan 6; compare text on p. 17b and "Eulogy" at the end of the essay on
p. 18a; see also chüan 9, "Shih-hsü," and chüan 10, "chih-ying."

statement that literary works had to be appreciated to reveal their beauty. If we apply this statement to his *Wen-hsin tiao-lung*, there is no doubt about its being one of the most beautiful, because it is one of the most admired, of works. During his own day Shen Yüeh, the literary lion of his age, kept it within reach on his desk. Liu Chih-chi (661-721), the great historiographer of the T'ang dynasty, spoke of him in his *Shih-t'ung* as the arbiter of taste during the Six Dynasties period. Huang T'ing-chien (1045-1105), one of the great poets of the Sung, considered Liu Chih-chi's *Shih-t'ung* and Liu Hsieh's *Wen-hsin tiao-lung* two works which all scholars aspiring to be literary writers must read. And Hu Ying-lin of the Ming, who flourished in 1590, ranked *Wen-hsin tiao-lung* above *Shih-t'ung*.

In the Ch'ing dynasty, the compilers of the *Ssu-k'u ch'üan-shu chien-ming mu-lu* spoke of *Wen-hsin* as the first literary critical work which contains the essence of literary and rhetorical principles. Chang Hsüeh-ch'eng (1738-1801), another great historiographer, expressed his enthusiasm and unbounded admiration for Liu Hsieh's *Wen-hsin* in his *Wen-shih t'ung-i*, a work which ranks with Liu Chih-chi's *Shih-t'ung* in importance. And Juan Yüan (1764-1849) who, because of his important official position, was able to make such an important contribution by fostering scholarship, considered Liu Hsieh the creator of literary laws.

As late as 1941, Fu Tseng-hsiang, a famous bibliographer, said, "*Wen-hsin tiao-lung* deals with the development of literature. It is the compass in the literary world, a handbook to all writers and scholars."[100] Then, in 1946, Fu Keng-sheng in his *Chung-kuo wen-hsüeh p'i-p'ing t'ung-lun* said of the *Wen-hsin*, "Its scope is comprehensive, the ideas it contains are subtle and penetrating, and its emphasis is balanced, without deviating from the norm. Clear in its definitions and logical and systematic in its categorization, it is the greatest literary critical work ever produced in the whole history of China."[101] Occasionally

[100] Fu Tseng-hsiang, "Hsü Hsin-kung chiao *Wen-hsin tiao-lung* pa," *Kuo-ming cha-chih*, X, 1941.

[101] Fu Keng-sheng, *Chung-kuo wen-hsüeh p'i-p'ing t'ung-lun* (Chungking, 1946, and Shanghai, 1947).

we hear some dissenting note. Ch'ao Kung-wu (flourishing in 1144) criticized the factual accuracy of certain statements made by Liu Hsieh. But most writers have stood by Liu Hsieh with unswerving faith.

Before I bring this introduction to a close, I would like to dwell briefly on the difficulty involved in a study of Chinese literary criticism and how this difficulty may, to a certain extent, be eliminated. One of the difficulties is to grasp firmly the meaning of the terms used by Chinese writers and critics. In general, all Chinese terms are subject to a change of meaning in different contexts; but this is especially true in literary criticism. Unless we know exactly what certain terms mean in certain contexts, we are at a loss how to interpret them. This difficulty is increased by the fact that many writers who have not formed their thought with any degree of precision take advantage of the confusion and use the terms with abandon in an effort to deck themselves with borrowed elegance. It is true that language is a fluid thing, subject to change of meaning in different periods; but for any specific period, there must be some kind of agreement as to the several possible meanings one term may have—in order to avoid utter chaos. One way to get out of this difficult situation is to find a way to define the terms by referring to the contexts in which they actually occur—a procedure similar to the one I. A. Richards has followed in his studies of Mencius. It is my hope that some day I may have an opportunity to devote myself to this task.

THE LITERARY MIND AND THE

CARVING OF DRAGONS

by Liu Hsieh

Preface[1]

The literary mind is that mind which strives after literary forms. In a similar sense, Chüan-tzu long ago wrote *Ch'ing-hsin* (The mind of the lute), and Wang-sun wrote *Ch'iao-hsin* (The artistic mind).[2] What an excellent term indeed is "mind!" And because it is, I have used it too.

And since from time immemorial literature has always been characterized by certain embellishments, I am not implicating myself in the type of "dragon carving" practiced by Tsou Shih and his group.[3]

Now with respect to the universe, it is everlasting and boundless, and in it we find people of all types. He who wants to stand out above the others must depend on his intelligence. Time is fleeting and life itself is transitory. If a man really wants to achieve fame, his only chance is to devote himself to writing. In his appearance, man resembles heaven and earth, and he is naturally endowed with five talents; his ears and eyes are comparable to the sun and moon; his voice and breath are like the wind and thunder; yet, as he transcends all things, he is really spiritual. His physical form may be as fragile as the grasses and trees, but his fame is more substantial than metal and stone. Therefore, a man of virtue, in his relationship with the people of the world, aims at establishing both his character and his words. So it is not that I simply happen to be fond of argument; it is that I cannot do otherwise than write.[4]

[1] This chapter, in which Liu Hsieh states his reason for the choice of the title and his reason for writing the book, originally appeared at the end of the work, according to common practice in ancient China.

[2] Both Chüan-tzu's *Ch'ing-hsin* and Wang-sun-tzu's *Ch'iao-hsin* are listed in the "I-wen-chih" in the *Han-shu*. *Ch'iao-hsin*, also known as *Wang-sun-tzu*, is listed under "Ju-chia," the Confucian School. See *Han-shu* (Taipei ed., 1956), chüan 30, p. 13b. *Ch'ing-hsin* is listed under "Tao-chia," the Taoist School. See *ibid.*, p. 15b.

[3] The term "Tiao-lung," or carving of dragons, was first used to describe the ornate quality of Tsou Shih's writing. The biography of Hsün Ch'ing in the *Shih-chi* speaks of him as "Tiao-lung Shih." P'ei Yin, in his commentary, quoted Liu Hsiang as saying that Tsou Shih's writing was patterned after the ornate style of Tsou Yen, and was like the carving of dragons' patterns. Hence he was known as "Tiao-lung Shih." *Shih-chi*, chüan 74, p. 5a.

[4] Paraphrasing *Mencius*. See *Meng-tzu yin-te*, 24/3B/9; 25/3B/9.

As a child of seven I dreamed of colored clouds like brocaded silk and that I climbed up and picked them. When over thirty years of age, I dreamed I had in my hand the painted and lacquered ceremonial vessels and was following Confucius and travelling toward the south. In the morning I awoke happy and deeply at ease. The difficulty of seeing the Sage is great indeed, and yet he appeared in the dream of an insignificant fellow like me! Since the birth of man there has never been anyone like the Master.[5] Now, insofar as I wished to propagate and praise the teachings of the Sage, nothing would have been better than to write commentaries on the Classics. However, Ma, Cheng,[6] and others have already given us their penetrating interpretations of these Classics. Even if I had had some profound ideas about them, it is unlikely that they would have been sufficient to establish an independent school. As a matter of fact, the function of *wen-chang*, or literary writing, is an offshoot of the function of the Classics. The Five Rites[7] are accomplished on the basis of literary writing, and the Six Government Functions[8] are also performed with its aid. The relationship between ruler and ministers is made clear through literary writing, and government and military affairs are clearly defined by means of it. And if one traces these written documents back to their source, it is found to be none other than the Classics themselves.

However, our time is far removed from that of the Sage, and orthodox literary style has declined. *Tz'u* writers love the exotic, and prize in their writing that which is superficial and eccentric. They try to "decorate the feather" just to be painting and will attempt to embroider even the leather handkerchief bag. All these writers deviate greatly from their true source in pursuit of the pretentious and the excessive. But in the *Book of History* in the discussion of *tz'u*, or language, it is

---

[5] Another paraphrase of Mencius. *Ibid.*, 12/2A/2.

[6] Ma Jung, 79-166; Cheng Hsüan, 127-200. Both are great classical commentators.

[7] See *Chou-i yin-te*, 3/19b, commentary. See note 5, Chapter III, for the list of the Five Rites.

[8] *Chou-i yin-te*, 1/9b. They are: *Chih* (in charge of over-all policy making), *chiao* (in charge of education), *li* (in charge of rites), *cheng* (administration), *hsing* (law), and *shih* (in charge of public works).

said, "In writing one should emphasize the essentials."[9] And when Confucius presented his *hsün*, or teachings, he showed a dislike for unorthodoxy. The uniqueness of the *tz'u* and the *hsün* is due to this emphasis on the essential. Therefore, I picked up my brush, mixed the ink, and began to write this essay.

In modern times there are many who discuss literature. But as for Wei-wen's *Shu-tien*,[10] Ch'en-ssu's *Hsü-shu*,[11] Ying Yang's *Wen-lun*,[12] Lu Chi's *Wen-fu*,[13] Chung-hsia's *Liu-pieh*,[14] and Hung-fan's *Han-lin*,[15]—each of these reflects a particular corner of the field; few have even envisioned the whole open vista. Some praise or belittle the talents of their times; some evaluate the works of writers of the past; some vaguely distinguish between the graceful and the vulgar style; and some summarize the themes of various essays. Wei-wen's *Tien-lun* is detailed but not comprehensive; Ch'en-ssu's letter is argumentative but irrelevant; Ying Yang's discussion is flowery but sketchy; Lu Chi's *Wen-fu* is artful but lacks unity; [Chih Yü's] *Liu-pieh* is fine but ineffectual; and Li Ch'ung's *Han-lin* is shallow and divorced from the essentials. There have also been Chün-shan [or Huan T'an], Kung-kan [or Liu Chang], Chi-fu [or Ying Chen], and Shih-lung [or Lu Yün], and their group, who discussed literature in vague and general terms; although occasionally they produce some creative ideas, they are unable to trace back from the leaves to the roots, or back from the tide to its source. They fail to transmit the teachings of the earlier sages, and are therefore of little help to writers to come.

In writing the *Wen-hsin tiao-lung* I attempt in Chapter I to show

[9] See note 19, Chapter II.

[10] Ts'ao P'ei's *Tien-lun lun-wen*, *Wen-hsüan*, chüan 52. It is an essay on style, with particular reference to the Seven Masters of the Chien-an period, 196-220.

[11] Ts'ao Chih's letter to Yang Te-tsu. See *ibid*., chüan 42.

[12] See *I-wen lei-chü*, chüan 22.

[13] See *Wen-hsüan*, chüan 17. *Wen-fu* is available in three English translations: *The Art of Letters*, trans. by E. R. Hughes (New York, 1950); *Essay on Literature*, trans. by Ch'en Shih-hsiang (rev. ed., Portland, 1953); and *Rhymeprose*, by Archiles Fang, Harvard Journal of Asiatic Studies, XIV [1951], 527-66.

[14] Chih Yü's *Wen-chang liu-pieh lun*. Fragments of it are found in the *Ch'üan-chin wen*, chüan 77.

[15] Li Ch'ung's *Han-lin lun*. Fragments are found in the *Ch'üan-chin wen*, chüan 53.

how literature has its source in the Tao, in Chapter II how it takes
its model from the Sage, in Chapter III how it adopts the pattern of
the Classics, in Chapter IV how it consults the apocryphal writings, and
in Chapter V how it experiences some changes in the *Sao*. I have dealt
with the crucial factors of literature exhaustively here.

In discussing *wen*, or writings which are rhymed, in Chapters V
to XIII, and *pi*, unrhymed writings, in Chapters XVI to XXV, I have
classified them into separate genres and traced each genre back to its
source in order to make clear its development, and I have defined a
number of literary terms in order to clarify their meaning. I have
selected several literary works for treatment under each specific topic,
and have advanced arguments to demonstrate their unity. Thus in the
first part of the book a clear general outline is presented.

In the analysis of emotions and their literary expressions, I have
sought in Chapters XXXI and XXXII to determine their scope systematically. I have elaborated on the theme of creative thinking in Chapter
XXVI, and dealt with the relation between style and nature in Chapter
XXVII. I have analyzed lyricism in Chapter XXVIII, and explained
how to choose the proper style in Chapter XXX. I have developed the
principle of flexible adaptability to changing requirements in Chapter
XXIX, and looked into the use of musical patterns in Chapter XXXIII
and the choice of words in Chapter XXXIV. The theme of literary development is treated in Chapter XLV, entitled "Shih-hsü," or "Literary
Development and Time," and my own evaluation of several literary
talents is presented in Chapter XLVII entitled "Ts'ai-lüeh," or "Literary
Talents." In Chapter XLVIII, entitled "Chih-yin," or "An Understanding Critic," I express my sad disappointment; and in Chapter XLIX,
entitled "Ch'eng-ch'i," or "Capacity of a Vessel," I set forth my impartial
verdict on the characters of several literary writers. In this "Hsü-chih,"
or "Preface," are contained the ideas which sum up all the succeeding
chapters. Thus in the second part, from Chapter XXVI on, the sub-
topics are made clear in all their details. The postulation of principles
and definition of terms are shown in the number of the Great Change;

but only forty-nine chapters are employed for the elucidation of literature.[16]

It is easy to evaluate and discuss a specific work of literature, but rather difficult to deal comprehensively and critically with all literary works. Some of them may have forms as light as fur and hair, but yet have content deeper than bone and marrow. There are also works without number whose ideas are implicit rather than explicit and whose source is hidden, neither ideas nor sources being directly expressed in words. In appearance they may look commonplace, but they are in fact very profound. As for my evaluation and ranking of the existing literary works, some of my conclusions are the same as those of former writers. It is not that I copied them, but that it is impossible to differ from them. And if some of my judgments differ from previous ones, it is not that I seek difference for its own sake, but that there are certain reasons why I must differ. But whether identical to or different from previous judgments, mine have not been influenced by either the modern or the ancient critics. My sole purpose has been to dissect the muscles and trace the veins of literature and endeavor to discover the proper standard. As for my achievement in coursing through the hunting grounds of literature and looping reins in the palace of rhetoric, I think my work is as exhaustive as can be expected.

However, words do not completely express ideas;[17] it is difficult even for the Sage to find it otherwise. If one's knowledge is by nature limited to the capacity of a jar or a tube, how can he be expected to offer all the general principles? Although my critical hearing has

[16] The total number of chapters of the book is fifty. As one chapter is a preface, only forty-nine chapters are actually concerned with literature. In the *Book of Changes*, we find the statement: "The number of the Great Operation is fifty; but only forty-nine are actually used." *Chou-i yin-te*, 42/Hsi shang/8. The operation refers to the process of divination, which is described in the *I-ching* or *Book of Changes*, the Richard Wilhelm translation rendered into English by Cary F. Baynes (Bollingen Series XIX, New York, Pantheon Books, Inc., 1955), I, 333-36. (All subsequent citations to the *I-ching* will be to this edition.) The numbers fifty and forty-nine refer to the number of yarrow stalks. The diviner begins with fifty yarrow stalks, but actually he uses only forty-nine. Some scholars believe that "the number of the Great Change" ["Ta-i chih-shu"] should be read as "the number of the Great Operation" ["Ta-yen chih-shu"].

[17] *Chou-i yin-te*, 44/Hsi shang/12.

been cleansed by the unlimited experience of past writers, how can I be sure that the unseen coming generations will not look upon this heritage of mine as dust?

The Tsan:
Life is limited;
Wisdom alone is without bound.
The pursuit of external things is difficult,
But one will easily succeed if he works in accord with his own nature.
Resolute, like a boulder in a creek I stand
Absorbed in the contemplation of literature.
If literature is truly a vehicle for the mind,[18]
My mind has found a place to rest.

I. On Tao, the Source

Wen,[1] or pattern, is a very great power indeed. It is born together with heaven and earth. Why do we say this? Because all color-patterns are mixed of black and yellow,[2] and all shape-patterns are differentiated by round and square.[3] The sun and moon like two pieces of jade manifest the pattern of heaven; mountains and rivers in their beauty

---

[18] See note 5, Chapter VI.

[1] The term "wen" has no simple English equivalent. As it is used here at the outset of the treatise, it signifies a wide variety of patterns that envelop all aspects of the universe. The fact that each aspect has its own particular pattern seems to have struck Liu Hsieh with great force. The use of a single term to cover all these different patterns suggests that in Liu's mind the presence of some kind of pattern is the common feature of all aspects of the universe.

[2] Conventionally, black is the color of heaven, and yellow the color of earth. See the *Book of Changes*, "Wen-yen," under Hexagram K'un; *Chou-i yin-te* (Peking, 1935), 4/2/yen. Taken together, black and yellow are used as a synecdoche to represent all colors. Synecdoche, the trope in which a part is used to stand for the whole, is often employed in Chinese writings.

[3] Another synecdoche: square, the conventional shape of the earth, and round, the conventional shape of heaven, are taken together to mean all shapes.

display the pattern of earth. These are, in fact, the *wen* of *Tao* itself.
And as one sees above the sparkling heavenly bodies, and below the
manifold forms of earth, there is established a difference between high
and low estate, giving rise to the two archetypal Forms.[4] Man, and
man alone, forms with these the Great Trinity, and he does so because
he alone is endowed with spirituality. He is the refined essence of the
five elements—indeed, the mind of the universe.

Now with the emergence of mind, language is created, and when
language is created, writing appears. This is natural. When we
extend our observations, we find that all things, both animals and
plants, have patterns of their own. Dragons and phoenixes portend
wondrous events through the picturesqueness of their appearance, and
tigers and leopards recall the individuality of virtuous men in their
striped and spotted variegation.[5] The sculptured colors of clouds sur-
pass paintings in their beauty, and the blossoms of plants depend on no
embroiderers for their marvellous grace. Can these features be due
to external adornment? No, they are all natural. Furthermore, the
sounds of the forest wind blend to produce melody comparable to that
of a reed pipe or lute, and the music created when a spring strikes
upon a rock is as melodious as the ringing tone of a jade instrument
or bell. Therefore, just as when nature expresses itself in physical
bodies there is plastic pattern, so also, when it expresses itself in sound,
there is musical pattern. Now if things which are devoid of consciousness express themselves so extremely decoratively, can that which is
endowed with mind lack a pattern proper to itself?

Human pattern originated in the Supreme, the Ultimate.[6] "Mysteri-
ously assisting the gods,"[7] the images of the Changes[8] are the earliest

[4] Referring to the two principles, yin and yang. The former is feminine, passive, and
earthly; the latter is masculine, active, and celestial.

[5] A conventional association. See *Chou-i yin-te*, 30-31/49/5 hsiang.

[6] A reference to a statement in the *Book of Changes*, "There is in the Changes the
Supreme Ultimate," *Chou-i yin-te*, 43/Hsi, shang/11 (12). The English version of
Richard Wilhelm's German translation renders "T'ai-chi" as "the Great Primal Begin-
ning." See *I Ching*, I, 342.

[7] *Chou-i yin-te* 49/Shuo/1.

[8] The *Book of Changes* is originally a book on divination. With the addition of later
commentaries, the ten wings, and particularly the "Hsi-ts'u," it becomes a philosophical

expressions of this pattern. Pao Hsi[9] began [the *Book of Changes*] by drawing [the eight trigrams], and Confucius completed it by writing the "Wings."[10] [One of these Wings], the "Wen-yen" or "Words with Pattern," was written especially to explain the "Ch'ien" and the "K'un."[11] Words with pattern indeed express the mind of the universe! From Ho-t'u, the Yellow River Map, were born the eight trigrams, and from Lo-shu, the Writing from the River Lo,[12] came the nine categories.[13] For these and for the fruits contained in the jade and gold decorated tablets and the flowers blooming in red words and green strips[14] was any one responsible? No. They are natural, organic expressions of the Divine.

When birds' markings replaced knotted cords, writing first emerged.[15] The facts about Yen and Hao are recorded in the *San-fen*,[16]

---

work of great importance. Many translations have been made, among which the English one by James Legge and the German one by Richard Wilhelm are the best known. References in these notes are to the English translation by Cary F. Baynes of the Wilhelm German translation.

The main text is composed of 64 hexagrams, each of which contains six lines. Commentaries, or "judgments" on these hexagrams and lines were attributed to King Wen.

[9] Better known as Fu Hsi, one of the three legendary Huang, or Emperors, identified as T'ai Hao in the Pai-hu-t'ung. See Ssu-ma Ch'ien, *Shih-chi*, "San-huang chi."

[10] See note 47, "Introduction."

[11] There are sixty-four hexagrams in the *Book of Changes*, of which Ch'ien and K'un are the most important two, treated at the beginning of the Book. "Wen-yen" is one of the ten "Wings," sometimes rendered as "Words," attributed by early scholars to Confucius, who devoted it to the explanation of the first two hexagrams because of their special significance. The term "wen" used here is the same "wen" used to designate "pattern." Since "Wen-yen" was supposedly from the pen of Confucius, Liu Hsieh seems to have authority for attaching importance to the term "wen."

[12] *Shang-shu Chung-hou wo ho chi*, an apocryphal work, quoted by Ma Kuo-han in the *I-shu*, is reported to have contained the statement, "A dragon in the Yellow River presented the Map, and a tortoise in the Lo River carried the Writing. These, with red words and green characters, were given to Hsüan-yüan" (the Yellow Emperor).

[13] *Chou-i yin-te*, 44/Hsi, shang/11. For the "nine categories," see "Hung Fan" in the *Book of History*. For the "Map" and the "Writing" see *I-ching*, I, 332-33.

[14] Jade tablets, red words, and green characters appear quite frequently in apocryphal writings purporting to supplement by elaboration the ideas advanced in the Classics. These writings were the works of the Han scholars.

[15] Hsü Shen, the first important Chinese lexicographer, said in the preface to his *Shuo-wen*, the first dictionary, that Ts'ang Chieh began to write on the basis of the markings of birds and animals. Hence by "birds' markings" is meant writing.

[16] *San-fen* and *Wu-tien* are mentioned in *Tso-chuan*, under the 12th year of Duke Chao; they were taken to mean the records of the three Huang and the five Emperors.

but since they took place in such a distant past, their sound and color are beyond our ken. It was during the T'ang and the Yü reigns that writing really began to flourish. The "Ode to the Chief"[17] is the first expression of poetic sentiment, and the narrative account of "I-chi" set a precedent for future memorials. Then the House of Hsia arose, with its lofty achievements and great merits. "The nine regulated accomplishments were written into songs,"[18] and the House became still richer in attainments and virtue.

By the time of the Shang and the Chou, literary form surpassed its substance. The contents of the "Ya" and the "Sung"[19] shine fresher daily in their flowery brilliance. When King Wen was in trouble, his oracular judgments glowed bright;[20] couched in rich and cryptic language, they contain subtle meanings, solidly grounded and profound. And Tan, the versatile Duke of Chou, gloriously surpassed even these achievements by writing poetry and compiling the "Sung," improving the literary qualities of all writing. Our Master [Confucius], standing without peer among the early masters, continued this tradition of the sages of the past. The six Classics, since he has cast and molded them, ring out the resonant music of bronze and jade; they present the refined principles chiseling human emotions and nature, as they furnish outlines for all literary forms. The clapping of his wooden bell[21] was answered for one thousand li around, and his influence will find an echo ten thousand years from now. He expresses in literary form the light of the universe, and opens the ears and eyes of all the people.

17 In the section entitled "I-chi" in the *Book of History*.

18 Quoted from "Ta-yü mu" in the *Book of History*, where the nine accomplishments refer to the regulation of the six treasures, water, fire, metal, wood, earth, and grain, and the three businesses, the rectification of the people's character, the conveniences of life, and the securing of an abundant livelihood. See Legge, *The Chinese Classics*, Pt. II, Bk. II, Ch. II, 7, p. 56.

19 Two of the three sections in the *Book of Poetry*, containing poetry of the upper classes and ceremonial or sacrificial songs respectively.

20 The judgments on the hexagrams and lines were attributed to King Wen, who was said to have written these when he was imprisoned by the ruler of the Shang.

21 Confucius was compared to a wooden bell, sounding warning to the people. See "Pa-i" in the *Analects*.

From the time of Master Feng[22] to the time of Confucius, both
Feng, the first sage, who invented writing, and the "King Without
Crown,"[23] who transmitted the teachings, drew their literary embellishments from the mind of *Tao*, and both taught by reference to divine
principles. Both took images from the Yellow River Map and the
Lo River Writing, and both divined by means of milfoil stems and
tortoise shells. Both observed heavenly patterns in order to comprehend
their changes exhaustively, and both studied human patterns of
behavior in order to transform them. It was in this way that they
were able to legislate for the universe[24] and to establish the principles
governing human society, to achieve gloriously in fact, as well as to
beautify literary forms and ideas. From these things we know that *Tao*
is handed down in writing through sages, and that sages make *Tao*
manifest in their writings. This principle may be extended to all
things without difficulty, day after day, without exhausting its applica-
tions. The *Book of Changes* says, "The stimulation of all celestial
movements depends upon the oracular judgments,"[25] and their power
to stimulate the celestial world is derived from the pattern of *Tao*.

The Tsan:[26]
The mind of *Tao* is subtle,[27]

[22] A commentator on the *Li-chi* (Book of rites) in connection with a passage in the
"Yüeh-ling" (Monthly guide for a ruler) gives Feng as the surname of Fu Hsi.

[23] "King Without Crown," a title given to Confucius by scholars—particularly scholars
of the New-script School during the Han and Wei periods, who held that Confucius,
with his virtue, should rule, although actually he did not.

[24] This idea of legislation on a cosmic scale need not be surprising; Immanuel Kant
speaks of the mind as the legislator of the universe; and a Sung philosopher, Chang Tsai,
aimed at establishing the Mind of the Universe.

[25] *Chou-i yin-te*, 44/Hsi, shang/12; *I-ching*, I, 348. The term rendered here as "judgments" is "tz'u," which means also term, statement, or proposition. Liu Hsieh seems to
have capitalized on this ambiguous association of these different meanings of the term
to facilitate his moving from the importance of the oracle judgments to the significance
of linguistic form.

[26] The Tsan, as used in this work, is a form of rhymed poetry with four-word lines,
treated by the author himself in Chapter 9, where he says that its functions are to assist
in the explanation of the subject, to pass value judgments on the subject, and to give a
summary of the subject treated.

[27] Quoted from "Ta-yü mu" in the *Book of History*; this chapter has been proved to
be a forgery, a fact not known to Liu Hsieh. Hsüntzu, in his chapter "Chieh-pi" (On

And it is taught through divine principles.
Glory to the first sage,
Who made articulate the principles of love and filial piety.
The Map the dragon carried presents the substance,
And the Writing the tortoise brought makes manifest the form
Here may be seen the patterns of heaven
Which serve all people as models.

II. Evidence from the Sage

The creative man is called a sage; the man who transmits, an understanding scholar.[1] To cultivate human nature and emotions is the mission of the great Sage. "The literary form of the teaching of the Master is available to us";[2]—we have the sentiments of the Sage expressed in writing. The wise teachings of former kings are recorded on wooden and bamboo strips, and the graceful expressions of the Master overflow in his aphorisms.[3] When praising the ancient T'ang dynasty [when literature first began to flourish], he described [its ruler Yao] as brilliant and great [in mastery of literary form];[4] he also praised the contemporary Chou [when literary form surpassed its substance], calling its culture rich and worthy of adoption.[5] This shows us what importance Confucius attached to literary form in government and education. When the Earl of Cheng entered Ch'en, Confucius

---

prejudice), quoted lines which differ from those found in the *Book of History* in only one insignificant particle from a *Tao-ching*. The *Tao-ching* was interpreted by the commentators on the *Hsüntzu* as an ancient work on moral principles.

[1] See *Li-chi yin-te* (Peking, 1937), 19/3.

[2] *Lun-yü yin-te* (Peking, 1940), 8/5/13, where Tzu Kung stated that the Master's literary form might be heard while his doctrine on nature and the way of heaven is hardly ever touched upon.

[3] Referring to *Lun-yü*, the *Analects*.

[4] *Lun-yü yin-te*, 15/8/19, where Confucius is recorded to have said of Yao, "brilliant with literary form."

[5] *Ibid.*, 5/3/14.

believed that it was his mastery of rhetoric which brought him success.[6]
And when the people of Sung entertained [Wen-tzu from Chao] by
preparing a formal feast, Confucius commended them for the observ-
ance of proper ceremony shown in their attention to the language
they used.[7] This shows us what importance Confucius attached to
literary form in practical affairs. In praising Tzu-ch'an, Confucius
said, "His words are adequate for the expression of his ideas, and his
literary forms are adequate to ornament his words,"[8] and in his general
discussion of a superior man he said, "One should be truthful in one's
sentiments, but also masterly in expression."[9] This shows us what
importance Confucius attached to literary form in self-cultivation.
Ideas adequately expressed by words combined into literary forms—
sincere sentiments embodied in masterly expressions: these are the
touchstones of literary composition.

Our Master was as discerning as the sun and the moon,[10] and as
sublime as the spiritual working of the universe. His literary forms
are perfect examples and his ideas are perfectly coherent. Sometimes
he employs only a few words to convey an idea, and sometimes he
indulges in a comprehensive discussion of all his sentiments. Sometimes
he reveals the nature of a thing by pointing out the pattern it exhibits,
and sometimes he implies the function of it through cryptic innuendo.
In the *Spring and Autumn* he uses one word to express both praise
and censure and in "San-fu" he expresses a greater category under
the form of a lesser.[11] These illustrate his expression of an idea in a
few words. In the "Pin" lyrics we find many verses with many lines
each, and in "Ju-hsing" there are long discussions and ornate rhetoric.[12]
These illustrate his indulgence in comprehensive discussions of all his
sentiments. Writing chiefly characterized by critical judgment he

---

[6] *Ch'un-ch'iu ching-chuan yin-te* (Peking, 1937), 307/Hsiang 25/7 Tso fu 2.

[7] *Ibid.*, 316/Hsiang 27/5 Tso.   [8] See note 6.

[9] *Li-chi*, 32/26.

[10] The sun and the moon have traditionally been considered to see as well as to
illuminate all they shine upon.

[11] Application of the principle involved in a fortiori reasoning.

[12] Confucius was assumed to be the author of the *Book of Poetry*, of which "Pin-feng"
(lyrics from the Pin region) is a section. "Ju-hsing" is a chapter in the *Li-chi*.

symbolizes by the hexagram *k'uai* [which means "to judge"],[13] and
writing chiefly characterized by logical clarity he symbolizes by the
hexagram *li* [which stands for fire and the sun].[14] These illustrate how
he reveals the nature of a thing by pointing out the pattern it exhibits.
In the Four Images[15] there is profound meaning which is delicate and
cryptic, and in the Five Illustrations[16] the language is connotative,
implicative. These illustrate how he implies the function of a thing
through cryptic innuendo.

From all these examples we can see how literary pieces differ in their
form, some being diffuse and others concise; and we see also that they
vary in their method of presentation, which is sometimes veiled
[suggestive, evocative], and sometimes lucid. The choice of either
method must depend on the occasion, remaining flexibly adaptable to
all changing circumstances. If one looks for examples in the writing
of the Duke of Chou and of Confucius, he will have obtained models
for his literary compositions. In discussing questions, one must seek
the guidance of the sages, and in one's efforts to understand the sages,
one must make the Classics one's teachers.[17]

The *Book of Changes* says, "When things have been correctly distinguished and the language expressing them has been made accurate,
then decisive judgments are complete."[18] And the *Book of History* says,
"In the choice of language one should emphasize the essential and
should not indulge in the extraordinary."[19] So we know that the way
to establish significant distinctions is by using language accurately; and
the way to perfect writing is to emphasize the essential. If the writing

[13] *Chou-i yin-te*, 46/Hsi, hsia/2. *K'uai* is hexagram 43, meaning to distinguish, hence
to judge.

[14] *Li* is hexagram 30.

[15] *Chou-i*, 44/Hsi, shang/11. There are many interpretations regarding the Four
Images. The following is Shao Yung's interpretation: *yin* or feminine principle, *yang* or
male principle, *Kang* or strength, and *jou* or softness.

[16] See Tu Yü's *Ch'un-ch'iu Tso-chuan hsü*, where the Five Illustrations are given:
(1) subtle although apparent; (2) full of meaning although unassuming; (3) pursuasive
although objective; (4) exhaustive but well-knit; and (5) both admonishing and
exhortatory.

[17] Reading with a handwritten version quoted by Sun I-jang in his *Cha-i*.

[18] *Chou-i yin-te*, 48/Hsi, hsia/5.

[19] *Shang-shu t'ung-chien* (Peking, 1936), 44/0218-0225.

is thus perfect, there will be no danger of succumbing to the love of
the extraordinary; and if significant distinctions are thus established,
decisive judgments will emerge. The fact that profound ideas may
be obscure will not mean that the language is not accurate; and the
fact that the subtlety of a thing's expression may merely connote or
imply meaning will not mean that the essential element is not stressed:
the essential element and the subtlety of the expression will be achieved
together; and accurate language and profound ideas will coexist. We
may observe these literary accomplishments in the works of the sages.

Yen Ho spoke of Confucius as "decorating feathers by painting them;
futilely employing florid language."[20] But in his deprecation of the Sage
he fails. The literary works of the Sage owe their grace and beauty
to the fact that they are full of both flowers and fruits. Even in the
case of the Way of Heaven [the obscure doctrine which the Master's
disciples themselves] hardly heard of,[21] we still try to find it out; in
the case of the literary forms which are accessible to us, should we
neglect to study these? No, for if one would follow the example of the
Sage in organizing his writing, his literary efforts would almost
certainly be rewarded with success.

> *The Tsan*:
> Superbly divine, he [Confucius] was born with knowledge;[22]
> Sagacious and wise, he ruled supreme.
> Profound reason shapes his literary theme,
> And his breath, full of talent, weaves itself into exquisite patterns.
> His discernment is comparable to that of the sun and the moon,
> And his expressions contain more wealth than mountains and seas.
> Though his shadow faded within a hundred years,
> After a thousand ages his mind still shines.

[20] *Chuang-tzu yin-te*, 89/32/27.
[21] See note 2.
[22] *Lun-yü yin-te*, 34/16/9, where Confucius speaks of three kinds of men, distinguished
by three ways of possessing knowledge: the highest type is he who is born with knowledge; next comes he who obtains it through learning; and lowest is he who slaves
to get it.

III. The Classics as Literary Sources

The works dealing with the universal principles of the Great Trinity [heaven, earth, and man] are known as *ching*.[1] By *ching* we mean an expression of the absolute or constant *Tao* or principle, that great teaching which is unalterable. Therefore, the *ching* faithfully reflect heaven and earth, spirits and gods. They help to articulate the order of things and to set up the rules governing human affairs. In them is found both the secret of nature and spirit and the very bone and marrow of fine literature.

First came the *San-fen* of the Three Sovereigns, followed by *Wu-tien* of the five emperors, *Pa-so* and *Chiu-ch'iu*.[2] As years passed, this main stream developed a great welter of branches and side-eddies. But after our Master edited and handed down this material, those great treasures, the Classics, began to shine through. The *Book of Changes* spread out its ten Wings, or Commentaries. The *Book of History* displayed its seven Views.[3] The *Book of Poetry* listed the four beginnings.[4] The *Book of Rites* described the five kinds of Rites.[5] And the *Spring and Autumn* presented the Five Illustrations.[6]

Here are principles which are absolute in regard to human nature and emotions, and here is language which conforms to the best literary

[1] *Ching* is rendered into English as "classics" in the sense that they have stood the test of time and are universal and constant.

[2] See K'ung An-kuo's "Shang-shu hsü," where the *Pa-so* is said to be about the eight trigrams, and the *Chiu-ch'iu* geographical accounts of the nine continents.

[3] In the *Shang-shu ta-chuan*, the *Book of History* is divided into seven sections, and through each section one is able to view one quality. These are: righteousness, benevolence, sincerity, capacity, affairs, good government, and beauty.

[4] There are several interpretations of these four beginnings. In the "Mao shih-hsü," the four beginnings mean "Feng," "Ta-ya," "Hsiao-ya," and "Sung." Cheng Hsüan commented, "By *shih* or the beginning is meant that by way of which the kingly way prospers and declines." Another view is expressed in "K'ung-tzu shih-chia" (the biography of Confucius) in the *Shih-chi* (The historical records): "Kuan-chü" is the beginning of the "Feng," "Lu-ming" the beginning of the "Hsiao-ya," "Wen-wang" the beginning of the "Ta-ya," and "Ch'ing-miao" the beginning of the "Sung."

[5] The Five Rites are: for sacrifice, for melancholy occasions, for hospitality, for military ceremonies, and for auspicious occasions.

[6] See note 16, Chapter II.

principles. As a consequence the *ching* can unfold the student's understanding and cultivate in him the proper principles; their "light shines far and wide."[7]

The mind of *Tao* is subtle, and the thinking of the Sage transcendent: when the walls and eaves are many and high, breathing is naturally deep: a bell of ten thousand weights will not ring out petty sounds.

The *Book of Changes* deals with *T'ien*; it has penetrated the divine order, to fulfill itself fruitfully.[8] Accordingly, the "Hsi-tz'u"[9] says that it has boundless implications, its critical judgments are of high literary quality, its language is accurate, and its symbolism deep:[10] "The leather cords broke three times"[11]—what a profound source of ideas this has proved to be for the Sage!

The *Book of History* truthfully records what has been spoken.[12] Although the terms used are hard to understand, if one masters the *Erh-ya*[13] the ideas will be comprehensible. Tzu-hsia, [a disciple of Confucius who specialized in literature], in his praise of the *Book of History* calls it "brilliant as the light of the sun and the moon and orderly as the configurations of the stars,"[14] which testifies to its clarity.

The purpose of the *Book of Poetry* is to express feelings and sentiments. The terms used in it are to be studied in the same way as those used in the *Book of History*. The way the lyrics are written and the metaphors forged, the way the theses are embellished and the parables contrived, create an effect of warmth and tenderness when these poems are recited, an effect which deeply moves the heart.

The *Book of Rites* aims at the establishment of traditions. It formulates the basic principles governing social customs. The principles and

---

[7] A line quoted from the *Book of Poetry*, *Mao-shih yin-te*, 63/247/3.

[8] *Chou-i yin-te*, 46/Hsi, hsia/3: "The profound idea has entered the divine state for the purpose of bringing about its fruitful functioning."

[9] *Ibid.*, 48/Hsi, hsia/5.

[10] *Ibid.*, 48/Hsi, hsia/5: "The meanings are far-reaching, the judgments are well ordered. The words are roundabout but they hit the mark. Things are openly set forth, but they contain also a deeper secret." *I-ching*, I, 370.

[11] Quoted from "K'ung-tzu shih-chia," the biography of Confucius, in the *Shih-chi*.

[12] The *Han-shu*, "I-wen chih": "The historian on the left records what is spoken."

[13] A dictionary of terms used in the Classics arranged according to meanings.

[14] Quoted from the *Shang-shu ta-chuan*.

corollaries are subtle and oblique, and become clear only through practical application. Every single phrase selected from it is a treasure.

The *Spring and Autumn* is characterized by its clear reasoning. Reason may appear in the choice of a single word. "Five meteorites" and "Six fishhawks"[15] are two examples of a pattern of composition marked by a thoroughness in reasoning. In the case of "The Chih gate and the two gates,"[16] reason appears in the order: precedence and sequence. To be so subtle and yet so apparent, so full of meaning yet so unassuming, is to be genuinely profound.[17]

In the case of the *Book of History*, its language may appear strange to the reader, but when he looks for its ruling principles he will find them indicated very clearly. In the case of the *Spring and Autumn*, its language may seem readily understandable, but when the reader seeks the meaning of it he begins to realize its depth. These two works illustrate different patterns of writing from the hands of sages, as well as different methods of approach, objective and subjective.[18]

---

[15] *Ch'un-ch'iu Ching-chuan yin-te*, 111/Hsi 16/1. "There were falling meteorites in the state of Sung, five in number. . . . And there were six fishhawks flying backward over the capital of Sung." Commentary by Kung-yang says: "Why is 'falling' first mentioned and then 'meteorites'? It is because this was a record about what one heard. First one heard the sound of falling. Looking at them, he found them to be meteorites. After a closer observation he discovered them to be five in number. Why is the number 'six' first mentioned and then 'fishhawks'? Because in the case of 'the six fishhawks flying backward' it was a record about what one saw. Looking at them, one found them to be six in number. Looking closer, he saw them to be fishhawks. After watching them at leisure, he discovered them to be flying backward." For these reasons, the *Spring and Autumn* is held to be logical, that is, a work characterized by reason.

[16] *Ch'un-ch'iu Ching-chuan yin-te*, 439/Ting 2/2 Kung-yang. "Chih gate and the two gates were destroyed by fire." "Chih gate" is the south gate of the royal palace, and the two gates are those outside the Chih gate where proclamations are posted. Chih gate is apparently more important than the two gates. The commentary by Kung-yang says: "Why does the record say 'Chih gate and the two gates were destroyed by fire'? It is because the two gates were not important. Why then does it not say Chih gate was destroyed by fire and the fire was extended to the two gates? It is because it was the two gates which were [first] destroyed by fire. Then why is it mentioned last? It is because [the historian] did not wish to proceed from the less important to the more important."

[17] See note 16, Chapter II.

[18] The whole section beginning with the line "The *Book of Changes* deals with *T'ien*" to this point is taken verbatim from Wang Ts'an's writing without acknowledgement by Liu Hsieh. However, such a practice was quite common in the early times, and should not be considered as plagiarism. Wang's writing is found in both *I-wen*

These Classics have deep roots and luxuriant branches and foliage. The language is concise but the content is meaningful; the facts are commonplace, but their metaphorical implications are unlimited. So, although they are ancient, their flavor remains fresh. Later scholars take them up and do not feel that they have become outmoded; scholars in the past long used them and never felt that they were ahead of their times. They may be compared to Mount T'ai, which waters all the lands about, or to the Yellow River, which moistens one thousand li.

Thus, the *Book of Changes* originates the *lun* or discursive, *shuo* or argumentative, *tz'u* or oracular, and *hsü* or prefatory forms of writing. The *Book of History* is the source of the *chao* or decree, the *ts'e* or edict, the *chang* or memorial expressing thanks, and the *tsou* or general memorial. *Fu* or narrative poetry, *sung* or sacrificial poetry, *ke* or folk song, and *tsan* or eulogy have their foundations in the *Book of Poetry*. *Ming* or inscription, *lei* or elegy, *chen* or admonition, and *chu* or prayer have their beginnings in the *Book of Rites*. And *chi* or chronicle, *chuan* or biography, *meng* or oath[19] and *hsi* or proclamation have their roots in the *Spring and Autumn*. All these Classics have reached great heights in establishing standards; they have also opened up vast new vistas. So that no matter how writers may leap and bound, they must eventually come home to the fold of the Classics. One may pattern his writing after the classical forms or enrich his diction by studying the *Book of Poetry* [with the same confidence with which] one may depend on a mountain's copper ores to suffice for coinage, or rely on sea water to make salt when boiled.

If one's writings were based on the Classics, his style would be especially distinguished by one of the following characteristics: deep feeling untainted by artificiality, unmixed purity of form, empirical truth untarnished by falsehood, moral ideas uninvolved in perversity, simple style free from verbosity, and literary beauty unmarred by excesses. Master Yang compared [the writing of the Classics] to the

---

Lei-chü, 38, and *T'ai-p'ing yü-lan*, 608. For a discussion of this practice of borrowing from other authors see Chang Hsüeh-ch'eng's *Wen-shih t'ung-i*, "Shuo-lin."

[19] Reading *ming* as *meng* with the T'ang hand-written version.

carving of jade into vessels, his idea being that literary pattern is innate in the five Classics.[20]

A man wins his mastery of literature through the excellence of his character, and his character is manifested in his literary excellence. In literature, first among the four elements of instruction,[21] both symbol and colorful pattern assist each other to teach. No one who aims at the improvement of his moral character and the establishment of his name fails to go to the Sage for his model; but when one develops an interest in a career of literature and rhetoric, he seldom realizes that he too should take the Classics as his starting point. The poetry of Ch'u has alluring charm and the poetic prose of Han is extravagant; but both are deviant forks which never return to the main stream. Would it not be a good thing to curb the tendency to deviate by returning to the source?

The Tsan:
The universal principles governing the Great Trinity
Are embodied in profound teachings and ancient learning.
To achieve transformation in order to return to the One,
These teachings are divided into five.
The five Classics are art masters moulding human nature and spirit,
And the great treasure house of literature,
Unfathomable and lustrous,
The Source of all literary forms.

IV. Emendation of Apocrypha

The Divine Way is plain and yet hidden; the Mandate of Heaven is subtle and yet manifest.[1]

---

[20] See chapter on "Kua-chien" in his *Fa-yen*.
[21] *Lun-yü yin-te*, 13/7/25: "The master taught *wen* [literature], *hsing* [character], *chung* [loyalty], and *hsin* [trustworthiness]."
[1] The Divine Way and the Mandate of Heaven: the subject matter of the apocrypha. The apocrypha also claim to explain the Classics.

Following the emergence of the horse-dragon, there developed the *Book of Changes*;[2] and with the appearance of the divine tortoise, the "Hung-fan" saw the light of day.[3] For this reason, "Hsi-tz'u" says: "From the Yellow River comes the diagram and from the River Lo comes the Book, and these the Sage followed as principles."[4] However, it has been so long ago, and records are so obscure, that a body of strange and fantastic literature has developed around these Diagrams and this Book. Although some truth is preserved by this apocryphal literature, its existence has permitted falsehood to creep in.

The six Classics are lucid and articulate, but the apocrypha [which have been attached to them] are disorganized and redundant; the *Book of Filial Piety* and the *Analects* are distinct and clear, but their apocrypha are profuse and chaotic. If we examine the apocrypha in the light of the Classics, we shall discover four proofs that their claims to authenticity are false. First, inasmuch as the apocrypha claim to complement the Classics, they bear to the Classics the same relationship that the woof bears to the warp in weaving. Now, only when the silk and hemp are not mixed with each other may one succeed in making either hempen cloth or silken fabric. But the Classics are rational while the apocrypha are incredible; they are one thousand li apart. So this claim of the apocrypha must be false. Second, the Classics, the teachings of the Sage, are clear; the apocrypha, supposedly divine teachings, are obscure. Now, sages' teachings would [ordinarily be comparatively] comprehensive, divine teachings more in the nature of unifying principles. But the apocrypha are more voluminous than the Classics, and the so-called divine principles are even more complicated than those of the sages. So this claim of the apocrypha must be false. Third, a real mandate from heaven is accompanied by physical signs and miraculous prophecies. But the eighty-one apocryphal

[2] A dragon in the form of a horse was believed to have brought out of the Yellow River certain diagrams which developed into the eight trigrams.

[3] The divine tortoise is believed to have carried the Book on its back out of the River Lo. K'ung An-kuo of the Former Han, a descendant of Confucius, identified this book as the "Chiu-ch'ou" found in the chapter entitled "Hung-fan" in the *Book of History* (Shang-shu t'ung-chien, 0063-0066).

[4] *Chou-i yin-te*, 44/Hsi, shang/11.

writings are all attributed to Confucius, Yao was made the creator of the "Green Diagram," and Ch'ang [King Wen of the Chou], was credited with the "Red Book."[5] So this claim of the apocrypha must be false. Fourth, and last, maps and diagrams appeared on several occasions before the Shang and Chou dynasties, but the Classics were completed only at the end of the Spring and Autumn period. For the woof to come before the warp is contrary to custom in weaving. So this claim of the apocrypha must be false. When the false beliefs have been isolated and rejected, true beliefs differentiate themselves and become established. Since the Classics are adequate as teachings, what contribution do the apocrypha make to them?

As a matter of fact, the appearance of the maps and diagrams was the manifestation of the good mandate of Heaven, the auspicious herald of a sage; they are not meant to supplement the Classics. This is why, when the Yellow River did not produce maps in his time, our Master heaved a sigh. If authentic maps could have been fabricated, why then the sigh?[6] From the circumstance that long ago King K'ang placed the River Maps in the Eastern Apartment,[7] we know that these physical symbols of prophecy were rare treasures handed down from one dynasty to another. Confucius' contributions to them were merely their prefaces. But later devotees of esoteric sciences constructed strange doctrines about the physical symbols. Some of them discoursed on the *yin* and *yang*, while others invented narratives of calamities and supernatural occurrences. The chirping of the birds was deemed to sound like human speech and the nibbling of worms on leaves was construed as a completed sentence.[8] These writings, voluminous and

[5] Both references are found in Ma Kuo-han, *Yü-han shan-fang chi i-shu.*

[6] *Lun-yü yin-te,* 16/9/9.

[7] *Shang-shu t'ung-chien,* 42/0328-0332. During the Hsia dynasty, the "Tung-hsü," or Eastern Apartment, was the academy where the aged were cared for.

[8] *Ch'un-ch'iu ching-chuan yin-te,* 330/Hsiang 30/3 Tso; see *Tso-chuan,* under the 30th year of Duke Hsiang: "Birds chirped on the temple at Po, and they sounded like 'Alas! Alas!' On the day of *chia-wu* the state of Sung had a great calamity, and Po-chi of Sung died." See also "Wu-hsing chih" in the *Han-shu:* "During the reign of Emperor Chao [86-74 B.C.] a big willow tree in the Palace of Shang-yüan broke in two and fell to the ground. One morning it stood up. Branches and leaves grew out. Worms nibbled its leaves to form the sentence: 'Kung-sun Pin-chi will be made emperor.'" Kung-sun Pin-chi was the Emperor Hsüan (73-49 B.C.) who succeeded Emperor Chao.

disorderly as they were, were all attributed to Confucius. Learned scholars, after much discussion and research, placed the date of their appearance during the reigns of the Emperors Ai [6-1 B.C.] and P'ing [A.D. 1-5].[9] The genuine secret treasures [which King K'ang] had stored in the Eastern Apartment of the Palace, were then mixed with forgeries. During the reign of Emperor Kuang-wu [A.D. 25-57] the emperor placed great faith in these apocryphal writings, a precedent which was followed by many, many scholars, competing shoulder to shoulder with one another. Prince P'ei-hsien [Fu] collected apocryphal writings to elucidate the Classics.[10] Ts'ao Pao wrote prophecies in setting the *Book of Rites* in order.[11] They had all gone far indeed in their deviations from the *Tao* and the orthodox. Huan T'an was disgusted with their nonsense and falsehood,[12] and Yin Ming ridiculed their superficiality and untruth;[13] Chang Heng exposed their errors,[14] and Hsün Yüeh drew attention to their oddity and perversity.[15] The judgments of these four worthies, who were both erudite and penetrating, are indeed fine and to the point.

As for the writings on Fu-Hsi, Shen-nung, the Yellow Emperor, and Shao-hao; or on the nature of *Shan, Tu,* and the *Chung-lü;*[16] or on the physical symbols of the white fish and red crow;[17] or on the auspicious omens of yellow gold and purple jade,[18] they record a great wealth of significant achievements in language both rich and brilliant.

---

[9] Hsü Yang-yüan disputed this point, maintaining that some of the apocryphal writings were done toward the end of the Western Han dynasty, but maps and statements of prognostication existed long before then. Hsü's essay is found in Yen Chieh's *Ching-i ts'ung-ch'ao.*

[10] Fan Yeh, *Hou-han shu* (Po-na ed.), 42/6a.

[11] *Ibid.,* biography of Ts'ao Pao.   [12] *Ibid.,* biography of Huan T'an.

[13] *Ibid.,* biography of Yin Ming. Reading with the T'ang manuscript *shen-hsia* as *fou-chia* to harmonize with the phrase in the previous line.

[14] *Ibid.,* biography of Chang Heng.   [15] Hsün Yüeh, *Shen-chien,* "Su-hsien."

[16] It is not possible to identify *Shan* and *Tu* with certainty. *Shan* may refer to *Tun-chia k'ai-shan t'u,* and *Tu* to *Ku-yüeh tu-ching. Chung-lü* is a work on natural calamities recorded in the "I-wen chih" of the *Han-shu.*

[17] Ssu-ma Ch'ien, *Shih-chi,* "Chou pen-chi," relates how a white fish jumped into King Wu's boat and a fire descended from heaven and turned into a red crow, all symbols indicating that King Wu had received the mandate of heaven.

[18] Omens of good government, recorded in *Tou-wei-i,* apocryphal interpretation of the *Book of Rites.*

While they add nothing to the Classics, they are a great help to literary composition. Therefore later literary men picked out and treasured the best elements in them. P'ing-tzu [or Chang Heng], greatly concerned lest these writings should mislead scholars, wrote a memorial urging that they should be banned, but Chung-yü [or Hsün Yüeh], because they also contain some truth, would not allow them to be burned. Since in all previous dynasties apocryphal writings have been treated as companions to the Classics, they have been here discussed in full.

The Tsan:
The mighty River and the mild Lo
Gave birth to maps and apocrypha,
Divine treasures to be stored for the use of posterity.
Although their principles are obscure, their literary patterns are
   valuable.
During the two Han dynasties
The red and the purple were one boiling mixture.[19]
But now, having deleted their odd and fantastic features,
We preserve only what is well-carved and beautiful.

V. An Analysis of Sao[1]

After the *feng* and *ya*[2] were no longer written, nothing worthy emerged to continue the development. Then a remarkable literary achievement arose in a burst of splendor: the *Li-sao*, soaring high in

---

[19] Red is a primary, hence pure, color, and purple a secondary or mixed color. In the *Analects*, Confucius once said, "I hate the manner in which purple takes away the luster of red." *Lun-yü* (Shih-san-ching chu-shu ed.), chüan 17, 7b. Since then red and purple have been interpreted as orthodox or refined and unorthodox or vulgar, respectively.

[1] Ch'ü Yüan, one of the greatest poets of China, flourishing in the fourth century B.C., was from the state of Ch'u. A member of the royal clan, he was at first a trusted minister

the wake of the Ancient Poets,[3] and in the van of the writers of *tz'u*.
Can it be because the time of the author of the *Li-sao* was not yet long
removed from the age of the Sage and Ch'u writers were men of
great talent?

Long ago Emperor Wu [140-87 B.C.] of the Han loved *Sao*, and
Prince [An] of Huai-nan [d. 122 B.C.] wrote an exegesis of it. To the
Prince, while the *Kuo-feng* expresses passion without sensuality, and
the *Hsiao-ya* social complaint without rebelliousness, the *Li-sao* may
be said to contain qualities of both. For, like a cicada, it molts in the
midst of muck and filth and then soars aloft beyond the dusty world,

---

of the King of Ch'u. But later he was alienated from the King by court intrigues and was
twice exiled. Finally he drowned himself. It was during his second exile that he wrote
the *Li-sao*, or *Encountering Sorrow*. Hence the term *sao* is roughly equivalent to the
English term "lament." Although the term occurs only in the *Li-sao*, it has often been
treated by later scholars as a genre, applied to the *Ch'u-tz'u*, or "Poetry of the State of
Ch'u," as a whole. This chapter discusses the merits or the demerits of the *Li-sao* and
Ch'u-tz'u in terms of their relation to the Classics, quoting and evaluating, in the
process, the literary opinions of the Han scholars on them. Liu Hsieh does not make
clear where the discussion of the *Li-sao* stops and where that of the *Ch'u-tz'u* begins.
At one moment he seems to be concerned with the *Li-sao* and in the next breath he is
found to be speaking about the *Ch'u-tz'u* as a whole. However, I try to mark the point
where Liu Hsieh shifts from the *Li-sao* to the *Ch'u-tz'u* as I do in the translation on the
basis of the content he quotes.

2 There are four versions of the *Book of Poetry* (also translated as *Book of Songs*,
Book of Odes) of which only the Mao version has come down to us intact. It is so
named because a Han scholar by the name of Mao Heng wrote a philological commentary on the Book, and this commentary was taught to another Han scholar whose
name was Mao Ch'ang. The former is known as the Great Mao, the latter as Lesser Mao.
The *Book of Poetry* is composed of three parts: (1) *feng*, folksongs and lyrics collected
from thirteen different localities; (2) *ya*, containing lyrics of a more polished type, and
narratives; (3) *sung*, ceremonial and sacrificial songs, which accompanied dances. The
term *feng* means wind, and, figuratively, is taken to mean either the gentle influence
of lyrical lamentation and complaints or the gentle way in which one remonstrates with
his superior, especially the ruler. The term *ya* means graceful. These two, together with
sung, have been used to designate the style of a literary piece which has the quality
of the *Book of Poetry*.

Then there are three literary elements employed in the *Book of Poetry*: (1) *fu*, narrative, (2) *pi*, metaphorical, and (3) *hsing*, allegorical. These three elements and the
previously mentioned three types of *feng*, *ya*, and *sung* form what are known as the
"six elements."

Finally we often come across the phrase "four beginnings." I have shown how the
Book of Poetry is composed of three parts: *feng*, *ya*, and *sung*. As the *ya* is subdivided
into the *Hsiao-ya* (minor *ya*) and *Ta-ya* (major *ya*), the book is considered to contain
four instead of three parts, that is, *feng*, *ta-ya*, *hsiao-ya*, and *sung*. For its different
interpretations, see note 4, Chapter III.

3 In most cases, Liu Hsieh uses *shih-jen*, the Ancient Poets, to refer to poets who
wrote the poems contained in the *Book of Poetry*.

its brilliance untarnished by its passage through the mud. The light it sheds may be compared to that of the sun and the moon.

It was the opinion of Pan Ku [A.D. 32-92] that Ch'ü Yüan was parading his talents and making an exhibition of himself in the *Li-sao*, that he drowned himself in the river out of resentment and bitterness, that the stories of I and Chiao and of the two Yao beauties[4] do not tally with those given in the *Tso-chuan*,[5] that references to K'un-lun and Hsüan-p'u[6] are not found in the Classics; but that nevertheless its language is beautiful and elegant, setting a standard for all *tz'u* and *fu*; and that the poet [Ch'ü Yüan], though not a man of comprehensive wisdom, possessed talent of exquisite quality.[7]

Wang I believed that the Ancient Poets persuade by sheer force[8] while Ch'ü Yüan is humble and unassuming, and that the ideas in the *Li-sao* are based on the Classics: for example the driving of dragons in fours and the riding of phoenixes are based on "He then rides on six dragons . . . ,"[9] [which is taken from the *Book of Changes*] and references to K'un-lun and Liu-sha are based on the "Division of Land" in the "Yü-kung" [in the *Book of History*]. There is no one among the famed scholars who did not take the *Li-sao* as a model for his formal literary writings. It is indeed gold in appearance and jade in substance, a work which has no peer in a hundred generations.[10]

At the time of the Han, Emperor Hsüan [73-49 B.C.] admired its consistency with the Classics,[11] and Yang Hsiung [53 B.C.-A.D. 18],

---

[4] Daughters of the ruler of Yu-yü, given to Shao-k'ang as wives when he was on his flight.

[5] The *Tso-chuan*, one of the three commentaries on the *Annals of Spring and Autumn*, a history of the state of Lu, edited by Confucius. This commentary was supposedly written by a contemporary of Confucius. Its authenticity has been debated, but Bernard Karlgren has convincingly demonstrated it.

[6] K'un-lun, a mountain range situated in the West of China. Hsüan-p'u, situated in the farthest reach of the K'un-lun mountains.

[7] See Pan Ku's "Preface to the *Li-sao*."

[8] The phrase *t'i-erh*, "lead by taking hold of the ear," is from the *Book of Poetry*: see the *Mao-shih yin-te*, 68/256/10. It is a figurative expression for a forceful method of remonstrating with a ruler.

[9] *Chou-i yin-te*, 1/1/t'uan, "He then rides on six dragons toward heaven."

[10] See Wang I's "Preface" to *Ch'u-tz'u chang-chü*.

[11] The *Han-shu*, biography of Wang Pao.

after critical and appreciative study, maintained that its style is the same as that of the Odes.[12] These four scholars accepted the *Li-sao* as consistent with the Classics, although Pan Ku criticized it for not agreeing with the *Tso-chuan*. But both in commendation and in censure all have been quite arbitrary, and both their blame and their praise have been exaggerated. In their judgments they may be said to be observant but not discriminating; they have been appreciative but uncritical.

In order to determine the truth of their statements, we should discuss concrete examples from the whole *Ch'u-tz'u*. When he describes the brilliance and greatness of Yao and Shun,[13] or speaks of the reverence and respect shown by Yü and T'ang,[14] [Ch'ü Yüan] is adopting the style of *tien-kao* [of the *Book of History*].[15] When he condemns the lack of discipline of Chieh and Chou,[16] or deplores the fall of I and Chiao,[17] he is adopting the formal remonstration.[18] When he uses dragons as a metaphorical expression for men of virtue, and clouds and rainbows as metaphorical expressions for sycophants, he is adopting the devices of metaphor and moral allegory.[19] When he wipes the tears which flow each time he looks at [the palace of] the ruler, which, to his grief, is closed to him by nine gates, he is adopting the formal expression of a repining loyal subject. Judged by its performance in

[12] Yang Hsiung's statement is unidentifiable.

[13] Yao and Shun, legendary sage-kings, whose reigns are known as T'ang and Yü respectively.

[14] This is according to the T'ang dynasty manuscript, but it should be T'ang and Yü according to the *Li-sao*. Yü and T'ang were also ancient sage-kings whose dynasties are known as Hsia and Shang respectively, and not to be confused with T'ang and Yü, the reign titles of Yao and Shun respectively.

[15] In the *Book of History* certain chapters are known as *tien* and a few others as *kao*. Hence the phrase *tien-kao* comes to stand for the style of the *Book of History* as a whole.

[16] Chieh was the last ruler of the Hsia, and Chou was the last ruler of the Shang. They are considered the symbol of wickedness just as Yao and Shun are considered symbols of virtue.

[17] I usurped Hsia, only to be usurped in turn by Chiao, and Chiao was destroyed when Shao-k'ang restored the Hsia rule in 2096 B.C.

[18] Remonstration was conceived in the ancient times to be a function of the poems in the *Book of Poetry*. Hence, by saying that Ch'ü Yüan is adopting the idea of remonstration, Liu Hsieh means that Ch'ü is adopting the style of the *Book of Poetry*.

[19] Devices traditionally linked with the *Book of Poetry*.

these four respects,[20] the *Li-sao* is in harmony with the spirit of *feng* and *ya*. But the references to riding on clouds and dragons and such narratives of the strange and fantastic as the sending of Feng-lung[21] to seek Fu-fei, or the commissioning of the venom-bearing falcon to act as go-between to obtain the hand of the daughter of Sung [Yu-sung]— all these are matters which are odd and strange. K'ang-hui's[22] causing heaven to collapse on the earth, the shooting down of the [nine] suns by I, the nine-headed uprooter of trees[23] and the earthly deity with three eyes[24]—all these are tales which are incredible and strange. When Ch'ü Yüan expresses his desire to follow the example of P'eng Hsien,[25] or to accept contentedly the fate of [Wu] Tzu-hsü,[26] he seems cowardly and small-minded. His pointing with great pleasure to men and women sitting together all mixed up without distinction and his considering an all-day and all-night drinking spree as the height of enjoyment speak of licentiousness and excess.[27] At these four points the *Ch'u-tz'u* is not in accord with the Classics. In some respects it possesses classic elegance; in other respects it is exaggerated and fantastic. We know, indeed, that its style cannot compare with that of the literary works of the Three Dynasties, and yet it is fuller of the qualities of *feng* and *ya* than that of the literature of the Warring States period. Though a ruffian in the realm of *ya* and *sung*,[28] it is a hero in the land of poetry. When we examine both the bone structure of the work and

[20] Of the four respects, the first refers to the style of the *Book of History*, and the remaining three to that of the *Book of Poetry*. The repining loyal subject, of which Ch'ü Yüan is a classic example, is first found in the *Book of Poetry*. He is conceived to be remonstrating with his lord by means of metaphors and allegories. Later this became a conventional type.

[21] Wang I's commentary to the *Li-sao* says: "Feng-lung is the god of clouds." But it is often thought to be the god of thunder.

[22] The *Ch'u-tz'u*, chüan III, "T'ien-wen." K'ang-hui is another name for Kung-kung.

[23] Found in "Chao-hun," by Sung Yü, in the *Ch'u-tz'u*.

[24] Also found in Sung Yü's "Chao-hun." The last two tales cannot be attributed to Ch'ü Yüan.

[25] A worthy of the Yin dynasty who drowned himself when his advice was not followed.

[26] Wu Tzu-hsü, who cut his throat when he was not listened to by the King of Wu. See Ssu-ma Ch'ien, *Shih-chi*, biography of Wu Tzu-hsü.

[27] Both references are to Sung Yü's "Chao-hun."

[28] The phrase "*ya* and *sung*" means here the *Book of Poetry*. See note 2, on the structure of the *Book of Poetry*.

the musculature and integument which that structure sustains, we see that, although the work adopts the basic idea of the Classics, there are yet magnificent literary expressions which are the original work of the authors themselves. Thus the *Li-sao* and *Chiu-chang,* brilliant and beautiful, communicate frustrated desires; the *Chiu-ko* and *Chiu-pien,* delicate and lyrical, express grief; the *Yüan-yu* and *T'ien-wen,* odd and eccentric, exhibit great artfulness; and the *Chao-hun* and *Ta-chao,* gorgeous and dazzling, are imbued with profound beauty. The *Po-chü* reveals the true manner of one in exile; and the *Yü-fu* manifests a talent that is without peer. For these reasons, their spirit is in harmony with the spirit of the ancients and their language meets the need of the present day. With their startling grace and unique beauty, they are indeed incomparable. From the *Chiu-huai* downward, all the poets have followed their steps, but, hopelessly outdistanced, not one could over-take Ch'ü and Sung.[29] As narratives of feelings and of wrong, Ch'ü Yüan's and Sung Yü's works are melancholy and moving; in recount-ing a life of isolation they communicate its almost unbearable sorrow; mountains and streams leap before our eyes when we listen to their melodic descriptions, and seasonal changes form part of our experience as we read their literary accounts of them. Mei [Sheng, ?-141 B.C.] and Chia [I, 200-168 B.C.] entered the realm of beauty by imitating their style; and Ma [Ssu-ma Hsiang-ju, ?-117 B.C.] and Yang [Hsiung, 53 B.C.-A.D. 18] attained the quality of the wondrous[30] by developing their forms. Those who were influenced by them include poets of more than one generation. Great talents have borrowed their main ideas; the clever, their elegant language; those who compose poetry, their descriptions of mountains and streams, and poetic novices such moral metaphors as that of "fragrant grass."[31] If one is able to lean on the

[29] Ch'ü Yüan and Sung Yü, the two major poets of Ch'u, authors of the works cited here. Traditionally, the *Li-sao, Chiu-chang, Chiu-ko, Yüan-yu, T'ien-wen, Po-chü,* and *Yü-fu* are attributed to Ch'ü Yüan, and *Chiu-pien* and *Chao-hun* to Sung Yü. The *Ta-chao,* however, is sometimes attributed to Ch'ü Yüan and sometimes to Ching Ch'a, another famous poet of the State of Ch'u.

[30] "Wondrous" is one of several rough classifications of literary quality.

[31] In the *Ch'u-tz'u,* particularly the *Li-sao,* fragrant grasses and flowers are meta-phorically used to stand for good moral qualities, and hence good men.

ya and the *sung* as one leans on the cross bar of a carriage, or to harness the *Ch'u-tz'u* poetry as one harnesses a horse, and if one can absorb their wondrous qualities without losing sight of their truths and appreciate their flowers without neglecting their fruits, then, just as effortlessly as he glances, he will be able fully to utilize his literary power, and just as spontaneously as he coughs, he will be able to reach the literary heights. He will have no need to go to Ch'ang-ch'ing [or Ssu-ma Hsiang-ju] for inspiration or to Tzu-yüan [or Wang Pao, ?-61 B.C.] for benefits.

The Tsan:
Without Ch'ü Yüan
How could there be a *Li-sao?*
His startling talent sweeps like wind,
And his vigorous patterns roll like clouds.
The mountains and streams he describes have no horizons,
And the emotions and ideas he expresses are those of one who has
 suffered much.
All the phases and forms of the works are of gold and jade,
And its minutest fragments overflow with beauty.

VI. An Exegesis of Poetry[1]

Great Shun[2] said: "Poetry is the expression of sentiments, and songs are these expressions set to music."[3] Of this explanation, given by the sage, the meaning is clear. That which is the sentiment within the mind becomes poetry when expressed in words.[4] It is here indeed that literary

[1] The purpose of this chapter is to give the origin, function, and development of poetry from its earliest traces at a time when it was not distinguished from music to Liu Hsieh's own time.
[2] See note 13, Chapter V.
[3] *Shang-shu t'ung-chien* (Peking, 1936), 02/068-0686.
[4] Mao's edition of the *Book of Poetry* (Shih-san-ching chu-shu ed., 1815), 5a.

form unfurls itself to communicate reality.[5] Poetry means discipline,[6] disciplined human emotion. The single idea that runs through the three hundred poems in the *Book of Poetry* is freedom from undisciplined thought.[7] The interpretation of poetry as disciplined human emotions is in thorough agreement with this observation.

Man is endowed with seven emotions. When stimulated by external objects, these emotions rise in response. In responding to objects one sings to express his sentiments. All this is perfectly spontaneous. In ages past, there was a metrical piece of Ke-t'ien-shih's called "Hsüan-niao," which was set to music;[8] and in the music of Huang-ti's "Yün-men" there is not one note which is empty of meaning.[9] At the time of Yao the song of "Ta-t'ang" was sung, and Shun created the lyric called "Nan-feng."[10] Examination of these two poems, however, shows that they have only the merit of communicating ideas.

When Great Yü completed his work, his nine regulated achievements

[5] Scholars usually attribute the first use of the term *tsai* (to convey) to Chou Tun-i of the Sung, and the idea of literary *form* as a vehicle conveying *tao* (moral principles) to Han Yü of the T'ang, whose term for this idea is *kuan* (to string together). In this chapter we see that Liu Hsieh was the first one either to use the term *tsai* or to advance the idea of literary *form* as being in itself a vehicle for ideas. In conceiving the function of literary form to be *kuan* or *tsai* (to string together or to convey) moral principles, Han Yü and Chou Tun-i are thought to have relegated the literary form to a secondary role and elevated moral principles to a supreme height. This idea may be fully justified in the case of Chou Tun-i and the Neo-Confucians after him; it is less applicable to Han Yü, who certainly valued literary form both as an instrument and for its own sake. But it is totally inapplicable in the case of Liu Hsieh, for whom literary form and moral principles are of equal importance.

[6] This is according to the *Han-shen-wu*, an apocryphal work purporting to explain the *Book of Poetry*.

[7] *Lun-yü yin-te*, 2/2/2.

[8] Ke-t'ien-shih is the title of an ancient ruler. See the *Lü-shih ch'un-ch'iu*, "Shan-t'ung chi": "He wins confidence while not uttering a single word, and the people follow his way though he makes no effort to transform them. Great indeed is he, and beyond name." The "Hsüan-niao" is second of the eight musical poetic pieces recorded in the *Lü-shih ch'un-ch'iu*, "Ku-yüeh p'ien" in "Chung-hsia chi," chapter on the ancient music. See *Lü-shih ch'un-ch'iu t'ung-chien*, 5/8b.

[9] "Yün-men" is a musical poem commemorating Emperor Huang-ti's achievements and virtue. See *Chou-li yin-te*, 6/1b, "Ch'un-kuan," "Ta ssu-yüeh," and the "Cheng-i"; the commentary to Cheng Hsüan's (127-200) "Preface of Shih-p'u."

[10] "Ta-t'ang" was written by Shun in praise of Yao's determination to abdicate. In the "Yüeh-chi" in the *Li-chi*, "Ta-chang" is mentioned as a song of the Yao period. For the poem, see the *Shang-shu ta-chuan*, attributed to Fu-Sheng of the Han. For "Nan-feng," see *Li-chi yin-te*, 19/7.

were sung in songs;[11] and when T'ai-k'ang lapsed from virtue, his five brothers complained in song.[12] To use poetry to eulogize good and set right evil behavior is a practice of long standing. From the Shang to the Chou, the *ya* and the *sung* are the most perfect examples. The four beginnings[13] are dazzling and brilliant, and the six elements[14] are exhaustive and profound. Tzu-hsia properly comprehended the verse containing the line "Be white in order to be beautiful";[15] and Tzu-kung, the stanza in which chiseling and polishing are mentioned.[16] For this reason Shang and Tz'u were considered by Confucius worthy to discuss poetry with.[17]

After the exhaustion of the royal grace of the Chou dynasty, the collecting of poems stopped.[18] During the Spring and Autumn period the old poetry was read or recited by men who wished to reveal their ambitions; it was pressed into service to glorify diplomatic guests at state functions, and to quote it with facility was sought as a personal ornament. In the state of Ch'u poetry was characterized by satires and laments, and the *Li-sao* may be considered a satirical allegory. Although the first emperor of the Ch'in burned classical writings, he had poems about the immortals written.[19]

At the beginning of the Han, Wei Meng, following the example of

[11] See note 18, Chapter I.

[12] Wu-tzu, "five persons," usually construed to mean five brothers of T'ai-k'ang, may also mean Wu-tzu or Wu Kuang, the youngest son of Ch'i, son of Yü and father of T'ai-k'ang, as reported in the *Chu-shu chi-nien*. If this rendering is correct, *Wu-tzu chih-ke* would be "The song of Wu-kuang, T'ai-k'ang's youngest brother." But there seems little doubt that Liu Hsieh took the phrase to mean the five brothers of T'ai-k'ang.

[13] See note 4, Chapter III.

[14] See note 2, Chapter V.

[15] *Lun-yü yin-te*, 4/3/8, where Tzu-hsia and Confucius were discussing lines from the "Shih-jen" in the *Book of Poetry*. The line quoted in the *Analects* and here is not contained in the Mao edition of the *Book of Poetry*. See *Mao-shih yin-te*, 12/57/2.

[16] *Lun-yü yin-te*, 2/1/15. The poem discussed is found in *Mao-shih yin-te*, 12/55/1. In both these cases, a moralistic interpretation of poetry is emphasized.

[17] Shang is another name of Tzu-hsia and Tz'u another name of Tzu-kung. See references in the *Analects* in notes 15 and 16.

[18] *Han-shu*, "I-wen chih": "In ancient times there was an office in charge of collecting lyrics and folksongs. From these poems the ruler learned of the conditions of the people. Such knowledge would acquaint him of the success and failure of his government and would serve as a basis for improvement."

[19] This happened in the thirty-sixth year of his reign (211 B.C.), but the poems are lost. See Ssu-ma Ch'ien, *Shih-chi*, "Ch'in-shih-huang pen-chi."

the Chou poets, first used the four-word-line form for the formal remonstration. Emperor Wu [140-87 B.C.] loved literature and, in the tower of Po-liang, crossed wits with his ministers to produce poetry.[20] And there were Yen[21] and [Ssu-]ma [Hsiang-ju] and the like who were limited by nothing in their poetic creativity. When Emperor Ch'eng [32-7 B.C.] ordered the selection and collection of the poetry of the time,[22] more than three hundred poems, including almost all the literary pieces of the day, were collected. In all these literary remains we find no trace of five-word-line poetry. Therefore scholars of later times cast doubt on the authenticity of [the poems attributed to] Li Ling[23] and Pan, a woman palace-official, during the time of Emperor Ch'eng.

In the "Hsing-lu" in the "Shao-nan"[24] we find half the lines [in the second and third stanzas] to be of the five-word type,[25] and the entire "boy's song," "Ts'ang-lang," is of five-word lines.[26] "Hsia-yü,"[27] a song of a court jester, appeared long ago during the time of the Ch'un-ch'iu period;[28] and the folk song "Hsieh-ching" was current in recent times.[29] So when we investigate the periods and look for evidence, it is clear that the five-word-line pattern has long been in existence. As for the "Ancient Poems,"[30] they are fine and beautiful.

[20] This reportedly happened in the year 108 B.C. The poetry may be described as "round robin" poetry. The emperor led off with a line, to be followed by his ministers one after another, each giving a line with the same rhyme or rhymes. Ku Yen-wu of the Ch'ing dynasty considered these lines to be later forgeries, because the titles affixed to many of the ministers who took part were created in later times. See his *Jih-chih lu*, chüan 21.

[21] Yen Chi, flourishing in the second century B.C.

[22] See the "Main Preface" of the "I-wen chih" in the *Han-shu*.

[23] Five-word line poems have been attributed to Li Ling and his friend Su Wu. Liu Hsieh seems to be the first one to question their authenticity. Later Su Shih (1036-1101) made the same point.

[24] "Shao-nan" is one of the fifteen sections in the *Book of Poetry* containing poems collected from among the states, and "Hsing-lu" is a poem under this section; its number is 17.

[25] *Mao-shih yin-te*, 1/17/2, 3.

[26] *Mancius*, 27/4A/9. Also found in the "Yü-fu" in the *Ch'u-tz'u*.

[27] The first two characters of a five-word-line poem used as a title.

[28] *Kuo-yü*, "Chin-yü."

[29] *Hsieh-ching* are the first two characters of the folk song. It was current during the time of Emperor Ch'eng. See the "Wu-hsing chih" in the *Han-shu*.

[30] The term "Ancient Poems" refers particularly to the group of nineteen five-word-

Some attributed them to Mei Shu of the Western Han,[31] except for the poem on "Ku-chu," which was believed to be from the pen of Fu I.[32] But if we compare their literary style, they seem to be the productions of the Two Han. Their composition and rhetoric are unadorned and yet not crude. Realistic in describing objective scenes and deeply moving in depicting inner emotions, they are indeed the crown of the five-word-line poetry.

The "Yüan-pien" or Lament of Chang Heng,[33] pure and elegant, is absorbing in interest; and those poems about the immortals, or those of a slow rhythm,[34] are graceful in the freshness of their sound-patterns.

At the beginning of the Chien-an reign [A.D. 196-220] the five-word-line pattern developed by leaps and bounds. Emperor Wen[35] and Ch'en Ssu[36] galloped ahead with a free rein, while Wang, Hsü, Ying, and Liu, with eyes fixed on the road, raced along in competition.[37] Their common themes are love for the wind and the moon, excursions to gardens and parks, royal grace and favors, drunken revelry and feasts. Heroic in giving free play to their vitality, open and artless in the application of their talents, never resorting to petty cleverness in the expression of their feelings or in their descriptions of what they saw, and in harnessing language for their descriptions, aiming simply at lucidity—in all these ways they manifest the same spirit.

During the reign of Cheng-shih [240-248] of the Wei, the trend

---

line poems, collectively known as "Ku-shih shih-chiu shou" (Nineteen ancient poems), of which the authorship and date have been matters of conjecture and debate.

[31] Mei Sheng (?-141 B.C.).

[32] "Ku-chu" means a lone bamboo, symbolic of a betrothed woman pining for her lover to come to take her as his bride. Fu I flourished during the reigns of Emperor Ming (A.D. 58-75) and Emperor Chang (A.D. 76-88) of the Later Han.

[33] A four-word-line poem entitled "Autumn Aster" by Chang Heng is quoted in the *Yü-lan* as a poem in his lament group. See *T'ai-p'ing yü-lan*, chüan 893.

[34] These poems are not identifiable.

[35] Ts'ao P'ei, 187-226, who usurped the throne and created the Wei dynasty.

[36] Ts'ao Chih, Ts'ao P'ei's brother, 192-232.

[37] Wang Ts'an (177-217), Hsü Kan (171-218), Ying Yang (?-217), and Liu Chen (?-217) are four of the seven poets known as "The seven masters of the Chien-an period." The remaining three are: K'ung Yung (153-208), Ch'en Lin (?-217), and Yüan Yü (?-212). They are also known as Seven Masters in Yeh, the place where they all resided, and are so grouped in Emperor Wen's literary critical essay, *Tien-lun lun-wen*. All of them used the five-word-line poem as their main literary form.

was to explain *tao*,[38] and poetry of this period contains elements of the
cult of immortality. Ho Yen [?-249] and his like are in general superficial and shallow. Only Hsi [K'ang, 223-262], whose works are characterized by pure and lofty emotions, and Yüan [Chi, 210-263], whose
ideas are far-reaching and profound, achieved outstanding stature. As
to the "Po-i"[39] by Ying Chü [190-252], that independent and coura-
geous man, its language is odd but the ideas are true. It retains the
spirit of the Wei.

In the Chin dynasty [266-316] the taste of most men of talent leaned
toward the trivial and ornate. Chang,[40] P'an,[41] Tso [Ssu] and Lu[42]
walked shoulder to shoulder in the lane of poetry. Their language is
more ornate than that of the Cheng-shih period, but they did not have
the vigor of the Chien-an masters. Some of them delighted in a
fastidious use of literary phrases, while others sought to embroider
[their literary reputations with] the conventional and trivial. These
were the general trends of the time.

During the period of the Chiang-tso [317-420][43] literary writings

[38] This is the *tao* of the religious sect, to be distinguished from philosophical Taoism;
although it was still discussed under the names of Lao and Chuang. Lao refers to
Laotzu, believed to have lived during the sixth century B.C. Before he retired, he left
behind a short work of about 5,000 words, expounding a mystical principle which is
called *tao*. About two hundred years later, Chuangtzu continued the *tao* philosophy,
a kind of naturalism with emphasis on absolute individual spontaneity and freedom.
Because *tao* was considered a metaphysical principle, the discussion on Lao and Chuang,
particularly during the Wei and Chin dynasties, is known as metaphysical talk. During the
Ch'in dynasty there arose a belief in the physical immortality of man. One of the
incentives that urged the First Emperor of the Ch'in dynasty to roam all over China
was to seek the elixer of life by exploring famous mountains in the hope of meeting
with the immortals. The Taoists of the Han and Later Han periods practiced alchemy
in an effort to produce the elixer.

[39] Poems so called because they express the idea that in *po-lü* or "one hundred ideas"
there may be *i-shih*, or "one miss"; this is the origin of the form known as "Po-i," or
"One hundred-one."

[40] There were three Chang brothers: Tsai, Hsieh, and K'ang, all flourishing in the
fourth century. See the *Chin-shu*, chüan 55, the biography of Chang K'ang. Another
theory groups Chang Hua (232-300) with Chang Tsai and his brother Hsieh to form
"Three Chang."

[41] There were two P'an: Yüeh (?-300) and his nephew Ni.

[42] The two Lu brothers were Chi (261-303) and Yün (262-303).

[43] Referring to the time when the Chin moved south under the pressure of the northern
barbarian tribes, to establish the Eastern Chin.

were burdened with metaphysical discussions.[44] Writers ridiculed the desire for worldly attainments and indulged in talks on complete spontaneity, or total obliviousness to mental machination and schemes. Although Yüan and Sun[45] and those who followed them had each his own particular way of carving and coloring his literary patterns, still, with respect to intense rhetorical interest, none was in the same class [with those who wrote prior to the Chiang-tso period]. For example, the poems by Ching-yang [or Kuo P'u, 276-324] on the immortals are distinguished and truly great.

At the beginning of the Sung [420-479] some development in the literary trend was evident. Chuang and Lao had receded into the background and the theme of mountains and streams then began to flourish. Writers vied in weaving couplets which might extend to hundreds of words, or in attempting to achieve the wondrous[46] by a single line. In expressing feelings, they always made them in complete harmony with the things they described; and in literary phraseology they tried their best to achieve freshness. These are the fields in which recent writers have been competing.

As we trace literary development through successive periods, we can detect a developing trend in literary sentiments. And as we single out which features are common to and which are unique in various periods, the main outline of the trend will become clear. In the four-word-line poetry, which is the orthodox form, grace and brilliance are the fundamental qualities; while in the five-word-line verse, which is a derived pattern, the important elements are purity and beauty. Flowers [the ornate or romantic elements] and fruits [the factual or realistic elements] are employed differently in accordance with individual talents. Thus P'ing-tzu [or Chang Heng, 78-135] achieved the grace of the ideal poetry, Shu-yeh [or Hsi K'ang, 223-262] its brilliance, Mao-hsien [or Chang Hua, 232-300] approached its purity, and Ching-yang [or Chang Hsieh] developed its beauty. Tzu-chien

[44] Discussions on Taoist conceptions found in the *Laotzu*, the *Chuangtzu*, and the *Book of Changes*.

[45] Yüan Hung and Sun Ch'o, both flourishing in the fourth century.

[46] See note 30, Chapter V.

[or Ts'ao Chih, 192-232] and Chung-hsüan [or Wang Ts'an, 77-217]
combined in their works all these good qualities; while T'ai-ch'ung
[or Tso Ssu] and Kung Kan [or Liu Chen, ?-217] each captured a
particular aspect of its beauty.

Although the form of poetry has a universal norm, the workings of
poets' minds are never stereotyped. Each writes according to his own
nature and gifts, and few are able to encompass all the good qualities.
If a poet has a shrewd understanding of the difficult, he will find his
course easy; but if he carelessly attempts to treat everything as easy,
the difficult will certainly remain there in store for him.

As for the mixed form containing three- and six-word lines, it has
its origin in the *Book of Poetry*. And the writing of the "Li-ho"[47] has
its beginning in the apocryphal writings. The "Hui-wen"[48] began with
Tao Yüan;[49] and "round-robin" poetry is modeled after the lines
produced in the Tower of Po-liang. Some of these forms are great and
others are petty, but they all aim at expressing emotions and ideas.
Hence we include them all in the realm of poetry. But we shall not
attempt to deal with all of them in detail.

   The Tsan:
People are born with feelings,
With instincts to hum and sing.
The stream of poetry took its rise during the time of ancient emperors,
And forks of it appear in the two "Nan."[50]
Poetry is in harmony with both the spirit and the reason,
And develops in accord with historical circumstances.
Glorious and rich,
It is a splendid spectacle for all time.

   [47] *Li* means to take apart and *ho*, to combine. In this form of poetry, some lines
take characters apart and others combine these parts to form new characters. Hence the
name "To separate and to combine." Here, poetic qualities are almost nonexistent, and
the reader is confronted with a set of riddles.
   [48] Another literary game of composing poetic lines which can be read from right
to left or from left to right, and from up downward or from down upward.
   [49] Not identifiable.
   [50] See note 24 for "Shao-nan."

VII. Musical Poetry (Yüeh-fu)[1]

The *Yüeh-fu* may be described as tones[2] prolonged according to rules of prosody and intervals[3] chosen according to rules of harmony.[4] The nine songs in the central heaven[5] are those of God, and the eight tunes of Ke-t'ien[6] belong to the times of ancient emperors. From the "Hsien"[7] and "Ying"[8] downward there is little evidence to discuss. The "Hou-jen" song of T'u-shan[9] marked the beginning of the music of the south. The folk song "Fei-yen" of Yu-sung[10] was the beginning of the music of the north. With the sighing of [K'ung-]chia of the Hsia dynasty at Tung-yang, the music of the east began.[11] And Yin Cheng's nostalgia for his old city when he moved to the West River

---

[1] Originally a government bureau established at the time of Emperor Wu (140-87 B.C.) of the Han dynasty to collect, write, and compose songs, probably for ritual purposes. The term *Yüeh-fu* then was used to stand for the songs collected or written by members of the bureau. In this chapter the musical aspect is emphasized, although it is quite plain that this aspect cannot be completely divorced from poetry itself.

[2] There are five tones: Kung (C), Shang (D), Chiao (E), Chih (G), and Yü (A), a whole tone scale.

[3] Twelve pitch pipes, producing a chromatic scale from C to A.

[4] This is a quotation from "Shun-tien" in the *Book of History. Shang-shu t'ung-chien*, 02/0687-0692.

[5] Ssu-ma Ch'ien, *Shih-chi*, "Chao shih-chia": Chao Chien-tzu reported his dream in which he went to the central heaven where he heard nine songs.

[6] See note 8, Chapter VI, where we have Ke-t'ien-shih.

[7] The music of Yao called "Hsien-ch'ih." See the *Pai-hu-t'ung*, "Ti-wang li-yüeh."

[8] The music of Emperor Kao, called "Wu-ying" according to the *Pai-hu-t'ung* and "Liu-ying" according to an apocryphal work on the Classic of music, quoted in a commentary on "Yüeh-chi" in the *Li-chi*.

[9] "Hou-jen" are the first two words of a song by a girl who waited for Yü of the Hsia dynasty on behalf of her mistress, the daughter of T'u-shan-shih. Literally, "hou-jen" means one who waits.

[10] There were two beautiful girls in the tribe of Yu-sung who were trying to catch a flying swallow sent to see them by God. When the swallow left and flew to the north never to return, they made a song, which ends in: "Swallow! Swallow! It flew away!" The phrase "fei-yen" means a flying swallow.

[11] K'ung-chia of the Hsia dynasty hunted at Tung-yang. A great gust of wind blinded him and he groped his way into a peasant's house. It happened that the peasant's wife was feeding her baby boy. Some people took this coming of the Hsia ruler as a good omen for the boy's future, while others thought it was a misfortune. K'ung-chia took the boy with him, saying that nothing would happen to the boy, now that he was a son of the ruler. When the boy grew up his feet were injured when a tent with a broken beam fell on them, and he was obliged to become a gate keeper. K'ung-chia sighed: "Alas! What a misfortune! Isn't that fate!"

initiated the music of the west.[12] There is no general rule for the development of musical patterns. Ordinary men and women express their feelings in local folk songs; these songs were gathered by official poetry collectors and set to music by blind music masters.[13] These feelings set silk strings and bamboo reeds vibrating while the living spirit informed the brasses and stone bells. Because of this bond between music and meaning Master K'uang could predict success and failure by testing the wind;[14] and Chi-cha could detect symptoms of a state's rise and fall in musical subtleties which he recognized.[15] How keen their perception was!

Music is organically related to one's moral nature. Its influence penetrates one's very fibres and marrow. Therefore, our early kings took great pains to check excesses in this realm. The education of noble sons included a requirement that they practice the singing of the nine virtues.[16] Therefore they were able to respond emotionally to the seven beginnings,[17] and their moral influence was capable of changing the "eight winds" [the empire].

After the decline of the *ya* [or orthodox] music, sounds that drowned one's soul prevailed. During the Ch'in musical classics were burned;

[12] Yin Cheng is another name for Ho-t'an-chia of the Shang (1542-1533 B.C.). As a reference for notes 9, 10, 11, and 12, see *Lü-shih Ch'un-ch'iu*, "Chi-hsia chi," "Yin-ch'u pien."

[13] For the practice of poetry collecting, see the *Kung-yang chuan*, commentary by Ho Hsiu of the later Han. Somewhat different versions are given in the *Han-shu*, "Shih-huo chih," in a letter from Liu Hsin to Yang Hsiung, quoted in the *Fang-yen*.

[14] *Ch'un-ch'iu ching-chuan yin-te*, 288/Hsiang 18/6 Tso.

Chin people heard that Ch'u was about to attack Chin. Master K'uang, a court musician in Chin, played the songs of eight winds (winds from eight directions). He noted that the south wind lacked vigor. He predicted that Ch'u, a state in the south, would never succeed.

[15] Chi-cha, a prince from the state of Wu, came to the state of Lu and listened to the music of different dynasties and states. He was able, through listening to the music, to pass judgments on the quality of government of these various dynasties or states. See *Ch'un-ch'iu ching-chuan yin-te*, 326-327/Hsiang 29/8 Tso.

[16] For the enumeration of the nine virtues, see "The Kao-yu mo" in the *Book of History*, 16a. *Shang-shu t'ung-chien*, 04/0139-0165. They are described as: "tolerant and yet dignified, gentle and yet independent, frank and yet polite, in control and yet respectful, yielding and yet effective, straightforward and yet mild, simple and pure, decisive and practical, and strong and acting according to principles."

[17] The beginnings of heaven, earth, man, and the four seasons. These beginnings find expression in the following respective notes: C, D, E, F#, G, A, and B.

however, at the beginning of the Han some were recovered. Chih [a Han musician] recorded the musical notes, and Shu-sun [T'ung] fixed the modes. Kao-tsu [the first emperor of the Han, 206-195 B.C.] created the "Wu-te wu" [a martial dance], and Emperor Wen [179-157 B.C.] initiated the Ssu-shih," [or "Four Seasons" dance].[18] Though these were made in the spirit of the "Shao-hsia,"[19] they also adopted some of the Ch'in patterns. But that melodious music is silent now, never to return. At the time of Emperor Wu [140-87 B.C.], who emphasized rituals, the *Yüeh-fu* was first established. Through that office songs of Chao and Tai were collected, and the melodies of Ch'i and Ch'u were preserved. [Li]Yen-nien composed flowing tunes, and Chu [Mai-ch'en] and [Ssu]-ma [Hsiang-ju] wrote songs in the style of the *Sao*. The "Kuei-hua" is a mixed tune; it is beautiful but not classical; and the "Ch'ih-yen" and other pieces are high-flown but not really elegant.[20] The music introduced by Prince Hsien of Ho-chien is graceful but seldom employed. It was apropos of the group just mentioned that Hsi An remonstrated against the writing of [comparative trivia, or, as he put it,] "songs in honor of the heavenly horse."[21] When Emperor Hsüan [73-49 B.C.] came upon the scene, he went back to the *ya* and the *sung*, and in poetry he tried to imitate the spirit of the "Lu-ming."[22] But by the time of the periods of Emperor Yüan [48-33 B.C.] and Emperor Ch'eng [32-7 B.C.], vulgar music had gradually spread. Orthodox music runs against the current of popular taste, and it is very difficult to maintain it. Later ritual anthems contain some graceful elements but, although their language may be elegant, their music no longer has the quality of the ancient music-masters K'uei or K'uang.

The three rulers of the Wei,[23] quick-witted and richly endowed,

[18] See the *Han-shu*, "Li-yüeh chih." "Wu-te wu" symbolized the happiness the world experienced when Kao-tzu brought peace to the chaotic world by means of his military campaigns; and "Ssu-shih wu" showed that the world was enjoying peace and prosperity.

[19] Name of an ancient musical piece. See *Chou-li yin-te*, 6/6a.

[20] These songs are given in the *Han-shu*, "Li-yüeh chih."

[21] Ssu-ma Ch'ien, *Shih-chi*, "Yüeh-shu."   [22] No. 161 in the *Book of Poetry.*

[23] Ts'ao Ts'ao, 155-220, Ts'ao P'ei, 187-226, and Ts'ao Jui, who ruled from 227 to 239.

often cut up both words and tunes to form trivial lyrics and common rhythms. As for their "Pei-shang" and "Ch'iu-feng" and so on,[24] the themes are either carousal or complaints against military campaigns; their minds are always preoccupied with inordinate pleasures, and their language expressive of mournful thoughts. Although their work is consistent with the three tunes of the Han, it is corrupt when compared with the "Shao-hsia."[25]

In the Chin dynasty there appeared Fu Hsüan with a profound understanding of music. He gave grace to the ritual songs he created, to be used in the ceremonies of ancestral worship. And Chang Hua's new compositions were also used in court dances. Tu K'uei, by retuning the pitch pipes, imparted ease and grace to the music of the time, while Hsün Hsü altered the measurement of the standard pitch, as a result of which the traditional tone and rhythm were made, respectively, more sad and more rapid. For this reason Jüan Hsien contended that it represented a deviation from the true traditional tone, and this opinion of his was later confirmed by the discovery of an authentic, ancient metal rule.[26] These string- and wind-accompanied songs[27] are

[24] "Pei-shang" are the first two characters of a song written by Ts'ao Ts'ao; and "Ch'iu-feng" the first two words of a song written by Ts'ao P'ei.

[25] See note 19 above.

[26] In his study of the music of the time, Hsün Hsü discovered some discrepancy between different notes. His inference led him to the conclusion that the ancient rule was about 4/10 of an inch shorter than the one in use since the Han. So he ordered a new rule made, according to which new pitch pipes were constructed. These pipes in turn served as standards for the tuning of various instruments. Then the rule was used to test ancient extant instruments. He found the measurements thus obtained agreed perfectly with the inscriptions on those instruments. And then a jade pipe, a musical stone of the Chou time, and a bell of the Han time were unearthed. When the new pipes were used to test their tune, they agreed. Now while all people looked upon Hsün's discovery with great admiration, Yüan Hsien objected that the note according to the new rule was too high. It happened that after Yüan's death a bronze rule was discovered. Its inscription was so vague that it was not possible to date it. But there was no doubt that it was an ancient rule. And it was 4/10 of an inch longer than that of Hsün's. But the writers of the *Chin-shu* (to which the reader is referred for further details) concluded in favor of Hsün because of the confirmation given him by those ancient instruments. See the *Chin-shu*, "Lü-li chih."

[27] "Ho-yüeh" is an abbreviated expression of "Hsiang-ho ko," a form of singing accompanied by string, wind (flute), brass, and stone instruments. Liu included in this category all the musical pieces he discussed in this chapter.

characterized by refinement and excellence; their external expressions
and inner sentiments accord perfectly. From this perfect accord we
know that poetry is the mind of music and sound is its body. Since
the body of music is sound, blind music masters tune the instruments;
since the mind of music is poetry, superior men perfect literary forms.
In "A love of music without indulgence in excesses"[28] lies the reason
why the customs of the state of Chin were praised;[29] while "[The
gallant and the girl,] they are going to sport together"[30] spelled the
downfall of the state of Cheng.[31] Therefore we know that when
Chi-cha made his judgments, he was listening to the language of the
songs, not merely the music.

As for love songs, tender and sentimental or mournful tunes
expressing final and fateful decisions,[32] they overflowed with sensuous
language. How, then, was it possible for proper music to emerge?
However, the popular taste reveled in the new and strange. In the
presence of classical music, which is mellow and full of dignity, people
would stretch and yawn; but when they listened to the eccentric
language [of the Liu Sung love-songs], they would slap the thigh and
begin to hop up and down like sparrows. This marked the first step
toward a state of affairs in which both poetry and music were tinged
by the influence of Cheng.[33]

The words which are set to a piece of music are poetry, and the
musical sounds of sung poetry are melody. In employing musical
sounds to accompany the words one often finds that poetry is too
complicated to be reduced to musical rhythm. Hence, Ch'en Ssu [or

[28] A line from the "Hsi-so" in "T'ang-feng," *Mao-shih yin-te*, 23/114/2. T'ang was
later the state of Chin.

[29] The praise was expressed by Chi-cha of Wu, who came to the state of Lu on a
diplomatic mission. See note 15 above.

[30] A line occurring in both stanzas of "Chen-wei" in "Cheng-feng." *Mao-shih yin-te*,
19/95/1, 2. The state of Cheng is known for its love of sensuous pleasure in both
poetry and music.

[31] Also a judgment expressed by Chi-cha.

[32] "Love songs" presumably refers to poetry by Pao Chao of Liu Sung, 420-479; and
"mournful tunes" refers to songs expressing the feelings of a deserted wife, such as
"Pai-t'ou yin."

[33] See note 30 above.

Ts'ao Chih][34] complimented Li Yen-nien[35] as well-versed in adding words to, or subtracting words from, the ancient lyrics [to make them fit the new music]. He deleted superfluous words, revealing the value of simplicity. The "Ta-feng" of Kao-tsu [of the Han][36] and the "Lai-ch'ih" of Emperor Wu[37] were set to music and sung by boys' choruses. In these songs there was no musical discord. Tzu-chien [or Ts'ao Chih] and Shih-heng [or Lu Chi] both wrote fine songs; but these were never given to the singers, nor accompanied by instruments.[38] For this reason they were considered discordant by the average listener with popular taste. As a matter of fact, the average listener lacks imagination. The military songs of Hsüan [the Yellow Emperor] and Ch'i [-po][39] and the elegies of Han times, though differing in their themes, the former military and the latter funereal, are both included in the *Yüeh-fu*. And those written by Miu Hsi [of the Wei dynasty] could be considered in the same class with these. Long ago, when Tzu-cheng [or Liu Hsiang of the Han; 77-6 B.C.] treated literary works, he distinguished poetry and songs into two categories. It is for this reason that a brief consideration has here been given to music, to define its place and function.

The Tsan:

The eight timbres[40] introduce musical patterns into literary works,
In which the words are implanted to express the form.
Folk songs were sung in the wild,

[34] Known as Prince Ch'en; Ssu was his posthumous title.
[35] A musician during the time of Emperor Wu of the Han.
[36] The first two words of a song Kao-tsu wrote. It is found in the "Yüeh-shu" in the *Shih-chi*.
[37] The last two words of a song written by the emperor mourning the loss of a beautiful concubine. It is found in the "Wei-ch'i chuan" in the *Han-shu*.
[38] The word "singers" in the phrase which is here rendered "never given to the singers" is actually "wu-chao ling-jen," literally, actors without royal edict. According to a note to this term by Chi Yün of the Ch'ing dynasty, all poets during the T'ang dynasty who wrote poems according to the patterns of the ancient *Yüeh-fu*, or created new titles for their poems, are known as "Wu-chao ling-jen." This would suggest that their poems were not written to be set to music.
[39] See the "Yüeh-chih" in the *Sung-shu*.
[40] Sounds from metal, stone, earthenware, leather, silk, wood, gourd, and bamboo, materials out of which musical instruments are made.

While melodies drawn from metal and stone filled the steps of the
  court.
It is difficult to recapture the spirit of the ancient music,
But it is all too easy to encourage a taste for the sounds of Cheng.
This is true not only for the appreciation of music,
But also for our grasp of the principle of conduct.

VIII. *Elucidation of Fu*[1]

The *Book of Poetry* contains six elements, the second of which is
called *fu*. *Fu* means to arrange; it signifies arrangement of the patterns
that give form to literature, and expresses the feelings that conform
to objective things.[2] Duke Shao once said that dukes and ministers
presented poetry, music masters presented *chen* [admonitions], and
the blind presented *fu*. In the *Commentary* it is said that, "One who
can write a *fu* when ascending to the height . . . may be made a
minister."[3]

In the "Preface" of the *Book of Poetry*, poetry is considered to belong
to the same category as *fu* [inasmuch as *fu* is there given as one element
of the book]; but in the commentaries *fu* is spoken of as a separate
genre.[4] However, if their ultimate purpose is considered, all are seen

[1] *Fu* is a genre developed from the poetry of the state of Ch'u, the *Ch'u-tz'u*. Liu
Hsieh in this chapter begins by referring to the various senses in which the term *fu*
is used, then traces it to its incipient forms in earlier times, determining its relation to
Ancient Poetry and the *Ch'u-tz'u*, and finally follows its development to his own time.

[2] The function of *fu* is to give direct narration, unhampered by either metaphor or
allegory. We often, however, find *fu* mixed with both metaphor and allegory. Hence
another interpretation given by Liu Hsiang: That which is chanted without being sung
is *fu*, suggesting thus that there is a special manner in which *fu* is chanted. For the six
elements of poetry, see note 2, Chapter V.

[3] *Commentary* refers to *Mao Commentary on the Book of Poetry*. The line quoted
here is taken from the commentary to poem no. 50, "Ting chih fang chung," in the
"Yung-feng" of the *Book of Poetry*.

[4] In the "Chou-yü" in the *Kuo-yü*, *fu* is mentioned along with *shih* (poetry), *chen*
(admonitions), and *chien* (remonstrances); in the *Mao Commentary*, it is separately
mentioned apart from *shih* (oaths), *shuo* (argumentative writings), and *lei* (elegy).

to be trunk and branches of one tree. [To emphasize the independence of *fu* as a coordinate rather than a subordinate form] Liu Hsiang showed clearly that it is chanted, not sung;[5] and Pan Ku pronounced it to be a later development of the ancient poetry.[6] As for the "Ta-sui" of Duke Chuang of Cheng[7] and the "Hu-ch'iu" of Shih Wei,[8] their expressions are terse and their lines are short, and all of their poetry is their own original creation; but although they follow the form of *fu*, they only marked its dawn, still far from daylight. It was Ling-chün [or Ch'ü Yüan] who, with his writing of the *Sao* style, first broadened the scope of both its sound patterns and its external expressions. If this summary is correct, then *fu* first received its mandate as a literary form in the works of the Ancient Poets and expanded its scope in the *Ch'u-tz'u*. Since then Hsün K'uang [or Hsüntzu] wrote the *fu* of "Li" and "Chih"[9] and Sung Yü[10] composed the *fu* of "Feng"[11] and "Tiao."[12] These writers first gave the name *fu* to their writings, consciously distinguishing it in this way from poetry. Originally a satellite among the six elements of poetry, it now assumed the status of a great independent state. The "guest-host" narrative was the first form of *fu*,[13] and an elaboration of sounds and external expressions followed, with the employment of all the known literary effects.[14] It was the first time a distinction was made between poetry and *fu*, the beginning of *fu's* receiving its distinctive name.

The Ch'in dynasty was not known for its literary achievements. At that time we find some *fu* in a mixture of forms. The poets at the

---

[5] The *Han-shu*, "I-wen chih." This chapter on literature in Pan Ku's *Han-shu* is based on the "Ch'i-lüeh," a bibliographical account of seven different categories, including classics, their commentaries, speculative writings, poetry, and *fu*, started by Liu Hsiang and completed by his son Liu Hsin of the Han.

[6] See preface of Pan Ku's "Liang-tu fu," in the *Wen-hsüan*.

[7] *Ch'un-ch'iu ching-chuan yin-te*, 3/Yin 1/3 Tso.

[8] *Ibid.*, 94/Hsi 5/1 Tso.

[9] The *Hsüntzu*, "Fu-pien" (Chu-tzu chi-ch'eng ed.), chüan 18, Chapter 26.

[10] Believed to be a disciple of Ch'ü Yüan, and flourishing during the third century B.C.

[11] In the *Wen-hsüan*.

[12] *Ku wen-yüan* (Wan-yu wen-k'u ed.), chüan II, pp. 63-5.

[13] The "K'e-chu" (guest-host) *fu* was first started by Hsün K'uang, in the form of a dialogue. Hence the name.

[14] This elaboration refers to Ch'ü Yüan.

beginning of the Han dynasty wrote them after the earlier pattern. Lu Chia attacked the problem very early; Chia I developed the trend; Mei Sheng and Ssu-ma Hsiang-ju made the style popular; and Wang Pao and Yang Hsiung brought it to powerful fulfillment. And writers from Mei Kao and Tung-fang [So] on down treated all kinds of subjects. Examples of *fu* multiplied in the time of Emperor Hsüan [73-49 B.C.] and were edited during the reign of Emperor Ch'eng [32-7 B.C.]. Those presented for royal perusal amounted to more than a thousand. When we examine their sources, we are convinced that they originated in the state of Ch'u and reached their height in the Han dynasty. The *fu* on the themes of capitals, palaces, parks, and hunting, as well as those describing travels and expressing thought,[15] are all works whose function is "to set the boundaries of a state and to mark the divisions in the country";[16] [in other words these works influenced the conduct of rulers] and their significance lies in their glorification of the state. They struck, in their preface, the right note, and concluded with summaries in logical order. In the former, the main themes are proposed and the fundamental feelings made articulate; and in the latter the logical pattern is given, showing its natural rhetorical flow. Since the last stanza of the "No"[17] had been called by Min-ma [Fu] the *luan* [conclusion][18] we know that both the *sung* compiled by the Yin people and the *fu* done by the Ch'u poets belong to the category of masterpieces and form the pivot of graceful writings. As to those works whose themes are plants, animals, and other miscellaneous things, they express feelings which arise in response to external situations, feelings which are reactions to chance experiences with various scenes. In describing the external situations, the language should be delicate and closely knit; and in forging metaphors in relation to the nature of things, appropriateness in principle should be emphasized.

---

[15] On capitals: Pan Ku's "Liang-tu" and Chang Heng's "Erh-ching"; on palaces: Wang Yen-shou's "Ling-kuang" and "Ching-fu"; on parks and hunting: *fu* by Ssu-ma Hsiang-ju and Yang Hsiung, such as "Shang-lin," "Kan-ch'üan," "Chiang-yang," and "Yü-la." Most *fu* are found in the *Wen-hsüan.*

[16] The functions of government offices as defined in the *Chou-li.*

[17] *Mao-shih yin-te*, 81/301.

[18] The *Kuo-yü*, "Lu-yü," hsia.

These are in the realm of minor works, but are crucial points in the achievement of the qualities of the wondrous and the skillful.

As for the following ten *fu* writers: Hsün [K'uang] used riddles to state his thought; Sung [Yü] first used the grandiloquent language which marked the beginning of the affected patterns; Mei Sheng's "T'u-yüan" combines the fundamental with what is new; Hsiang-ju's "Shang-lin" employs a variety of images to create the beautiful; Chia I in his "Fu-niao" shows keen perception in his analysis of feelings and ideas; Tzu-yüan [or Wang Pao] in his "Tung-hsiao" is most accurate in imitating the ever-changing patterns of sound and appearance; the "Liang-tu" of Meng-chien [or Pan Ku] is clear and graceful; Chang Heng's "Erh-ching" is lively and grand; the "Kan-ch'üan" of Tzu-yün [or Yang Hsiung] set the style for profound themes; the "Ling-kuang" of [Wang] Yen-shou is filled with images of flight and movement. They were all heroes in the realm of the *tz'u* and *fu*.

The works of Chung-hsüan [or Wang Ts'an] are fine and detailed and they always start out with vigor. Wei-ch'ang [or Hsü Kan] is learned and comprehending, and his writings occasionally fall into bold colorful patterns. The *fu* of T'ai-ch'ung [or Tso Ssu] and An-jen [or P'an Yüeh] established great models for composition on stately themes; and those of Shih-heng [or Lu Chi] and Tzu-an [or Wang Kung-sui] are solid achievements on popular subjects. Ching-ch'un [or Kuo P'u] was sophisticated and clever and his flow of rhetoric was bountiful; and Yen-po [or Yüan Hung] dealt in generalities and was never exhausted but always full of feelings. These were also the leaders of the *fu* in the Wei and the Chin dynasties.

The reason for making "ascension to the height" the peculiar quality of *fu* is that it is the sight of concrete objects which excites the emotions. Since the emotions have been excited by concrete objects, the ideas associated with the objects always remain clear; and since the objects are viewed with feeling, the language used to describe them is always beautiful. Beautiful language and clear ideas complement each other as the symbol and the symbolized. They are like red and purple silk in weaving, and black and yellow pigments in painting. The patterns, though mixed, possess substance, and the colors, though variegated, are fundamentally based. This is the main principle of the *fu* writing.

However, for those who run after the secondary and overlook fundamentals, even if they did read one thousand *fu*, they would only sink deeper in their perplexity about its essential qualities.[19] As a result, profuse flowers would tend to ruin the branches and rich viands to damage the bone, offering neither the values necessary to maintain moral principles nor any aid in the form of admonition and warning. It was for this reason that Master Yang [Hsiung] regretted his youthful indulgence in the "art of worm-carving," and ridiculed the beautiful patterns of fog and clouds.[20]

  The Tsan:
The *fu* was derived from poetry
And developed into several different forms.
In describing objects and picturing appearances
The richness of its patterns is like that of carving and painting;
It casts lustre over the dull,
And paints the commonplace in language that has no limitations.
In style, its ultimate achievement is beauty under control,[21]
And its language is the result of the cutting out of weeds.

IX. Ode and Pronouncement (The Sung and the Tsan)

In the list of the "Four Beginnings," the *sung* occupies the final

19 Huan T'an, *Hsin-lun*, quoted Yang Hsiung as saying: "One who has read one thousand *fu* will be good at it."

20 Yang Hsiung, *Fa-yen*, "Wu-tzu pien": "Someone asked, 'When you were young you loved *fu*, did you not?' 'Yes, but it was the worm- and seal-carving of a child.' In a little while he continued, 'An adult will not do it.' . . . Someone said, 'But it has the beautiful patterns of fog and clouds!' [Yang] said, 'That would be just moth-worm to a seamstress's work.' "

21 Yang Hsiung, *Fa-yen*, "Wu-tzu,": "The *fu* of the ancient poets has beauty which is under control; and that of later literary men has beauty which is infected with abandonment."

position. *Sung* means to describe a spectacle; its function is to praise great virtue and describe the performance of rites honoring it.[1] During the time of Ruler K'u, Hsien Mo wrote *sung* to be set to the music of "chiu-shao."[2] Since the Shang dynasty, the genre has been complete with words and form.

Feng is that form whose influence reaches the limit of a state; *ya* is that form whose corrective influence reaches the four directions of the realm; and *sung* is that which is used in ceremonies before, and prayers to, the spirits. The *feng* and the two *ya*, concerned with human affairs, are of two types: the modified and the correct.[3] But the *sung's* main function is to appeal to the spirits; hence it should be perfect. The *sung* of Lu glorifies Duke Tan [of Chou], and the *sung* of Shang records the merits of earlier kings. Both are songs proper for temple rites and are not ordinary pieces to be sung during feasts. The "Shih-mai"[4] was written by Duke Chou;[5] and in the *sung* of this sage we find the model of the genre. But all people have their own minds, and there is no stopping their mouths. The Chin carriage driver's praise of the fields on the plain[6] and the satire of the people of Lu on [Confucius' leather] knee guard[7] were originally straightforward statements which were not sung: they were short exhortations or satires. But [Tso] Ch'iu-ming[8] and Tzu-kao[9] turned them into *sung*.

---

[1] Cf. note 4, Chapter III. The *sung* refers particularly to the last section of the *Book of Poetry*, which consists of songs sung in accompaniment to dances during ceremonial rites in honor of the ancestors of the dynasty makers. It is here that we find poetry, music, and dance linked together to perform one function.

[2] See *Lü-shih ch'un-ch'iu*, "Chung-hsia chi," "Ku-yüeh p'ien."

[3] For the explanation of the ideas of the modified and correct forms, see "The Great Preface" in the Mao version of the *Book of Poetry*, attributed first to Tzu-hsia, a disciple of Confucius, and later to Wei Hung of the later Han.

[4] The *Mao-shih yin-te*, 75/273.

[5] About the affairs of King Wu. See the *Kuo-yü*, "Chou-yü," and *Ch'un-ch'iu ching-chuan yin-te*, 199/Hsüan 12/3 Tso.

[6] *Ibid.*, 132/Hsi 28/5 Tso.

[7] In *K'ung-ts'ung-tzu*, "Ch'en wang-i pien," it is stated that when Confucius first served the state of Lu as its prime minister, the people of Lu ridiculed him for his leather kneecap. But three years later, when Confucius succeeded in bringing about the transformation of the land, the people began to sing their praise of him.

[8] The supposed author of the *Tso-chuan*.

[9] Alias K'ung Ch'uang, and not the man our author wanted to refer to. He seems to

These are cases of "plain *sung*," in which the *sung* form was modified to include subject-matter from the affairs of men. When San-lü[10] wrote his "Orange *Sung*" he imparted to it a colorful language of exquisite fragrance and taste, steeped in metaphor and allegory. Here even the orange, a thing of little importance, received the treatment of *sung*.

Emperor Cheng of the Ch'in had *sung* engraved on tablets to commemorate his own achievements. Emperor Hui and Emperor Ching of the Han, too, had the virtues of their ancestors sung. This practice of *sung*-writing was continued generation after generation.

As for the *sung* by Tzu-yün [or Yang Hsiung] in honor of Ch'ung-kuo,[11] the *sung* by Meng-chien [or Pan Ku] to Marquis Tai,[12] Wu-chung's [or Fu I's] commemoration of Hsien-tsung [Emperor Ming of the later Han], and Shih Ts'en's eulogy of Empress Hsi,[13] they either imitated the style of the "Ch'ing-miao,"[14] or modeled themselves on the "Chiung"[15] and the "No";[16] although they differ in depth and detail, they have the same function in that they commemorate the virtuous and describe their ceremonial rites, and are thus alike in being elegant documents of the state.

In the "Pei-cheng" of Pan [Ku] and the "Hsi-cheng"[17] of Fu [I], we find that what are designated as *sung* have been transformed into mere prefaces. And is this not to praise the erroneous, and thus do violence to the form? And the "Kuang-ch'eng" and "Shang-lin" of Ma Yung [79-166] are graceful like *fu*. How he sacrificed the substance in his love for rhetoric! On the other hand, both Ts'ui Yüan's "Wen-hsüeh" and Ts'ai Yung's "Fan-ch'ü" give beauty to prefaces and are brief and simple; Chih Yü's critical writing is fine and clear, but when

---

have made a mistake about the identity of his man: the one he wanted is Tzu-shun, quoted in *K'ung-ts'ung-tzu*, the source of his information.

[10] The title of Ch'ü Yüan's office, the function of which was to be in charge of the education of the young nobles of the royal clans in the state of Ch'u.

[11] The *Han-shu*, biography of Chao Ch'ung-kuo.

[12] The title of Tou Jung. See the *T'ai-p'ing yü-lan*, chüan 588, where the *Wen-chang liu-pieh lun* by Chih Yü is quoted on this point.

[13] She became empress in A.D. 102.   [14] *Mao-shih yin-te*, 75/266.

[15] *Ibid.*, 79/297.   [16] *Ibid.*, 81/301.

[17] *Ch'uan-hou-han wen* contains Fu I's "Hsi-cheng."

[passing judgments on Yang Hsiung's "Ch'ung-kuo" *sung* or Fu I's "Hsien-tsung" *sung*] he treated the *sung* together with both *feng* and *ya* without discriminating between their purposes, he was advancing unsound theory, similar to the absurd discussion of yellow and white.[18]

During the Wei and the Chin few *sung* got out of the rut. Of the works by Ch'en-ssu [or Ts'ao Chih], the "Huangtzu" is outstanding; and among the many pieces by Lu Chi, the "Kung-ch'en" is the most prominent. The fact that they mixed praise and censure in the same piece is indeed an example of the corrupt style of an age of decline.[19]

The *sung* must possess the qualities of elegance and grace, and its language has to be clear and bright. In its narration it is similar to the *fu*, but it must not succumb to florid and excessive language. It has the spirit of reverence and prudence which characterizes the *ming*, or inscription, but differs from it in not being admonition or warning. In its praise and honoring of its subject, it formulates beautiful expressions, but its content has the broadest scope. It has finesse and artifice adapted to the feelings aroused. This is the essence of the *sung*.

The term *tsan* means "to pronounce and assist." Formerly, during the worship of Yü-shun,[20] the music master repeated the *tsan*, which was the initial pronouncement of the ceremony. When I[21] "assisted" Yü, and I Chih[22] "assisted" Wu Hsien,[23] they both made laudatory pronouncements in a loud voice, giving assistance by rendering in exclamations that which was beyond language. Therefore, when the Court of State Ceremony was first created during the Han, such pro-

[18] *Lü-shih ch'un-ch'iu*, "Pieh-lei pien": "A sword expert said, 'Its [the sword's] white color means that it is hard, and its yellow color means that it is strong. Now the yellow color is mixed with the white; it must be both hard and strong. It is a good sword.' The objector said, 'Its white color means that it is not strong, and its yellow color means that it is not hard. Now the yellow color is mixed with the white; it must be neither hard nor strong. How can it be a good [sharp] sword?'"

[19] The original function of the *sung* is to praise, and never to censure.

[20] See note 13, Chapter V.

[21] I was Yü's minister, to whom Yü tried to give his rule in the manner of Yao and Shun.

[22] Another name for I Yin, a minister of T'ang of the Shang dynasty.

[23] There were three persons of this name: a sorcerer at the time of the Yellow Emperor, a sorcerer during the Shang, and a medical doctor of Yao. Since I Chih is I Yin, we shall assume that the second Wu Hsien is meant. A sorcerer in ancient times was prominent in ceremonies.

nouncements were designated *tsan,* an ancient term. But [Ssu-ma] Hsiang-ju was the first author to try his brush on a *tsan,* one which commemorated Ching K'o.[24] In the historical works of Ssu-ma Ch'ien and Pan Ku, *tsan* were employed to express both praise and censure. These gave summaries in terse language and adopted the style of the *sung* for pronouncing judgments. And the critical remarks at the end of *chi,* or chronicles of rulers, and *chuan,* or biographies, are also given the same name *tsan.* And yet Chung-ch'ia [or Chih Yü][25] erroneously called them *shu,* or narratives. This was indeed wide of the mark. When Chin-ch'un [or Kuo P'u] made his commentary on the *ya* he wrote *tsan* for all animals and plants. What he treated included both the praise and the censure. This type of *tsan* may be likened to the modified type of *sung.* But the original idea of the *tsan* developed out of the desire to express praise or admiration. For this reason its style has always been terse, allowing little room for expansion. Its lines are always in the four-word pattern, and its rhymes are limited. Its guiding principle is to employ brevity of language to portray adequately the feelings involved and to develop its literary expressions with emphasis on lucidity. Although its roots strike deep into the past, it has seldom been put to use. In general it may be considered a branch of the *sung.*

The *Tsan*:
To give dignity to ceremonies the *sung* is the proper form,
And to perpetuate achievements one employs the *tsan.*
Both carve colorful designs and spread out literary patterns;
Both are sonorous and brilliant.
Old in years and distant in time,
Their beautiful music may still be likened to the dawn.
But when they are applied to common things,
Their dazzling language soon invites boredom.

[24] A heroic soul during the Warring States period, who was sent as an assassin to kill the King of Ch'in.
[25] Flourishing in the third century.

X. Sacrificial Prayer and Oath of Agreement (The Chu and the Meng)[1]

The position of heaven and earth having been fixed, sacrifice is offered to all the deities. After the worship of the six subjects[2] has been performed and sacrificial ceremonies to the hills and streams have been properly administered, there will be seasonal rain and gentle breezes, giving life to corn and millet. For this reason the people pay these deities whom they worship good measure in return. The fragrance of great sacrifice[3] arises from one's enlightened virtue; and the words of faith offered by the sacrificial officials must be of literary excellence. Long ago I Ch'i[4] initiated the twelfth-moon sacrifice to be offered to the eight deities. Its words are: "Let earth return to its habitat and water to its gully, and let no insects appear, and may all grasses and plants return to their marshy place." These are the words of the sacrificial prayer of Shen Nung.[5]

The words of Shun's prayer to the deity of the field run: "I carry this plough to till the southern field. May all the people within the four seas share this abundance." His devotion to the interest of the people is clearly shown in these words. And Li [T'ang] of Shang, with his sage reverence increasing day by day, sacrificed to heaven with a black bull, pleading that if any sin should be committed anywhere within the realm he might assume the responsibility for it. These are the words of his prayer to heaven. During the time of drought T'ang again prayed in a carriage of white,[6] and in the prayer he chided himself for six things.[7] These are the words of prayers for seasonal rain and the proper regulation of other elements of nature.

[1] In this chapter, Liu Hsieh traces the *chu* and the *meng* to their earliest forms. Since both involve an appeal to deities, they are grouped together.

[2] The four seasons, cold and heat, the sun, the moon, the stars, and flood and drought.

[3] Referring to the acceptance of the sacrifice by deities.

[4] Identified as either Shen Nung, the divine farmer, or Yao, the legendary emperor.

[5] See *Li-chi*, "Chiao t'e sheng." *Li-chi yin-te*, 11/21.

[6] White is symbolic of grief.

[7] The prayer is preserved in the *Hsüntzu*, "Ta-lüeh p'ien." The six things are: (1)

The officer of sacrifice during the Chou dynasty was in charge of the six prayers offered in the six sacrifices: "Myriads of things all have their life"[8] was presented before the sacrifice of heaven and earth; "Universally acting in dignity" was sung at the ceremonies to welcome the sun; "Rising early and retiring late" was a prayer said before the ancestral temples; "Happiness bountiful and without limit" was included in the prayer offered while sacrificing sheep to the deities; and during the sacrifice offered either to the god of earth, or to the supreme Deity on the battlefield, there were always literary expressions. For it was in these expressions that the ancients showed reverence to gods and respect to ancestors.

Since the time of *Ch'un-ch'iu*, sacrilege has been committed in the adulation and flattery practiced at sacrifices. Officers of sacrifice were corrupted by bribes, and historians indulged in ornate rhetoric which dispersed the deities, who ceased to honor the sacrifices by descending.

When Chang Lao congratulated [Chao Wu-tzu] on the completion of his house, his words of congratulation were considered good prayers either for rejoicing or for mourning.[9] K'uai K'uei was blessed because of his prayer in battle about his tendons and bones.[10] Even under adverse circumstances, people always resorted to prayers.

As for the "Chao-hun" in the *Ch'u-tz'u*, it may be considered the pattern of beauty for prayers. The various sacrifices of the Han[11] revealed the functions of prayers and the manner in which they were performed. They contain in them the ideas of great scholars, but include also some suggestions from necromancers. So, the secret prayers to shift calamities [from the royal person to the people] were vastly

---

intemperate government, (2) causing the people to suffer, (3) luxury in the palaces, (4) interference in government by palace women, (5) bribery, and (6) employment of sycophants. In his prayer T'ang asked if these were the reasons for the drought.

[8] A line of the prayer during a sacrifice to heaven; similar ideas are expressed in the prayer to earth. See *Ta-tai li-chi*, "Kung-kuan p'ien."

[9] See *Li-chi*, "T'an-kung," hsia. *Li-chi yin-te*, 4/64.

[10] *Ch'un-ch'iu ching-chuan yin-te*, 469/Ai 2/7 Tso. K'uai K'uei was the heir to the throne of Wei. There was a rebellion in the state and he took part in the suppression. About to go into battle, he prayed that his tendons and bones might suffer no mishap.

[11] See *Shih-chi*, "Feng-shan shu."

different in spirit from those of T'ang.[12] And the practice of using little children to drive away the imps of pestilence was similar in spirit to the curse of the sorcerers of Yüeh.[13] The principle of conduct was gradually losing its hold on society.

Since the Yellow Emperor's malediction against the perverse, and Tung-fang So's scolding of the ghosts, later imprecations upon evil have all been characterized by clever anathema, the only exception being Ch'en-ssu's [or Ts'ao Chih's] prayer against the calamity of storm, which was offered in a spirit of righteousness.[14]

According to the accepted rule, the function of a sacrificial prayer was limited to the reporting of events. But the sacrificial pieces of the middle periods[15] contain praises for good words and conduct. This inclusion of the act of praising in a sacrificial piece was an expansion of the function of the genre.

Again, during Han times there were elegiac edicts on occasions of royal mourning; and when Chou [or King Mu] lost his concubine Sheng-chi, the historian of the inner palace presented the elegiac edict. According to these evidences, the elegiac edict was originally an edict whose purpose was to confer honor, but since the occasion was a sad one, the language was chosen to accord with that mood. So the elegiac edict has the same significance as the *lei*, or simple elegy, except that its words are addressed to spirits. It begins like the *lei* and ends on an elegiac note; it has the style of a *sung* and the form of a prayer. [This last is true because] the grand historian[16] modeled his pronouncement after the prayer of Chou times.

Whenever words are purposefully grouped together, flowery patterns are developed; but in the invocation of the spirits, real feeling must be stressed. Both for refining the language and for establishing one's sincerity, the necessary condition is to have a clear conscience. The spirit in which a prayer is said must be one of sincerity and

12 See note 7 above.
13 The people of Yüeh believed in ghosts and sorcery. See *Han-shu*, "Chiao-ssu chih."
14 The piece is quoted in the *I-wen lei-chü*, chüan 100.
15 Apparently referring to the Han and the Wei periods.
16 In ancient China a grand historian was in charge of mourning ceremonies.

reverence; and the form in which sacrifices are offered should be one of respect and contrition. These are the main ideas. The sacrificial piece offered to the Meng-shan by Pan Ku is the very model of sincerity and reverence in a prayer;[17] and P'an Yüeh's elegy on his wife Yü expresses the essence of respect and grief in sacrifice.[18] If these pieces are studied thoroughly, the secret of their success will be clearly seen.

The term *meng* means to make clear [or to declare]. With red bull, white horse, pearl tray, and jade vessel,[19] the parties declared their intentions at dawn before the spirits. During the times of the Three Ancient Kings,[20] the forms of oath and declaration[21] were not used. When they found it necessary to swear in signing an agreement, they gave their words and withdrew. During the decline of the Chou dynasty, there were many declarations of agreement; at times these were concluded by force. The practice started with Ts'ao Mo[22] and was finally resorted to by Mao Sui.[23] King Chao of the state of Ch'in made an oath promising the I tribe a gift of yellow dragons in his agreement with them;[24] and the first ruler of the Han swore by the mountains and rivers in the statement he made when he created the dukedoms.[25] But only when the righteous principle underlying it was maintained was it possible to fulfill the conditions of the agreement. As soon as the principle came to be neglected, the agreement was also thrown to the winds. Whether an agreement is to be respected or ignored lies completely in the hands of men: the oath has nothing to

[17] Fragments of this piece are preserved in Yen K'o-chün's *Ch'üan-hou-han wen*, chüan 26.

[18] Fragments of this piece are preserved in *I-wen lei-chü*, chüan 38.

[19] At a ceremony where intentions were declared in a treaty to be signed, a red bull or white horse was used. The tray was used to hold the blood and the vessel the food. The ears of the bull were cut and put in the tray, which was held in the hands of the leader of a confederation. Hence the term "holding the ears of a bull" means leadership.

[20] The first kings of the Hsia, Shang, and Chou.

[21] The declaration is in the form of an oath, stating that if either party should break the contract agreed upon that party should be destroyed by heaven, spirits, and men.

[22] See *Shih-chi*, "Tzih-k'o lieh chuan." [23] See *Shih-Chi*, biography of P'ing-yüan Chün.

[24] Ch'ang Chü, *Hua-yang kuo-chih*. King Chao promised the I tribe a pair of yellow dragons should Ch'in attack I.

[25] *Shih-chi*, "Kung-ch'en hou nien-piao."

do with it. The oath Tsang Hung wrote to accompany the ceremony of
dipping the fingers in blood has enough righteous force to shatter the
clouds;[26] the iron oath of Liu K'un [of the Chin] possesses spirit so
subtly moving that it even affected the sleet and frost.[27] But these oaths
did no good to either the Han or the Chin: on the contrary, the parties
to the agreement became enemies. Therefore we know that when sincerity is not at the bottom of one's heart, there is no use in agreements.

The main points to cover in drawing up an agreement are these:
state the crisis, encourage loyalty and filial piety, pledge each other to
share the same fate of life or death, pledge each other to work together,
pray to the spirits to witness the agreement, invoke the nine heavens
as judge,[28] establish sincerity with earnestness, and express all these
things with all soberness in literary language. They are the elements
common to all agreements. However, it is not the language which is
difficult to produce; what is difficult is to keep the agreement expressed
in that language. Let all people coming afterward note that loyalty and
sincerity are enough, and that there is no need to depend on the spirits.

The Tsan:

Worship with piety and conclude declarations of intention with
    solemnity.
The sacrificial officers furnish words for these acts.
The attainment of sincerity depends on the attitude of reverence,
And the language must be sweet.
In later periods writers indulged in excessive ornamentation,
And their words are spun into tapestries of red and blue.
But to get the spirits to come and accept the sacrifice
It is important that one's conscience be clear.

---

[26] *Hou-han shu*, biography of Tsang Hung. All forces joined together against Tung
Tso at the end of the Han dynasty, and this was an occasion for all of them to stick
their fingers in the blood of the bull. Tsang Hung was the one who came forward to give
the oath when nobody else seemed to dare to assume the responsibility, for it required a
great deal of literary talent.

[27] The Chin was under the threat of barbarian invasion. Liu and Tuan P'i-ti swore
to come to each other's assistance in defending the Chin against the barbarians. The
oath is quoted in *I-wen lei-chü*, chüan 33.

[28] This phrase is quoted from the *Li-sao*.

XI. Inscription and Exhortation (The Ming and the Chen)

The Yellow Emperor long ago carved sayings on his carriage and desks to admonish himself lest he should falter; and the Great Yü of the Hsia dynasty chiseled sentences on drum and bell frames to serve as remonstrances. Ch'eng-t'ang of the Shang cut the "Rule for Daily Renewal" on his trays and basins;[1] and King Wu of the Chou wrote on the doors and mats teachings that would keep him vigilant. The Duke of Chou left on a bronze statue words urging caution in speaking; and Confucius made an about-face at the warning of a tilted vessel.[2] The sages long ago recognized the necessity of keeping oneself admonished.

The term *ming* means to name; to distinguish an article necessarily entails calling it by name. To make this appellation correct and assay its connotation, great moral development is essential.[3] Tsang Wu-chung, in his discussion of the *ming*, said, "They deal with the virtues of the Son of Heaven, the achievements of the lords, and the military merits of the ministers."[4] The writing on the tripod which the Hsia dynasty cast from the tribute bronze offered by the chiefs of the nine districts[5] and the Chou inscription on the buckthorn arrow presented by the Su-shen tribe[6] are examples of inscriptions commemorating virtues of the Son of Heaven. The epigraph for Lü Wang[7] on the

[1] This rule exhorts one to renew oneself, that is, to improve, with the coming of each new day. See *Li-chi*, "Ta-hsüeh p'ien."

[2] The lesson of the tilted vessel: when empty, it tilted; when filled to the middle, it sat up straight; and when full, it toppled.

[3] The name, as here used, must not only denote the article to which it is given but also connote a virtue which the name of the article suggests. Hence, "to name" actually means to suggest a moral exhortation in an inscribed appellation. For these moral achievements are what the name connotes. Without these connotative contents the name cannot be considered as correct.

[4] See *Ch'un-ch'iu ching-chuan yin-te*, 289/Hsiang 19/4 Tso fu 2.

[5] The tribute was an expression of appreciation on the part of the nine chiefs for the virtue of the Hsia ruler. See *ibid.*, 182/Hsüan 3/5 Tso.

[6] King Wu triumphed over the Shang, and the Su-shen tribe came to court with the buckthorn arrow as tribute. King Wu ordered that the good virtues of the early kings be commemorated in an inscription on the arrow. See *Kuo-yü*, "Lu-yü," hsia.

[7] Lü Wang was King Wu's chief adviser.

vessel cast by K'un-wu[8] and the inscription on the conquered tribe's Chung-shan Fu tripod[9] speak of lords' achievements. And Wei K'o's record of military exploits on the Bell of Ching[10] and K'ung K'uei's register of the merits [of the ancestors of Wei] on the Wei tripod[11] are concerned with ministers' military merits.

The bestowal on Fei Lien of a stone sarcophagus[12] and the discovery of the posthumous title of Duke Ling [of Wei] in his burial ground[13] are indeed weird tales, dealing as they do with inscriptions on underground stone. And there are also quite ridiculous examples: King Wu-ling of the state of Chao had footprints carved on the city wall of Po-wu, and King Chao of the state of Ch'in ordered a chess game made on the top of Mount Hua; both were bent on showing off to posterity by these absurdities.[14] After examining these examples, the proper significance of an inscription must have become clear to us.

Ch'in Shih-huang's inscriptions on mountains are beautiful and erudite; although his government was ruthless, these inscriptions have real literary brilliance. Pan Ku's epigraph on Mount Yen-jan and that left by Chang Ch'ang on the slab at Hua-yin[15] may be considered the

---

[8] A great metallurgist in ancient times.

[9] The Southern Huns; during the Later Han period, they were brought under control by Tou Hsien, to whom they presented this tripod.

[10] See *Kuo-yü*, "Chin-yü." The event took place in the fifteenth year (?) of Duke Hsüan of Lu. "Ching" refers to Duke Ching of Chin.

[11] See *Li-chi*, "Chi-t'ung." *Li-chi yin-te*, 25/23.

[12] The *Shih-chi*, chronology of Ch'in State. Fei Lien, a minister of the Shang dynasty, was building an altar at Huo t'ai-shan when a stone coffin was unearthed, on which was found an inscription saying that the coffin was given to Fei Lien for his loyalty.

[13] See *Chuangtzu*, "Tse-yang p'ien," and Chang Hua's *Po-wu chih*, "I-wen p'ien."

[14] Po-wu is a city in modern Ho-pei; Chao's footprints are said to be three feet wide and five feet long; with the caption: "Chu-fu [the title the king conferred upon himself while still living] frequented this place." King Chao's chess game consisted of six *chien* (I am not quite sure what a *chien* or a *chu*, a dictionary definition of *chien*, would be.) each eight feet long, and twelve chessmen, each eight inches tall, with the inscription: "King Chao often played the game with heavenly deities at this spot." In the case of King Wu-ling, we know he made up his own posthumous name; but in the case of King Chao, no such information is available. From this consideration, the tale seems to be a later forgery.

[15] Tou Hsien, a general of the Later Han, after pacifying the northern frontier, ascended Mount Yen-jan and had slabs erected for the recording of his military achievements. Pan Ku was responsible for the text of the inscription. See *Hou-han shu*, biography of Tou Hsien. Chang Ch'ang's text is found in the *Ku-wen-yüan*, chüan 18.

best of epigraphs. Ts'ai Yung's works are characterized by a fullness
of feeling, standing all alone in all times. His words on the halberd
of General Ch'iao breathe the classical spirit, and his words on the Chu
Mu tripod are a perfect model of stone inscription. For here he indulged
in that in which he was particularly well-versed. The words of Ching-
t'ung [Feng Yen] put on various weapons follow the prosodic form
of *wu-ming*,[16] but they deal with events which are not pertinent to the
weapons, and furthermore, they are either too verbose or too brief,
never managing to strike a happy medium. And Ts'ui Yin's weapon
inscriptions are mostly laudatory; only a few are admonitory. Li Yu's
writings are limited in ideas and lacking in rhetorical organization; he
mixed inscriptions on the divine milfoil plants and tortoise shells with
those on games and chess, and placed those on balance and bushel, important in measurement, after those on mortars and pestles. Since he
did not even take time to distinguish the proper categories and relative
importance of the articles he treated, how can we expect him to have
paid attention to the inner structure [or moral connotations] of these
things? The nine precious weapons of Emperor Wen of Wei[17] are sharp,
and yet their inscriptions are blunt. Chang Tsai alone, in the piece he
inscribed at Chien-ke,[18] reveals a talent of crystal beauty. Fleet-footed,
he arrived ahead of others, though he had a slow start. In inscribing
this work on the Min and the Han[19] he indeed attained what was
appropriate to the genre.

The function of the *chen*, or exhortation, literally "needle," is to
attack sickness and prevent disease [of character], as the therapeutic
puncture does in medicine. This form of writing flourished during the
Three Dynasties. Only fragments of two pieces from the Hsia and
the Shang are still extant; and in the Chou dynasty, of the "Pai-kuan
chen," or "Exhortations to the King by a Hundred Officials" ordered
by Hsin Chia,[20] only the "Yü-chen" or "Exhortation by Hunters" is a
piece perfect in both form and ideas. By the time of the Ch'un-ch'iu

16 Inscription on a military weapon.   17 Ts'ao P'ei.
18 In Szechuan, bordering on Shen-hsi.   19 Two rivers flowing through Szechuan.
20 Hsin Chia was a grand historian during the time of King Wu.

period, the form had declined, but its tradition was still continued. Thus we have a *chen* of Wei Chiang, who warned his ruler[21] by referring to the conduct of Hou-i[22] and the *chen* of the ruler of Ch'u, who counseled his people to work hard.[23] Since the Warring States period, the inculcation of virtue has been discarded and the recording of achievements emphasized, so that the *ming* has taken the place of the *chen*, which is now neglected. But to Yang Hsiung, who delved into the tradition of ancient times, the *Yü-chen* became the model for his twenty-five pieces on the minister, magistrate, prefect, and governor. Later Ts'ui and Hu[24] filled the lacunae and completed what is collectively known as the "Pai-kuan," or the "One Hundred Offices." These pieces define the functions and ranks of the hundred offices, like a pendant mirror[25] giving definite warnings and admonitions; they, indeed, were written in the purity of style of ancient times [the Hsia and the Shang], and ascended to the height attained by Hsin Chia in a later period [the Chou]. We do have also P'an Hsü's compositions on tallies, which are pertinent but shallow, and the piece by Wen Ch'iao, which is learned but overburdened; Wang Chi's work on "Kuo-tzu"[26] teems with quotations, but the facts are unsystematically arranged; while P'an Ni's piece on carriages, though containing correct moral principles, is full of weeds.[27] Few of these later works are able to achieve the proper standard. As to Wang Lang's *chen* on miscellaneous articles, those on napkins and shoes may have the spirit of warning, but they are, in fact, inappropriate. They do conform to the rules of the *chieh*, or warning[28] and the *ming* or inscription, in that they are

[21] The Duke of Chin.

[22] Hou-i lost his kingdom because he loved hunting, and the Duke of Chin loved hunting, too. Hence the reference to Hou-i, who is mentioned in the *Yü-chen*. See *Ch'un-ch'iu ching-chuan yin-te*, 258/Hsiang 4/7 Tso fu 1.

[23] See *ibid.*, 197/Hsüan 12/3 Tso.

[24] Ts'ui Yin and Ts'ui Yüan; Hu Kuang.

[25] A mirror used as a pendant, with the function of showing if one is properly groomed. By extension it becomes a symbol for warning or admonition.

[26] The National Academy, of which Wang Chi was once the chancellor.

[27] Verbose in style.

[28] Previously Liu Hsieh used *chieh* as a verb, i.e., to warn, which has affinity with exhortation, i.e., *chen*. Apparently it is introduced here as a synonym of *chen*.

terse and concerned only with essentials; but the *chen* on water, fire, well, and stove are loquacious without end. All this is due to his personal idiosyncrasy.

The *chen* is intended to be recited at court,[29] while the *ming* is to be inscribed on vessels. Though they differ in name and function, they share a common quality in their spirit of warning. The sole purpose of the *chen* is to prevent mistakes, hence its language is solid and pertinent; but the *ming* has the additional function of giving praise, hence its style must be grand and brilliant. The matters selected for treatment must be appropriate and clearly presented; and the language used should be simple and yet profound. In these requirements are summed up the main ideas of these genres. However, as the pieces inscribed on the arrow and the tripod of the conquered states[30] have been scattered, the difference in the uses of the *chen* and the *ming* have seldom been applied in later times. It is up to the writers to judge for themselves in selecting important subjects.

The Tsan:
The *ming* expresses the moral ideas implied in the name of articles,
While the *chen* suggests moral principles.
There are some words we may well wear as our "inscriptions,"
But water can never be used as a mirror can [either to reflect truly or
    to bear an inscription].
Hold fast to this principle of truthfulness and self-admonishment,
And be reverential in word and deed.
Ideas of classic grace are naturally grand,
And the pithy phrase is always a thing of beauty.

[29] Music masters presented the *chen* at court. See the *Kuo-yü*, "Chou-yü."
[30] See notes 6 and 9 above.

XII. Elegy and Stone Inscription (The Lei and the Pei)

The Chou was a dynasty of great virtues, and *ming*, or inscriptions, and *lei*, or elegy, were written to commemorate them. Those who can write an elegy on the occasion of a death are capable of being ministers. To write an elegy is to sum up, that is, to sum up the virtuous conduct of the deceased and immortalize it. Very little is known to us about the writing of elegy before and during the Hsia and the Shang. During the Chou dynasty elegies were written, but they were never written for a *shih*.[1] Furthermore, it was not the practice for a person inferior in social status to write an elegy for his superior, or for a younger man to write an elegy for an older one.[2] In the case of the ruler, heaven was invoked to write his elegy.[3] To read an elegy before the dead and to confer upon him a posthumous title is a ceremony of very great importance. It was after the battle of Ch'eng-ch'iu, where the Duke of Lu fought [the forces of the state of Sung], that an elegy was first written in honor of a *shih*.[4] When Confucius died, Duke Ai of Lu wrote the elegy. Although it is not a work of profundity, in the depth of feeling expressed it has preserved for us the ancient tradition of this form of writing.[5]

With the elegy written for Huitzu by his wife, the language became sad and the rhythm prolonged.[6] During the Han dynasty, elegies were written in this latter vein. The one by Yang Hsiung for Empress Yüan tends towards verbosity.[7] Its important lines, including the one which mentions "Sha-lu,"[8] have been quoted, but Chih [-yü] suspected that

[1] Member of the lowest rank in the official hierarchy.

[2] *Li-chi yin-te*, 7/28.   [3] *Ibid.*, 7/28.   [4] *Ibid.*, 3/17.

[5] The elegy is preserved in the *Tso-chuan*, Duke of Ai, sixteenth year, *Ch'un-ch'iu ching-chuan yin-te*, 492/Ai 16/4 Tso. See also *Li-chi*, 3/107.

[6] Preserved in Liu Hsiang's *Lieh-nü chuan*. It may not be authentic. "Huitzu" is the posthumous name given to Chan Ch'in by his wife. He flourished during the Ch'un-ch'iu period and lived at Liu-hsia in the state of Lu; hence he was known as Liu Hsia. The posthumous name "Hui" means benevolence.

[7] The empress was the consort of Emperor Yüan, 48-33 B.C., and the mother of Emperor Ch'eng, 32-7 B.C. The elegy is found in *Ku wen-yüan*, chüan 20.

[8] Four lines of the elegy are found in the biography of Empress Yüan in the *Han-shu* by Pan Ku. Sha-lu is the name of a mountain in Ho-pei.

this quotation was the whole piece.[9] As a matter of fact, would it be possible to give a full account of the collected virtues of, and do proper honor to, a royal personage in four brief lines? Elegies written by Tu Tu[10] have achieved fame before the time of the present generation. But though the piece for Wu [Han] is good, his other pieces are rather weak. Could it be that Emperor Kuang-wu's[11] praise of him changed people's evaluation of his works?[12] Fu I's elegies are well-organized and well-proportioned. And those by Su Shun[13] and Ts'ui Yüan are logical and clear. Their narratives read like biographies, their language is beautiful, and their tonal arrangements have a pleasant effect. They were unquestionably talented writers of the elegy. P'an Yüeh, in organizing his ideas, followed especially the example of Hsiao-shan [or Su Shun]; he is good at expressing sorrow, and creates fresh and felicitous expressions with ease. For this reason he is looked upon by people of later dynasties as one who brightened the beauty of the genre. Ts'ui Yin's elegy for Chao and Liu T'ao's for Huang[14] both capture the spirit of the genre, and their beauty lies in their brevity and relevance. Those of Ch'en-ssu [or Ts'ao Chih] have achieved a great name, but their style is long-winded and drawn out. In the last part of his elegy for his brother, Emperor Wen, for about one hundred lines he indulged in talking about himself. This is a serious departure from the ideal standard.

The ministers of the Yin sang praises of T'ang to commemorate the blessings of the black bird,[15] and the Chou historians chanted songs in honor of King Wen to recount the great achievements of Hou-chi.[16]

[9] Chih-yü, in his *Wen-chang liu-pieh*, made this statement, unaware of the existence of the complete piece.

[10] His biography is in the *Hou-han-shu*.   [11] The first ruler of the Later Han.

[12] Tu's elegy for Wu Han is found in the *I-wen lei-chü*, chüan 47.

[13] Biography in the *Hou-han-shu*.

[14] Biographies of both men are in the *Hou-han-shu*, but their works are not contained in them, nor are they found elsewhere.

[15] Probably referring to "Hsüan-niao," No. 393 in the *Book of Poetry*. Hsüan-niao, a bird of black color, identified as a swallow, is supposedly the agent through whose blessings Shang, the ancestor of the Shang people, was born. The elegy, however, seems to refer to "Ch'ang-fa," whose number in the *Book of Poetry* is 304.

[16] Referring apparently to "Sheng-min," No. 245. Hou-chi was the first ancestor of the Chou people, and his birth is described in this poem.

The description of the summed up virtues and merits of ancestors is indeed the principle followed by the Ancient Poets in the writing of the *lei*.

Such a piece of writing, in expressing mournful feelings, develops according to the circumstances to which these feelings are the responses. Fu I's elegy written for Pei-hai[17] begins: "The light of the sun was darkened, and the whole Huai district was blanketed in rain." This expression of feeling at the beginning of the elegy became a model for later writers. And his imitators were often attracted to him by his cleverness.

With respect to its organization, the elegy consists of a selection of the sayings and an account of the life of the deceased. It is biographical in form, and the language it adopts is that of the *sung*, or ode, beginning in glory and ending in sorrow. In its portrayal of the deceased as a man, it brings him affectingly before us; and in expressing grief, its mournful tune suggests profound sorrow. This is the main idea of the elegy.

Pei, or stone monument, means *pei*, or walled terrace. Emperors and kings of ancient times erected *pei*, or stone monuments, on which to keep records of their reigns, or as places to render sacrifices to heaven and earth, and erected *pei*, or walled terraces, on the mountains. Because of this homophone they called the walled terrace *pei*.[18] The record of King Mu of the Chou inscribed on the stone of Yen-shan gives us an inkling of the function of the *pei* in ancient times.

Then there were the monuments in ancestral temples, erected [in the central courtyard] between the two rows of side rooms; these monuments served merely as hitching posts for sacrificial animals, and were not used at first for inscriptions recording merits and achievements. When in later times bronze articles became scarce,[19] stone monuments were used instead of bronze; both signify the immortal.

17 Prince Ching. Fragments of this piece are found in *Ku wen-yüan.*

18 *Pei* meaning a stone monument, the sense in which the term in the title is used, and *pei* meaning a terrace signify each other because of their homophone. This principle of linking semantically two homophonous characters is often resorted to by scholars for the explanation of many characters found in the ancient Classics.

19 Bronze was generally used for the purpose of recording merits and achievements.

[Later, monuments were also erected over the tombs.] From the monuments erected in the temples to those erected over the tombs, all had somewhat the significance of the piling up of earth to build a foundation.[20]

After the time of the Later Han, *pei* and *chieh* rose like clouds.[21] But of all the carvings from the blades of these later talents those by Ts'ai Yung stand out without peer. Among the stone inscriptions for which he was responsible, the "Yang Tz'u Pei," or "Monument to Yang Tz'u," is marked by strong character and classic beauty, the two pieces on Ch'en [T'ai-ch'iu] and Kuo [Yu-tao] are completely free from any flattery, and those on Chou [Hsieh] and Hu [Kuang], pure and balanced. In recounting events, they are comprehensive and yet brief and to the point; and in rhetoric, they are graceful and smooth. We find in them an inexhaustible flow of translucent phrases, and also brilliant ideas which are unique. All these are a result of a talent which is natural and spontaneous.[22]

The works of K'ung Yung were modeled after those of Po-chieh [or Ts'ai Yung]. The two pieces on Chang [Chien] and Ch'en,[23] clear-cut and beautifully phrased, may be considered as being in the same class as those by Ts'ai.

Sun Ch'o[24] intended his works for *pei* and *lei*. But his pieces on Wen [Ch'iao], Wang [Tao], Hsi [Chien], and Yü [Liang][25] are wordy and without order. His only well-written piece is the one on Huan I.[26]

[20] The "piling up of earth to build a foundation," an activity common to the erection of all monuments, is here used to signify their common quality—an indication of immortality.

[21] Both *pei* and *chieh* mean stone slabs or monuments. A square stone slab is called a *pei*, and a round stone is called *chieh*. See *Wen-t'i t'ung-shih*. See also *Hou-han-shu*, commentary in the biography of Tou Hsien.

[22] For Ts'ai's works, see *Ts'ai Chung-lang chi*. Ts'ai's dates are A.D. 132-192.

[23] Fragments of K'ung's inscription on Chang are preserved in *Ch'üan hou-han wen*, chüan 83. The one on Ch'en is lost.

[24] Flourishing during the fourth century.

[25] All of the Eastern Chin.

[26] Fragments of the pieces on Wang and Hsi are found in *I-wen lei-chü*, chüan 45, and of that on Yü in chüan 47. The piece on Huan I, however, has completely disappeared.

The writing of the *pei* requires the talent of a historian. In organization it is biographical, and its language is that of the *ming*. From its description of great virtues the reader should be able to visualize the benign countenance taking shape in the subtle breezes; and in its account of a successful life he should be able to perceive the glory of the craggy height which the one commemorated had attained. In these we have the substantial features of the *pei*.

A stone monument is in fact an inscribed article, and the inscription is the literary pattern of the monument. To select a name for the article in accord with its nature was an activity prior to that of composing the elegy. Therefore, all writings inscribed on stone to honor merits are included in the genre of *ming*, or inscription, and those of them which give accounts of the deceased on upright stone slabs are classified under *lei*, or elegy.

  The Tsan:
To give an account of facts and recapture what has passed into noth-
     ingness
Are reasons for the creation of the *lei* and the *pei*.
In them, virtues are inscribed and life commemorated
In clusters of colorful literary modes.
The style in which the deceased is described gives one the feeling of
     seeing him in person,
And listening to its language is like listening to mournful sobs.
The flower incised in stone and ink
Will not fade because of the collapse of the shadow [physical body].

XIII. Lament and Condolence (The Ai and the Tiao)

According to the rule of conferring posthumous titles, one who dies young is given the title of *ai*, or lamented. *Ai*, or to lament, means *i*, or to adhere; sorrows adhere to the heart; hence the term *ai*, or to lament, or simply sorrow. One gives vent to one's sorrows by means of writing, which is tearless lamentation. Therefore this form of writing does not apply to the death of older people, but always to those who meet an untimely death.[1]

Long ago, three good generals were buried with King Mu of Ch'in as sacrifices, not having been allowed to be ransomed even by the lives of a hundred; these deaths may be considered as untimely and unjust. The poem "Huang-niao" sings its grief for them. Is this not the example of lament from the Ancient Poets themselves?[2] At the time when Emperor Wu of the Han [140-87 B.C.] sacrificed to heaven and earth, Huo Tzu-hou[3] suddenly died. The emperor expressed his grief in a poem which may also be included in the genre of lament. It was the lamentation of Ts'ui Yüan for Prince Ju-nan[4] of the Later Han which gave the genre a new form. But in the violence of its onset upon the gate of the realm of ghosts, its language becomes grotesque and uncultured; and in its references to dragons and cloud-riding, it may succeed in suggesting a desire for immortality, but it entirely lacks the emotion of sorrow. The last five stanzas are in five-word form, the style of folk songs, and are more or less moulded after the pattern set up by Emperor Wu.

Both Su Shun and Chang Sheng also wrote lament. Though they began to see its subtle flowers, they had yet to penetrate to the core of its fruit. Of all the lament writers during the Chien-an period [196-220], only the work of Wei-ch'ang [or Hsü Kan] may be considered good. His "Hsing-nü," or "Lamentation for a Daughter," has occasional bursts of real feeling. Then came P'an Yüeh, whose laments were patterned after the beauty of Hsü's style. With his clear thought, his flexible language, his deep sentiments and profound sorrows; with his account of events reading like a biography, his composition in the

---

[1] Literally, *yao* and *hun*, meaning "dying young" and "dying an infant less than three months old," respectively.

[2] See *Mao-shih yin-te*, 27/131.

[3] Huo Shan, the son of Huo Ch'ü-pin, a great general. [4] Unidentifiable.

spirit of the *Book of Poetry*, and his four-word pattern, short and rhythmic, never a line loose or sluggish, he was able to state his ideas simply in words that are gentle, and to grace an old form with a fresh interest. His "Chin-lu" and "Tse-lan" are without heir.[5]

In general, the main things to consider in a lament are, on the one hand, sorrowful feelings and, on the other, a language capable of expressing love and regret. The dead was young and had not had a chance to establish his virtue; hence, in commending him, one does not go beyond speaking of him as intelligent and bright; since he was weak and unable to shoulder any responsibility, one mourns for the loss of his physical form. When the composition springs from a heart full of grief, it will be fine; but if one manipulates one's heart to conform with literary expressions, the piece must be characterized by excess. An excessively ornate piece may contain beautiful expressions, but it is not the right vehicle for expressing sorrow. The important thing in writing a lament is that genuine feeling be the basis of one's mournful tone and that the expression be moving enough to bring forth one's tears.

The term *tiao*, or to condole, means *chih*, or to arrive. A line in the *Book of Poetry* runs:

"Shen chih tiao i," meaning "The Spirits have arrived."[6]

The occasion on which a posthumous title is being fixed upon a man of virtue who has lived out his natural term is a time of extreme importance, an occasion full of sorrow. Therefore the arrival of guests to condole with the bereaved is termed *chih-tao*. But when a death is caused by crushing or drowning, an event contrary to the normal course, no condolence is given.[7] When Sung suffered from flood and

---

[5] "Chin-lu" mourning a son, and "Tse-lan" a girl. The second piece was written for his friend's wife, whose daughter died when she was three.

[6] "T'ien-pao" in the *Book of Poetry*, *Mao-shih yin-te*, 35/166/5. *Tiao* is a modern pronunciation. According to *Shuo-wen*, it should be pronounced *ti*, and according to Karlgren, *tiog*, which is phonetically linked to *tao*, the ancient pronunciation of which is *tog*, meaning to arrive. As *tao* and *chih* are semantically linked, *ti* and *chih* become synonyms.

[7] See "T'an-kung," shang, in the *Li-chi* for the three conditions in which no condolence is to be offered, i.e., no guests are to come. *Li-chi yin-te*, 3/25.

Cheng from fire, envoys from other states came to express their sympathy; for both when calamities fall upon a state and when people die, condolences are in order.[8] When Chin built Ssu-ch'i terrace and Ch'i attacked Yen, Shih Chao and Su Ch'in offered condolences immediately after expressing their congratulations.[9] For whether it was the oppression of the people [as in Chin's building of the Ssu-ch'i terrace] or the provocation of an enemy state [as in Ch'i's attack upon Yen during the latter's mourning period], both were ways leading to destruction. All these cases were fit occasions for offering condolence.

Some people lose their lives because, while occupying high positions, they are arrogant; some lead perverse lives because they are impatient and filled with resentment; some have great ambitions and yet are born out of their times; and some possess talents but find themselves burdened with too many distractions. All expressions imparting sympathy to the spirits of people like these are designated *tiao*.

When Chia I floated down the River Hsiang,[10] full of resentment, he wrote to condole with the spirit of Ch'ü Yüan. This piece is perfect in style and clear in its narrative. Its language is pure and its thought sad. It is indeed an outstanding work of its kind.[11] [Ssu-ma] Hsiang-ju's expression of sympathy to Erh-shih[12] is entirely a specimen of *fu*,[13] although Huan T'an considered it full of mournful feeling, causing the reader to heave a sympathetic sigh. Its last section is particularly

[8] For the Sung flood, see *Ch'un-ch'iu ching-chuan yin-te*, 59/Chuang 11/3 Tso; and for the Cheng fire, see *ibid.*, 394/Chao 2 Tso.

[9] The building of Ssu-ch'i terrace, while an occasion for celebration, was considered a fit subject for condolence by Shih Chao, who accompanied the Earl of Cheng to Chin for that occasion, because such construction served no useful purpose, but added to the burden of the people. See *Tso-chuan*, Duke Chao, the eighth year, or *Ch'un-ch'iu ching-chuan yin-te*, 368/Chao 8/3 Tso. Ch'i attacked Yen when the latter had lost its king and the new king, I, had just been inaugurated. As Yen was in no position to resist, Ch'i took ten cities. While this expansion of territory on the part of Ch'i was an occasion for congratulations, it also revealed the ruthless nature of the ruler of Ch'i, which could prove his own downfall. Therefore, Su Ch'in offered condolences immediately after having expressed congratulations. See *Chan-kuo ts'e*, "Yen-ts'e."

[10] Ch'ü Yüan had drowned himself in the River Hsiang in Hunan.

[11] Chia I, like Ch'ü Yüan, was alienated from his ruler because of slanderous sycophants. In this condolence he was in fact giving vent to his own resentment.

[12] The second emperor of the Ch'in dynasty.

[13] See Chapter VIII.

pertinent, for it is concise and capable of evoking sad thoughts. As
to the condolence offered by Yang Hsiung to Ch'ü Yüan, it was a work
of great labor but little merit. Yang was deeply intent on reversing the
point of view found in the *Li-sao*; and for this reason his work is
characterized by clumsy expressions and uncouth rhyme. Both Pan
Piao[14] and Ts'ai Yung were proficient in the manipulation of words;
however, they followed Chia I as shadows and can hardly be considered his equals. Then there are the condolences to [Po-]i and [Shu-]
ch'i[15] written by Hu [Kuang], Yüan [Yü], and Chung-hsüan [or
Wang Ts'an]. Those by Hu and Yüan are all praises and no blame;
the one by Chung-hsüan, however, expertly criticized them.[16] Hu and
Yüan praised Po-i and Shu-ch'i for their integrity, while Wang Ts'an
regretted their narrow-mindedness; each was expressing his personal
view. Ni Heng's[17] expression of sympathy to P'ing-tzu [or Chang
Heng],[18] although elegant and decorative, is light and pure; and that
offered by Lu Chi[19] to Wei Wu [or Ts'ao Ts'ao] has an expertly written preface, but a wordy text. None besides these cited here is of any
consequence.

   Tiao, or condolence, although in use in ancient times, was adorned
with beautiful language only in later times; indeed, when ornamented
unduly and slowed in tempo, it becomes *fu*. To write condolence properly, one should have correct ideas, in conformity with the nature
of the case; one should bring to light the virtues of the deceased and
block the tendency to indulge in what is perverse; one should carefully
consider what to praise and what to censure; and one's language

---

   [14] A.D. 3-54.

   [15] Two brothers of the Shang dynasty who signified their refusal to acknowledge
the sovereign power of the Chou by declining to eat Chou grains. They removed themselves to the foot of Mount Shou-yang, feeding on weeds. When reminded that even
weeds belonged to the Chou dynasty, they starved themselves to death. They are known
in Chinese history as examples of loyalty and integrity.

   [16] Wang Ts'an served under Ts'ao Ts'ao, whose intention to usurp the throne at the
end of the Han dynasty was evident, though it was his son, Ts'ao P'ei, who finally took
the throne. It was natural for him to criticize Po-i and Shu-ch'i, who failed to see the
effect of the revolution of King Wu in exterminating the ruthless government of the
last ruler of the Shang dynasty.

   [17] 173-198.   [18] 78-139.   [19] 261-303.

should be sad and yet accurate. Then, no one can deny one the ability to write in perfect form.

The *Tsan*:
The *Ai* grieves
For those who die young;
Sprouting grain that fails to flower
Has since old times been mourned.[20]
But even a man of comprehensive talents
Has often lost his bearings in this form and failed to put it under
    control.[21]
What is worthy of being mourned one thousand years later
Is here clothed in words.

XIV. Miscellaneous Writings

The works of men of intellect and wide learning are characterized by colorful expressions which are brought to life by their vigorous spirits. Rich in literary ideas, these men bring forth productions that are always fresh and new. Sung Yü, a man of talent, was often subject to the ridicule of the vulgar. So he wrote *tui-wen*, to let out his feelings. It was due to his vigorous spirit that he was able in his writing to soar with absolute freedom in the boundless expanse of the universe.[1] And Mei Sheng, the master of exquisite phraseology, first wrote "Ch'i-fa,"[2] whose language is as rich as the patterns of clouds and whose beauty

[20] See the *Analects*, "Tzu-han," *Lun-yü yin-te*, 17/9/22, where Confucius used this metaphor to illustrate the untimely death of Yen Hui, his most beloved disciple, whose death Confucius deeply mourned.

[21] This refers to the fact that with over-adornment and slow-moving rhythm, *tiao*— or lamentation—becomes *fu*.

[1] Sung Yü flourished in the third century B.C. *Tui-wen*, literally "answering questions," is a form of writing. His "Tui Ch'u-wang wen" (Answer to the question of the king of Ch'u) is in Hsiao T'ung's *Wen-hsüan*.

[2] Mei Sheng died in 141 B.C. "Ch'i-fa" literally means seven shots, that is, to arouse

surprises us like gusts of wind. In this piece of *ch'i,* Mei first touches
on sensual pleasures and desires; he begins with the perverse, but con-
cludes with the proper; his purpose was to give warning to one who
was brought up in ease. Yang Hsiung, contemplating in the [T'ien-lu]
ko,[3] and deeply occupied in writing, collected familiar words and
trivial phrases to form *lien-chu,*[4] whose language, though frivolous,
is bright and smooth. These three [*tui-wen, ch'i,* and *lien-chu*] are in
fact branches of literature, inferior pieces produced in times of leisure.

Once *tui-wen* was created, Tung-fang So took it and expanded it,
giving it the title "K'e-nan," or "Objections by a guest or an opposition
party." By citing cases from the past, he explained away his own
frustrations. The work is clear and logical. Yang Hsiung wrote "Chieh-
ch'ao,"[5] in a vein which contains a great deal of humor. He doubles
back and forth, trying to explain away his failure in life, and does so
with moderate success. We have also Pan Ku's "Pin-hsi," containing
flowers of wonderful colors; Ts'ui Yin's "Ta-chih," displaying a language of classical elegance; Chang Heng's "Ying-wen," close-knit and
graceful; Ts'ui Shih's "Ta-chi," well ordered although slightly crude;
Ts'ai Yung's "Hsi-hui," profound in thought and brilliant in expressions; and Ching-ch'un's [or Kuo P'u's] "K'e-ao," overflowing with
feeling and rich in colors. Though these writers followed one another's example, their works may all be considered great. On the other
hand, although the "K'e-wen" of Ch'en-ssu [or Ts'ao Chih] may
contain wonderful expressions, it is rather loose in reasoning; and
Yü K'ai's "K'e-tzu" has ideas in abundance, but is weak in literary
expression. Writings of this quality are numerous, and none is worthy

---

one to action by seven stimulating cases. In the present piece, Mei Sheng tried to
stimulate the heir apparent to actions appropriate to his status. The origin of this
particular style is a moot question. But many scholars since the time of Han had
employed it as a vehicle. It is known as *ch'i,* or "seven."

[3] A royal library of the Early Han, built by Hsiao Ho, the first prime minister of the
Han dynasty.

[4] *Lien-chu* means "continuous string of pearls." A piece of writing in which phrases
and ideas are threaded together like pearls on a string is given this name. In his biography in the *Han-shu,* Yang is said to have been an editor in the royal library.

[5] "Chieh-ch'ao," literally, to explain away people's ridicule, is faithfully patterned
after Tung-fang So's "K'e-nan," although in it he spoke ill of Tung-fang's character.

of our attention. For the purpose of this type of writing is to give vent to one's frustrated feelings. If one finds himself in adversity, he will conquer his disappointment by dwelling on the principle of life; if one finds himself at odds with his times, he will console himself by cultivating peace of mind. One always maintains a frame of mind both deep and lofty, and expresses it in the colorful patterns of a unicorn or a phoenix. These are the fundamentals in the writing of this literary form.

Since the writing of "Ch'i-fa," many have followed in Mei's footsteps. A look at this initial attempt of Mei's will convince us that it is truly outstanding, indeed a work of great beauty. We have Fu I's "Ch'i-chi," which exhibits the art of combining the pure and the pertinent; Ts'ui Yin's "Ch'i-i," which has contrived to enter the realm of learning and grace; the "Ch'i-pien" of Chang Heng, which abounds in variegated figures; the "Ch'i-su" of Ts'ui Yüan, in which moral principles find their place; Ch'en-ssu's [or Ts'ao Chih's] "Ch'i-ch'i," whose beauty lies in its grandeur and vigor; and Chung-hsüan's [or Wang Ts'an's] "Ch'i-hsi," which handles facts and their *raison d'être* with clarity. Between the "Ch'i-shuo" of Huan Lin and the "Ch'i-feng" of Tso Ssu, there were more than ten writers who attached themselves to them like branches or like shadows. Some of their works are rich in literary patterns but weak in ideas, while others expound moral principles in all their purity but are impure in language. In general, they all describe palaces and hunting, and in grand style. They are concerned with outlandish costumes and exotic wood, describing with extreme dexterity heart-enchanting songs and women. Their delightful conceptions stir one to the bone and marrow, and their bewitching phrases captivate the soul. Although they begin with the lustful, they conclude with what is right. But for every person to whom they may have succeeded in bringing the moral lesson home by means of satirical metaphors, there are hundreds who are encouraged to lead licentious lives, and are unable to return to simplicity. It was for this reason that Yang Hsiung ridiculed the idea of beginning with the lustful notes of Cheng and Wei, and striking up the refined music only at the end of the singing.[6] The only piece that speaks of ancient worthies, basing its thought on Confucian principles, is the "Ch'i-su" [by Ts'ui Yüan]; although it is not outstanding in its literary quality, the ideas it contains are really lofty and profound.

Many writers have also imitated the *lien-chu*. Tu Tu, Chia K'uei, Liu Chen, P'an Hsü, and their group intended to make strings of pearls, but only succeeded in stringing fish eyes.[7] They may be compared to the crawling of the youth from Shou-ling, a far cry from the gait of Han-tan which he had set out to acquire.[8] [Their act of imitation is as ugly as that of] the homely neighbor woman who held her hands over her heart in imitation of the beautiful Hsi-shih, [with a grimace that created an effect] totally different from that of Hsi-shih's knitted brows.[9] But Shih-heng [or Lu Chi] alone, through careful consideration, brought to the form new ideas couched in swift-moving language, and extended its scope by neat organization and firm sentence structure. Need he indeed envy the four-inch pearl of Chu Chung?[10] It is easy to be perfect in writing short literary pieces, and easy too to make one's thoughts presentable when they are not formed in haste. Any piece which is so written as to have clear ideas and neat expressions, coherent narrative, and melodious sounds which always ring clear-cut and clean, is worthy of the name *chu*, or pearl.

Since the Han many terms have been employed to designate miscellaneous writings. These are: *tien*,[11] or important documents; *kao*,[12]

---

[6] See his biography in the *Han-shu*.

[7] A figure connoting falsehood, for fish eyes look like pearls but are not.

[8] A certain youth from Shou-ling, in the state of Yen (modern Peking), came to Han-tan, the capital of the state of Chao (in modern Ho-pei), to learn the Han-tan gait. But before he succeeded in his study, he lost all he had known. Hence he had to crawl back to Shou-ling. The figure is found in the *Chuangtzu* (*Chuangtzu yin-te*, 45/17/79), and ridicules the folly of an imitation of others which results in the loss of one's own originality.

[9] Another reference from the *Chuangtzu*, "T'ien-yün" (38/14/42), where it is said that long ago Hsi-shih, a great beauty, was afflicted with a bad heart. In her pain, she held her hands over her heart and knitted her brows. An ugly neighbor, seeing that she was very beautiful in such a posture, tried to imitate her.

[10] See *Lieh-hsien chuan*, by Liu Hsiang of the Early Han.

[11] Originated in the "Yao-tien" and "Shun-tien" of the *Book of History*.

[12] Also originated in the *Book of History*.

or to inform; *shih*,[13] or to take an oath, or military proclamation; *wen*,[14] or to inquire; *lan*,[15] or to peruse; *lüeh*, or a précis; *p'ien,* or a piece of composition, or simply a book; *chang*, or a chapter; *ch'ü*, or a ditty; *ts'ao*, or a piece of instrumental music; *lung*, or a short song; *yin*, or a prelude; *yin*, or a sad chanting [to be distinguished from the previous *yin*]; *feng*, or a satirical writing; *yao*, or a folk song sung without instrumental accompaniment; and *yung*, or a song. These different names may all be classified together under the category of miscellaneous writings. But if we distinguish among them with respect to their meanings, each may be included in its appropriate group.[16] And since each has a logical place, we shall not deal with them here out of their proper contexts.

The Tsan:
Great were the earlier scholars,
Men of solid learning and overflowing talents.
Their surplus energy they devoted to sheer literary virtuosity,[17]
Dashing off light, beautiful phrases, showing off their cleverness.
These display themselves in clusters like branches,
Twinkling as if they were Orion or the Pleiades.
But those who tried to imitate the "brow-knitting"
Succeeded only in unsettling their own minds.

[13] Also originated in the *Book of History*.
[14] Originated during the Han time.
[15] It is found in the *Lü-shih ch'un-ch'iu*, which is also known as *Lü-lan*, that which is perused by Master Lü.
[16] For example: *tien* may be included in "Feng-sh'an" (Chapter XXI), *kao* in "Chao-tz'e" (Chapter XIX), *shih* in "Chu-meng" (Chapter X), *wen* in "I-tui" (Chapter XXIV), *ch'ü, ts'ao, lung, yin, yin, feng, yao,* and *yung* in "Yüeh-fu" (Chapter VII), *chang* in "Chang-piao" (Chapter XXII).
[17] See *Lun-yü yin-te*, 1/1/6. "When there is energy left after moral practice, then take up literature."

XV. Humor and Enigma (The Hsieh and the Yin)

A poem of Jui Liang-fu's contains these lines:

> [The king] has his own private thoughts,
> And he exhausts and enrages the people.[1]

The mental processes of the people are as precipitous as mountains, and their mouths, when stopped, are like dammed-up rivers. As their resentment and anger differ, their ways of expressing these feelings in jests or derision also vary. When once long ago Hua Yüan left his armor in the field after his defeat, the soldiers guarding the city ridiculed him in a song gibing at his protruding eyes.[2] And when Tsang Ho lost his army, he was the subject of a satirical tune referring to him as a pigmy.[3] In both cases the people mocked the appearance of the subjects of their songs in order to express their inner resentment and scorn. Again there were the rude popular songs using the figures of the silkworm and crab and the inappropriate song referring to the colorful pattern of a raccoon.[4] Crude though these may be, in case they could be of service in the way of giving warning to people, they were all recorded in the *Book of Rites*, or the *Li-chi*. These examples show

---

[1] *Mao-shih yin-te*, 69/257/8. According to the preface to the poem, Jui was criticizing King Li of the Chou dynasty, who paid no attention to the people but followed his own intentions. "He has his own lungs and intestines."

[2] *Ch'un-ch'iu ching-chuan yin-te*, 179-180/Hsüan 2/1 Tso.

[3] *Ibid.*, 259/Hsiang 4/Tso *fu* 2. Tsang Ho was a very small man.

[4] *Li-chi yin-te*, 4/72. A man of Ch'eng—a city of Lu, in present day Shangtung— would not wear mourning for his elder brother. But as soon as he heard that Tzu-kao, a disciple of Confucius known for his filial piety, was appointed the magistrate of Ch'eng, he started to wear mourning for his brother. The people of Ch'eng sang a song, which runs: "A silkworm has silk, while a crab has a basket; . . . and when his brother died, he wore mourning for Tzu-kao." Just as the basket, that is, the house the crab carried, was not for holding the silk the silkworm produced, so the mourning of the man of Ch'eng was not for his own brother. The same chapter of the *Li-chi*, 4/69, tells us that while Confucius was working on the coffin for the mother of an old friend by the name of Yüan Jang, the latter sang that the carving of the wood was as beautiful as the pattern of a raccoon's head. This was highly inappropriate for the occasion, but Confucius forgave him because he was his old friend. Some scholars with a Taoist bent considered Yüan Jang a man of great achievement because he succeeded in freeing himself from his emotions, which are the human bondage.

us that even humorous sayings and enigmatic statements are not to be discarded.

Hsieh, or humor or jest, means *chieh,* or all,[5] that is, something expressed in crude language to the taste of the common people, which is enjoyed by all. In ancient times King Wei of Ch'i indulged in drinking and feasting, and Ch'un-yü [K'un] admonished him by means of a comic story about good wine.[6] And during a feasting party given by King Hsiang of Ch'u, Sung Yü wrote a [witty] *fu* arguing that he was not fond of women.[7] Both of these aimed at subtle advice and may be commended. Then we have jester Chan's ironic comment on [Erh-shih's proposal to] paint the city walls,[8] and jester Meng's sarcastic remonstrance against the funeral service for a dead horse;[9] in both cases clever speeches and witty arguments were employed to suppress what would have been stupidity and ruthlessness. For this reason, Tzu-ch'ang [or Ssu-ma Ch'ien], when compiling his history [the *Shih-chi*], included

[5] *Chieh* (meaning "all") is a component in *hsieh,* giving it its phonetic element. The signific element of *hsieh* is furnished by the radical *yen,* meaning "to talk." But Liu Hsieh was apparently treating the phonetic *chieh* as a signific element. However, since by a signific is meant merely a general area within which the meaning of the word may fall, and since in many cases specific meaning is furnished by what is usually taken to be a phonetic, Liu may be correct here. In that case, we have to translate the term *chieh* (all) to mean "some kind of harmony among all people."

[6] Ssu-ma Ch'ien, *Shih-chi,* "Ku-chi lieh-chuan." Ch'un-yü K'un told the king that sometimes he was drunk after drinking a *tou* (about a liquid pint), and sometimes he was drunk after drinking a *shih* (ten times a *tou*). He described how drinking loosened up his morals, and brought the king to his senses, so that he promised to give up all-night drinking sprees.

[7] The *fu* is found in the *Wen-hsüan.*

[8] When Erh-shih, the second emperor of the Ch'in dynasty, planned to have the city walls painted, jester Chan said, "Good. Even if your majesty did not speak about it, I would have petitioned for it. Though the painting of the city walls might prove a great sorrow and burden to the people, it is indeed fine! The city walls would be bright and slippery, and no enemy could climb them; and even if they did climb them, they would all be easily tarnished. However, this would hardly give shelter to your own home." Erh-shih laughed and gave up his plan. See *Shih-chi,* "Ku-chi lieh-chuan."

[9] *Ibid.*: A favorite horse of King Chuang of Ch'u died. The king ordered all his ministers to wear mourning, and planned to give it a funeral service fitting a high official. When his subordinates advised against it, he decreed, "Those who dare to advise against the funeral of the horse shall die." Jester Meng heard of it, came before the king, and started to cry. When asked why, he said, "The horse was the king's favorite. In a state as great as Ch'u, nothing is impossible. It would indeed be too much of a slight to bury it with a service only befitting a minister; it should be buried with a service befitting a ruler . . . for only thus would the lords know that your majesty values horses and despises human beings." The king gave up his plan.

in it a chapter on the humorists ["Ku-chi lieh-chuan"], because in spite
of their wandering and devious speeches they always aim toward the
right principle. However, what is by nature not of the purest easily
leads to the faulty. Thus we have Tung-fang [So] and Mei Kao, who
"feed on the dregs of the wine," [that is, they had a tendency to sink
to the level of the common herd].[10] They did nothing to correct the
tendency and, instead, indulged in raillery and took indecent personal
liberties. Thus, even if they referred to their works as *fu*, they knew
very well that these are no better than comic préces. Mei showed some
measure of regret when he saw that he had been looked upon as a
jester.[11] Thus Wei-wen [or Ts'ao P'ei] used comic themes to write
jokes;[12] and Hsüeh Tsung jested sarcastically during a diplomatic
reception.[13] These jokes, though effective in producing merriment
during a feast, serve no practical purposes. And yet good writers often
went out of their way to join in the fun; P'an Yüeh's joke on an ugly
woman and Shu Hsi's on a pastry peddler are good examples.[14] And
those who followed in their footsteps number more than a hundred.
The humorists during the Wei and the Chin accentuated the trend by
their mutual influence. We find the nose of Ying Yang compared to
an egg whose end has been cut off by a thief, and the physical form
of Chang Hua compared to the handle of a pestle.[15] These loquacious
writings are a disgrace to moral principles. Are they not as unseemly
as laughter from a drowning man or riotous songs from a criminal?

Yin, or enigma, literally means to hide: to use obscure language to
hide ideas or to employ an artful parable to point to certain facts.

[10] A figure taken from the "Yü-fu" in the *Ch'u-tz'u*, meaning to follow the trend
of the crowd.

[11] See the *Han-shu*, the biographies of Tung-fang So and of Mei Kao.

[12] His joke book is not reported in his biography in the "Wei-chih" in the
San-kuo-chih.

[13] See his biography in the "Wu-chih" in the *San-kuo-chih*.

[14] Pan's work is not identifiable. Shu's work is found in *Hsü Ku Wen-yüan*.

[15] The reference to the case of Ying Yang (A.D. ?-217) cannot be identified. That
of Chang Hua (A.D. 232-300) is found in the *Shih-shuo hsin-yü* by Liu I-ch'ing, "P'ai-
tiao p'ien" (Chu-tzu chi-ch'eng ed.), chüan 6, Chapter 25, p. 206. Six persons are
mentioned together with six descriptions. Since the correlation between the persons
mentioned and the subsequent descriptions is not specified, Liu Hsieh must have some
other source as the basis for his statement.

When Hsüan [Wu-] she [of Hsiao] asked Ch'u generals to save him [when Hsiao was under attack by Ch'u, and Hsüan knew that the Hsiao army would be routed], their talk about "yeast" really referred to the dry well [in which Hsüan hid while waiting to be rescued].[16] And when [Shen] Shu-i [of Wu] begged for food from the ministers of Lu, he sang of pendant jade, while the ministers told him to call for *keng-k'uei*.[17] Wu Chü[18] satirized the king of Ch'u with the parable of the great bird,[19] and a Ch'i gentleman gibed at the Lord of She with the parable of a sea fish.[20] And Chuang Chi [Chih] used the allegory of the tail of a dragon,[21] while Tsang Wen[-chung] sent a

[16] Yeast was good for prevention of getting wet; see *Ch'un-ch'iu ching-chuan yin-te*, 200/Hsüan 12/5 Tso.

[17] Shu-i, in his song, told the Lu people that while everybody in the Ch'u camp had a jade pendant, he alone had to go without; and while everybody had good wine to drink, he and other commoners could only look on as they drank. The Lu ministers told him to call for *keng-k'uei*, which is a riddle meaning food and water, for in the army food was not to be given out to the enemy.

[18] Flourishing during the seventh century B.C.

[19] *Shih-chi*, "Ch'u shih-chia." For three years after King Chuang of Ch'u ascended the throne, he gave no orders. Day and night he passed in revelry. His only proclamation to the people runs: "Those who dare remonstrate with me shall die." Then came Wu Chü, who said he had a riddle to present before his majesty. "On a mound there is a bird which for three years would neither fly nor cry. What is that bird?" King Chuang said, "For three years it may not have made a single flight, but once it flies, it will penetrate the sky; for three years it may not have cried, but once it cries, its cry will startle all the people. Go home, Chü. I now know."

[20] *Chan-kuo ts'e*, "Ch'i-ts'e." Ching-kuo-chün was about to build the city walls of She. Annoyed by objectors, he ordered that no one should be admitted to his residence. A Ch'i gentleman pleaded that he be given a chance to say only three words, saying that if he should say a word more, he was willing to accept the death penalty. Ching-kuo-chün saw him. The gentleman rushed in and said, "Sea big fish," and rushed out. When called on to explain, he refused, saying that he was not willing to play with death. Chün told him to forget about his agreement and give the explanation. So he said, "Have you not heard of the big fish? No net can get it, and no hook can catch it. However, if ever it is out of water, even ants can do anything they wish with it. Now the state of Ch'i is your water. Having Ch'i, why should you build walls for She? If ever you should lose Ch'i, even if you heightened the walls of She to the sky, it would be of no use to you." Chün said, "Good." He gave up building walls for She.

[21] *Lieh-nü chuan* (Ssu-pu pei-yao ed.), chüan 6, p. 46. Chuang Chih said to King Ch'ing-hsiang of Ch'u, "The big fish is out of water; the dragon is without a tail; the walls are about to fall in, and yet Your Majesty will not take a look." When told to explain, she said, "The fish out of water is Your Majesty, who is now five hundred li from the capital. The dragon without a tail points out the fact that you are now forty years of age and yet without an heir. . . . The walls about to fall in at which Your Majesty will not take a look mean that confusion is about to reign and yet you will not change your way."

cryptic message using the figure of a sheepskin.[22] Historical records
abound in cases of the employment of *yin*; some of the important ones
served to bring about good government and helped develop personality,
and some of the minor ones also assisted in recalling the erring and
in dissolving doubts. For a guiding principle of the *yin* is expediency,
and it is employed at critical moments. Enigmas and humorous writings may be considered to be two aspects of the same thing. There were
eighteen collections of enigmas during the Han dynasty, and Liu Hsin
and Pan Ku placed them at the end of "Songs."[23]

King Chuang of Ch'u and King Wei of Ch'i in ancient times loved
enigmas. After their time came Tung-fang Man-ch'ien [or Tung-fang
So], who was particularly clever in making them. But his are mostly
absurd statements and calumnious jests, which serve no moral purpose.

Since the time of Wei, jokers and jesters have been disparaged. Men
of culture, ridiculing *yin*, transformed them into riddles.[24] A riddle is
a piece of writing so circuitous that it leads people into a maze. Some
riddles are based on the structure of characters, and some on the
pictures and forms of articles. They show refinement and cleverness
in the manipulation of thoughts, and simplicity and clarity in the
array of expressions; their ideas are indirect and yet correct, and their
language is ambiguous and yet suggestive. We find the beginning of
this development already evident in Hsün-ch'ing's "Ts'an-fu." The
riddles by Wei-wen [or Ts'ao P'ei] and Ch'en-ssu [or Ts'ao Chih]
are terse and close-knit; those by Kao-kuei-hsiang-kung are comprehensive in citing illustrations but, while cunning and clever, they miss

[22] *Ibid.*, chüan 3, p. 25. Tsang Wen-chung of Lu was sent to Ch'i as an envoy. Ch'i
detained him and raised an army to attack Lu. Wen-chung sent a cryptic message to
the Duke of Lu. The language was so ambiguous that only his mother knew how to
decipher it. The message contains many figures meaning various things. Among them
is the one about sheepskin mentioned in the text, which means that Ch'i was feasting its
troops and getting ready for an assault against Lu. Liu Hsieh picked this one out as
representative.

[23] According to the arrangement given in the "I-wen chih" in the *Han-shu*, these
enigmas are placed below *fu*, and not "Songs." Perhaps Liu Hsieh was using the term
fu loosely, as he and most writers of the time so often did.

[24] It seems that an enigma attempts to hide ideas from those for whom they are not
intended, and a riddle is to puzzle people's minds generally.

the important point. When we re-examine the enigmas of the ancients, we find that they are perfectly logical, concerned with what is important. When did they indulge in childish burlesques, aiming at thigh-slapping merriment?

However, the place of the *hsieh* and *yin* in literature is comparable to that of the "Small Talk" [anecdotal writings which were considered as of no great importance] in the midst of the Nine Schools.[25] For the petty officials collected these anecdotes to broaden their scope of observation. If one should allow himself to follow in their steps, would he be more advanced than [Ch'un-yü] K'un and [Tung-fang] So and the firm friends of Chan and Meng, the jesters?

> *The Tsan:*
> The satires and enigmas of the ancient times
> Aimed at getting people out of critical situations and relieving them of
>   boredom.
> "Though silk and hemp exist,
> One does not discard straw and rush."[26]
> If the ideas are appropriate and fitting to the situation,
> They may help give admonition and warning;
> Should they be mere farce and jokes,
> They would have a very damaging effect upon moral living.

XVI. Historical Writings

The beginning of human history lies so far back in time that it is shrouded in primitive darkness. For us who live in modern times, are

---

[25] See the "I-wen chih" in the *Han-shu*. Actually ten schools are listed: Confucians, Taoists, the School of Yin-yang, Legalists, the School of Vertical Alliance and Horizontal Confederacy, Logicians, Mohists, Miscellaneous, Agriculturists, and the School of Small Talk. But "I-wen chih" also states that, of these ten schools, only nine are worthy of attention.

[26] A quotation from a poem preserved in *Tso-chuan*. See *Ch-un-ch'iu ching-chuan yin-te*, 229/Cheng 9/12 Tso.

not written records the only sources of learning about the ancient
world? During the time of Hsüan-yüan [the Yellow Emperor] lived
Ts'ang Chieh, who served as a historian. So it has apparently been a
practice since time immemorial to keep an office in charge of records.
In the "Ch'ü-li" it is said, "Historians carry brushes in attendance on
the king's left and right."[1] *Shih*, or a historian, literally means *shih*, or
to employ, one who waited on the left or right of the king and who
was employed to keep records. In ancient times, the left-hand historian
kept records of what was done, and the right-hand historian, of what
was said. The classic of what was said is in the *Book of History* and
the classic of what was done is in the *Annals of Ch'un-ch'iu*. In the
T'ang and Yü dynasties were developed the *Tien* and the *Mu*,[2] and
during the Shang and Hsia[3] were developed the *kao* and *shih*.[4] When
the Chou received the new mandate of heaven, Duke Chi [of Chou]
laid the foundation of all institutions. He considered the three methods
of determining the first month of the year,[5] and formulated the Chou
calendar; he also employed the system of using the four seasons for
the orderly recording of events.[6] When the lords established their
states, each had his own state history, the purpose of which was to give
distinction to the good and ill fame to the evil, so as to establish certain
norms governing mores.

When the Chou declined during the reign of King P'ing,[7] there was

---

[1] See *Li-chi yin-te*, 1/37. The phrase "in attendance on the king's left and right" was
added by Liu Hsieh.

[2] In the *Book of History*, the first two chapters have the titles "Yao-tien" and "Shun-
tien," and the next two chapters, "Ta-yü mu" and "Kao-yao mu."

[3] The order should be Hsia and Shang. Liu's choice was probably influenced by the
tones of the characters in the first line, so he changed the order for pleasant tonal effect.

[4] In the *Book of History*, Chapters 11, 12, 27, 29, 30, 32, 33, and 34 are *kao*, and
Chapters 7, 10, 21, 49, and 50 are *shih*.

[5] From the time of Emperor Wu of the Han dynasty until 1912 when the solar
calendar was adopted, China had used the Hsia method of determining the first month
of the year. The Shang dynasty arranged its first month to fall on the twelfth month
of the Hsia calendar; the Chou dynasty, on its eleventh month. These three ways of
determining the first month are known as *san-cheng*, or "three first months."

[6] In recording events, *Ch'un-ch'iu* first gives the year of the reigning duke of Lu,
then the seasons—spring, summer, autumn, and winter—, then the month, and then
the day. The last two items are sometimes omitted.

[7] King P'ing (770-720 B.C.) moved Chou's capital to the east (the present Lo-yang
in Honan) under the pressure of the western barbarians.

nothing in the government that was morally worthy of being sung in the Odes;[8] laws and regulations were discarded, and moral principles collapsed. The Master [Confucius], grieving for the disappearance of the kingly way and the fall of orthodox principle, was smitten with sadness, when he resided at home, because of the failure of the phoenix to arrive; and shed tears, while loitering on the street, on hearing of the capture of a unicorn.[9] So he retired to the place of the Great Master of Music for advice to rectify the trends of music and bring them back to the *ya* and the *sung*,[10] and he edited *Ch'un-ch'iu*, on the basis of the history of Lu. In this work, he dealt with successes and failures in history to illustrate his approval and disapproval [of various facets of the contemporary scene], and exposed the factors governing the destinies of states to show what was to be encouraged and what warned against. One word of praise from him was worth more than the carriage and official cap of high government position; and one word of censure cut deeper than hatchet and halberd. However, the purpose of the work is deep and profound, and its language connotative and terse. As [Tso] Ch'iu-ming was a contemporary, he knew the secrets of its subtle words. He therefore traced its roots and followed all its important ramifications to the end, and in so doing created a style of writing known as *chuan*, or commentary. By *chuan*, or to comment, is meant *chuan*, or to transfer, that is, to transfer the ideas of the Classics

[8] One of the literary principles advocated in the preface to the *Book of Poetry* and reinforced by numerous later attempts (Cheng Hsüan's *Shih-p'u hsü*, preface to the chronology of poetry, being the best known) is that the quality of poetry is intimately related to the quality of the government. By "quality" here is meant mainly moral quality. For the function of poetry is assumed to be didactic.

[9] For a reference to the phoenix, as an omen of a wondrous event, see Chapter I above; and for the significance of the unicorn, see *Ch'un-ch'iu ching-chuan yin-te*, 487/Ai 14/1 Kung. Both phoenix and unicorn are symbols indicating the prevailing of a kingly way, or signs that a sage is in command. In the case of the phoenix, Confucius mourned that there was no such sign, meaning that he was not at the helm of the government, hence the figure of residing at home; and in the case of the unicorn, its appearance was at a time when there was no kingly government to correspond to the auspicious prognostication. This appearance is symbolized by Confucius' loitering on the street. Of course, both the phoenix and the unicorn were used with reference to his own political fortune in life.

[10] *Ya* and *sung* constitute the orthodox music as contrasted with the Cheng, or licentious music, which prevailed at that time.

one receives to those who come after one. *Chuan*, or the commentary, is indeed the wings of the sage's writings, and the crown of all written records.

The office of historian was still in evidence during that period peculiarly characterized by [the political sophistry of] the Vertical Alliance and Horizontal Confederacy [of the Warring States period].[11] When the state of Ch'in unified the seven states, it was found that each of the warring states had its own *ts'e*, or records. Since these were simple records without running commentaries, they used the term for bamboo slips, or *ts'e*, to designate them.[12] When the Han destroyed the houses of Yin and Hsiang,[13] the first years witnessed a parade of military achievements. Lu Chia [228-140 B.C.], steeped in the ancient models, wrote *Ch'u-han ch'un-ch'iu* [History of the Struggle between Ch'u and Han].[14]

Then came the grand historian [Ssu-ma] T'an,[15] whose family for generations had served in the capacity of "holders of bamboo slips" [or historians]. [T'an's son] Tzu-ch'ang [or Ssu-ma Ch'ien] continued the tradition, and enumerated the achievements of the rulers. [Here he was faced with a problem.] Should he compare all rulers to Yao and designate the chapters on them *tien*?[16] But not all the rulers were worthy ones; in their midst were some who were unworthy. Should he follow the example of Confucius and give the title *ching*, or classic, to his writings? But his style of writing could not compare with that of the First Sage. So he adopted the title used in the *Lü-lan* [or *Lü-shih*

---

[11] During this period, political speculators fell into two groups, one maneuvering to line up the states, now reduced to seven in number, for Ch'in, known as the Vertical Alliance, and the other maneuvering them against Ch'in with Ch'i as their leader, known as the Horizontal Confederacy.

[12] For the *Chan-kuo ts'e*, see A. Wylie, *Notes on Chinese Literature* (Shanghai, 1922), p. 32, under *Chen kwo ts'ih*.

[13] The House of Yin refers to the Ch'in dynasty and the House of Hsiang, to Hsiang Yü, Liu Pang's chief rival for power at the end of the Ch'in dynasty.

[14] King of Ch'u was Hsiang Yü's title and King of Han, Liu Pang's.

[15] T'an was the father of Ssu-ma Ch'ien, the first great historian.

[16] The first chapter of the *Book of History* deals with the accomplishments of Yao and is called "Yao-tien." The term *tien* thus acquires a specific significance as a style, generally characterized by archaic flavor, which was taken to be a sign of elegance. Later it came to mean what is really elegant without being archaic.

ch'un-ch'iu], and gave the general title of *chi*, or annals, to all these chapters.[17] This is a grand title, as it has the meaning of "a principle."[18] [The whole work includes:] the *chi*, or annals, which treat of all sovereigns and kings, the *lieh-chuan*, or biographies, of lords and titular personages, the eight treatises on the various aspects of the government, and the ten charts of chronologies and titleholders.[19] This arrangement, though differing from the ancient form, serves to relate historical facts in neat order. His merits include his effort to create a factual record without evasion or omission, his comprehensiveness in covering his sources, his purity of style, his extensive observations, and his logical clarity; and his faults include his love for the strange, contrary to the spirit of the Classics, and the absence of order in his arrangement of certain materials. These merits and faults have been discussed in detail by Shu-p'i [or Pan Piao, A.D. 3-54]. Pan Ku followed in his steps in writing the history of the Han dynasty, and a knowledge of Ssu-ma Ch'ien's literary quality will carry us over half the distance in understanding Pan Ku's work. His ten treatises are all-inclusive and rich in sources; his *tsan*, or concluding remarks of praise or censure, and *hsü*, or prologues, are grand and beautiful; the work is a specimen of the combination of scholarship and literary grace which gives the reader a taste that lingers on. He wrote in the tradition of the Classics and looked to the Sage as his example; his narratives are both rich and brilliant; these are his merits. He was accused of passing over his father and plagiarizing his work, and of demanding payment of gold as a compensation for writing the history. But these false accusations were eloquently disposed of by Kung-li [or Chung Ch'ang-t'ung, 180-220].[20] Narratives of historical events by Tso [Ch'iu-ming] are attached to the main text of the Classic [of

---

[17] *Lü-shih ch'un-ch'iu* contains 12 *chi*, 8 *lan* (perusal), and 6 *lun* (essays).

[18] "Principle" is another connotation of *chi*, in the sense that it serves, like the annals, as a general outline in which all events fall into place.

[19] Liu Hsieh seems to have unwittingly omitted the "shih-chia" (or the biographies of members of high families), and placed under the *lieh-chuan*, which deal with prominent men, what should have been placed under the "shih-chia."

[20] Chung's work is lost; only three items are preserved in Ma Kuo-han's *Yü-han shan-fang chi-i*.

Ch'un-ch'iu]. His language is succinct; yet it is rather difficult to get a clear idea of clans and families. It was the biographical section of the history by [Ssu-ma] Ch'ien that first presented a clear picture and easy view of the prominent men. This served as an example for all later historians. When Emperor Hsiao-hui [of the Han, 194-188 B.C.] was gathered to his fathers, his mother, Empress Lü, acted as a regent, and both Pan Ku and Ssu-ma Ch'ien devoted a *chi* to her. This is contrary to the principle found in the Classics, and did not do justice to the actual fact. Why? Because since the time of Pao-hsi,[21] nobody has ever heard of a female ruler.[22] The hard fate the Han met with should not be made a basis for a general way of viewing all later dynasties. It was King Wu who first swore that a hen should not herald the approach of morning;[23] and Duke Huan of Ch'i, in a conference, stated that no woman should be allowed to interfere with the affairs of the state.[24] Queen Hsüan of Ch'in[25] brought moral chaos to her state,[26] and [the violent interference of Empress Lü] threatened to end the life of the Han.[27] Not only should state affairs not be entrusted to the hands of a woman, but even names and titles[28] should be applied to them with discretion. But when Chang Heng [A.D. 78-139] was in charge of the records, he committed the same mistake that Ssu-ma Ch'ien and Pan Ku had committed. His idea of devoting a *chi* to Empress Yüan and Empress P'ing[29] is indeed absurd. Although

[21] Better known as Fu-hsi, one of the three legendary sovereigns.

[22] *Chi*, annals, is a title reserved for rulers. To call the biography of an empress *chi* and use it as a framework in which other events of the time fall into place is, by implication, a moral indorsement of a female sovereign. Since the function of a historian, according to this ancient tradition, was to give implied value judgment by means of certain loaded words or phrases, Liu Hsieh considered Pan Ku's and Ssu-ma Ch'ien's application of the term *chi* to the biography of the empress highly censurable.

[23] See the *Book of History*, "Mu-shih," *Shang-shu t'ung-chien*, 0091-0094.

[24] *Ch'un-ch'iu ching-chuan yin-te*, 100/Hsi 9/4 Ku.

[25] Queen Hsüan of Ch'in had illicit relations with a barbarian king.

[26] *Shih-chi*, "Hsiung-nu lieh-chuan."

[27] Empress Lü, the consort of the first emperor of the Han, removed emperors from the throne, murdered princes of the Liu family, and made members of her own Lü family princes, an act in direct defiance to the will of the deceased first emperor.

[28] In the present case, Liu had in mind the application of the term *chi*.

[29] Empress Yüan was the consort of Emperor Yüan [48-33 B.C.] and Empress P'ing, the consort of Emperor P'ing [A.D. 1-5].

Tzu-hung was not really [born of the royal concubine Chang], he was
after all the heir of Emperor Hsiao-hui; and although Ju-tzu [Ying,
A.D. 6-8] was raised from a lowly status, he was, nevertheless, a successor to Emperor P'ing. Both of these are legitimate subjects of *chi*;
why be concerned with the two empresses?[30]

The *chi* and *chuan*, or annals and biographies, of the *Hou-han-shu*
originated in the Tunk-kuan.[31] The works of Yüan [Shan-sung] and
Chang [Ying] are one-sided, confused, and without order; and those
of Hsüeh [Ying] and Hsieh [Ch'eng] are full of loopholes and mistakes and generally are unreliable; but those of Ssu-ma Piao [A.D.
?-306], which are both comprehensive and authentic, and those of
Hua Ch'iao, which are both accurate and appropriate, may be considered the crown of the group.[32] The three great historical figures
of the Wei dynasty[33] were given *chi* treatment in some writings and
chuan in others. The *Yang-ch'iu*,[34] and *Wei-lüeh*,[35] and the *Chiang-
piao*[36] and *Wu-lu*[37] are characterized alternately by emotional bias
which made them difficult to authenticate, and by perfunctory and
loose treatment, a failure to grasp the essential. The three Records

[30] Referring to Empress Lü, for whom both Ssu-ma Ch'ien and Pan Ku wrote *chi*,
and to Empress P'ing, for whom Chang Heng proposed a *chi*. According to Liu Hsieh,
a *chi* should be devoted to Tzu-hung instead of to Empress Lü, and one to Ju-tzu instead
of to Empress P'ing. But Liu mentioned, in fact, three empresses. His carelessness sets
later scholars to wonder which two empresses are intended in the final sentence.

[31] An academy where scholars did their writing, and where the royal library was
housed.

[32] Yüan wrote *Hou-han-shu*; Chang, *Hou-han-nan-chi*; Hsüeh, *Hou-han-chi*; Hsieh,
Hou-han-shu. With the exception of Hsieh, who belonged to the Wu period, they were
all of the Chin Dynasty.

[33] Ts'ao Ts'ao, Liu Pei, and Sun Ch'üan, rulers of Wei, Shu, and Wu respectively.
The period is known as the Three Kingdoms period, extending roughly from 220-265.
In considering all three as within the framework of the Wei, Liu Hsieh was apparently
committed to the view that the Wei faction of the three kingdoms is to be considered
as the legitimate and orthodox dynasty succeeding the Han.

[34] By Sun Sheng (*c.* 302-373). The full title is *Wei-shih Ch'un-ch'iu* (History of the
Wei Dynasty). "Ch'un" was later changed to "Yang," because the character "ch'un" was
part of the name of Empress Chien-wen of the Chin, hence under taboo.

[35] A brief history of the Wei, by Yü Huan of the Wei.

[36] Historical records of the Yangtze valley, that is, the state of Wu, by Yü P'u of
the Chin.

[37] Records of Wu, by Chang Po of the Chin.

[of the Three Kingdoms] by Ch'en Shou,[38] however, are lucid in their
language, and sound in their selection of material. Hsün and Chang
correctly compared them to the works of Ssu-ma Ch'ien and Pan Ku.[39]

Records about the Chin dynasty are numerous. Lu Chi [261-303]
made a start, but did not cover the whole field. Wang Shou[-chih]
completed his own project, but did not bring it to the conclusion
requested of him.[40] Kan Pao [of the Chin] wrote *Chi*, or *Chin-chi*
which, because of his good judgment in choosing the right criterion
for historical composition, has been well praised;[41] and Sun Sheng's
Yang-ch'iu has been pronounced an able piece of work on account of
its conciseness.

I have observed that the writers of commentaries on the Classic of
Ch'un-ch'iu formulated certain principles and general schemes governing the writing of history. But from *Shih* [*-chi*] and *Han* [*-shu*]
downward, no criteria were established. It was Teng Ts'an [of the
Chin] who in his *Chin-chi* first created a set of general principles. He
was able to shake himself loose from the influence of the Han and
the Wei and reach back to the Yin and the Chou for his principles.
Although he was a rustic scholar from the valley of Hsiang,[42] he took
the forms of *tien* and *mu*[43] as his ideals. When An-kuo [Sun Sheng]
later formulated his principles, he was using the principles Teng
had prescribed.

In writing a historical record, one has to keep in mind [a number

[38] The histories of the three kingdoms, Wei, Shu, and Wu, by Ch'en Shou of the
Chin, 233-297.
[39] Chang refers to Chang Hua, (232-300), who was known to have great admiration
for Ch'en Shou. See Ch'en's biography in the *Chin-shu*. But it is difficult to identify
Hsün. The only person who comes to mind is Hsün Hsü (?-289); however, he spoke
disparagingly of Ch'en (see Ch'en's biography). It is barely possible that Hsün might
have changed his opinion about Ch'en over a period of time.
[40] Wang Shou-chih, 380-435, of Liu-Sung, using his father's notes on the T'ai-yüan
(376-396) and Lung-an (397-404) periods, wrote the *Chin An-ti Yang-ch'iu* (History
during the reign of Emperor An of the Chin Dynasty [397-404]). It was so good that
he was asked to continue it to the end of the dynasty, which lasted until 419. But Wang
brought it up only to the ninth year of I-hsi, 413.
[41] Kan followed *Tso-chuan* as his example.
[42] Teng was from Ch'ang-sha, in modern Hunan, watered by the River Hsiang. See
his biography in the *Chin-shu*.
[43] See note 2 above.

of things]: the record must include sources collected by hundreds of
authors; stand the test of time for thousands of years; show the
evidences of rise and decline of a state, and demonstrate the reasons
for its rise and decline; through such a record the institutions of a
dynasty may be made to last as long as the sun and the moon, and
through it the accomplishments of a government, whether ruled by
moral suasion or by force, may become as great and lasting as heaven
and earth. It was for this reason that at the beginning of the Han
dynasty the office of historian was considered one of extreme importance: all documents and statistical reports were first collected in the
office of the grand historian, the purpose being to acquaint him with
the laws and institutions of the nation, and he was expected to look
into the stone building [the royal library] and the metal [book] chests
and to unroll broken pieces of silk and examine fragments of bamboo
slips[44] in order to gain extensive experience in the art of inquiring
into antiquity.

In forming ideas and selecting words to express them, he was to
establish his rules on the basis of the Classics; and in giving encouragement or warning, approval or disapproval, he was to rest on the
principles formulated by the Sage. For only so would his judgments
be clear and precise, free from both acrimony and unwarranted
generosity.

The *chi* is a form of chronology and the *chuan* a framework for
arranging events; they are not inconsequential writings, but factual
records. However, when chronology stretches out too long, it is difficult to list with any precision events happening either at the same time
or at a different time; and when events are accumulated in mass, it
is easy to be careless about their beginnings and endings. This is why
it is difficult to obtain a synoptic view. Sometime the same achievement
is shared by many characters; if it is recorded in every case, the work
will suffer from redundancy; and if it is mentioned only once, the
work will suffer from being perfunctory. This is why it is not easy to
have a general arrangement of material. These are the kinds of argu-

---

[44] Both silk and bamboo slips were writing materials.

ments on which were based Chang Heng's criticisms of Shih [Ch'ien]
and Pan [Ku], and Fu Hsüan's [217-278] sarcastic remarks about the
records of the Later Han.

In recapitulating the life of the distant past, the farther back the
past is, the more chances there will be that the reports are unreliable.
Kung-yang Kao[45] made the remark, "What is transmitted differs in
different versions";[46] and Hsün K'uang said, "Recording the distant,
they are neglecting the recent."[47] As a matter of fact, when in doubt,
do not record, because it is essential to have reliable historical records.
However, people in general love what is strange, and pay no attention
either to facts or to what ought to be. In transmitting what they hear,
they magnify it in pompous style, and in recording the distant past,
they describe it in detail. They throw out what is commonplace and
pick out what is unusual, boring and digging to find support for
unwarranted views, bragging that "in my book is recorded what
cannot be found in earlier histories." This is the source of all error
and exaggerations, the greatest of poisonous influences in writing about
the past.

When we come to the treatment of contemporaries, many facts are
often distorted. While Confucius' judgments concerning the periods
of Duke Ting and Duke Ai[48] are couched in subtle language [his
example is too seldom followed]; secular opinions are still influenced

---

[45] Who wrote the Kung-yang commentary on the *Ch'un-ch'iu*.

[46] The *Ch'un-ch'iu ching-chuan yin-te*, 4/Yin 1/6 Kung; 25/Huan 2/4 Kung;
487/Ai 14/1 Kung.

[47] This phrase is not found in the *Hsüntzu*. What is found there is the view that,
because of the nature of circumstances, an account of the distant past is necessarily brief,
and that of recent times is in greater detail. See *Hsüntzu*, chüan 3, Chapter 5, p. 52.
See also *Han-shih wei-chuan* (Hsüeh-tsin t'ao-yüan ed.), chüan 3, p. 15a. There may
be a textual corruption, and the text might be emendated to read "brief in recording
the past and detailed in the account of the present." This would be more in line with
Hsüntzu's idea and also with what follows in the text. Liu Hsieh could have misquoted
Hsüntzu to support his own view, although the misquoted statement, when viewed as
a critical remark, is not necessarily contrary to Hsüntzu's view.

[48] Duke Ting, 509-495 B.C.; Duke Ai, 494-468 B.C. They were the last two dukes
of Lu treated in Confucius' *Ch'un-ch'iu*, who were his contemporaries. Confucius
stopped writing in 481, the fourteenth year of Duke Ai, when he heard that a unicorn,
a symbol of sage government, was captured.

by selfish interests. If the subject is from a family of great prestige and honor, he tends to be eloquently adorned, even though he may be a mediocrity. But should the subject be a frustrated scholar, all his virtue will not save him from ridicule. This blowing on the already frostbitten and puffing at the already bedewed,[49] or fabrication of hot and cold with the brush is a common distortion involved in writing about a contemporary, and a thing to be deeply deplored. So we see that historical accounts of the past are characterized by errors of one sort, and those of our own times by distortion of another kind. To be able to give a rational account of a matter and keep rigidly to what is true, one has to have a pure mind.

It is true that Confucius advocated giving honor to the virtuous and protecting one's dear ones by hiding their faults, because a tiny flaw will not disfigure a beautiful jade. But straightforward writing by a good historian consists [partially] in the censure of the villainous and the wicked, just as a farmer roots out weeds when he sees them. This is a principle which will remain valid for all time. With respect to the art of systematically handling a mass of material of all sorts, with respect to the importance of devoting oneself to the reliable and getting rid of the strange, with respect to understanding of proper sequence, and with respect to the careful choice of concepts to be employed in dealing with the facts, one must have a perfect grasp of the general principle. With the perfect understanding of this principle, one will be able to comprehend systematically all the related factors.

Indeed, the responsibility of a historian involves the ordering of a dynasty; he is responsible to all the people within the boundaries of the seas, in his shouldering of the burden of pronouncing moral judgments. What other labor can compare to this burden of the writer's in magnitude? With all the learning of [Ssu-ma] Ch'ien and [Pan] Ku, they have been the subjects of criticism for generation after generation. When one lets his private prejudices lead him astray, that is the graveyard of his writing.

---

[49] To make one who is cold feel colder.

The Tsan:

Historical writing began during the time of the Yellow Emperor,
And its form was perfected by Duke Chou and Confucius.
History relates the development of events from generation to generation,
And it is the final book of judgment on what is good and what is evil.
In it the good is honored and the evil censured,
An act which stirs the soul of all times.
For the beauty of historical writing, we go to [Tso] Ch'iu-ming,
But for the courage of calling a spade a spade, we pay tribute to Nan
    [Shih] and Tung [Hu].[50]

XVII. Speculative Writings

Speculative writings are works by men who have entered into the
realm of *Tao* and have seen the Truth. Of these men, those of the
highest order aim at the establishment of virtue; men of a lower order
seek to immortalize their convictions in words.[1] The masses of people,
living in herds, are plagued by the reflection that they are lost in oblivion

---

[50] Both Nan and Tung exhibited great courage in recording facts. *Ch'un-ch'iu ching-
chuang yin-te*, 305/Hsüang 25/2 Tso: In 548 B.C., Ts'ui Chu murdered Duke Chuang
of Ch'i. The historian put the record in the book: "Ts'ui Chu murdered his ruler." He
was killed by Ts'ui. The brother of the historian picked up the brush and wrote that
Ts'ui had murdered his ruler. He too was killed by Ts'ui. Another brother was also
killed by Ts'ui for attempting to put his regicide on record. When the fourth brother
came to do his duty, Ts'ui let him alone. At that time Nan Shih came with his brush,
fearing that all the Ch'i historians had been killed and that no one was left to put the
regicide on record. While on his way, he heard that the record had been made and
returned home. Reference to Tung Hu is also found in the same source, 181/Hsüan
2/4 Tso: In 607 B.C. Chao Ch'uang murdered Duke Ling of Chin. Chao Tun was
then the prime minister. To show that the minister had failed in his duty of keeping
order in the state and dealing out just punishment to the criminal, Tung Hu, who was
the historian, wrote in the book that Chao Tun murdered his ruler. When Chao Tun
tried to argue with Tung, he received a severe moral lesson.

[1] An abbreviated quotation from the *Tso-chuan*, where Shu-sun Pao, when visiting
Chin, was engaged in a discussion of immortality. See *Ch'un-ch'iu ching chuan yin-te*,
302/Hsiang 24/1 Tso. The original text gives three types of immortality: virtue, achievements, and words.

among their many petty activities; and even gentlemen, in finding a place for themselves in the world, are vexed that their names and virtues are not known. Only those with outstanding talents and unique power of comprehension are able to perpetuate their brilliance in words, so that their names are suspended on high like the sun and moon. *Feng-hou, Li-mu,* and *I-yin* were all by men of this type.[2] These writings contain the words of the ancient sages and were recorded during the Warring States period. Yü Hsiung, a man who understood *Tao,* was an adviser to King Wen [of Chou], and his words and the records of his life were collected to form the *Yützu* [or Master (Philosopher) Yü]. The practice of designating a work as *tzu,* or a philosophical or speculative work, began with this *Yützu.* Then came Po-yang [or Laotzu], an expert on ceremonial rites, to whom Confucius went for instruction; his speculation about *tao* and *te* heads the list of all philosophical works.[3] Now, Yü [Hsiung] was King Wen's friend, while Li [Erh, that is, Laotzu] was Confucius' teacher; and from these sages and worthies, all contemporaries,[4] issued the two distinct streams, of the Classics and the *Tzu,* philosophical or speculative writings.[5]

[2] See *Han-shu,* "I-wen-chih."

[3] *Tao* means the first principle of the world, and *te* the particular principles of *tao* which are embodied in particular things. Roughly, *Tao* corresponds to the Platonic Idea, and *te,* to Plato's ideas of individual things. There was a tradition that Laotzu, when he was about to go into retirement, wrote at a friend's request a book of five thousand words known as *Tao-te-ching* (A classic of *Tao* and *Te*).

In referring to Laotzu as Confucius' teacher, Liu Hsieh was giving a view which has been repeatedly questioned since Ts'ui Tung-pi's *Shu-ssu K'ao-hsin lu* and Wang Chung's *Laotzu k'ao-i* of the Ch'ing times. In modern times, with the possible exception of Hu Shih, most scholars believe that the *Tao-te-ching* emerged in book form during the Warring States period, 481-222 B.C., and could not have come from Laotzu who gave Confucius advice. As to the authenticity of Laotzu as a historical figure, nothing definite has been established. In the *Shih-chi,* Ssu-ma Ch'ien was already uncertain about him. He talked about at least three different persons, and was not sure whether they were one and the same person who wrote *Tao-te-ching.* No further fact has emerged since then which could even remotely hint at a possible solution of the entangled problem.

[4] Yü, who was considered a worthy, was a contemporary of King Wen, considered a sage, and Li, a worthy, was a contemporary of Confucius, a sage.

[5] *Yützu* and *Laotzu* are philosophical writings, while the *Book of Changes,* in whose completion King Wen had a part, and the books of *Poetry, History, Rites, Music,* and the *Ch'un-Ch'iu,* with which Confucius was considered by our author as being intimately connected, are Classics.

During the period of Ch'i-kuo [the Warring States, 480-222 B.C.], when might was the principle of government, able men swarmed like bees. Meng K'o [or Mencius], who embraced Confucianism, won respect; Chuang Chou attained freedom and spontaneity in his elucidation of the *Tao*; Mo Ti upheld the virtues of frugality and simple living; Yin Wen discussed the problem of correspondence between name and fact; Yeh-lao based his theory of government on good utilization of land, and Tsoutzu [or Tsou Yen] based his on astronomical observations; Shen [Pu-hai] and Shang [Yang] instituted the laws through the application of the sword and saw as instruments of punishment; Kuei-ku won success by means of casuistry;[6] Shih Chiao was versed in all the miscellaneous arts; and as for the *Ch'ing-shih,* it was woven out of the street talk of the times. And the works written under the influence of these are numerous. All of them are characterized by flights of rhetoric and moving artfulness, and their authors were overwhelmed with honor and glory.

The devastating fire lighted by the ruthless Ch'in emperor destroyed much ancient literature;[7] it burnt more furiously than that on the ridge of a jade-producing mount;[8] but its enveloping flames left the writings of the various philosophers untouched.

During the reign of Emperor Ch'eng of the Han [32-7 B.C.], thought was given to the problem of salvaging books from oblivion, and Tzu-cheng [or Liu Hsiang] was entrusted with the task of editing and collating the variant texts. As a result, the *Ch'i-lüeh*[9] give forth their profuse fragrance, and the works of the Nine Schools[10] were collected

6 This probably refers to Kuei-ku's disciples, Su Ch'in and Chang I, who became prime ministers because of their ability to persuade people to accept their views.

7 The first emperor of the Ch'in, to tighten his totalitarian rule, burnt in 213 B.C., with few exceptions, all Classics, histories of the states he had destroyed, and works which were not in harmony with the spirit of his rule. One year later he buried alive scholars who disputed his policy.

8 Meaning, the fire destroys at one stroke both the jade and rocks, making no distinction between what is valuable and what is not, a figure taken from the "Yin-cheng" in the *Book of History. Shang-shu t'ung-chien,* 09/0204-7. Liu changed the first word of the phrase without, however, changing the meaning.

9 Seven Epitomes of Literature, which include classics, philosophy, poetry, military tactics, divination and numerology, and the skills of technicians, including medical practitioners. See the "I-wen chih" in the *Han-shu.*

10 See note 25, Chapter XV.

and put together like the scales of a fish. After the selecting and editing, there remained the collected works of over one hundred and eighty authors.

During the Wei and the Chin, many writers arose; they preserved all of the speeches that had gone unrecorded and wrote down all of the miscellaneous sayings. These they arranged according to categories, and what they obtained filled their boxes and graced their carriages.[11] But although a great many sayings were accumulated, their main ideas can easily be summed up. For all works dealing with morals and government developed out of the five Classics. Those which are pure conform to the classical pattern, and those which are impure do not. The "Yüeh-ling" in the *Li-chi*[12] was the model for the *chi* of the *Lü-shih ch'un-ch'iu*;[13] and the chapter "San-nien-wen-sang" [Inquiry into the three year mourning, in the *Li-chi*] is described in the *Hsüntzu*.[14] The *Lü-shih ch'un-ch'iu* and the *Hsüntzu* may be classified as pure. But as for minister [Hsia] Chi's talk about thunder in the eyebrow of a mosquito in answer to a question by T'ang of Shang,[15] and Hui-shih's answer to the king of Liang about a war fought between two states each occupying one antenna of a snail, leaving many dead on the field,[16] and the discussion about removing mountains and stepping over the sea in the *Liehtzu*,[17] and the story of the fall of heaven

[11] People filled their carts or carriages with books in boxes when they traveled.

[12] Listing the various activities to be performed during the twelve months, corresponding to the twelve *chi* in the *Lü-shih ch'un-ch'iu*.

[13] See note 17, Chapter XVI.

[14] See the latter part of the "Li-lun" (Discourse on rites) in the *Hsüntzu*, chüan 13, Chapter 19.

[15] Liu Hsieh refers here to the *Liehtzu*, in whose chapter "T'ang wen," or "T'ang's questions," a number of absurd things are discussed, including the one quoted here. Although Liu stigmatized this and the others he mentions as impure, many of them actually should be viewed as metaphorical or allegorical. In the present case, Hsia Chi was merely trying to show the relativity of all things, and that what appeared to man to be minute beings, such as mosquitoes, were immense to other, more minute beings, which could live in a mosquito's eyebrow and hear the rolling sound of thunder.

[16] Found in the "Tse-yang p'ien" in the *Chuangtzu*. See *Chuangtzu yin-te*, 70/25/27: A Ch'u clan established its state on the left antenna of a snail, and a Man clan on the right. They went to war, leaving tens of thousands of dead on the field. The victors followed the enemy in hot pursuit for five days and then returned.

[17] Found in the "T'ang Wen" in the *Liehtzu*.

and collapse of the earth in the *Huai-nan-tzu*[18]—these are all examples of the impure.

For this reason the world has always thought ill of speculative works because they are adulterated with empty and absurd discussions. For example, the *Classic of Kuei-tsang*[19] displays a great array of examples of the unbelievable and strange: there is mention of I's shooting ten suns to death, and the fleeing of Ch'ang-o to the moon.[20] If the *Book of Changes* of the Yin [or Shang dynasty] is of this nature,[21] what can one expect of the rest of the speculative writings? In the *Book of Lord Shang* and the *Han-fei-tzu* respectively are discussed "Six Lice"[22] and "Five Worms,"[23] in which filial piety is neglected and virtue abandoned. It was no accident that Lord Shang was torn to pieces and Han Fei was poisoned.[24] The arguments about the white horse and the orphaned calf by Kung-sun [Lung-tzu] are exercises in casuistry, but they lack logical validity;[25] and it was not without reason that Wei Mou compared them to the notes of the owl.[26] When Prince Tung-p'ing asked to see the speculative works and the *Shih-chi*, the Han court did not grant him the request[27] because the *Shih-chi* contains a great deal of military strategy and the speculative works abound in sophistry. But men of wide learning should try to get the gist of these writings,

---

[18] In the "T'ien-wen hsün" in the *Huai-nan-tzu*. Also in *Ch'u-tz'u*, "T'ien-wen."

[19] Supposedly a divination book of the Shang dynasty, corresponding to the *Book of Changes* of the Chou. See note 21 below.

[20] Ch'ang-o, a girl, swallowed an immortality pill; she fled to the moon and became the goddess of the moon.

[21] There are three books of *Changes*, all dealing with divination. That of the Hsia is known as *Lien-shan*, that of Shang as *Kuei-tsang*, and that of the Chou as *Chou-I*.

[22] "Six Lice" are discussed in two chapters in the *Book of Lord Shang*, Chapters 4 and 20. They are yearly crops, food, good things, pleasures, ambition, and career. Yearly crops and food are the worries of farmers; good things and pleasures, the evil influences of merchants; and ambition and career, the concerns of officials.

[23] "Five Worms" is the title of Chapter 49 in *Han-fei-tzu*, discussing five types of evil forces which may cause the downfall of a state and, therefore, should be eliminated.

[24] The death of Lord Shang is recorded in *Chan-kuo ts'e* (Kuo-hsüeh chi-pen ts'ung-shu ed., T'aipei), chüan 3, p. 15. Han Fei's death is recorded in his biography in the *Shih-chi*, "Erh-shih-wu-shih" (T'aipei, 1956), chüan 63, p. 5a.

[25] See *Kung-sun lung-tzu*, Chapter 2 on "White Horse" (Chu-tzu chi-ch'eng edition), pp. 4-7; and *Chuangtzu yin-te*, 93/33/77-78.

[26] *Ibid.*, 45/17/68-77. But here the comparison is made between Kung-sun Lung-tzu and a frog in a well, whose outlook is necessarily limited—not an owl.

[27] This took place in the first year of King Hsüan of the Han dynasty (73 B.C.).

giving a casual glance to the flowers but enjoying the fruits, weeding out the false and accepting the true. A panorama of all the different views contained in these writings would be a great scholarly spectacle.

After examination, we find that the works of Mencius and Hsüntzu are characterized by their sound moral ideas and graceful style; those of Kuan [Chung] and Yen [Ying] by the clarity of their factual accounts and the purity of their language; that of Lieh-yü-k'ou [or Lieh tzu] by its vigorous spirit and wonderful rhetoric; that of Tsoutzu by its wild imagination and forceful expressions; those of Mo-ti and [his disciple] Sui-ch'ao by the clarity of their ideas and the simplicity of their language; those of Shih Chiao and Wei Liao by their full understanding of the arts and the bluntness of their words. The *Ho-kuan-tzu*, continuous and unbroken, contains deep utterances, and the *Kuei-ku-tzu*, vast and boundless, returns to profound ideas. To articulate his feelings with sparkling clarity is a special gift of Wentzu; Yin-wen knows the secret of forging phrases which are both terse and refined. Shen Tao was clever in analyzing intricate syllogisms, and Han Fei was known for his wealth of parables and fables. Lü-shih was prescient in ideas and perfect in style, and Huai-nan, whose selection of his materials was unusually broad and extensive, couched them in beautiful language. These writers are the flowers of the whole profession of philosophy, and the language they employed is, in general, the very essence of literary writing.

As to Lu Chia's *Hsin-yü*, Chia I's *Hsin-shu*, Yang Hsiung's *Fa-yen*, Liu Hsiang's *Shuo-yüan*, Wang Fu's *Ch'ien-fu*, Ts'ui Shih's *Cheng-lun*, Chung Ch'ang[-t'ung's] *Chang-yen*, and Tu I's *Yu-ch'iu*, some of these are discourses on the Classics, while others deal with the art of government. But although they are all known as *lun*, or discourse, they should be classified as philosophical works. Why? Because a philosophical treatise is concerned with a comprehensive elucidation of all things, while a discourse is devoted to the study of a specific subject. Therefore, since the works quoted here are complex in subject matter, they should be classified as philosophical treatises. Prior to the Six States [or Warring States] period, writers were not very far removed in time from the Sage, so that they could discourse in high style over the heads of their contemporaries, and each could open up a new vista for himself. The years after the two Han periods witnessed a gradual decline in vigor of this form of writing. The writers, while perfectly clear about the "broad highway" [of the Confucian school] before them,[28] had generally become dependent and eclectic. This signalized the gradual change taking place between the time close to the Sage and that farther away.

Alas! Only when a man is out of tune with his times is it possible for his ideas and orthodox principles to find a chance for expression.[29] He places himself in his mind among the ancients and transmits his thought to people who come thousands of years after him. Musical instruments of metal and stone may have perished; but must their music be silenced too?

The Tsan:

Men of character have a certain way of conducting themselves in the
　　world:
Endowed as they are with precious gifts and outstanding excellence,
And with power to bring all things to expression,
And with intellect enough to comprehend the universe.
They establish virtue; they allow nothing to remain hidden;[30]
They instruct, being in possession of *Tao*.[31]
They follow each his own inclination in his particular development,
Because their several fields are clearly delineated.

---

[28] By the time of Emperor Wu of the Early Han, the Confucian school had achieved a position of eminence in the thought-life of the Chinese people.

[29] Philosophers in ancient China were often frustrated scholars who, failing to win the ears of the rulers and make themselves serviceable to some court, and consequently failing to find a way to put their ideas and principles into practice, retreated to a quiet spot either to teach or to write, thus giving these ideas a better chance to survive. Confucius and Mencius are two of the most conspicuous examples.

[30] Liu Hsieh was trying to reconcile the apparent difference of two ways of life: one, that of establishing virtue, and the other, that of establishing words. Liu attempted here to make a man of virtue also a man of letters.

[31] Expressing thought similar to the previous line.

XVIII. *Treatise and Discussion (The Lun and the Shuo)*

The principles propounded by the Sage are known as *ching*, or Classics, and the works which explain the Classics and set forth their underlying ideas are known as *lun*, or treatise or discourse. *Lun*, or to discourse, literally means *lun*, or to set in order. If in the process of setting these ideas in order one has not gone amiss, he will have succeeded in keeping the purpose of the Sage from failing.

Long ago, the subtle words of Chung-ni [or Confucius] were recorded by his disciples from recollection. With the Classics in mind, they termed their recordings *Lun-yü*, or the *Analects*. This was the first instance of the application of the term *lun* to all similar treatises. Prior to the *Lun-yü* the character *lun* did not appear as a title to any Classics.[1] May not the two *lun* which are found in the *Liu-t'ao* have been so entitled at a later date?[2]

A study of the genre *lun* reveals that it has developed into many types: when it treats of government, its style is in harmony with that of the *i*, or discourse, and *shuo*, or discussion; when it comments on the Classics, it has the same form as the *chuan*, or commentary, and *chu*, or note; as a historical judgment, it is used together with the *tsan*, or generally complimentary comment, and the *p'ing*, or critique; as an attempt to elucidate a certain text, it is treated like the *hsü*, or prologue, and *yin*, or introduction. Thus, *i* means to talk properly; *shuo*, to speak; *chuan*, to transmit the master's instruction; *chu*, to give explanatory notes; *tsan*, to express one's judgment; *p'ing*, to evaluate the validity of arguments; *hsü*, to give a preliminary arrangement of

---

[1] The text originally runs: "Prior to the *Lun-yü* the character *lun* did not appear in any Classics." But in the light of the context, Liu Hsieh must have meant that no works about the Classics had been termed *lun*, as Fan Wen-lan contends. Moreover, the character *lun* is found in the *Book of History* and the *Chou-li*.

[2] The *Liu-t'ao* is a treatise on strategy attributed to Lü Shang, assistant to King Wu of Chou. The modern edition does not contain the term *lun* as part of two titles as indicated by Liu here. From Chang-huai T'ai-tzu's commentary to the biography of Ho Chin, in the *Hou-han shu*, we know that the term still occurred at that time as part of the first and second chapters. We do not know when the text became corrupt.

things; and *yin*, a preface, or foreword. They are eight distinct forms, but all have the same ultimate import as the *lun*. *Lun* means to take into consideration a variety of statements for the purpose of examining minutely a specific idea. Therefore, Chuang Chou [or Chuangtzu] entitled his chapter on the equality of all things *lun*, and in the *Ch'un-ch'iu* of [Lü] Pu-wei, there is an orderly arrangement of six *lun*.[3] The discussions on the Classics, once held at Shih-ch'ü palace [a royal library, in 51 B.C.] and once in Pai-hu hall [in A.D. 79] were participated in by a group of scholars, the results of whose discussions were entitled *lun*, a most proper designation. Pan Piao's "Wang-ming [lun]" and Yen Yu's "San-chiang [-chün lun]" give a vivid expression of their thought, and may be included in the genre of historical writing.

During the period when the Wei first came into power, logic and law were the studies of the day. Fu Ku [209-255] and Wang Ts'an were experts in the logical analysis of name and reason. By the time of Cheng-shih [240-248], literature became the first concern. It was Ho Yen [?-249] and his group, however, who were responsible for beginning the writing of the metaphysical treatises. At this time, Tan [or Laotzu] and Chou [or Changtzu] came into focus and competed with Ni-fu [or Confucius] for the highway. The "Ts'ai-hsing" of Lan-shih [or Fu Ku],[4] the "Ch'ü-fa" of Chung-hsüan [or Wang Ts'an],[5] the analysis of sound by Shu-yeh [or Hsi K'ang],[6] the "Pen-hsüan" of T'ai-ch'u [or Hsia-hou Hsüan],[7] the two "Elucidations" of Fu-ssu [or Wang Pi],[8] and the two treatises of P'ing-shu [or Ho Yen][9] are all the results of profound and unique insights, original with each author, and all

---

[3] See note 12, Chapter XVI.

[4] A treatise on talent. See his biography in "Wei-chih."

[5] On the elimination of self-conceit. The treatise has not been preserved.

[6] A treatise on the theme that human voice has no intrinsic quality expressing sadness or happiness. See his collected works.

[7] On the originally mysterious. The character "hsüan," meaning mysterious, seems to be a clerical error. According to all other available sources, it should be "wu," meaning nothingness. The treatise deals with the Taoist concept of nothingness or void. See his biography in the "Wei-chih," in the *San-kuo chih*, and also Chang's commentary in the "Chung-ni p'ien" in the *Liehtzu*.

[8] Only one is recorded, "The Elucidation of the *Book of Changes*," although he wrote commentaries on both the *Book of Changes* and *Laotzu*.

[9] On two important Taoist concepts: nonaction and the unnamable.

are characterized by penetrating and sparkling arguments creating logic that is close-knit and flawless. These authors were indeed men of outstanding talents.

Then we have Li K'ang's "Yun-ming [lun],"[10] which deals with a theme similar to that dealt with in the *Lun-heng*[11] but surpasses the latter in quality, and Lu Chi's "Pien-wang,"[12] which was modeled after the pattern of the "Kuo-ch'in [lun],"[13] but fell short of it. However, both pieces may be considered beautiful.

In the Sung dynasty [420-479] Kuo Hsiang, whose mystical insight penetrated the realm of the mysterious,[14] and I-fu [or Wang Yen] and P'ei Wei, who had a controversy over the problem of being and nonbeing[15] dominated their day, leaving their names behind them. However, those who saw only the principle of being were tied to physical manifestations; while those emphasizing nonbeing confined themselves to the silent and the void. Each may have had a penetrating vision of one aspect of the problem, but neither group arrived at the final truth. May not the condition in which one's thought is able to penetrate the source of the mystery be the ultimate state of *prajñā*?[16] The common discussions during the period of the Eastern Chin were all centered around metaphysical subjects. Although not a day lacked its new arguments, the principles were taken from previous writers.

As to Chang Heng's "Chi-shih," which reads like a piece of comic

[10] On fate, of which the main themes are: peace or confusion are the result of natural evolution; one's life, whether frustrated or successful, the result of fate; and honor or humble station, the result of accidents in time.

[11] By Wang Ch'ung of the Later Han, *c.* A.D. 27-100.

[12] Expressing the idea that Wu, one of the three kingdoms where Lu's family was a very prominent one, should not have fallen to the Chin.

[13] The faults of the Ch'in, by Chia I of the Early Han.

[14] Kuo, A.D. ?-312, wrote a commentary on the *Chuangtzu*.

[15] Wang, 255-311, a Taoist scholar, advocated that nonbeing was the first principle of things; while P'ei, 267-300, a Confucian, wrote an essay adhering to the principle of being. However, during this period, a controversy such as this usually took on a Buddhist tinge.

[16] *Prajñā* means wisdom or understanding, which is the principal means, by its enlightenment, of attaining to nirvāṇa. Liu Hsieh was a Buddhist scholar, and took the Buddhist vow shortly before he died. However, in the *Wen-hsin*, this is the only occasion on which we find him using a Buddhist term explicitly.

writing, K'ung Yung's "Hsiao-lien," which indulges in satires,[17] and
Ts'ao Chih's "Pien-tao," which looks like a copybook,[18] these are not
written in the orthodox terms, and it seems better that no *lun* of this
type be written at all.

As a genre, the *lun* performs the function of establishing what is
true and what is not. It goes over all available tangible evidence and
pursues truth to the realm of the intangible. It bores hard to get understanding and drops its hook deep to obtain profundity. It is the "net
and hoof" of all thought, and it is also the measure of all things.[19]
Hence its ideological content should be coherent and its language free
from verbosity; it should bring the mind and the reason together in
perfect accord and leave no sign of patchwork in the organization;
the expressions it employs should be so intimately coordinated with
the thought that the enemy is baffled as to where to attack. In these
qualities consists the essence of the *lun*. In a *lun*, it is as if one were
splitting wood; the main thing is to split it according to its grain.
When the axe is sharp it often cuts across the grain; just so, when
one's language is clever, he often violates the reason in order to
rationalize and reach an understanding. Sometimes a *lun* may appear
to be a clever piece on the score of its language, but in view of the
evidence it adduces it will be seen to be absurd. Only a man of virtue is
able to comprehend the desire of the people of the world. Why should
one resort to sophistry in writing a *lun*?

As to commentaries, in these the *lun* perforce disintegrates as a
genre, although throughout the wide variety of such miscellaneous
writings the ultimate purport remains the same. However, the commentary by Ch'in Yen-chün [or Ch'in Kung] on the "Yao-tien" runs
to over one hundred thousand words and Chu P'u's on the *Book of
History* to three hundred thousand. Men of learning, impatient with
such wordy details, have kept themselves clear of laboring with philo-

17 Neither piece is preserved.
18 Quoting and refuting fantastic stories from the religious Taoists, who believed in
the immortality of man and the effect of an elixir of life.
19 The figures of the net and the hoof are taken from the *Chuangtzu*, where they are
used as external symbols for the capturing of the inner mystery of things.

logical and textual problems. Nevertheless, the philological elucidation of the *Book of Poetry* by Master Mao,[20] the commentary on the *Book of History* by [K'ung] An-kuo [of the Early Han], the commentary by Cheng [Hsüan] on the *Book of Rites*, and Wang Pi's commentary on the *Book of Changes* are precise and illuminating. These may be considered paragons of the *lun* as commentary.

The character *shuo*, or to speak or to discuss, has the sense or meaning of *yüeh*, or to please.[21] And as *tui*, or to please, is a mouth and tongue [according to the "Shuo-kua" in the *Book of Changes*], then the way to please is by means of one's words. But when one's attempt to please goes beyond his actual state of feeling, he is guilty of hypocrisy. For this reason Shun abhorred flattery. Some of the fine examples of *shuo* are I Yin's talk on taste, which was responsible for the prosperous rule of the Yin [or Shang],[22] T'ai-kung's discussion on fishing, which caused the Chou to rise,[23] the diplomatic speech of Chu Wu [or Chu Chih-wu], which relieved Cheng of impending invasion,[24] and the persuasive address of Tuan-mu [Tz'u, or Tzu-kung], which saved Lu.[25]

During the Warring States period [481-222 B.C.] sophists rose like clouds. They indulged in the so-called "vertical and horizontal intrigues,"[26] and competed in what have been termed the "long and

[20] There were two scholars by the name of Mao who specialized in the *Book of Poetry*: the Great Mao, whose personal name was Heng, and the Lesser Mao, whose name was Ch'ang. The former flourished during the Six States period and was responsible for the commentary on the *Book of Poetry*, which was later handed down to the latter, who lived in the Early Han.

[21] The character *shuo* is composed of two elements: *yen* (to speak) on the left, and *tui* (to please) on the right. Hence *shuo* has two senses: to speak or to please. Later, the *yen* radical is replaced by a heart radical, when it is taken to mean "to please" and is pronounced *yüeh*. But the original form persists, though its pronunciation is identical with *yüeh*, when it means "to please."

[22] I Yin, a minister of T'ang of the Shang, used taste, the aim of culinary art, as a parable to illustrate the quality of good government. See note 90, Introduction.

[23] See *Shih-chi*, "Ch'i T'ai-kung Shih-chia."

[24] See *Ch'un-ch'iu ching-chuan yin-te*, 138/Hsi 30/6 Tso.

[25] A disciple of Confucius. See *Shih-chi*, biographies of the disciples of Confucius.

[26] Under the leadership of Chang I, an intrigue was put into operation to persuade the six states to line up in support of the state of Ch'in, which is known as *heng*, or horizontal alliance; and under that of Su Ch'in, the states were persuaded to form

short tactics."[27] The "Chuan-wan" charges forward with its clever phrases, and the "Fei-ch'ien" is the embodiment of tactical dexterity.[28] The eloquence of one man was more weighty than the precious nine tripods; a tongue three inches long was stronger than a million troops.[29] Brilliant and scintillating, [Su Ch'in] carried the six seals;[30] rich and opulent, [Chang I] was enfeoffed with five cities.[31]

After the Han had disposed of Ch'in and Ch'u,[32] the sophists slowed their pace. Li [I-chi, ?-203 B.C.] was boiled alive in Ch'i;[33] and K'uai T'ung barely escaped the Han cauldron.[34] Although we have Lu Chia,

---

a league in opposition to the state of Ch'in, which is known as *tsung*, or vertical federation.

[27] The "long and short tactics" refers to the tactics adopted by the warring states in upsetting one another's plans, tactics which were somewhat Machiavellian in character. In his preface to the *Chan-kuo ts'e* (The tactics of the warring states), Liu Hsiang of the Han said that "kuo-ts'e" (state tactics) were also known as "tuan-ch'ang" (the short and the long). *Chan-kuo ts'e*, "Preface," p. 1. Liu Hsieh in Chapter XVI interpreted *ts'e* as "bamboo slips," and *Chan-kuo ts'e* as "records of the warring states." See p. 86. But Liu Hsiang apparently took the term *ts'e* in a different sense, meaning tactics. Here Liu Hsieh seems to have the same idea in mind, although the term *ts'e* does not actually appear.

[28] "Chuan-wan" and "Fei-ch'ien" are two chapters in *Kuei-ku-tzu*, on techniques of roughly Machiavellian character. Kuei-ku-tzu was the teacher of Su Ch'in and Chang I, leaders of vertical federation and horizontal alliance, respectively.

[29] See *Shih-chi*, biography of Prince P'ing-yüan. Mao Sui, a guest in the household of Prince P'ing-yüan of the state of Chao, by sheer talking, persuaded the king of Ch'u to come to Chao's rescue, when the latter was attacked by the state of Ch'in. The prince spoke of his eloquence as more weighty than the nine tripods, and of his three-inch tongue as stronger than a million troops.

[30] Su was entrusted with the premiership by the rulers of the six states in cementing the vertical federation against Ch'in. The seal was emblematic of the premiership.

[31] Chang's policy to form a horizontal alliance to support Ch'in was so successful that Ch'in made him this enfeoffment in gratitude.

[32] The Ch'in was destroyed in 207 B.C. by the combined forces of Han and Ch'u. In the ensuing struggle between Han and Ch'u, which lasted until 202 B.C., Han emerged as the victor and established a new dynasty.

[33] With powerful eloquence, Li succeeded in persuading the ruler of Ch'i to surrender more than seventy cities to Han without shooting an arrow. But another general of Han, Han Hsin, ?-200 B.C., goaded by K'uai T'ung, attacked Ch'i, partly for the purpose of occupying the territory of Ch'i, and partly for the destruction of Li I-chi. Having been softened by Li's talk, Ch'i was an easy prey. However, Li was boiled alive by Ch'i, as Han Hsin's attack made him a conspirator. This took place in 204 B.C.

[34] Later K'uai T'ung persuaded Han Hsin to revolt against the Han. When Han Hsin was about to be executed, he deplored the fact that he had not listened to K'uai T'ung. On hearing this, Kao-tsu, the first emperor of the Han, ordered K'uai to be boiled alive. But K'uai was spared when he made the point that at the time when he persuaded Han Hsin to revolt, the situation of the empire was still unsettled. Anybody was entitled to his ambition. And it was entirely due to Han Hsin's stupidity and unwillingness to

famed for his literary ability, Chang Shih [-chih], so effective in his discourse, Tu Ch'in, lucid in his literary expression, and Lou Hu with his eloquence, some proudly making their points on the steps of the royal court and some "attacking the defective"[35] at the table of the nobles, they all tended to bend with the wind, and none dared go upstream against the flow. The important thing in employing the *shuo*, or discussion, is to grasp the opportune moment, sometimes discussing with leisurely ease and sometimes with tension; further, the *shuo* need not always be effected in speech, for it can also be executed in writing. Fan Sui's [letter to King Chao of Ch'in], discussing affairs of state, and Li Ssu's [memorial to the first emperor of the Ch'in], arguing against the latter's order to get rid of all guest ministers, drive home the important points, and every word in them hits the right mark. Although [in tendering these memorials both men] were touching the reversed scales [of the dragon],[36] they succeeded in putting over their ideas. These may be considered the best examples of *shuo* as embodied in memorials. Tsou Yang's attempts to warn Prince Wu and Prince Liang were expressed in clever metaphors and irrefutable arguments; therefore, although in danger, he came out unscathed. But Ching-t'ung's [or Feng Yen's] addresses to influence the minds of Pao [Yung] and Teng [Yü] are slow in narrative and progression and verbose in language, so that in all his attempts he failed to win confidence.[37]

The crucial requirement in a *shuo* is to present at an opportune moment ideas which are crystal-clear and true. Positively, one's ability in the art of *shuo* should help him execute his duty with success; and negatively, it may enable him to avoid disgrace. Except when dealing with a deceitful enemy, its principles have always been loyalty and

---

listen to advice that Han Hsin had met his sorrowful fate and Kao-tsu had become what he was. See Han Hsin's biography in the *Shih-chi*.

[35] "Attacking the Defective" is a chapter in the *Kuei-ku-tzu*, pointing out the importance of detecting and attacking any defects that we might have and planning to mend them.

[36] It is certain death to touch the reversed scales of a dragon. This figuratively expresses being caught in a fit of anger of the ruler, aroused by adverse criticism.

[37] See his biography in the *Hou-han-shu*.

truthfulness. In it one opens his heart before the ruler and conveys his ideas in winged words. These are the fundamentals of a *shuo*. Master Lu [Chi] spoke of *shuo* as "brilliant and yet deceitful";[38] one might well ask, Why?

The Tsan:
Logical reason takes form in words,
And their account of this reason forms a *lun*.
Words probing the depths of man and nature
Reach far, though originating in the "square inch" [of the human heart].[39]
Whether the prospect is dark or bright, [a *lun* writer] follows one single principle,
And without evasion faces the ghosts and spirits.
Exercising control through speech,
Exhaling and inhaling, he restrains and encourages.

XIX. Edict and Script (The Chao and the Ts'e)

Translator's note: From the text of this chapter, it seems obvious that no one of the terms used to stand for different types of writing has a specific sense in which it is used consistently in different contexts; and it is also obvious that our author made no attempt to clarify this confusion. As a matter of fact, this tendency to treat a term, which has many senses, as if it had only one sense, and to raise it to the status of a genre, while using it as inconsistently as it originally was used in different settings, is one of the major faults of Liu Hsieh, against which we have a legitimate complaint. Mark how the terms *chao* and *ts'e* are treated in this chapter. At first they are treated as if they were technical terms, serving to designate specific types of writing. But as we go along, we find to our grief that

38 A line from Lu Chi's *Wen-fu*. See note 13, "Preface."
39 The ancient Chinese, like Aristotle, believed the human heart to be the seat of reasoning.

in addition to using *chao* specifically as a royal pronouncement, the author also uses it as a general term for all royal edicts; and the term *ts'e*, in addition to being used as a script of enfeoffment, is also used to mean writings in general. The same is true with the terms *chih, ch'ih, kao, ming*, etc. This seems to have originated from a deliberate policy of ignoring the semantic distinction between different senses of a term, and of effecting by means of ambiguity a loose and easy flow in literary associations of ideas. This explains in part the unscientific manner in which the genres are classified. They are neither mutually exclusive nor independently comprehensive. We find, for example, the genre of poetry discussed in Chapters V, VI, VII, and VIII. The genre *lun* is discussed specifically in Chapter XVIII; but it is also touched upon in Chapters III, IV, V, XVII, and many others. In Chapter XVII the *lun* is defined as a discourse devoted to the study of a specific subject; and works by Lu Chia, Chia I, Yang Hsiung, Liu Hsiang, Wang Fu, Ts'ui Shih, Chung Ch'ang-t'ung, and Tu I are classified as philosophical writings, in spite of their having been named as *lun*, because some of them discourse on the Classics. But in Chapter XVIII, the *lun* includes not only philosophical works by the Taoists of the Wei and Chin, but also Mao's commentary on the *Book of Poetry*, K'ung An-kuo's commentary on the *Book of History*, Cheng Hsüan's commentary on the *Book of Rites*, and Wang Pi's commentary on the *Book of Changes*—a direct contradiction by Liu Hsieh of his own statement in the previous chapter. Here then, we find the major task of a student of Chinese literary criticism: to try to penetrate beyond the veil of literary terminology and feel his way through the labyrinth of the minds of Chinese authors, which are very inadequately expressed in words. Thus we may also find out why it is not possible for the ancients to do otherwise, and we may see the necessity of intuitive insight so often insisted upon by them and so clearly demonstrated by Chuangtzu in numerous figures, parables, and anecdotes. Perhaps one has to be a mystic before one can really understand the minds of the ancient Chinese authors.

As an emperor rules over his empire, his words have a mysterious effect. Though he himself remains deep and silent in front of an embroidered screen,[1] his voice is heard to the limits of the four borders. To accomplish this, he depends on the *chao*, or edict, and the *ts'e*, or script. Long ago, during the time of the Yellow Emperor, of T'ang

[1] The ruler sits before the embroidered screen, which becomes a symbol of the royal personage.

[or Yao], and of Yü [or Shun], all royal pronouncements were called *ming*, which means "the authority which defines nature."[2] During the period of the Three Dynasties [Hsia, Shang, and Chou], the *ming* had the further function of a proclamation or an oath. An oath was used in connection with the conduct of military affairs, and a proclamation in connection with the prosecution of governmental activities. The *ming*, or mandate, is revealed by heaven; hence, it is employed for appointing officers and conferring blessings. Under the hexagram of *hou* in the *Book of Changes*, it is said, "The ruler despatches his *ming* to be proclaimed to the four directions."[3] The mandate thus proclaimed would stir the people as the wind under heaven stirs the grass.[4] Later, during the Seven States period, the term *ling* was used. It means "to commission." When the Ch'in unified the empire, the term *ming* was dropped and in its place *chih*, or to institute, was used. In the early years of the Han when rules and regulations were first formulated, the *ming* were classified under four categories: the *ts'e-shu*, or script of enfeoffment; the *chih-shu*, or ordinance; the *chao-shu*, or pronouncement; and the *chieh-ch'ih*, or warning. The "royal warning" was issued to the local officials; the "royal pronouncement" was issued to the hundred central officials; the "ordinance" was issued to declare an amnesty, and the "royal script" was issued to invest princes and lords with fiefs. The term *ts'e*, or script, has the literal meaning "a bamboo slip"; *chih*, or ordinance, "to institute"; *chao*, or pronouncement, "to proclaim"; and *ch'ih*, or warning, "to correct." The *Book of Poetry* says, "Reverence this bamboo slip";[5] the *Book of Changes* says, "Men of virtue on the basis of this [image of limitation] *institute* measures and regulations";[6] the *Chou-li* speaks of the proclamation of

---

[2] According to Fan Wen-lan, *hsing* (nature) should be emendated to read *hsing* (surname), because in ancient China only a noble had a surname; each was granted by the ruler. Hence, the term "pai-hsing" (one hundred names) meant "one hundred officers." However, there does not seem to be any necessity for this reading. In *Li-chi* (see *Li-chi yin-te*, 31/1) it is stated, "Heavenly mandate, or *ming*, is called nature, or *hsing*." It makes perfect sense to think of royal pronouncements as defining the nature of each function or appointment.

[3] *Chou-i yin-te*, 27/44/hsiang.   [4] *Lun-yü yin-te*, 24/12/19.

[5] *Mao-shih yin-te*, 36/168/4.   [6] *Chou-i yin-te*, 36/60/hsiang.

an enlightened ruler;[7] and the *Book of History* speaks of "keeping oneself correct in the carrying out of the mandate of heaven";[8] all these terms are grounded in the Classics. The restriction of the use of *chao*, or proclamation, to "reach afar" and that of *ming*, or oral dictate, to "control the *near*" are practices instituted in the Ch'in. The *Li-chi* says [that "the words of a ruler are like] silk [fibers, when unspoken] and like thread [when spoken],[9] and these words are instruments for the successful management of the ruler's relations with the various chieftains. Yü [Shun] emphasized the importance of the office whose responsibility it was to receive the ruler's words,[10] and the Chou considered that office the throat and tongue of the kings.[11] The two Han, therefore, made responsibility for the *chao-kao*, or pronouncement and proclamation, part of the office of the grand historian. The words spoken by the king were always set down in the historical records, for when spoken, the words of the king become rope[12] and, like sweat, once out they can never be recalled.[13] Therefore, Emperor Wu [of Han, 140-87 B.C.], because [his uncle] Prince Huai-nan was a man of literary distinction, had [Ssu-ma] Hsiang-ju look over the letters he drafted to this prince.[14] And as in Lung-yu [in present Kansu], there were many literary scholars, Emperor Kuang-wu [of the Later Han, A.D. 25-57] paid particular attention to the literary quality of his messages to them. This was done not merely to win praise of the day, but also to show a reverent care for the opinion of later times.

The style of the *chao* prior to Emperors Wen [179-157 B.C.] and Ching [156-141 B.C.] was frivolous and impure, but during the time of Emperor Wu, who inclined towards Confucianism, it was grand

---

[7] *Chou-li yin-te*, 9/28b. "Ming-chün" (an enlightened ruler) should be read "ming shen" (bright spirits).

[8] *Shang-shu t'ung-chien*, 5/0534-7.

[9] The *Li-chi*: "The words of the ruler are like silk fibers, but when they are spoken they are like threads; the words of a ruler are like threads, but when they are spoken they are like ropes." The great effect of words, especially when spoken by the ruler, is given a figurative treatment here. See *Li-chi yin-te*, 33/7.

[10] *Shang-shu t'ung-chien*, 2/730-4.   [11] *Mao-shih yin-te*, 71/260/3.

[12] See note 9 above.

[13] See the biography of Liu Hsiang in the *Han-shu*.

[14] See Prince Huai-nan's biography in the *Han-shu*.

and profound. His scripts of enfeoffment to the three princes [Ch'i, Yen, and Kuang-ling][15] have the same literary quality as the *hsün* and *tien*;[16] the lesson and warning they conveyed were both profound and graceful, good examples for later generations to imitate. In his letter to Yen Tsu, Emperor Wu mentioned that Yen had tired of his duty in the Ch'eng-ming lu;[17] this, in fact, shows in what great favor the emperor held Yen. Later, the epistle of Emperor Hsüan [73-49 B.C.] to Governor Ch'en Sui expresses the depth of his feelings for his old friend.[18]

When Emperor Kuang-wu [25-57] brought order to the chaotic world, he was deeply concerned about his language. However, in the heat of the moment, he often lost his poise in expressing his joy or anger. In his letter to Teng Yü, he described the office of Ssu-t'u as that of Yao,[19] and in his threatening letter to Hou Pa [also a Ssu-t'u], he referred to the execution axe.[20] Royal letters like these are indeed contrary to the form of *chao* demanded by good taste. Emperors Ming

15 See the biographies of the three princes in the *Shih-chi*.

16 Both the *hsün* and the *tien* are chapter titles in the *Book of History*. Hsün means to give instruction. The *History* has a chapter entitled "I-hsün" (The instruction of I Yin) by a T'ang minister. When T'ang died, his grandson ascended to the throne, and I wrote this for the benefit of the young ruler. As to the *tien*, the first two chapters of the History include this term in their titles. *Hsün-tien* may be rendered simply as "classical."

17 See Yen Tsu's biography in the *Han-shu*. Yen Tsu had gone away from court to be the governor of K'uai-chi, in modern Chekiang, his native place. The emperor apparently let him go with reluctance. Ch'eng-ming lu was a hall in the palace where attendant ministers stayed.

18 Emperor Hsüan, when humble, often lost to his friend Ch'en Sui in games and was unable to pay. After he became emperor, he made Ch'en an official, and eventually wrote him a letter mentioning jokingly that the appointment was in payment of his gambling debts to Ch'en.

19 In the Chou time, Ssu-t'u was one of the six Chief Ministers; in the Han, a prime minister was known as Ssu-t'u, one of the three Grand Ministers. Teng was made Ssu-t'u by Kuang-wu. In A.D. 25, when Kuang-wu ascended the throne, Teng was in charge of the military expeditions in the west. When he delayed his operation against Ch'ang-an, the old capital, Kuang-wu sent him a stiff letter, in which he declared that a Ssu-t'u was, in effect, a Yao (the exemplary ruler of the past), and that he should therefore make all haste to bring his campaign to a successful completion, in order to give succor to the long-suffering people of the west. See his biography in the *Hou-han-shu*.

20 Hou Pa recommended a certain person whom Emperor Kuang-wu hated; suspecting that Hou was bribed, he sent him a letter threatening to execute him. See the biography of Feng Ch'in in the *Hou-han-shu*.

[58-75] and Chang [76-88] emphasized learning, and consequently issued some graceful *chao*.

During the reigns of Emperors An [107-125] and Ho [89-105],[21] government declined and in the Hall of Rites [where scholars were gathered], there were few scholars with talent. When a royal *chao* or *ch'ih* [that is, pronouncement or warning] was to be drafted, a scholar from outside the Hall was often summoned to do it. At the end of the reign of Chien-an [196-220], we find a rise in interest in literature. The "Chiu-hsi" of P'an Hsü[22] was elegant and graceful, outstanding in its group. Wei K'ai's edict of abdication[23] is marked with brilliant rhetoric, quite unsurpassed.

Since the times of Wei and Chin, the drafting of royal edicts had been one of the functions of the royal secretary. Liu Fang [of the Wei] and Chang Hua [of the Chin] were both appointed to this position. Edicts and orders flowed from their brushes, wonderful to listen to. The edicts of Emperor Wen of Wei are for the most part grand in both language and ideas, and his inappropriate use of the phrase "to exercise awesome authority or to confer blessed happiness" may be considered the one black spot in his well-considered works.[24] When the Chin dynasty obtained a second lease on life,[25] Emperor Ming [323-325] alone patronized the talented. Wen Ch'iao, because

---

[21] Liu Hsieh reversed the order for euphonic reasons.

[22] "Chiu-hsi" means conferment of nine honors to the virtuous lords by the Son of Heaven. Often we find that a minister grew too powerful, and the Son of Heaven conferred these honors under duress. This was the case when Emperor Hsien, the last emperor of the Han, conferred these honors on Ts'ao Ts'ao in 213. On this occasion, P'an Hsü was commissioned to write the royal edict for the emperor.

[23] Emperor Hsien, the last emperor of the Later Han, abdicated in favor of Ts'ao P'ei, the eldest son of Ts'ao Ts'ao, in A.D. 220. The royal edict proclaiming the abdication was written by Wei K'ai.

[24] The phrase is taken from the *Book of History* (see *Shang-shu t'ung-chien*, 24/0602-9), where it is pointed out that one should not "exercise his awesome authority" or "confer blessed happiness" without good reason. Here the emperor was using the phrase to describe the kind of behavior he expected of the general, to whom he was sending the edict. When Chiang Chi remonstrated with him, he had the edict recalled before it reached its destination, and had the phrase dropped. See the biography of Chiang Chi in the *Wei-chih*.

[25] Referring to the Eastern Chin, after the Western Chin collapsed under the pressure of the invasion of the northern tribes.

of the purity of his literary style, was appointed royal secretary. From this time on, interest in their literary quality became a strong influence on the composition of edicts.

The words of a ruler are lofty and laden with meaning; hence they are suspended on high for all to look up to, they are the laws to all chieftains, and they are pledges capable of winning the confidence of all states. Therefore, in making appointments and selecting the virtuous for such appointments, an edict should contain ideas as bright as the sun and the moon; in enfeoffment, it should be rich in literary quality, with the grace of the breeze and the timely rain; in warning or ordinary decree, it should have brilliance that flows from the brush, sparkling like stars in the Milky Way; in connection with the conduct of military expeditions, it should thunder forth in rolling majesty; in giving pardon, it should be as gracious as the dews in the spring; and in the just application of law and punishment, its language should be as sharp as the autumn frost. These are the main principles governing the royal edict.

Chieh-ch'ih, or royal warning, are edicts written in language which is sharp and cutting. The order given by King Mu of the Chou [1023-983 B.C.] to Chiao-fu to receive regulations governing the royal warning may be cited to illustrate this point.[26] King Wu [or Ts'ao Ts'ao] of Wei said that in writing a warning, the language should be directed to the facts, and no vagueness should be allowed. This remark manifests his wisdom with respect to government administration. And Emperor Wu of the Chin served all his ministers with warnings; he warned the military governors of the importance of military affairs; he warned the civil governors of the importance of handling subordinates; he warned prefects of the importance of being kind to the people and not too observant of their faults; and he warned the guard of their duty in defense. His are warnings which may be considered classical.

Chieh, or to advise against, means literally "to take care." Yü [of the

26 See the *Mu-t'ien-tzu chuan.*

Hsia] spoke of the function of a *chieh* as good. Now, the ruler and the father rank first among the respected, among the three with boundless grace [which it is impossible for one to repay];[27] and both the advice of Emperor Kao-tsu of the Han [202-192 B.C.] to the heir apparent and Tung-fang So's admonishment to his son are of the same nature as the "Ku-ming."[28] From Ma Yüan [14 B.C.-A.D. 49] downward, each writer has left behind his advice to his family. And the advice to her daughters by Pan Chi [or Pan Chao, ?-*c.* 116, sister of Pan Ku, the historian] may be considered words from the mouth of a woman teacher.

Chiao, or to teach, literally means *hsiao,* or to imitate. Words once spoken form the models for people to imitate—for example, the five teachings disseminated by Hsieh;[29] therefore the words of kings and lords have come to be grouped under the general term *chiao,* or teaching. Cheng Hung's teachings during his tenure as the prefect of Nan-yang were well remembered by later generations,[30] because they were clear statements of his administration. On the other hand, when K'ung Yung was the prefect of Pei-hai, his declarations to the people were marked with literary embellishments but lacking in rational substance. His is a practice contrary to the right principle of government. As to both the skill in detail and the succinctness of Chu-ke K'ung-ming [that is, Chu-ke Liang, a great strategist of the Three Kingdoms period] and the brilliant judgments of Yü Chih-kung [or Yü I], both are well grounded in reason and have achieved the right standard in language. They furnish the best examples of *chiao.*

In addition to *chiao,* there is also *ming,* or mandate. It is said in the *Book of Poetry,* "There is *ming* from heaven," showing the importance

[27] The third one from whom we receive boundless grace is the teacher.

[28] In the *Book of History,* Chapter 42, the advice which King Ch'eng of the Chou, on his deathbed, gave to his son King K'ang.

[29] Hsieh was a minister of Shun, who appointed him to be the Ssu-t'u, a minister in charge of education. The five teachings are: father's justice, mother's love, elder brother's kindness, younger brother's respect, and son's filial piety. See *Shang-shu t'ung chien,* 2/0478-98, and *Ch'un ch'iu ching-chuan yin-te,* 176/Wen 18/9 Tso.

[30] This is not mentioned in the biography of Cheng Hung in the *Hou-han-shu.*

of *ming*.[31] And in the *Chou-li*, the Shih-shih had the duty of keeping
the ruler informed or *chao*,[32] showing that the *chao* was then relatively unimportant.[33] In our own day, the *chao* is important and the
ming unimportant; this indicates the change from ancient to modern
times.

  The Tsan:
The august king, in giving orders,
Shows inner reverence and outer respect in his pronouncements.
His words are like silk,[34]
And all the people love to hear them.
Their brilliant sound soars high,
And on mighty winds is carried to a distance.
Vigorous ideas and lively language
Decorate these, his majestic commands.

XX. War Proclamation and Dispatch (The Hsi and the I)

As lightning precedes thunder, so awesome proclamations precede
military expeditions. Just as the sight of lightning evokes a fear of the
ensuing thunder, so the hearing of a proclamation makes the listener
freeze with fear of military strength. It has long been a practice to send
out proclamations before military expeditions. Yu-yü [Shun] was the
first to sound the warning to his state; the ruler of Hsia was the first
to take the oath in the army; Yin [or Shang] took the oath outside
the army camp; and the Chou took the oath immediately before the

---

[31] *Mao-shih yin-te*, 59/236/6.

[32] An office whose function was to inform, or *chao*, the ruler of what is good. See
Chou-li, "Ti-kuan" (Shih-san ching chu-su ed.), chüan 14, p. 2a.

[33] Relatively unimportant because it was used by the official and was not used like
ming as a mandate from heaven, nor as royal decree.

[34] See note 9 above.

battle.[1] Thus we know that during the time of the [Five] Emperors [one of whom was Shun], warning was sent out before a military campaign; and during the time of the Three Kings [of the Hsia, Shang, and Chou], an oath was taken at the time the expedition was launched. In all these cases, the instructions were directed to their own troops, and nothing was said to the enemy. But when King Mu of Chou launched an expedition to the west, Lord Ts'ai Mou-fu remarked that in ancient times there were both proclamations to set forth the purpose of the expedition and proclamations in which the crimes of the enemy were enumerated. This may be considered the beginning of the *hsi*, or war proclamation.

During the period of the Ch'un-ch'iu, all military expeditions were initiated by the lords.[2] Mindful that the enemy might not acknowledge their authority, these lords, in order to maintain it, had to give their expeditions noble justifications in order to inspire awe, and this they accomplished by exposing in proclamations the evil done by the enemy. This was just what Liu Hsien-kung had in mind in his advice [to Shu-hsiang of Chin, when the state of Ch'i was reluctant to come to terms]: "Inform them of the reason by proclamation, and support it with troops."[3] Duke Huan of Ch'i, on his expedition against the state of Ch'u, rebuked it for failing to send tribute [to the Chou court];[4] Duke Li of Chin seized upon the burning of [the Chin city of] Chi-kao as his reason for attacking Ch'in,[5] and Kuang Chung and Lü Hsiang both wrote proclamations before their military expeditions.[6] A careful examination of their content shows that they are actually what we now call *hsi*, or war proclamations.

It was during the Warring States period that such proclamations

[1] Taken from the *Ssu-ma Fa*, military regulations. The purpose of the oath is to prepare the people for the forthcoming expedition.

[2] This was a sign of the decline of the Chou, because normally all military expeditions should have been initiated by the king.

[3] See *Ch'un-ch'iu ching-chuan yin-te*, 382/Chao 13/5 Tso.

[4] *Ibid.*, 92/Hsi 4/4 Tso. At this time the Chou was so weak that the king was a figurehead. Strong vassal lords acted in the name of the Son of Heaven. So Ch'i, the strongest state of the time, took Ch'u's failure to send tribute to Chou as an excuse for attacking it.

[5] *Ibid.*, 235/ Ch'eng 13/4 Tso.   [6] Kuan against Ch'u, Lü against Ch'in.

came to be known as *hsi*. *Hsi* means clear, clearly revealed, clearly understood. Chang I, when sending a *hsi* to Ch'u, wrote it down on a bamboo slip only one foot and two inches long.[7] The clearly expressed language of the *hsi* is grasped as a poster is grasped when it is presented before the eyes and ears.

The purpose of a military expedition is to restore peace, and it must not be initiated on one's own account. Formerly when the Son of Heaven took charge of an expedition in person, he would say: "I respectfully execute this act of punishment in the name of heaven."[8] And when it was a vassal lord who launched the campaign, he would say: "Reverently I impose this penalty in the name of the king."[9] In this way the Son of Heaven shared his responsibility with his generals and gave them encouragement,[10] and the generals received orders from the emperor himself to undertake punitive expeditions. This was done not only to insure success in destroying the enemy, but also to provide the utmost opportunity for couching the orders in severe language expressive of a militant spirit. Such proclamations would have a resounding impact, like that of stormy winds, and their militant spirit would destroy the enemy's morale like the comet sweeping away [evils with its tail]. They expressed martial indignation and constrained the spirits of the malefactors. They gave evidence indicating the ripening moment of evil, and pointed out that the days of the malefactors, whose crime had reached its limits, were numbered. They struck terror to the hearts of the evil, but gave confidence to those who were

---

[7] Chang I was wrongly accused of stealing jade cups while being entertained at the Ch'u court and was consequently lashed. When he became the prime minister of Ch'in, he sent Ch'u a *hsi* to the effect that he now would steal Ch'u cities. A *hsi* is sometimes defined as "a foot and two."

[8] *Shang-shu t'ung-chien*, 21/0702-13; 22/0165-73.

[9] See K'ung Yin-ta's commentary on *Shang-shu t'ung-chien*, 22/0165-73.

[10] Literally, "division by the city gate threshold and a push to the chariot," paraphrase of a line from the biography of Feng T'ang in Pan Ku's *Han-shu*. The original line in the *Han-shu* runs: "Your servant—addressing Emperor Wen—heard that in ancient times when a king dispatched a general on an expedition, he would kneel down to give the general's chariot a push and say: 'Within the threshold of the city gate I assume responsibility, and beyond the threshold, you, my general, assume full responsibility.'" Later "division by threshold" came to mean division of responsibility, and "to give the chariot a push" meant to give encouragement.

faithful and obedient. They caused hundred-foot chariots to break before a written note scarcely a foot long and a city wall of ten thousand *chih*[11] to crumble under the weight of a *hsi*. Wei Hsiao's *hsi* recounting the three crimes [of Wang Mang][12] caused the Hsin dynasty[13] to collapse. Though unembellished, its language is succinct and its narrative clear. In it the scholars of Lung-yu[14] found a model for the *hsi*. Ch'en Lin's *hsi* against Ts'ao Ts'ao is marked with strength and courage; although its exposé of the family background is exaggerated, as in its assertion that Ts'ao's grandfather was a eunuch and his father a beggar receiving support from others; and although it contains the allegation, more false than acrimonious, that Ts'ao had the imperial tombs dug up for their treasure, its strong language in describing Ts'ao's crimes is as stark as exposed bones. With great courage he braved the anger of Ts'ao Ts'ao; and it was a sheer stroke of luck that he was not destroyed along with the clique of Yüan [Shao].[15] Chung Hui [225-264], in his *hsi* to the generals in Shu, cited his evidence convincingly, and the *hsi* of Huan Wen [312-373] against the barbarians[16] is even more telling in recounting their ruthlessness. These are all products of vigorous brushes.

In general a *hsi* speaks either of one's own kindness and fair judgment, or of the enemy's ruthlessness and cruelty. It stresses salient factors of timeliness and human relations, and discusses comparative military strengths and strategic positions; it refers to oracular revelations of the future, and to the lessons reflected in the pendant mirror of the past.[17] Although it is based on the realities of the national situation, it utilizes the deceptive tactics always involved in military art.

[11] About fifty miles.

[12] Crimes against heaven, earth, and men. See Wei Hsiao's biography in the *Houhan-shu*.

[13] Created by Wang Mang, who usurped the throne in A.D. 9. His dynasty lasted until A.D. 23. He chose Hsin as his dynastic title because he was enfeoffed Lord Hsin-tu.

[14] Present-day Kansu.

[15] He wrote the *hsi* for Yüan Shao, who was planning a punitive expedition against Ts'ao Ts'ao.

[16] Referring to Shih Le, who was overrunning North China at the time.

[17] For the meaning of the pendant mirror, see note 25, Chapter XI. "The pendant mirror of the past" means history.

To put over its ideas, it makes use of deceit; and to give force to its claim, it employs brilliant language. These tactics are imperative in all *hsi* writing. Therefore, in formulating ideas for a *hsi* or in attempting to make its words fly home, the important thing to remember is strength. To make the words fly home is essentially to give them speed, to avoid a slow-moving style; and, as a *hsi* is to be posted for all to see, never to allow its ideas to be vague. Its facts should be evident, its reason sound, its spirit high, and its language clear-cut; these are the essentials of a *hsi*. As to involved style or delicate and clever content, they are not materials for the genre.

We might add that when local officials call for recruits their proclamations are also known as *hsi*, since their idea is to announce an intention clearly.

I, or to transform or dispatch, means literally to change, to transform ways and change mores, to dispatch an order for people to follow. [Ssu-ma] Hsiang-ju's dispatch refuting the opinions of the people of Shu [who opposed contacting the southwestern tribes] is lucid in language and comprehensive in arguments; it may be considered the very bone of both *i* and *hsi*. Liu Hsin's dispatch rebuking scholars in the T'ai-ch'ang ministry[18] is couched in strong language, contains ideas which are clear, and may be considered the best of all civil dispatches. Lu Chi's dispatch to the hundred officials[19] is simple in language and plain in recounting facts, and may be said to be the best of all military dispatches. These examples demonstrate that the *hsi* and the *i* may be used on both civil and military occasions. In a military situation, the *hsi* is used to address the enemy and the *i* to address the allies; the distinction is made for the purpose of rooting out any suspicion in the

18 The T'ai-ch'ang ministry was in charge of rites, a function similar to that of a modern ministry of education. Scholars who were experts in the study of particular classics were appointed Po-shih (learned men) in the ministry. Liu Hsin proposed to create three new Po-shih for the three classics: the *Book of History*, particularly the chapter "T'ai-shih," the great oath King Wu made at the beginning of his expedition against the Shang, the thirty-nine chapters of the newly recovered *Book of Rites*, and the *Tso-chuan*, Tso's commentary on the *Ch'un-ch'iu*. He was vehemently opposed by the Po-shih in the T'ai-ch'ang ministry, and he rebuked them in the dispatch referred to here.

19 Not recorded, presumably lost.

minds of the people and planting in its stead firm concord. Between
the two terms there is thus a slight difference in application, but they
are similar in form and content. To know the *i* we need only refer to
the *hsi*. We shall not, therefore, deal with it again here.

The *Tsan*:

[In hunting, ancient kings] used beaters on three sides, and [T'ang of
    Shang also ordered] the net to be loose [on three].[20]
Therefore all punitive expeditions are preceded by proclamations.
Look into the pendant mirror of the past for lucky and unlucky omens;
And depend on milfoil stems and tortoise shell to predict the success or
    failure of a campaign.
Suppress the overbearing and ruthless,
And exterminate the poisonous.
Transform ways and change mores;
The grasses incline under the strength of the wind of proclamation.[21]

XXI. Sacrifices to Heaven and Earth (Feng Shan)[1]

[A ruler] is situated as the Big Dipper[2] and confronts the brilliant

---

[20] In the *Book of Changes* under the hexagram *pi* (☰☷), it is said, "In hunting
the king uses beaters on three sides only and foregoes game that runs off in front."
See *Chou-i yin-te*, 8/8/5. And in the *Lü-shih ch'un-ch'iu*, T'ang of the Shang dynasty is
said to have ordered the game warden to let loose three sides of the net. See *Lü-shih
ch'un-ch'iu* (Chu-tzu chi-ch'eng ed.), chüan 10, p. 102. These figures are used here to
indicate the reluctance of a good ruler to use force. A proclamation is here conceived
to be an attempt to correct wrongs without resorting to force.

[21] A figure taken from the *Analects*, where the wind refers to the influence of the men
of virtue, while the grasses are the people. See *Analects*, 24/12/19. The proclamation is
then the vigorous wind and the enemy is the grass.

[1] One of the things done during these sacrifices was to inscribe on stone tablets the
achievements of the ruler.

[2] The Big Dipper or Ursa Major was thought to be the chariot of the Supreme Being,
and it occupies the center of heaven around which all heavenly bodies revolve, a position
similar to that of a ruler on earth.

south;[3] he moves Polaris[4] and gives support both to the common people and to the virtuously eminent. Has such a ruler ever failed to inscribe his imperial achievements by weaving together the *Tao*, or first principle, and the *te*, or particular principles, as the warp and the woof are woven together? The "Green Diagram" says, "Through whirl and permeation, the ten thousand things are evolutionally transformed," expressing the effect of the influence of great virtue. And the "Red Book" says, "The way will be smooth if righteousness overcomes selfish desires, and disastrous if selfish desires overcome righteousness," showing the importance of extreme reverence and vigilance.[5] Such reverence and vigilance serve to build the ruler's virtue up to its majestic height; and this high moral quality of his achieves the evolutional transformation referred to. Accordingly there have been seventy-two monarchs who in the past have offered sacrifices to heaven and earth.[6]

Long ago the Yellow Emperor, because of the spirituality of his personality, was the recipient of most auspicious blessings, and he inscribed a record of his merit on the lofty Mount [T'ai] and had tripods cast at Mount Ching. Shun's sacrifice to T'ai-shan is clearly recorded in the "Yü-tien."[7] And we hear of the sacrifices to heaven and earth made by King Ch'eng and King K'ang [of Chou] as recorded in the apocrypha of the *Classic of Music*. When Duke Huan of Ch'i had become drunk with power, he cast his eyes toward imperial rule. But I-wu [or Kuan Chung] shrewdly remonstrated with him by detailing the extraordinary omens necessary for assuming the imperial

[3] In the *Chuangtzu* (for "Nan-mien," i.e., facing south, see *Chuangtzu yin-te*, 6/2/62, 30/12/26, 81/29/19; in 47/18/27, we have the phrase "Nan-mien-wang," a king who faces south, and in the "Shuo-kua" of the *Book of Changes* (see *Chou-i yin-te*, 50/shuo/4), we find mention of the ruler facing south, but nowhere has a satisfactory explanation for this practice been found. In the "Shuo-kua" it is merely said that the south is bright, hence the sage faces south in audience with the people of the world, as he faces the light in his rule.

[4] Supposedly the first star in the Ursa Major constellation, conceived in ancient China as the first heaven. If the ruler moves this first star, around which all other heavenly bodies revolve, he is evidently the prime mover in the world.

[5] Both the "Green Diagram" and the "Red Book" have been mentioned in Chapter IV, p. 23. See note 5, Chapter IV.

[6] Reporting to heaven and earth on their achievements, the expression of extreme reverence and vigilance.

[7] "Shun-tien," the second chapter of the *Book of History*.

role, and forestalled his attempt.[8] From this incident, we learn that jade tablets and gold inscriptions are the special omens of an emperor. But what has been said of the *chien*,[9] appearing in the west, and the *tieh*,[10] appearing in the east, is idle chatter without basis; what is really meant is the ruler's great virtue.[11] The monograph "Feng-shan" (Sacrifices to heaven and earth) among the eight treatises in the *Shih-chi* of Shih-ch'ien [or Ssu-ma Ch'ien] is about special rites of sacrifices which were also occasions for recording the merits of the rulers and offering secret prayers.[12] We find in this monograph a truly grand spectacle of heaven worship. The inscriptions of Ch'in Shih-huang-ti [first emperor of the Ch'in] on Mount T'ai were from the brush of Li Ssu; written in the language of a legalist, their style is neither elevated nor smooth. However, clean and vigorous, they were the best literary efforts of the time.

During the height of the two Han, Emperor Wu performed sacrifices to heaven and earth at Mount Su-jan and Emperor Kuang-wu performed sacrifices to heaven and earth at Mount Liang-fu; both records are masterpieces, glorifying their virtue and preserving their merits in memory.[13] The "Feng-shan" of [Ssu-ma] Hsiang-ju is elegant and leads the genre in beauty. It traces its origin, narrates successive performances of the sovereigns and kings at sacrifices, mentions clearly the physical symbols of the mandate of heaven, and makes the great achievements of past rulers shine. In it Hsiang-ju reached back to antiquity for evidence that was of service to the contemporary ruler [Emperor Wu], and extolled his good and brilliant reign above those

---

[8] The duke's ambition to assume the position of the Son of Heaven was frustrated through the failure of certain omens to materialize. These omens were then construed to be the prerogatives of a ruler mandated by heaven.

[9] A *chien* is a one-winged bird. These birds fly only in pairs.

[10] A *tieh* is a one-eyed fish. These fish swim only in pairs.

[11] The *chien* and *tieh*, the jade tablets and gold inscriptions, are, according to Kuan I-wu, some of the things which must appear as symbols of investiture by the mandate of heaven.

[12] See *Shih-chi*, "Feng-shan shu" (Taipei, Erh-shih-wu-shih ed.), chüan 28, p. 106. In 167 B.C., Emperor Wen abolished secret prayers by means of which the sacrificial officials attempted to shift calamity from the emperor to the people. *Ibid.*, p. 12a.

[13] Strictly speaking, they sacrificed to heaven at Mount T'ai and to earth at Mount Liang-fu. See "Wu-ti chi" in the *Han-shu* and "Kuang-wu chi" in the *Hou-han-shu*. Liu Hsieh's statements are elliptic for the purpose of euphony.

of previous sage kings. He sang his praise of the reign by citing auspicious omens, and pleaded with the emperor to go to offer sacrifices
to heaven and earth at the great mountain. Such a piece is without
peer, a creation completely new.[14]

The stone inscription extolling Emperor Kuang-wu's virtue was
from the brush of Chang Ch'un. Its first part is in the [classical] style
of *tien-mu*, and its last part in the style of a prayer, or *chu*. It cites
prognostications from the apocrypha, describes the chaotic times,[15]
and gives an account of Kuang-wu's military merits and civil virtues.
Lucid in narrative and articulate in reasoning, although it is somewhat
lacking in embellishment, it is more than adequate in its content.
These two writers [Ssu-ma Hsiang-ju and Chang Ch'un] left behind
concrete evidence on stone on Mount T'ai.[16] Although Yang Hsiung's
"Chü-ch'in"[17] and Pan Ku's "Tien-yin"[18] have not been inscribed, they
are in the style of the *chi*, or chronicle of rulers, and *shan*, or sacrificial
writings. "Chü-ch'in" was patterned after the work of Ch'ang-ch'ing
[or Ssu-ma Hsiang-ju]; it embodies strange stories told in a sophisticated language and touches the supernatural. However, with its close-
knit structure and coherent and smooth language, it is indeed the
result of the utmost intellectual effort. The subject matter dealt with
in the "Tien-yin" has the qualities of grace and beauty. Based on the
experience he obtained through a study of previous writings, it seems
to have achieved the right principle. It succeeds with flying colors in
expressing ideas in adequate language: for example, it speaks of
"Feng-shan" as "beautiful and not elegant," and of "Chü-ch'in" as
"elegant and not true." This seems to illustrate the truth that hindsight
is easily clearer than foresight and that taking advantage of an existing
situation gives one a better chance for success than creating anew.

When we come to the "Shou-ming" (Reception of mandate) of
Han-tan [Ch'un], we find it only the echo of former sounds; for like

---

[14] This piece is found in *Shih-chi, Han-shu,* and *Wen-hsüan.*

[15] Referring to the time of confusion subsequent to the usurpation by Wang Mang.

[16] The stone inscription of Hsiang-ju's writing is not mentioned elsewhere.

[17] The full title is: "Chü-ch'ing mei-hsin," criticizing Ch'in and extolling Hsin—
Wang Mang's dynastic title.

[18] Extolling the virtue of the Han.

the tail of a wind its strength is about spent. It just collects rhymes to form a *sung*, or song. Although smooth in language and logical in order, it lacks the vigor for flight. The "Wei-te"[19] of Ch'en-ssu [or Ts'ao Chih] postulates a host as protagonist and a guest as antagonist, but the question and answer dialogue becomes so devious and slow-moving that it consumes thousands of words: it is most laborious but of little merit, lacking both swiftness and flaming force.

Feng-shan, or "sacrifices to heaven and earth," serve to document the institutions of an age. Before laying down the general plan of the genre, one should first understand the main features of its construction. Its bone structure should be erect and in the realm of the *hsün-tien*, or classical, and it ought to be clothed in a language that is elegant and rich; its ideas may be old and yet not be so deep that they become obscure, and its language, though modern, should betray no sign of shallowness. It will be a masterpiece if it contains ideas that shoot forth tongues of fire and its language is as clear-cut as a sword blade. Even if imitation should become the order of the day, when the development of the genre has reached its limit, if one is able to give it a freshness of ornamentation, his works would exceed his predecessors' in excellence.

The Tsan:

In sacrifices to heaven the ruler's merits are emblazoned on stone,
As a report to heaven from whom he has received such heavenly grace.
Heard afar from high mountains
Is his fame, noble and bright.
Monuments are erected, penetrating the nine heavens,
Their inscriptions emblazoned in gold,
Cut according to the norm set by the geese [that is, to none],[20]
And to the patterns of twisted trees,
As lively as dragons.

[19] Extolling the virtue of the Wei.

[20] In *T'ai-hsüan ching*, by Yang Hsiung, it is said, "The pattern of the geese conform to no norm," used here along with the next figure to illustrate the rugged style of stone inscriptions.

XXII. Memorial, Part I (The Chang and the Piao)

Offices are created to carry on the various functions of government, and officials of all ranks work together. While the Son of Heaven, with fringes of pearls on his crown, holds court, lords and vassals come to seek audience, tinkling with jade pendants. They report orally in words whose validity is openly checked by reference to their actual accomplishments. Thus, when Yao consulted the four chiefs who were in charge of the vassal lords, or when Shun recommended the eight worthies [to Yao], or when officials repeated their courteous refusal of their appointments,[1] or when the ruler dispatched his ministers on missions—in all these cases, the words were uttered at court without resort to paper and brush. Hence the meaning of the term *chang-piao* is a report [that is, *tsou*] by word of mouth, and an examination of the validity of the words by reference to accomplishments stands for the ceremony of bestowing a title of nobility. When T'ai-chia [T'ang's grandson; 1738-1725 B.C.] ascended the throne, I Yin wrote a memorial warning him of certain pitfalls;[2] and when T'ai-chia again became heedful of the constant principle of right and returned to Po,[3] I Yin again wrote memorials to praise his effort.[4] This was the first instance we find of such advice offered as written memorials.

The Chou, having the advantage of the experiences of the previous two dynasties, witnessed further literary developments. It was customary to express one's gratitude by kowtowing and lauding his majesty's gracious mandate, or to express one's sense of humility before the great, enlightened order of enfeoffment orally; for at the time oral and written forms were not yet clearly distinguished, but expressions of gratitude can be readily seen.

During the period of the Seven States no change in the old form took place. When memorializing the throne, one was said to present

---

[1] This includes the declining of the offer of the throne.
[2] See note 16, Chapter XIX.   [3] Capital of Shang.
[4] The three chapters in the *Book of History* entitled "T'ai-chia," grouped together as Chapter 14 in the *Shang-shu t'ung-chien*.

a *shu*, or letter. It was the Ch'in which first instituted the change from
shu to *tsou*, or memorial. According to the Han institution, there were
four categories: *chang*, or to make clear or articulate; *tsou*, or to memorialize; *piao*, or to express; and *i*, or to discuss. The purpose of the
chang was to make clear one's feeling of gratitude; of the *tsou*, to
investigate and to impeach; of the *piao*, to express one's own feelings;
and of the *i*, to maintain a difference of opinion. *Chang* literally means
"clear or articulate." In the *Book of Poetry* there is a line: "forming
chang in heaven,"[5] which means that its pattern is made articulate. As
an example of an application of the idea to material things, a mixture
of red with white is called *chang*.[6] *Piao* means literally "to post."
[Chapter 32] in the *Book of Rites* is entitled "Piao-chi," meaning that
one's inner virtue is posted outside in one's manners. As an example of
the application of this idea to material things, to measure the shadow
on a sundial is known as *piao*. Thus the term *chang-piao* seems to
have originated.

We find included in the "Ch'i-lüeh" and "I-wen [chih]"[7] records
of all poetic writings; and yet the *chang, piao, tsou*, and *i*, all crucial
in the conduct of government, are omitted, because they were concerned with the affairs of various organs of government and were kept
in the files of their government offices. Few of the *piao* of the Early
Han period are still extant. And during the Later Han one of the
conditions for being selected for official appointment was to pass an
examination in the *chang* and *tsou*. Tso Hsiung's *tsou* and *i*, which
set the pattern for documents of the Grand Secretariat, and Hu Kuang's
chang and *tsou*, the best in the country, were both great literary productions.[8] A perusal of Po-shih's [or Hu Kuang's] *chang* on his visit
to the royal tombs will convince us of the elegance of his classical style.[9]

[5] The *Book of Poetry*, 60/238/4.
[6] The line is quoted from *K'ao-kung chi*, which means to give form or to make
articulate. See also *Chou-li*, chüan 40, p. 25a: "[A mixture of] red with white is called
chang."
[7] See note 9, Chapter XVII.
[8] Tso Hsiung flourished during the beginning of the second century; Hu Kuang
lived from 91 to 172.
[9] The work is lost.

Long ago, Duke Wen of Chin [636-628 B.C.] accepted the order of enfeoffment only after declining it three times. Hence, since the end of the Han no one has memorialized more than three times in declining his appointment. And Ts'ao [Ts'ao] considered it unnecessary for an official to memorialize three times in courtesy declining, and also felt that the memorial should not contain any superficial and flowery rhetoric. For this reason, the *piao* and *chang* during the first years of the Wei dynasty were written in a matter-of-fact style. If one's interest is in the beautiful, then there is little here that may be considered praiseworthy. But Wen-chü's [or K'ung Yung's] memorial recommending Ni Heng[10] is marked with lively spirit and flying colors, and those of K'ung-ming [or Chu-ke Liang], bidding farewell to the young ruler,[11] fully express his ideas, which were couched in smoothly flowing language. These writings may differ in that Wen-chü's is beautiful while Chu-ke's are factual, but both are heroes in the genre of *piao*. The *chang* and *piao* of [Ch'en] Lin and [Juan] Yü won them great fame during their time; K'ung-chang's [or Ch'en Lin's] was particularly known for its literary vigor. His *piao* is indeed the standard of its kind. Ch'en-ssu's [or Ts'ao Chih's] *piao* is the best of all these talented works, elegant in style, melodic in prosody, pure in language, and clear in thought. He artfully adapted his talents to things as they were, and always described the changing situation with the same life and spirit. Just because he was in full control at the rein, he was able to maintain an equally even pace whether he was slowing down or speeding up his tempo.

During the first years of the Chin dynasty, Chang Hua [232-300] was the leader among writers of this genre. The three memorials in which he declined the investiture of a lordship are comprehensive in reasoning and succinct in language; in elaborating ideas and in comparing facts, he always succeeded in producing a matched pair. The

---

[10] Flourishing during the Chien-an period, 196-220.

[11] Liu Ch'an, the second ruler of Shu, one of the three kingdoms. He ruled from 223 to 263, when he surrendered to the Wei. In these memorials, K'ung-ming outlined his plans for the invasion of Wei and gave advice to the young ruler concerning the affairs of the state.

world has valued his "Chiao-liao Fu" [Ode to the wren], and has overlooked his *chang* and *piao*. The memorial by Yang [Hu, 221-278] declining the office of a grand general has been greatly praised, and that of Yü [Liang, 289-340] declining the position of the royal private secretary has been highly lauded. Clear and orderly in declaring their minds, theirs are works marked with literary grace. The memorial by Liu K'un [270-317] beseeching [Emperor Yüan] to assume the throne[12] and Chang Chün's about himself[13] are clear and straightforward, both memorials especially excelling in their narrative accounts.

The functions of *chang* and *piao* are, respectively, to praise royal virtues and to express one's own opinion before the imperial court. They are both the ornaments of the person responsible for them and the flowers of the state. With the *chang* one lays bare one's heart before the imperial gate; therefore its rule is explicitness; and as the *piao* is a request to halt a certain action, there should be brilliance in its basic structure. If we seek after the reality implied in the names of both forms, we shall find that the *chang* is the fundamental form. Therefore, the form of a *chang* is highly articulated, and its aim is to achieve the classical; it gives the essentials without being sketchy, and is clear without being circumstantial. The genre of *piao* deals with a wide variety of matters. As the relative positions of truth and falsehood are always changing, the *piao* must have intellectual delicacy in order to insure that its influence will prevail, and purity of style to drive home the effect of its beauty. However, when one has genuine feelings, his outward expressions are dependent upon his mental attitude; while superficial writers' feelings become cramped by the literary form. If one can achieve a proper balance between embellishment and compendiousness, so that flowers and fruits are in good proportion to each other, and if there is complete freedom from stammering, one will have achieved the right standard. Tzu-Kung [a disciple of Confucius] said, "Use your mind to control ideas and your words to win confidence";

[12] This was in 317 when North China was overrun by the invading tribes from the north. The ascension of Emperor Yüan to the throne marked the beginning of the Eastern Chin dynasty.

[13] This piece has not been identified.

his idea is that literary expressions and ideas should be made one.[14] Hsün Ch'ing once remarked that it was more satisfying to see a man's beautiful literary expressions than woven patterns of silk.[15] Did he not express an idea similar to Tzu-Kung's?

   The Tsan:
In presenting *piao* at the imperial gate
Or offering advice before the embroidered screen,[16]
Words should be pure and clear
And ideas stately and grand,
Respectful in the narrative of details,
And neatly ordered, in putting first things first and last things last.
When endowed with literary talent, a man of virtue
Produces works which are truly works of art.

XXIII. Memorial, Part II (The Tsou and the Ch'i)

The ministers of the T'ang and Yü dynasties memorialized the throne by word of mouth. During the Ch'in and the Han, the memorials of the officials were known as *tsou*. Whether the memorial was concerned with political affairs, institutions and rites, a report of an emergency, or an accusation and impeachment, its general name was *tsou*. *Tsou* means to present, that is, to present in words the feeling of the masses of the people before the throne. The form *tsou* was created by the first emperor of the Ch'in. The writings of the [Ch'in] legalists,[1] however, were not known for their literary quality. If we examine [Prime Minister] Wang Wan's memorial lauding the military merits

---

   [14] *Ch'un-ch'iu ching-chuan yin-te*, 484/ai 12/3 Tso.
   [15] *Hsüntzu chi-chieh*, chüan 3, Chapter 5, p. 53. Liu Hsieh modified the statement to suit his purpose.
   [16] See note 1, Chapter XIX.
   [1] The Ch'in built its rule on legalist principles.

and virtue of [the first emperor], with its terse expressions and simple ideas, or that of Li Ssu about [the tomb at] Mount Li, brief in narrative and absurd in ideas, we shall see that the lack of grace and benign spirit in government has found expression in the writings of the dynasty.[2] Since the Han, memorials have also been known as *shang-shu*[3] [that is, presentation of a *shu*]. As there have been good scholars in great number, the literary quality of the *shu* has been most commendable. Chia I's memorial on the importance of agriculture, Ch'ao Ts'o's on military affairs, K'uang Heng's on sacrificial rites to heaven, Wang Chi's on the principle of conduct, or *li*, Wen Shu's on mitigating criminal punishment, and Ku Yung's remonstrating against the belief in the immortals[4] are works marked by clear-cut and effective reasoning, and smooth and readable literary style. These writers may be said to have known the main fine points of the genre.

The Later Han witnessed the emergence of many worthies, the brilliance of whose magnificent utterances has not been dimmed. Yang Ping's urgent remonstrance with the emperor on the basis of a natural calamity,[5] and Ch'en Fan's indignation about discriminatory grants of royal favor[6] are works [characterized by advice so frank as to be painful in the ear] as a fishbone [in the throat].[7] Chang Heng's criticism of earlier historical works,[8] and Ts'ai Yung's concern about court rituals[9] are specimens of erudition and lucidity.

[2] A good illustration of the assumed literary principle that the quality of a government is reflected in the literary writings of the time.

[3] *Shu* means to analyze systematically.

[4] A belief advocated by the religious Taoists. Many Chinese rulers, desperate for immortality, succumbed to it.

[5] Emperor Huan, 147-167, overindulged in pleasures. One day when he was out visiting, a great tree was blown down, roots and all, by a big wind. Yang Ping took this as an omen which augured ill for the emperor if he did not mend his ways. See his biography in *Hou-han-shu*.

[6] Also written during the reign of Emperor Huan.

[7] Straightforward advice hurts one's ear as a fishbone in one's throat hurts his throat. Hence a fishbone in the throat becomes a figure for frank advice.

[8] Chang Heng, in his memorial to Emperor An, 107-125, listed over ten items in Ssu-ma Ch'ien's *Shih-chi* and Pan Ku's *Han-shu* which were not in accord with historical facts, and expressed the desire to work in the Tung-kuan where all historical records were kept. See his biography in the *Hou-han-shu*, chüan 89.

[9] See his biography in the *Hou-han-shu*, chüan 90 hsia.

In the Wei dynasty there arose many prominent ministers, who produced a large number of literary works. Kao T'ang's [or Kao T'ang-lung's] astrological memorial,[10] Huang Kuan's memorial on education, Wang Lang's on economy, and Chen I's on the competitive examinations dealt with their subject matters exhaustively, and with a thorough knowledge of government.

The Chin dynasty was afflicted with a great deal of trouble, and under these adverse circumstances masses of people were forced to take to the road. Liu Sung's memorial expressing his concern about the situation of the times, and that of Wen Ch'iao expressing his anxiety about the lavish expenditures on construction, set the pattern of loyalty for those in charge of the management of the state.

The *tsou* as a form of writing demands as its foundation the qualities of lucidity, truthfulness, simplicity, and sincerity; and it opens with an approach which is analytical and systematic. The ideas expounded should be cogent enough to fire enthusiasm for carrying the task to completion, and the experience of the author broad enough to enable him to follow out all the ramifications of the reasoning. He should consider the principles prevailing in ancient times in his management of the present, and keep the mass of details under control and reduce them to the essential. It is in these that the substance of this form of writing consists.

The *tsou's* function in accusation and impeachment is to clarify the law and rid the state of evil. The T'ai-p'u of the Chou checked a criminal act and corrected evil conduct; the Yü-shih of the Ch'in enforced the law; the Han created the Chung-ch'en to be in charge of accusation and impeachment.[11] These officers occupied a position similar to that of a striking hawk,[12] and so had to grind and sharpen their spirits to such a point that stormy winds would whirl from the

---

[10] Certain astronomical phenomena were taken to be a warning given by the August Heaven to the Son of Heaven for his misconduct.

[11] T'ai-p'u, Yü-shih, and Chung-ch'en were law-enforcing offices of the respective dynasties.

[12] Hawk is used as a figure for a law-enforcing officer because of the similar nature of ruthlessness.

tips of their brushes and cutting frosts settle on their bamboo strips.[13] K'ung Kuang's memorial accusing Tung Hsien is a factual narrative of the latter's crime, while that of Lu Ts'ui accusing K'ung Yung is false and mudslinging libel. The heart of a great scholar is indeed different from that of a treacherous man.[14] Fu Hsien [of Chin, 239-294] was a man of strong and candid character, and his memorials are marked with firm and biting statements. Liu Wei [of Chin, flourishing about 317] was stern and just, and yet his impeachment memorials are often vague and sketchy. Each seems to have his own way of doing things. Later writers of impeachment memorials used these as their references, and although new forms were emerging every day, the old pattern has been preserved unchanged.

While the aim of an armorer is to protect, that of a maker of arrows is to kill.[15] Since it is its purpose to expose evil, an impeachment memorial cannot help but be severe and harsh. In the *Book of Poetry*, when censuring a sycophant, it says, "Throw him to the wolf and tiger";[16] in the *Book of Rites*, when showing displeasure toward those who are unprincipled, it compares them to parrots or chimpanzees;[17] Mo Ti, in denouncing the Confucians, looked upon them as sheep and hogs; while Mencius, when ridiculing the Mohists, compared them to birds and beasts.[18] If we find such cutting expressions in *Poetry, Rites, Mencius*, and *Motzu*, how can we expect impeachment memorials, whose very nature is severeness, to be free from them? Thus, writers in general vie with one another in the art of upbraiding. They blow aside the fur to seek faults[19] and penetrate the bone to find crimes.[20] They

---

[13] These were necessary paraphernalia for rendering a court judgment.

[14] See Tung Hsien's biography in *Han-shu*, chüan 93, and that of K'ung Yung in *Hou-han-shu*, chüan 100.

[15] *Mengtzu yin-te*, 13/2A/7. [16] *Mao-shih yin-te*, 48/200/6.

[17] The *Book of Rites. See Li-chi yin-te*, 1/6, "Ch'ü-li." Both parrots and chimpanzees can talk, but they are not men because they do not live according to moral principles (*li*). If a man failed to live according to moral principles, he would be just another parrot or chimpanzee.

[18] *Motzu*, "Fei-ju," hsia; *Mengtzu yin-te*, 25/3B/9.

[19] A phrase used in the biography of Prince Ching of Chung-shan in *Han-shu*, meaning to go out of the way to discover weak points.

[20] This line may also be interpreted as: ". . . and are cruel and ruthless in their bone-penetrating accusations."

seem to be good at scolding, but often miss the golden mean. If only they could open wide the gate of morals and post high principles, or erect a standard by pointing to the road of righteousness, then those who climbed over forbidden walls would have their legs broken and those who sought unsanctioned short cuts would lose their toes.[21] And where would be the necessity for hot words and scandalous utterances, or the desire to blame and censure? Thus, in an effort to establish a standard and to apply its criteria for this form of writing, one should first understand its essential nature. Its structure should conform to a certain classic form and its language possess a style worthy of becoming a prevailing standard. In order to be an outstanding hero among the feasting guests, upright and reverent within and righteous and impartial without, a writer in this genre should possess the legalist spirit of law and the literary vigor of the Confucians; he should be able to oppose powerful and ruthless forces unafraid[22] and convey his convictions through ink, giving no quarter to crooked elements;[23] indeed, his voice should be a moving influence beyond the bamboo strips.

Ch'i, or to inform, means literally "to open." When Kao-tsung [Emperor Wu-ting of the Shang; 1339-1279 B.C.] said, "Open your heart and fertilize my mind,"[24] he was using the term in this sense. The name of Emperor Ching [of the Early Han] was Ch'i, hence it was taboo during the Han and the term *ch'i* was not used.[25] It was during the Wei period that short notes to the throne were called *ch'i*. Sometimes at the end of a memorial, *ching-ch'i* ["I respectfully open my heart," or "respectfully submitted"] was used as a closing phrase. Since the time of Chin, *ch'i* has become current in use. It is used either as a *piao* or as a *tsou*. In presenting political views it is used as an

---

[21] Climbing walls and taking short cuts are figures for behavior which does not conform to the recognized moral standard.

[22] *Mao-shih yin-te*, 71/260/5.   [23] *Ibid.*, 66/253/5.

[24] Kao-tsung procured the services of Fu Yüeh, an able minister who had appeared to him in a dream. The line quoted was addressed to Fu. The term for "open" is *ch'i*. *Shang-shu t'ung-chien*, 17/0160-5.

[25] The people are not allowed to speak or write the character which happens to be part of the name of their ruler or of their father. To violate this taboo is considered an act of sacrilege.

alternate to the *tsou*, and it becomes a substitute for the *piao* when it is used to decline the conferment of a title of nobility or to express gratitude for royal grace. It is of the very essence of its nature to be pure, to be conformable to the principles of rhetoric and swift in tempo, to be distinct and clean in presenting arguments, and to be in beautiful literary form but without excessive ornamentation. These, in general, are some of the ideas governing the genre *ch'i*.

Again, the *piao* and *tsou* contain ideas which are firm and to the point; they are known as "frank speaking," and [because it is frank, aims at correcting the] bias; of course, if the kingly way itself is infested with personal bias, the spirit of the broad and grand is violated.[26] [But at any rate, it is because of] its [aiming at correcting] the personal bias[27] [that this form] is known as frank speaking. And Emperor Ch'eng of the Han highly praised Pan Po's frank address, just because he valued straightforwardness.

Ever since the establishment during the Han dynasty of the eight talented scholars,[28] there have been secret memorials concerning the principles of *yin* and *yang*. These memorials were submitted in sealed black pouches, a circumstance which earned them the name of "sealed memorials." Now, when Ch'ao Ts'o had received instruction in the *Book of History* [from Fu-sheng], he came back and reported to the emperor on *pien-i* [that is, on all that was convenient (*pien*) to the government and all that was suitable (*i*) to the people]. And later such *pien-i* were often attached to the "sealed memorials," the idea being to keep the reports a top government secret. The king's ministers, unselfish in motive,[29] will always speak frankly. So when there

---

[26] In the "Hung Fan" of the *Book of History* we have: "There is neither one-sidedness nor partisan spirit, for broad and grand is the kingly way; and there is neither partisan spirit nor one-sidedness, for the kingly way is level and plain." *Shang-shu t'ung-chien*, 24/0490-505.

[27] The text is corrupt. The interpretation given here is based on the emendated readings of Fan Wen-lan and Wang Li-ch'i.

[28] Each of these was entrusted with one special duty: some in charge of harmonizing the *yin* and the *yang* principles, some in charge of the calendar, music, etc. See "Hsü li-yüeh chih" in *Hou-han-shu*, and Chang-huai's commentary.

[29] An abbreviated quotation from the *Book of Changes*, statement attached to line two of the hexagram *chien*. See *Chou-i yin-te*, 24/39/2. The full line: "The king's minister

are good ministers, there will be good government. Therefore it is not necessary to dwell at length on this form of writing.

   The Tsan:
The Ssu-chih[30] in black garb
Keeps government clean of all evil influences.
With brush sharp as a sword
And ink deadly as poisonous wine,
His censorious cut may penetrate the bone,
And yet it will not mar the complexion.
In offering political views or suggesting policies,
He is the man to trust.

XXIV. Discussion and Answer (The I and the Tui)

On the Plain of Chou [King Wen's grandfather, the ancient lord Tan-fu] asked questions and discussed [matters],[1] and "discussion" is the meaning of the term *i*. The literal meaning of *i*, or to discuss, is *i*, or appropriate, [so that the complete concept is] "an examination of matters to find out what is appropriate." In the *Book of Changes* under the hexagram *chieh*, or limitation, it is said, [Guided by hexagram *chieh*] the superior man creates measures and discusses the nature of virtue and conduct.[2] Now the "Book of Chou" [in the *Book of History*] says, "When affairs are discussed according to certain rules

---

is beset by obstruction upon obstruction, but it is not due to his selfish motive."

   [30] An office created in the Han to assist the prime minister in exposing the corrupt elements in the government.

   [1] A combination of ideas contained in two lines in Poem 237 in the *Book of Poetry*. In this poem the first effort in the building of the Chou dynasty is described. Tan-fu was discussing problems with those who chose to follow him to Mount Ch'i, to which they removed under the pressure of the western tribes. As is true in so many cases, it is the term "discussing" which attracts our author in whatever context it occurs.

   [2] *Chou-i yin-te*, 36-37/60/hsiang.

[or *chih*], the government will be free from error."³ So according to the principles laid down in the Classics themselves, in this type of discussion *chieh-chih* [that is, "limitation and regulation," or simply "the exercise of control"] must be emphasized.

Kuan Chung once said that Hsüan-yüan [the Yellow Emperor] instituted the practice of *i* in the Tower of Enlightenment.⁴ So it is deeply rooted in the distant past. During the difficult times of inundation, Yao asked the four chiefs for advice; and Shun, in selecting men to fill the hundred offices, asked for the opinion of the five ministers. The rise of the three dynasties [Hsia, Shang, and Chou] was due to their efforts in seeking advice from the woodcutters [or the common people]. In the *Ch'un-ch'iu* it is related that when [Ch'u] freed the duke of Sung, Duke Hsi of Lu took part in the discussion.⁵ When King Wu-ling of Chao was planning to adopt barbarian dress,⁶ his policy was contested [*tseng-lun*] by his uncle [Prince Ch'eng].⁷ And the reform policy of Shang Yang was hotly argued [*chiao-pien*] by Kan Lung.⁸ Although the forms [*i*, or discussion; *lun*, or discourse; and *pien*, or argument] are all different, it is easy to see in what ways they agree and differ.

It was in the Han dynasty that *po-i* became an independent term.⁹ *Po* means mixed [originally, mixed of different colors]. When the *i*

³ *Shang-shu t'ung-chien*, 40/0318-25.

⁴ See *Kuantzu*, "Huan-kung wen" (Chu-tzu chi-ch'eng ed.), chüan 18, Chapter 56, p. 302.

⁵ *Ch'un-ch'iu ching-chuan yin-te*, 117-118/Hsi 21/8, 8 Kung-yang.

⁶ This took place in 306 B.C. See "Chao Shih-chia" in *Shih-chi*.

⁷ *I* has been defined in Chapter XXII as "to maintain a difference of opinion." So even though the term *i* does not appear in this and the following instance, this sense of the term is apparently meant when the author speaks of "contesting" or "arguing."

⁸ See the biography of Lord Shang in *Shih-chi*. Lord Shang was a legalist and, like all the legalists, advocated changes in the government, to meet the need of the time, which were based upon a concept of history closer to that of modern times than any other in ancient China. But Kan Lung, arguing on the basis of ancient sages' principles, tried to wreck his reform policy. In all these cases, what interests the author is the fact of arguing or discussing. The various forms of arguing or discussing represent for him the different moments in the development of the form of writing called *i* in this chapter.

⁹ See the four forms of memorials in Chapter XXII, of which the fourth is *i*, an abbreviated form of *po-i*. *Po-i* is the kind of memorial which maintains a personal opinion differing from the opinion of others.

is not pure but mixed, it is characterized as *po*. With the explicit definition of the *i* during the two Han periods, it achieved a distinct form. As the court was crowded with talented scholars, it was filled with their discourse. Chia I, in his effort to express the ideas for the old scholars at court, was an example of a nimble talent for discussion.[10] As for Chu-fu's *i* arguing against the prohibition of carrying bows,[11] [Han] An-kuo's argument about the Huns,[12] Chia Chüan-chih's contention over the expedition against Chu-yai,[13] and Liu Hsin's *i* on the controversy over the worship of the royal ancestors,[14] they may differ in content as well as in language, but they have all achieved the essential aims of the genre.

Then there were Chang Min's judgment on the law governing insult,[15] Kuo Kung's argument about exercising the power of execution on one's own authority,[16] Ch'eng Hsiao's condemnation of the

[10] See his biography in *Shih-chi*.

[11] "Chu Fu" should be "Wu-ch'iu." See the biography of Wu-ch'iu Shou-wang in *Han-shu*, where the *i* is recorded.

[12] See his biography in *Han-shu*.

[13] See his biography in *Han-shu*. Chu-yai is the present Hai-nan island south of Kuangtung province. The natives rebelled against the Han rule, and there was talk of sending an expedition against them. Chia Chüan-chih argued against it.

[14] During the first year of Emperor Ai (6 B.C.), after a long controversy over the problem of how many ancestral halls were to be maintained by the ruling house and which were to be discontinued after a certain period, Liu Hsin came forth with the proposal, based on the "Wang-chih" (the King's Institution) in the *Li-chi*, that the Son of Heaven maintain seven ancestral halls, which he defended against various other proposals, including one that only five halls be maintained. Liu Hsin also believed that a ruler with great achievements should have a hall maintained permanently. He included in this category the hall of Emperor Wu, which it had previously been urged should be discontinued at a given time.

[15] During the reign of Chien-ch'u (76-83) a son killed a man who had insulted his father. Emperor Chang (76-88) pardoned him, saving him from execution, the punishment for killing. During the next reign, that of Emperor Ho (89-105), this precedent became established as law, known as the law governing insult. Chang Min, afraid that this might lead to lawlessness, argued against it. Emperor Ho accepted his advice.

[16] During the reign of Yung-p'ing (58-59), Ch'in P'eng, a subordinate of General Tou Ku, was given a separate command. He executed people on his own authority. Tou Ku reported it to the throne as a case of insubordination. The emperor had the ministers at court discuss the matter. With the exception of Kuo Kung, all ministers were in favor of Tou Ku's opinion that Ch'in P'eng had no authority to execute people without first reporting the case to his superior. Kuo argued that since P'eng had been given a separate command, he should also exercise the authority of control over his forces, as it would be impossible for him to carry out his duty with any degree of efficiency if he had to

chiao-shih,[17] Ssu-ma Chih's discussion about the use of coin,[18] Ho Tseng's proposal to exempt married daughters from being involved in the crime of their father's family,[19] Ch'in Hsiu's suggestion on Chia Ch'ung's posthumous title;[20] all these are good and appropriate in view of the facts they were dealing with. The authors may be said to have understood the principles of the form of *i*.

During the Han period Ying Shao led the group of the best disputants; and during Chin times it was Fu Hsien who stood out among the able *i* writers. Chung-yüan [or Ying Shao], a learned scholar of antiquity, was systematic in explanation and organization; Ch'ang-yü [or Fu Hsien], on the other hand, though possessing considerable knowledge of government, was rather loose and verbose in his presentation. Lu Chi's judgment in his discussion [of the proper form for the biographies of the first three rulers of] the Chin dynasty[21] is

---

consult his superior in matters which required immediate decision. The emperor accepted his opinion.

[17] The chiao-shih were all-purpose officials created during the reign of Emperor Wu of Han to meet a certain emergency; they became very powerful and arrogant during the time of Chia-p'ing (249-254) of the Wei dynasty. They interfered with every office, simply because there was no clear-cut definition of their functions. As a result of Ch'eng's argument against them, the office was abolished.

[18] In 221 Emperor Wen of the Wei dynasty abolished the use of coin and ordered grains and silk to be used in its stead. During the next reign, speculators wet the grain and reduced the weight of the silk, creating a great deal of confusion. Ssu-ma Chih counseled returning to the use of coin. Emperor Ming ordered that the use of coin be restored.

[19] Previously a woman had been criminally implicated if either her father's family or her husband's had committed a crime. Ho Tseng, in the memorial prepared for him by Ch'eng Hsien, argued that it was against the spirit of the law to place a woman in double jeopardy. His final contention was that an unmarried woman should be involved only in her father's crime, and a married woman only in that of her husband's family.

[20] Chia Ch'ung, one of the strong men who helped the house of Ssu-ma in usurping the throne from the house of Ts'ao and establishing the Chin dynasty, died without male issue. His wife adopted the son of their daughter, whose surname was Han, to carry on the line. Ch'in Hsiu ridiculed this act. When the imperial order came that a posthumous title be suggested for Chia Ch'ung, Ch'in Hsiu proposed *huang*, a title traditionally conferred upon those whose conduct was not in accordance with the correct principles. The proposal was not accepted.

[21] Lu's opinion in this matter is preserved in *Ch'u-shüeh chi*, a collection, edited by Hsu Chien *et al.* of the T'ang under the auspices of the imperial personage. Lu Chi believed that the first three rulers of the Chin dynasty had been ministers of the Wei dynasty throughout their lives, and hence their lives should be written in the form of "true records," but that since they enjoyed the name of rulers the style should be that of *chi*, or annals. See Chapter XVI on History.

sharp and keen. However, its literary vigor suffers from his verbosity. But nevertheless each writer has his own beauty and has preserved for us his characteristic style.

Action should be preceded by discussion[22] and understanding must come from investigation of the doubtful;[23] for it is thus that one is enabled to approach the task of dealing with affairs of state in a spirit of reverence and vigilance capable of rendering his statescraft widely effective. Therefore, in substance, the *i* must be based on an adoption of the Classics as pivot; on a selection of facts from previous times, adapted to the changing needs of the present; on reasoning which does not try to complicate matters by adducing inconsequential ramifications, and must use rhetoric which does not elaborate any embellishment unnecessarily. When dealing with worship and sacrifice, the writer should know thoroughly the rites connected with it, and in military matters, he should be versed in the art of war. A knowledge of agriculture is a prerequisite for dealing with agricultural matters, and a thorough understanding of law is the *sine qua non* of any attempt to pass a legal judgment. When all these requirements have been met, the writer may bring forth ideas which are transparently clear, succinctly couched in language which is both accurate and proper. His ability to use language should appear in the lucidity and purity of his style, and he should not aim at artifice through excessive ornament. In dealing with events he should strive for clearness and thoroughness, and he should never seek originality by seemingly profound but vague presentation. This is the general outline of the form of *i*. If a writer ignorant of the art of government wields his brush and plays with literary composition, piling random phrase upon phrase, fabricating and concocting to show his cleverness, not only is his empty rhetoric refuted in the face of facts, but even the little reason he may have is buried under the pile of his own aimless rhetoric. Long ago, the Marquis of Ch'in, who was marrying his daughter to the Prince of Chin, sent along [seventy] beautifully dressed maids-in-

[22] *Chou-i yin-te*, 41/hsi hsiang/6.   [23] *Shang-shu t'ung-chien*, 24/0137-40.

waiting, and the Prince of Chin preferred the maids to the princess.[24]
A man from Ch'u sold pearls in a cassia-tinted magnolia case to a
man of Cheng, and the man of Cheng bought the case and returned
the pearls.[25] If one's language surpasses his ideas, permitting the un-
essential to outshine the fundamental, it is simply a repetition of the
cases of the Ch'in princess and the Ch'u pearls.

In a *tui-ts'e*,[26] one expresses his political opinion in answer to questions given in an edict; and in a *she-ts'e*,[27] one makes an investigation
of the matter in question and then presents his opinion. When one's
words are to the point, it is like hitting the mark in archer target-
practice. Though these terms are different from *i*, they are, in fact, *i*
under new garb.

In ancient times the selection of accomplished scholars was made by
choosing those able in practical affairs and investigating their words.
It was in the middle of the reign of Emperor Wen of the Han [179-157
B.C.] that the recommendation of the *hsien-liang*, or the virtuous and
good, was first put into practice.[28] And Ch'ao Ts'o, in his *tui-ts'e*,[29]
proved himself the best of all. Emperor Wu [140-87 B.C.], bent on a
more enlightened government, sought men of eminent ability. At that
time, in the *tui-ts'e* competition, the first man on the list received immediate official appointment, and in the *she-ts'e* competition, the one
who was in the *chia* or the highest category[30] entered officialdom. These
were important among the methods used for the selection of men of
ability. Ch'ao Ts'o in his *tui-ts'e* drew evidence from both ancient and

[24] See *Han-fei-tzu*, chüan 11, Chapter 32, "Wai ch'u-shuo," tso, hsiang, p. 198.
[25] *Ibid.*, pp. 198-99.
[26] A memorial in which one answers specific questions in an edict.
[27] Literally, to shoot an edict, a memorial in which one gives an answer to a question
he chooses from among a number of questions, the nature of which is not previously
revealed.
[28] This occurred in the year 165 B.C., when Ch'ao Ts'o came out first on the list.
Early in the second year of the reign of Emperor Wen, 178 B.C., the first imperial edict
went out for the recommendation of the virtuous and good, but it was the second edict
which brought in the first crop of them.
[29] In this memorial Ch'ao gave an answer to the emperor's question on the problem
of establishing peace and prosperity.
[30] The questions to be answered in a *she-ts'e* are classified into different categories
according to the degree of their difficulty. The most difficult are in the *chia* category.

modern sources; his language is clear-cut and effective, and the facts
he cites are pertinent and well chosen. His placement at the top of the
list was very well justified indeed. [Tung] Chung-shu's *tui-ts'e* continued the tradition set forth in the *Ch'un-ch'iu*. His was grounded
in the transforming principles of the *yin* and the *yang*, and he was
fully cognizant of the changes which took place in succeeding dynasties.
He had to deal with a large mass of material, but he remained free
from distraction. This was because he thoroughly understood the
principles of things. Kung-sun [Hung's] *tui-ts'e* is brief, showing no
sign of learned scholarship; but in view of his concentration on essentials and expression of them in succinct language, and the pertinence of the facts he cited to make clear the true nature of the situation,
he deserved his elevation to the top by the Son of Heaven in spite of
his low rating by the T'ai-ch'ang.[31] Tu Ch'in's *tui-ts'e* was sketchy
and left some of the imperial questions unanswered, but it pointed
out the real source of the emperor's trouble;[32] he wrote to express his
views on politics and government; he was not writing simply for
writing's sake. In the Later Han, Lu P'ei's *tui-ts'e* was sincere and
simple in language and in spirit. He brought to the form the grace
and elegance of a great Confucian, and [from among more than a
hundred scholars] he alone was placed at the top. The five writers
listed above set the bright standard of former times. Since then Wei
and Chin writers have gone in for literary embellishment. We can
expect a great deal of difficulty when one whose chief interest is in
embellishment tries to record facts; and those selected to answer imperial questions in later times often pleaded illness and kept away from
the tests. Thus it became impossible to get writing which was even
literary. During the Han time when a feast was given in honor of the
po-shih, or learned scholars, pheasants gathered in the court,[33] but

[31] An office in charge of ceremonial rites, which traditionally is also in charge of
education and state examination.

[32] The questions for answers came from Emperor Ch'eng (32-7 B.C.), who indulged
in women. At the end of Tu Ch'in's answer, he admonished the emperor about his
indulgence, which was the emperor's real trouble.

[33] This happened in 18 B.C., the third year of Hung-chia (20-17 B.C.) during the

when the Chin [emperor] examined the *hsiu-ts'ai*, or outstanding talents, only *chün*, or a species of deer, appeared.[34] There is nothing strange about these [contrasting] circumstances, because in one case the examination system was well kept, while in the other case it showed signs of neglect.

A *po-i*[35] is a memorial in which one argues one-sidedly, and each arguer holds to his own opinion. In a *tui-ts'e*, one develops his point of view in answer to the imperial questions in order to bring forth the principles of government. In dealing with the events of the day, he shows his deep understanding of the art of ruling, and in presenting his reasons, he proves to be a man of insight with respect to the current situation. He goes back to the Three Sovereigns and the Five Emperors for suggestions to mould the present world, and his is not circuitous high-sounding empty talk. He recommends measures which are expedient under changing circumstances to get the people out of difficulty, and his is not the sharp eloquence of a sophist. Like winds sweeping over the vastness of space and reaching far, or a river full and yet not overflowing—a *tui* such as this is an excellent answer in the court of the king.

Difficult indeed is the task of evaluating the talent of a scholar. He may be versed in the art of ruling but lack the ability to write, or he may possess literary ability and yet be inexperienced in government.

---

reign of Emperor Ch'eng. The gathering of pheasants was considered a good omen, happening only at a time when there was good government and peace, and when art and literature were patronized at court.

[34] The connotation of the term *chün* is not clear. Sun Sheng took it to be an auspicious omen, indicating patronage of art and literature at court. See *Chin-shu*, "Wu-hsing-chi." In this sense, its appearance could be considered as untimely, as in the case of the appearance of the unicorn, which prompted Confucius to give up editing the *Ch'un-ch'iu*. From the context, however, the term *chün* seems to augur ill, perhaps to symbolize a lack of patronage of art and literature. In Chapter XLVIII Liu Hsieh contrasted *chün* with *lin*, the legendary unicorn. But this is hardly sufficient evidence to establish the connotation of the term *chün*, because in that chapter he also contrasted *chih*, a pheasant, which means a good omen in our present context, with *feng*, a phoenix, thus making *chih* necessarily a symbol for something not auspicious. Perhaps, this is another case of our author's looseness in the use of terms.

[35] See note 9 above.

The object of selection through *tui-ts'e* should be men of versatile talents, men full of ideas who have enough literary ability to communicate them far and wide. Rare indeed is such talent!

    The Tsan:
The object of the *i* is political planning,
And there should be a complete accord between the word and the fact.
There should always be a valid reason for making any judgment,
And the language in which it is expressed should never be weak.
In answering imperial questions at court,
Many minds meet at the same time to reach concord.
The principles of government are held in high esteem,
And are conveyed far and wide in elegant form.

XXV. Epistolary Writing (The Shu and the Chi)

The great Shun [of the Yü dynasty] said, "The function of *shu* is to keep records,"[1] that is, to record the events of the day. For *shu* is the general name for the words of sages and men of virtue. It is the nature of the *shu* that its principal emphasis is on words. Yang Hsiung said, "Words are the sound of the mind; and *shu* is its picture."[2] When the mind's sound and picture take form, we shall be able to see in them the character of the man, whether he is a man of virtue or a petty man. Thus by *shu* is meant to express, that is to express one's mind in words and put them down on bamboo or wooden slips. This is the result of taking a suggestion from the hexagram *kuai*,[3] whose emphasis is on clear-cut lucidity.

[1] *Shang-shu t'ung-chien*, 5/0271-4. *Shu* here means writing in the form of a book. Later it came to mean letter writing.
[2] *Yang-tzu fa-yen* (Chu-tzu chi-ch'eng ed.), chüan 5, p. 14. Here *shu* apparently means writing down the words.
[3] Hexagram no. 43. See *I-ching*, I, 177.

During the Three Dynasties[4] the function of the government was simple, and there was little epistolary writing. During the period of Ch'un-ch'iu, international relations became more complicated, and the volume of letters and number of emissaries greatly increased. Jao-ch'ao presented Shih-hui a *ts'e*,[5] Tzu-chia [of Cheng] wrote a letter to Chao Hsüan-tzu [of Chin],[6] Wu-ch'en left Tzu-fan a note,[7] and Tzu-ch'an [of Cheng] sent a letter to Fan Hsüan-tzu of Chin remonstrating [against Chin's demanding heavy tribute from smaller states].[8] Reading these four letters, one feels he is talking face to face with the authors. Again when [Duke Ch'eng of] T'eng died, Tzu-shu Ching-shu [of Lu] presented T'eng with a letter of condolence.[9] From the existence of these examples, we know that words entrusted to envoys were often put down in the form of epistles.

The epistolary writings during the Seven States period were clever and beautiful, and there were many of them. And the body of writing of this type dating from the time of Han presents a profuse variety of expressions and spirits. Shih-ch'ien's [or Ssu-ma Ch'ien's] letter to Jen-an, Tung-fang So's letter arguing with Kung-sun [Hung], Yang Yün's answer to [Sun] Hui-tsung, and Tzu-yün's [or Yang Hsiung's] reply to Liu Hsin are all works characterized by grand ideas and a lofty spirit, each having its own particular pattern; each is an em-

[4] Traditionally, the three dynasties of Hsia, Shang, and Chou. Here the author apparently used it to include Hsia, Shang, and the first part of Chou.

[5] There are two interpretations of the term *ts'e*: a horsewhip and a bamboo slip containing a political message. The author apparently adopted the second interpretation. But the first interpretation is more fitting with the situation of a departing man. See *Tso-chuan*, Duke Wen, thirteenth year (Shih-san-ching chu-su ed.), chüan 19 hsia, p. 10b, commentaries.

[6] In the seventeenth year of Duke Wen of Lu, Chin met with the lords at Huang-fu in a conference. The Duke of Chin refused to see the Marquis of Cheng because Cheng had shown some tendency to align itself with the state of Ch'u. Cheng Tzu-chia wrote the letter to explain Cheng's earlier dealings with Ch'u. See *Ch'un-ch'iu ching-chuan yin-te*, 174/ Wen 17/ 5 Tso.

[7] Wu-chen, a minister of Ch'u, who fled to Chin when Tzu-fan and Tzu-chung, on account of old grudges, massacred Wu-ch'en's clan, wrote a note to Tzu-fan and Tzu-chung from Chin, stating that he would not give either of them any rest. He then went from Chin to Wu, an undeveloped state neighboring Ch'u, and taught the Wu people the art of war. After this, Wu became a constant threat to Ch'u, giving Tzu-fan and Tzu-chung no rest at all. *Ibid.*, 225/Ch'eng 7/ 10 Tso.

[8] *Ibid.*, 302/Hsiang 24/fu 1.   [9] *Li-chi yin-te*, 4/46.

broidery on a foot of silk,[10] expressing all the flutterings and oscillations of the square-inch heart.[11]

In the Later Han period, Ts'ui Yüan was especially good at the art of letter writing. During the Wei, Yüan-yü [or Juan Yü ?] was described as "light and swift."[12] And the writings of Wen-chü [or K'ung Yung] were all preserved, including fragments [in recognition of their excellence].[13] Hsiu-lien [or Ying Chü] loved letter writing and paid much attention to its perfection, but his must be ranked as secondary. Hsi K'ang's letter severing friendly relations [with Shan T'ao; 205-283] is one marked by lofty ideas and a grand style.[14] Chao Chih's letter [to Hsi Fan] depicting his sadness at separation is expressive of the eagerness and impatience of youth. As to the hundred letters dictated by Ch'en Tsun, each conveys his feelings in exactly the right measure, and as to those written by Ni Heng [for Huang Tsu], each is appropriate in expressing sentiments toward relations of all degrees of closeness. These two were especially talented in the art of letter writing.

A general survey of the nature of *shu* reveals that its purpose is to state one's feelings in words without reserve, and its function is to unburden the mind of its melancholy thought in the form of elegant colors. Therefore its style should be orderly and smooth, capable of expressing the spirit of the writer, easy and soft and pleasant to the reader. With its language clear and natural, it is indeed the presentation of the sound of the heart.

The distinction of men of honor and nobility is brought out by the attitude of reverence expressed in the ceremonial form. Before the Warring States period, the epistles of both the ruler and the ministers were styled *shu*. With the establishment of Ch'in institutions, we ob-

10 Silk was then the writing material.

11 See p. 108 above, and note 39, Chapter XVIII.

12 A term Wei Wen-ti—Ts'ao P'ei—used in his letter to Wu Chih (?-230) to describe Juan Yü's letter writing. See *Wen-hsüan* (Ssu pu pei-yao ed.), chüan 42, p. 421.

13 Wei Wen-ti liked K'ung Yung's writing so much that he ordered everything written by him to be presented to the court for prizes of gold and silk.

14 Shan T'ao, about to retire, was going to recommend Hsi K'ang to take his place. On hearing this, Hsi wrote a letter swearing to have nothing to do with him. Hsi, who had a Taoist bent, was afraid to be mixed up in the politics of that tumultuous time.

serve the first appearance of *piao* and *tsou*.[15] In the case of the epistles
to princes and dukes, the term *tsou-shu*, or memorial letter, was also
used. The *tsou-shu* of Chang Ch'ang to the mother of Prince Chiao-
tung expresses excellent ideas.[16] Various terms appeared during the
Later Han. In the office of the [San-]kung [the three highest ministers],
the term *tsou-chi*, or letter presenting the record, was used [for corre-
spondence], while in the headquarters of local generals, *tsou-ch'ien*, or
letter presenting the note, was used. *Chi* means to express one's ideas,
that is, to present his ideas. *Ch'ien* means to express, that is, to express
and indicate one's feelings. Ts'ui Shih's *tsou-chi* [to Liang Chi][17]
sounded the moral tone of self-effacement and yielding; while Huang
Hsiang's *tsou-ch'ien* at Chiang-hsia[18] left behind a pattern in expressing
reverence. Kung-kan's [or Liu Chen's] *ch'ien* and *chi*, or letters to
high ministers and local generals, or letter writing in general, are
beautiful and contain ideas which prove to be beneficial advice to
the receivers. And yet Tzu-huan [or Ts'ao P'ei] left him out [of his
essay on literature], a fact which accounts for his neglect by the world.
If we overlook the reputation and concentrate on the fact, we shall see
that Liu Ch'en's epistolary writings are much more beautiful than his
poetry. Liu I's letter expressing his gratitude for royal grace contains
pertinent similes reflecting his sincere sentiment, and Lu Chi's letter
defending himself is thorough in expressing his feeling and artful in
form. Both may be considered good specimens of the *ch'ien*. *Ch'ien*
and *chi* are related to the *piao*, or the memorial expressing gratitude,
on one hand, and to the *shu*, or memorial letter, on the other. They
should be written in a spirit of reverence without any sign of fear,
and should be succinct without showing any arrogance, pure and
graceful in unfolding the wealth of the writer's talents, and bright and
colorful in embodying their sounds in a literary form. These characteristics form the special province of *ch'ien* and *chi*.

[15] See Chapters XXII and XXIII.
[16] The prince's mother indulged in hunting. Chang Ch'ang cited good examples from
the past to warn her concerning her indulgence.
[17] Ts'ui served under Liang Chi. The letter is lost.
[18] Also lost.

The scope of *shu-chi*[19] is vast, covering a number of forms. Since days of old there have been many terms used to designate various kinds of notes and records. For those used in ruling and guiding the people, we have: *p'u*, or chronicle; *chi*, or register; *pu*, or warrant; and *lu*, or record; in medicine, chronology, astrology, and divination, we have: *fang*, or prescription; *shu*, or operation; *chan*, or divination; and *shih*, or formula; in proclaiming laws and military movement, we have: *lü*, or law; *ling*, or order; *fa*, or regulation; and *chih*, or ordinance; in creating confidence in trade relations, we have: *fu*, or tally; *ch'i*, or contract; *chüan*, or bond; and *shu*, or sales slip; in government requests for information, we have: *kuan*, or credential; *tz'u*, or to pierce; *chieh*, or record of settlement; and *tieh*, or memorandum; and in expressing their feelings, the people use: *chuan*, or notice; *lieh*, or narrative account; *tz'u*, or *viva voce*; and *yen*, or proverb. All these give utterance to the reasons formed in the mind and present it in words. Although they are insignificant as literary forms, they precede everything else in importance in handling government affairs.

P'u, or chronicle, means literally *p'u*, or comprehensive. [This form] presents the order of successive generations; it is comprehensive in its inclusion of all events. Cheng Hsüan, in preparing a *p'u* for the *Book of Poetry*[20] apparently adopted this sense of the term for his composition.

Chi, or register, means literally *chieh*, or to borrow. Every year the government borrows a labor force from the people, and keeps a classified census on a wooden slip. During the Ch'un-ch'iu period, an office was established in charge of the census register, an instance of *chi*.

Pu, or warrant, means literally, *p'u*, or a vegetable garden; the classified collection of government documents is similar to the planned planting of grasses and trees in a garden.[21] Chang T'ang and Li Kuang

---

[19] This expression has been rendered as "epistolary writing." But from what may be gathered from this last section of the chapter, it seems to have a broader scope, suggesting the English term "memo." This is another case of the loose use of terms.

[20] The work is known as *Shih-p'u*—a chronicle of the *Book of Poetry*.

[21] Apparently *pu* is also used in the sense of a file. How this is connected with the sense of warrants is not clear.

were both served by the officials with warrants, the function of which is to apprehend the fraudulent.

Lu, or record, means literally *ling*, or topic. An ancient history entitled *Shih-pen*[22] keeps records on bamboo slips, with titled topics; hence the use of the term *lu* in regard to it.

Fang, or prescription, means *yü*, or a corner. Each medicinal herb, in healing, has its particular virtue, particularly effective in one corner of the realm of medicine; hence the medicinal formula is known as *fang*.

Shu, or operation, means *lu*, or a road. When we have applied number to the calculation of the calendar, our view of the road [or way] will then become clear. The *Chiu-chang* [Nine chapters on arithmetic] deals with calculus; so it is known as *shu*, or the way of operation. *Wan-pi*[23] of Huai-nan [or Prince An of the Han] also belongs to this group.

Chan, or divination, means literally *chan*, or to spy or watch. Sometimes the stars are observable and sometimes not. Only by waiting and watching is one able to see them. [Duke Hsi of Lu] ascended the terrace and had the astrological changes recorded.[24] So this was called *chan*, or to divine.

Shih, or formula, means literally *tse*, or principle. The waxing and waning of the *yin* and the *yang* principles, or the passing away and coming into being of the five elements, though they appear to be changes which occur without any regularity, may be seen to be obeying certain principles when they are put under observation.

Lü, or law, or pitch pipe, means *chung*, or middle or norm.[25] With the establishment of *huang-chung*[26] the five tones are set correctly.

---

[22] Containing the records of rulers and great ministers from the time of the Yellow Emperor to the end of the Ch'in, together with their posthumous titles.

[23] A work dealing with the calendar and arithmetic.

[24] *Ch'un-ch'iu ching-chuan yin-te*, 94/Hsi 5/ Tso supplement 1.

[25] A pitch pipe is a bamboo tube, whose length determines its tone, used as a tuning fork. There are twelve pitch pipes of various lengths so adjusted that they give twelve semitones, forming a chromatic scale of twelve notes, starting with C. Since they are used for tuning the other instruments, they furnish the law by which tones are determined. Hence law becomes part of the meaning of *lü*.

[26] The first note on the chromatic scale, equivalent to C.

And with the formulation of laws for governing the people, the eight kinds of punishments may be justly applied. To call such laws *lü* shows that they aim at the golden mean or the norm.

Ling, or order, means literally *ming*, or mandate. A mandate proclaims certain prohibitions, as if on the authority of heavenly origin. The order given by Kuan Chung prevailed like a flowing stream because he had the ability to get the people to obey it voluntarily.

Fa, or regulation, means literally *hsiang*, or sign or signal. Military tactics do not confine themselves to following a prescribed plan; but whether an operation is going to be a surprise, or to follow orthodox procedure, there must always be some sign [or signal] to indicate its course. Hence the use of the term *fa*, or regulation or sign.

Chih, or ordinance, means literally *ts'ai*, or to cut or tailor. A *chih* is issued by the superiors to prescribe the conduct of the subordinates, in the same manner as a craftsman manufactures his vessels.

Fu, or tally, means literally *fu*, or authenticity. In calling and summoning troops, one has to guard against false orders; so the command has to have evidence of inner authenticity.[27] During the Three Dynasties, jade was used as a tally, while during the Han times metal and bamboo were used. In later times, these were discarded, and written tallies were substituted for them.

Ch'i, or contract, means *chieh*, or to tie a knot. Life was simple in remote antiquity, and knotted cord was used to make a contract binding. The way modern tribes in the west count and the way peddlers keep records of their money are reminiscent of this practice.

Chüan, or bond, means literally *shu*, or to bind or control, that is, to state binding conditions clearly to avoid possible fraud. Because the characters on a *chüan* are cut into halves, in Chou times a *chüan* was known as halved writing.[28] In ancient times there was also an iron bond, to strengthen one's credit. The bond Wang Pao wrote when he

[27] "Inner authenticity" is a rendering of *chung-fu*, the sixty-first hexagram in the *Book of Changes*.

[28] The phrase "p'an-shu" occurs in "Hsiao-ssu-k'ou" in *Chou-li* (*Chou-li yin-te*, 9/24a). According to a commentator, *p'an-shu* means halved writing.

bought the bearded slave may be considered a humorous pattern of a bond.[29]

Shu, or sales slip, means literally *pu*, or to spread out, in the sense of spreading out sales articles and itemizing them with rough descriptions. Hence small bonds and short writings are known as *shu*.

Kuan, or pass or credentials, means *pi*, or to close. People enter and go out through a gate, and one must be careful in keeping the gate closed. In government it is important to know thoroughly the conditions promoting smooth working or bottlenecks in government operations. When Han Fei asked, "[Kung-]Sun T'an-hui was a virtuous minister, so why was he confined to his district?" he had in mind this kind of carefulness.[30]

Tz'u, or to pierce, means literally *ta*, or to convey. The Ancient Poet pierced wrongdoing by means of satires; and in the *Chou-li* we find three situations in which *tz'u* was employed:[31] When a narrative account of things is successfully conveyed, it is like the piercing of a stoppage by means of a needle.

Chieh, or to untie, or a record of settlement, means literally *shih*, or to resolve, that is, to untie and resolve [or settle] a knotty problem by citing facts as evidence.[32]

Tieh, or memorandum, means literally *yeh*, or a leaf. Short bamboo slips bound into *tieh* are like leaves on the branch. [Lu] Wen-shu [of Han] cut the leaves of rushes [to form a *tieh* for the purpose of keeping records]; this illustrates what is meant by *tieh*.[33] Before a decision is

---

[29] When Wang Pao stopped at the house of a widow, a slave that had belonged to her dead husband refused to go out and buy wine for him. Enraged, Wang suggested that he should buy the man. The slave said that he would not do anything which was not explicitly stated in the bond. So Wang drafted the bond, describing in detail the man's duties, which included all forms of service imaginable. After reading the bond, the slave kowtowed and apologized, saying that he would rather die than become Wang's slave. He then obediently went out to buy wine for Wang. See Sun Hsing-yen, *Hsü ku-wen-yüan*, chüan 20.

[30] See *Han-fei-tzu*, chüan 17, Chapter 42, p. 302.

[31] See *Chou-li*, "Ch'iu-kuan" under "Ssu-tz'u"—officials in charge of piercing. The three *tz'u*: to get information governing high ministers, to get information about lower officials, and to get information about the people. See *Chou-li yin-te*, 9/14b, 26b.

[32] For example, a record of settlement of a quarrel over some territorial boundary.

[33] For Lu Wen-shu, see his biography in *Han-shu*.

reached in government planning, short *tieh* are kept for reference and discussion. So a more detailed *tieh* is known as a *ch'ien*, or note. *Ch'ien* literally means fine or detailed.

Chuan, or notice, including obituary, means literally *mao*, or description, that is, to describe according to the original source in order to establish the facts. Memorials suggesting posthumous titles for men of virtue of previous times all contain obituaries describing the characters of these men. This is the most important form of *chuan*.

Lieh, or narrative account, means literally *ch'en*, or to exhibit, exhibiting true situations so that they will be clearly discernible.

Tz'u, or *viva voce*, means literally word of mouth, by means of which one conveys his ideas to others. Tzu-ch'an [of the state of Cheng] was gifted with *tz'u*, and the various lords profited from it. Indeed, it is impossible to do without *tz'u*.[34]

Yen, or proverb, means literally a straightforward statement. As condolences are also unadorned, they too are known as *yen*.[35] A simple expression of the market place is: "Fruits without flowers." Duke Mu of Tsou made the statement: "A leaking bag still holds things."[36] These are examples of *yen*. In "T'ai-shih" it is said, "There is an ancient saying 'A hen should not herald the approach of morning.'"[37] And in "Ta-ya" is the statement: "People used to say, 'Through grief I grow old.'"[38]

[34] See *Ch'un-ch'iu ching-chuan yin-te*, 335/Hsiang 31/6 Tso: The various lords came to pay respects to Chin, and were quartered in humble dwellings. When the Duke of Cheng arrived, he was not given an audience. Tzu-ch'an, a minister of Cheng, through his eloquence, convinced the Chin of their mistake in neglecting their duty of treating the lords properly. As a result, the Chin ordered proper quarters built to house the visiting lords.

[35] *Yen* meaning proverb and *yen* meaning condolence are two different characters. Our author uses only one character, the former one, for both meanings, because of their phonetic and probably semantic link. This is the first known instance where the word is used in both senses.

[36] Chia I, *Hsin-shu*, "Ch'un-ch'iu p'ien."

[37] This statement is found in "Mu-shih," Chapter 22 in the *Book of History*, and not in "T'ai-shih," which is Chapter 21. *Ch'un-ch'iu ching-chuan yin-te*, 22/0091-4.

[38] This line is found in the "Hsiao-ya" section of the *Book of Poetry*, in poem no. 197, entitled "Hsiao P'an," and not in the "Ta-ya" section. Furthermore, the first part of the quotation, "People used to say," is not in the original text. *Mao-shih yin-te*, 46/197/2.

Both these are proverbs coming down to us from antiquity, quoted in the Classics.

Then Ch'en Lin, in his remonstrance, said, "Catch sparrows blind-folded"; and P'an Yüeh, in his lamentation, quoted, "Like pearls on one's palm, intimate as husband and wife"; both are proverbs employed in literary pieces. If the *Book of Poetry* and the *Book of History*, which are works from the hands of the sages, quote proverbs which, as literary expressions, are the most vulgar imaginable, how can one overlook these writings which are superior to the proverbs?

A survey of these types of letters shows that they all may be subsumed under the general category of the *Shu* and the *Chi* [which is the title of this chapter]. Some which deal with identical subject matter vary in their literary expressions: some emphasize only the simple content, while others also employ literary embellishment. The form varies with the type of material under treatment, the important thing being the grasp of essentials. Sometimes for the lack of one word the meaning is left incomplete, and sometimes one word too many in a sentence renders it awkward: these pitfalls should receive the careful attention of those in charge, and yet are often overlooked by those whose interest is in superficial beauty of expression. However, superb talents and great writers often neglect the art of letter writing. Such men are like Chiu-fang Yen, whose knowledge of a steed did not include a knowledge of its color or sex.[39] Words, which are the ornament of a man's person, are also an auspicious decoration of a state. Scholars in the "forest of brush"[40] should give thought to the form and structure of this genre.

[39] *Hui-nan-tzu*, chüan 12, "Tao-ying hsün," p. 198: "Duke Mu of Ch'in . . . sent him [Chiu-fang Yen] in search of a steed. He returned after three months and reported that he had got one, and it was in Sha-ch'iu. Duke Mu asked, 'What kind of a horse is it?' The answer was: 'A male, yellow in color.' a messenger was sent to fetch it and found that it was a female horse, and its color was black. Duke Mu was displeased. He sent for Po-lo [the most famous horse expert in antiquity] and told him, 'It is an utter failure! The one you recommended to go in search of a steed does not even know the animal's color or sex! How can he know anything about a horse?' Po-lo heaved a long sigh and said, '. . . What Yen was impressed by was the inner spirit. He grasped the subtle factor and neglected the vulgar detail.' "

[40] That is, the literary world.

The Tsan:

Literary writing develops into many forms,

Of which one is the epistolary:

It appears like a galloping steed caparisoned in gold,

But fulfills its function through simple utterances.

From the time of antiquity its sound has been heard,

And it brings response from a thousand *li* away.

The mass of entangled affairs

Becomes comprehensive through their being recorded.

XXVI. Spiritual Thought or Imagination (Shen-ssu)

An Ancient said, "One may be on the rivers and sea in body, but his mind remains at the palace gate."[1] This is what I mean by *shen-ssu*, or spiritual thought or imagination. One who is engaged in literary thought travels far in spirit. Quietly absorbed in contemplation, his thinking reaches back one thousand years; and with only the slightest movement of his countenance, his vision penetrates ten thousand *li*; he creates the music of pearls and jade between his poetic lines, and he witnesses the rolling of wind and clouds right before his brows and lashes. These things are possible because of the work of the imagination.

Through the subtlety of the imagination, the spirit comes into contact with external things. The spirit resides in the mind, and the key to its secret is controlled by both the feelings and the vital force. Physical things reach our minds through our ears and eyes, and the key to their apprehension is the skilled use of language. When the key works smoothly, there is nothing which will not appear in its true

---

[1] *Chuangtzu yin-te*, 79/28/56. In its original context, the line speaks of the worldly ambition of a man who is in retirement. However, Liu Hsieh ignores this implication and is concerned only with the amazing power of thought which transports one to places where his body is not.

form; but when its operation is obstructed, the spirit loses its rationale. For this reason, vacancy and tranquility are important in the development of literary thinking: the achievement of this state of vacancy and tranquility entails the cleansing of the five viscera and the purification of the spirit. One has also to acquire learning in order to maintain a store of precious information, and to contemplate the nature of reason so as to enrich his talents; he must search deeply and experience widely in order that he may exhaustively evoke the source of light; he must master literary traditions in order to make his expressions felicitous and smooth. It is only then that he commissions the "mysterious butcher"[2] [who dwells within him] to write in accord with musical patterns; and it is then that he sets the incomparably brilliant "master wheelwright"[3] [who dwells within him] to wield the ax in harmony with his intuitive insight. This, in short, is the first step in the art of writing, and the main principle employed in the planning of a literary piece.

When *shen-ssu* [or spiritual thought] is in operation, all possible vistas open up before it. Rules and principles become mere formalities and there is not the least trace of carving or engraving.[4] When one ascends mountains [in such an inspired state], the whole mountain will be tinged with the coloring of his own feelings; and when his eyes rove over the seas, the seas will be saturated with his ideas. He can roam as companion of the wind and the clouds according to the measure of his talents. At the moment when a writer first picks up his pen, and before anything has yet been written, he feels as if his creative vigor were doubled; but at the completion of the piece, he usually

[2] *Ibid.*, 7-8/3/2-12. The "mysterious butcher," in his cutting of a bull, exhibits such profound understanding of the bull that his knife swims between the joints and is still as sharp as if newly honed, even after nineteen years of service. Although Chuangtzu, a Taoist, was theoretically opposed to all expressions, literary or otherwise, this butcher has become the symbol of the highest achievement in literary creation. He is one who works through the spirit rather than through the senses.

[3] *Ibid.*, 36/13/68-74. The master wheelwright wields his ax to make a wheel in a manner absolutely unique, and hence not communicable. He is another example of the artistic height which is reached not by effort but by intuitive insight.

[4] Referring to laborious effort.

has succeeded in conveying only half of what he had at first contemplated. Why is this so? Because one's ideas may easily be extraordinary
when he is free to work in the realm of fancy, but it is very difficult
for one to give beauty to his language when he is tied down to the
factual details. Therefore, although the idea takes shape from spiritual
thinking, and the language receives its form from the idea, idea,
thought, and language may be so closely related that they are experienced as one, or they may differ as strikingly as if they were a thousand
li from each other. A writer may go beyond the world in search of
patterns which are there in the square inch of his heart, and sometimes
his thought strays over mountain and river for ideas which are only a
few inches or feet away. So be vigilant over your heart and cultivate
the intuitive method; there is little need of onerous mental effort, for
one who is endowed with natural excellence balanced as a harmonious
whole has no need to strain himself.

Individuals vary with respect to their natural talents; some are slow
and some are quick. And when they express themselves in literary
forms, they also excel in many different ways. [Ssu-ma] Hsiang-ju
chewed his brush to bits, Yang Hsiung had nightmares because of his
inability to continue writing, Huang T'an fell ill because of onerous
thinking, Wang Ch'ung exhausted his vitality in his intellectual labors,
Chang Heng took ten years to study the capitals [for his *fu*],[5] and
Tso Ssu took twelve years to collect material for the writing of his
fu on capitals.[6] It is true that all of these men's works are of immense
magnitude, but they are all the result of thinking which is slow and
laborious. On the other hand, Prince Huai-nan [or Liu An] completed
his *fu* on *Encountering Sorrow* before the morning was spent, Mei
Kao had his piece ready as soon as he received the royal commission,
Tzu-chien [or Ts'ao Chih] wrote poetry as easily as if he were reciting,
Chung-hsüan [or Wang Ts'an] let his brush fly as if copying from a

---

[5] He wrote one *fu* on the western capital and one on the eastern capital. See *Wen-hsuan*, chüan 2 and 3.

[6] He has three *fu* on the capitals of the three kingdoms known collectively as "San-tu-fu": Shu, Wu, and Wei. See *Wen-hsüan*, chüan 4 and 5.

ready-made draft, Juan Yü penned a letter on the saddle, and Ni Heng produced memorials while at meals. These pieces, all brief and terse, are all works of quick thinking.

A spirited scholar, with the essentials of the art of writing in his mind, is quick to meet situations with an instantaneous response even before he has time for consideration; while a man of profound thought, whose emotional reactions are complicated and who is ever aware of all possible alternatives, achieves light and maps plans only after prolonged questioning and inquiring. A man whose mechanism of response is quick does his work in a hurry; but it takes a long time for a man of deliberation to show his accomplishments. Though these two groups of people differ in their ways of writing, one group writing with ease and the other with great labor, both types must be men of comprehensive learning and broad experience. The mind which is only laborious without the support of learning resembles the empty quick-witted mind devoid of talent in that neither has ever been known to accomplish anything. There are two dangers besetting the man who stops to ponder while writing: if he is not clear about principles, his work will seem diffuse and insubstantial; but if he is prolix, his work will suffer from confusion. Comprehensive learning and broad experience are the only foods that will nourish writing afflicted with poverty of substance, and coherence and unity are the only medicines which will cure confusion. To be coherent and unified as well as comprehensive is also one way to reduce mental effort.

As emotional situations vary in complexity, literary forms vary with them. Unpolished expressions may make brilliant ideas concrete, and from commonplace things may be coaxed new revelations. Compare the finished cloth with the hempen thread. Although the cloth is the same in substance as the hemp, the added processes of weaving and spinning have given the cloth beauty and made it precious. But the subtle meanings beyond our thought and the profound inner workings of the heart inexpressible in words are not to be reached by language; here one should know enough to halt his brush. Only the most subtle soul understands their secret, and only the most spiritual mind comprehends their number. The [master chef] I Chih was unable to tell people how he cooked,[7] and wheelwright Pien could not inform people how he wielded his ax.[8] [Great art] is infinitely subtle.

> *The Tsan:*
> Under the operation of the spirit the phenomenal world becomes articulate,
> But does so responsive to varying emotional situations.
> Things are apprehended by means of their appearances,
> And the mind responds by the application of reason.
> It carves and engraves in accordance with sound patterns,
> Forging metaphors and allegories as it goes.
> It gathers together all its ideas and works them into harmony,
> And [like General Chang Liang] wins victory afar while sitting in its tent.[9]

XXVII. Style and Nature (T'i-hsing)

When the emotions are moved, they express themselves in words; and when reason is born, it emerges in a pattern. For we start with the imperceptible and follow through to the revealed, and on the basis of inner realities seek external realities in harmony with them. However, people differ in talent, in physical vitality, in scholarship, and in manner: in talent some are mediocre and some brilliant; in physical

---

[7] *Lü-shih ch'un-ch'iu* (Chu-tzu chi-ch'eng ed., Shanghai, 1935), chüan 14, pp. 140-41. "I Chih" is another name for I Yin, who, in answer to T'ang's question, says, ". . . The changes which take place in a cauldron are subtle and delicate, neither expressible in words by the mouth nor conceivable by the mind."

[8] See note 3 above.

[9] It was said of Chang Liang of the Han that, although remaining in his army tent when he mapped out his campaign strategy, he won victories one thousand *li* away. See his biography in the *Han-shu*. The parallel position of the mind or the spirit is hinted at here.

vitality some are strong and some weak; in scholarship some are superficial and some profound; in manner some are graceful and some
vulgar. All these are partly the outcome of temperament and nature,
and partly the result of a process of training. For this reason, we find
in the domain of the brush forest various grotesque forms taking shape
like rolling clouds; and in the garden of literature different activities
burgeon forth as waves surge upon waves. Thus, in the use of language and in the grasp of content, a man is destined to be either
mediocre or brilliant, and no one can make him what is contrary to
his talent; in temper and disposition, he is destined to be either vital
or spiritless, and no one can change the degree of his physical vitality;
in his reactions to things and grasp of meanings, he is destined to be
either superficial or profound, and no one has ever heard of achievement out of proportion to a man's scholarship; and in style and form,
he is destined to be either graceful or vulgar, and few can be what
is contrary to their training. Each follows the way he cherishes in his
heart, and people's hearts differ as much as their faces. All in all, we
may enumerate eight different styles: first, elegant and graceful, or in
the style of *tien* and *ya*;[1] second, far-ranging and profound; third,
polished and concise; fourth, lucid and logical; fifth, profuse and
flowery; sixth, vigorous and beautiful; seventh, fresh and extraordinary;
and eighth, light and trivial.

The style which is defined as elegant and graceful models itself
after the classical forms and adopts the Confucian principles; the far-
ranging and profound couches its content in cryptic phrases and obscure
expressions, treating of truths deep-seated in the nature of things; the
polished and concise has mastered the problems of diction and sentence structure, analyzing them down to the minutest details; the lucid
and logical employs straightforward language to express clear ideas
with reasoning so pertinent that it satisfies our minds; the profuse and
flowery indulges in creating beautiful patterns through a wealth of
metaphors, aiming at brightening and illuminating all branches and

---

[1] That is, the style of the *Book of History* and the *Book of Poetry*.

ramifications of its subject; the vigorous and beautiful distinguishes itself by eloquent discourse and grand composition glowing with remarkable colors; the fresh and extraordinary shuns the hackneyed and competes for success in the vogue of the moment, devoting itself to the unconsidered, the biased, the diverting and the strange; and the light and trivial is characterized by its frivolous language weakly organized, following the lead of the vulgar, without any strength of its own. As we see, the graceful contrasts with the extraordinary, the profound differs from the lucid, the profuse conflicts with the concise, and the vigorous clashes with the light. When we understand these styles, we can make the plant of literary composition grow, roots, leaves, and all, in the garden of literature.

Since the eight styles are constantly interchanged,[2] success depends on scholarship. Talent resides within, and is born of the physical vitality of the blood. This physical [and hence temperamental] vitality gives substance to our feeling and ideas, and these determine the form language will take. The beauty one imparts to his language depends, therefore, entirely on his temperament and nature. The sharp and quick-witted Chia I produced literary pieces with a clean and pure style; Ch'ang-ch'ing [or Ssu-ma Hsiang-ju], proud and eccentric, over-burdened his works with exaggerated reasoning and excessive wordiness; the writings of Tzu-yün [or Yang Hsiung] are abstruse, although giving the reader a taste which lingers, because of his retiring and reticent nature; Tzu-cheng [or Liu Hsiang] was clear in his ideas and exhaustive in his treatments of facts, because he was unassuming and simple; Meng-chien [or Pan Ku], a man of grace and excellence, was careful in composition and resourceful in thought; P'ing-tzu [or Chang Heng], widely learned, was thorough in investigation, and well-organized as well as colorful in expression; Chung-hsüan [or Wang Ts'an], hasty and spirited, exhibited outstanding works, indicating a fruitful talent; Kung-kan [or Liu Chen], narrow-minded and biased,

---

[2] This seems to refer to the possible changing from one style to another by an individual.

used strong language and showed startling emotion; as to Ssu-tsung [or Juan Chi], who was easy and free, he sang in the spirit of a recluse a tune wafted into the distance; Shu-ya [or Hsi K'ang], romantic and gallant, gave us high spirit and bright colors; An-jen [or P'an Yüeh], light and swift, was poignant in his remarks but rhythmic in prosody; and Shih-heng [or Lu Chi], reverent and decorous, couched his [more] exuberant feelings in obscure expressions. From these examples, we draw the clear inference that the outer and the inner realities always correspond. Is this not the general principle which we constantly find exemplified in nature as well as in the realm of talent and vitality?

Talent is bestowed by heaven, but in learning one must be very careful in choosing the first step in the course of his training. It is like carving or dyeing, in which the success depends on the first step of the process. When a vessel has been made, or a color printed, it is difficult to change. So when a child learns how to carve, he should first learn the graceful way. From mastery of this root he may proceed to acquire the leaves; and in this way his thought will be perfectly comprehensive in itself. Although the eight styles are all different, there is a common denominator, and once this denominator is understood, the writer will have in his grasp the center of the circle, and all radii will meet at this center like spokes gathering at a hub. So it is important that a man imitate one certain style to initiate his training process and continue to develop his talent in a way which conforms to his nature. This is the principle to be used as a guide in literary composition.

The Tsan:

There is a great variety of talents and natures, and a great variety of
    literary styles.
Verbal expressions are the musculature and integument,
But feelings and ideas are the bone and marrow.
There are forms which are graceful and beautiful like silk broideries;

And there are forms which are the result of laborious artifice, but
   [only succeed in turning the vermilion into the vulgar] purple.[3]
By training a writer may achieve a result as true as [nature itself],
And this kind of beauty is reached by a gradual process of labor.

XXVIII. The Wind and the Bone (Feng-ku)

The *Book of Poetry* contains six elements, and of these *feng*, or wind,
stands at the head of the list. It is the source of transformation, and
the correlate of emotion and vitality. He who would express mournful
emotions must begin with the wind, and to organize his linguistic
elements he must above all emphasize the bone. Literary expressions
are conditioned by the bone in much the same way as the standing
posture of a body is conditioned by its skeleton; feeling gives form to
the wind very much as a physical form envelops the vitality which
animates it. When expressions are organized on the right principles,
literary bone is there; and when the emotion and vitality embodied
are swift and free, there we find the purity of the literary wind. If a
literary piece has nothing but rich and brilliant colors, without wind
and bone to keep it air-borne, then one shaking is enough to destroy
its splendor, lacking as it does the vigor which can justify fame. Therefore, a condition for organizing one's thought and planning one's
composition is to develop to the full one's vitality; for when one is
strong and whole, he will shine with fresh brilliance. The concept here
applied to literary composition is enriched by comparison with our
observation of the use of wings by a bird of prey. He whose bone
structure is well exercised will always be versed in rhetoric; and he
who is deep of wind will always be articulate in expressing his feelings. To be firm and exact in diction, and in resonance sure without

[3] See note 19, Chapter IV.

being heavy: this is what is meant by vigor of wind and bone. Now to be thin in ideas and fat in words, or confused and disorganized, without unity, are sure signs of lack of this kind of bone. And when ideas are incomplete and incomprehensive, lifeless and without vitality, it is an evidence of the absence of the wind. Long ago, when P'an Hsü wrote his edict conferring the nine honors on Prince Wei,[1] he patterned his thought after the Classics. All other talents, on seeing his work, hid their brushes, because his had this vigor of bone and marrow. The *fu* on the immortals by [Ssu-ma] Hsiang-ju[2] exhibited a vitality which soared to the clouds. He was proclaimed poet laureate because his work possessed such powerful strength of wind. If one has the ability to see the essentials illustrated in these cases, he may be able to succeed in his literary pursuits. But no amount of embellishment will do him any good, if he fails to follow these essential principles.

It was for this reason that Wei-wen [or Ts'ao P'ei] said, "Vitality is the main factor in writing. The substance of this vitality is either clear or turbid, and its states cannot be achieved by effort."[3] In dealing with K'ung Yung, he said, "The substance of his vitality is lofty and exquisite"; in the case of Hsü Kan, he said, "Occasionally Hsü exhibits the [rather low] vitality which is known to characterize the district of Ch'i";[4] and in the case of Liu Chen, he said, "He possesses transcendent vitality." Kung Kan [or Liu Chen] also remarked, "Master K'ung's style is lofty and stately, definitely possessing extraordinary vitality, a vitality not expressible in brush and ink."[5] These writers laid a common emphasis on vitality.

A pheasant, with all its colorful feathers, is limited in its scope of flight to a hundred paces, because it is fat-fleshed and has little or no

---

[1] See note 22, Chapter XIX.

[2] Referring to his "Ta-jen fu," which was presented to the emperor. The emperor was so enthralled that he felt he was floating upon clouds, making an excursion through the universe. See Ssu-ma Hsiang-ju's biography in the *Han-shu*.

[3] This and the following statements are found in Wei-wen's "Essay on Literature." See *Wen-hsüan*, chüan 52.

[4] Li Shang, the commentator of *Wen-hsüan*, said that the district of Ch'i was known for a slow style in writing. *Ibid.*, chüan 52.

[5] Kung Kan's essay is lost.

vigor. An eagle may not have beautiful plumage patterns, but its wings carry it high in the sky, because of its strong bone structure and mighty vitality. Strength of literary talent is comparable to these cases. If we had the wind and the bone without colors, we would have a group of eagles in the forest of literature; but if we had colors without the wind and the bone, we would have a crowd of pheasants jumping about in a garden of letters. Only when a literary piece has both beautiful colors and the ability to soar high do we have a singing phoenix in the world of literature.

When a writer casts and molds his works after the patterns of the Classics, soars and alights in the manner in which philosophers and historians have soared and alighted,[6] and is equipped with a profound knowledge of the ever-changing emotions and the ability to display with a delicate touch styles suitable to them, he will be able to conceive new ideas and carve extraordinary expressions. For the writer who knows what style is fitting will be able to form new ideas without introducing confusion; and he who knows the ever-varying emotions will be able to adopt extraordinary expressions without ever overdoing it. But if before the bone and the emotional patterns are full-grown, or if before the wind and the rhetoric have been sufficiently cultivated, a writer should pass over the old rules and run after new creations, he would more often than not meet with failure, although he might occasionally come up with some clever ideas. For a piece which is constructed of mere extraordinary phrases is a mistake, and how can one consider it a constant principle? The *Book of Chou* says, "In writing one should emphasize the essential and should not indulge in the extraordinary."[7] The purpose of this statement is to prevent excessive literary embellishment. But the art of writing has many avenues, and each scholar may choose what delights him. However, because those who know do not instruct and those who really study have no teachers,[8]

6 Philosophical works and histories have always been held as examples of good literary style. See Chapters XVI and XVII above.

7 See note 19, Chapter II.

8 The art of writing is to be grasped intuitively and not discursively.

one may become accustomed to the flowery and pursue the excessively ornamental, drifting along aimlessly, forgetting to return. But if one will make sure that his form is correct and that he has a clear and vigorous style, he will possess pure wind and strong bone, and his whole work will gleam with brilliance. If one pays attention to these considerations, why should the art be beyond his reach?

The Tsan:
Emotion and vitality are one,
And so are rhetoric and style.
If one's language is clear and vigorous,
He will be showered with the honors of a jade tablet.
So cultivate the vigor of the wind,
And make the bone more robust;
When talent stands out sharply in all its ruggedness,
It may then be clothed in colors that glow and gleam.

XXIX. Flexible Adaptability to Varying Situations (T'ung-pien)

The genres to which literary compositions may belong are definite; an individual composition is permitted stylistic flexibility. How do we know this is so? Because in the case of genres, like *shih*, or poetry; *fu*, or poetic narrative; *shu*, or epistolary writing; and *chi*, or memoir, their names and content correspond; therefore, they are definite. But as for literary expressions and vital force, they must adapt themselves to varying situations in order to endure; therefore, they are flexible. The genres, because of the definite correspondence between their names and content, have to base themselves on established principles; but because the style must maintain its flexible adaptability to varying situations, its very essence is its sensitivity to new modes and cadences.

Only by observing this truth can a writer gallop on a road that does not end in an impasse, or drink out of a spring which is inexhaustible. When one has to endure his thirst because the well rope is too short, or give up the road because his legs are tired, it is not because he has exhausted the applicability of literary principles, but because he is inexperienced in the art of flexible adaptability. Literature may be looked at as very much like grasses and plants: their roots and trunks, which are attached to the soil, are all of the same nature; their smells and tastes, which are exposed to the sun, differ from individual to individual.[1]

In the lyrics and songs of the nine dynasties,[2] we find that feeling tone and literary pattern agree with each other in each one. The "Tuan-chu" of the period of the Yellow Emperor is an example of emphasis on extreme simplicity;[3] the "Tsai-hsi"[4] of the T'ang then developed beyond it. The "Ch'ing-yün" of the Yü is more richly embellished than that of the T'ang, and the "Tiao-ch'iang" of the Hsia is even more lavishly ornamented than that of the Yü. When we come to the Shang and the Chou, we find their poetry vastly more beautiful than that of the Hsia. But they all agree in being the expressions of genuine feeling and the narratives of their times. During the Ch'u period, *sao* was produced on the pattern of the Chou poems; and the *fu* and *sung* of Han times reflect the forms of the Ch'u songs. Wei's poetic composition defers to the style of the Han in a spirit of admiration, and Chin's literary writings pattern themselves after the colorful works of the Wei. A careful analysis will show that the literary productions during

[1] Attachment to the soil refers to the definite correspondence between the name and content of a genre, and the exposure to the sun refers to adaptability to varying situations.

[2] Two lists of dynasties follow. The first list contains: Yellow Emperor period, T'ang, Yü, Hsia, Shang, Chou, Ch'u, Han, Wei, and Chin, ten in all. The second list contains, in addition to these, Sung—a total of eleven. As Liu Hsieh's work was completed in Ch'i, the dynasty which followed the Sung, the latter should be included. It seems that the period of the Yellow Emperor and that of Ch'u should both be eliminated: the Yellow Emperor period, because it was a predynastic time, and Ch'u, because it was a part of the Chou. Without these, we have altogether nine dynasties.

[3] "Tuan-chu," a folk song, consists of four two-word lines, of which the meaning is not clear. It runs: "Bamboo broken; Bamboo continued; Dust flying; Chasing meat." The song is recorded in the *Wu-yüeh ch'un-ch'iu*, by Chao Yeh of the Han dynasty.

[4] Not identifiable.

the times of the Yellow Emperor and the T'ang are pure and simple; during the Yü and Hsia, simple and rational; during the Shang and Chou, beautiful and graceful; during the Ch'u and Han, exaggerated and alluringly charming; in the times of the Wei and Chin, superficial and ornamental; and at the beginning of the Sung, pretentious and novelty-ridden. Declining from the simple to the pretentious, literary taste becomes thinner and thinner as it approaches our own time. The reason for this is found in the fact that a rivalry in producing something new, to the neglect of the ancient values, has lulled the wind and sapped vitality. At present, most of the outstanding talented scholars who devote themselves to literature overlook the Han pieces and emulate the examples of the Sung period. Even if they have read all the standard literary works both ancient and modern, they seem to attach themselves to the recent and avoid the remote. But the color blue is prepared from indigo and the color red is prepared from madder. And although blue and red are better colors than their sources, they are incapable of further change. Huan Chün-shan [or Huan T'an] said, "As I read the much ornamented works of recent writers I feel that they may be beautiful, but I attach no weight to them. But when I read works by Liu [Hsin][5] and Yang [Hsiung], I often profit by them." This is an example in point. If one wishes to refine upon the blue and purify the red, one must return to the indigo and the madder and begin there; just so, to correct pretentiousness and cure superficiality, a writer must come back to the Classics and begin there. Only when a writer is able to strike a middle road between the demands of substance and of form, and to follow the right principles when confronted with a choice between a graceful and a vulgar expression, is he a man with whom we can discuss the problem of flexible adaptability.

At the beginning of the Han dynasty, there was already strenuous effort to perfect the descriptions of the sounds and outward appearances of nature. Later writers pursued this tendency. Although occasionally they soared beyond the old course, they invariably came to rest in the

[5] Liu Hsiang's son, a great bibliophile of the Han dynasty. He died in A.D. 23.

cage of the traditional. Mei Sheng in his "Ch'i-fa" wrote, "As I look over the Eastern Sea, I see unrolled before me the vast space merging with the blue sky." Then [Ssu-ma] Hsiang-ju wrote in his "Shang-lin fu," "As I look at [the plain], there is no beginning to it; and when I investigate it, there is no edge to it: the sun rises from its eastern pool and the moon emerges on its western slope."[6] Ma Yung[7] wrote in his "Kuang-ch'eng sung," "Heaven and earth merge into one; there is no beginning and no edge; from the east rises the great luminary [the sun], and on the western slope is born the moon."[8] Yang Hsiung wrote in his "Chiao-lieh,"[9] "Here rise and set the sun and moon, and heaven and earth meet." And finally Chang Heng wrote in his "Hsi-ching fu," "Just here the sun and moon rise and set, the symbols of *fu-san* and *meng-ssu*."[10] These five writers, in their several attempts to describe what is vast and unbounded, seem to breathe one spirit. There are many such examples; the writers always try to emulate one another. And to know which elements to preserve and which to change, in a complicated situation, is to possess flexible adaptability.

Therefore, in laying down principles governing literary traditions, one must have a broad view of the literary forms. He should first broaden his experience in order to deepen his perception, and acquire a synthetic outlook which creates harmony among all the literary precepts; then he may open up new vistas and create pivotal points of his own. [These accomplishments won], he will be in a position to keep his art under harness, controlling it as if from a distance, and progress at his leisure; [these accomplishments won], he will be able to achieve an artistic harmony perfectly in accord with his temperament and sustain his vitality, adapting it to varying situations. To his work will

[6] The line here differs from the original, which says: ". . . the moon sets down the western slope." This is a description of the vastness of the plain on which the author's eyes feast.

[7] A great Han commentator of the Classics (79-166).

[8] A description of the vastness of the universe.

[9] The original title is "Yü-lieh fu."

[10] A description of the vastness of the universe. *Fu-san* is the mythical tree the top of which the sun first touches in its course from the eastern sky; and *meng-ssu*, the mythical pool into which it sets.

belong the colors of the curving ridge of a rainbow or the splendor of the spreading wings of a red bird.[11] Writings of this quality will be, without exception, outstanding. But a writer who confines himself to a narrow conception of his art and feels proud of his one limited achievement will be good for nothing but to toddle in a circle in a court; how could such a man be expected to gallop over ten thousand *li*?

The Tsan:

It is the law of literature both to move along and to come to full circle;
The merit of literature renews itself from day to day.
If it changes, it will endure;
If it adapts itself to the changing tide, it will lack nothing.
Success will be his who follows the changing times,
And he will have no need of fear if he can take advantage of his opportunities.
With an eye on present circumstances, create what is extraordinary,
And establish laws by reference to ancient practice.

XXX. On Choice of Style[1]

One's emotion has a number of different moods, and each must be expressed in a particular literary style. All writers choose the genres[2] which accord with their emotional moods, and adopt the styles proper

---

[11] For the curving ridge for a rainbow, see Chang Heng's "Hsi-ching fu," and for the red bird, see his "Ssu-shün fu." Both are found in the *Wen-shüan*, chüan 2 and 16 respectively.

[1] The term *shih*, which is here rendered as "style," means situation or condition, as in the phrase *ti-shih*, the topographical condition or strategic situation of a place. It also means bent or tendency, as in the phrase *shan-shih*, the contour or tendency of a mountain. Figuratively it means power on account of position or situation. As used in this chapter, it means the tendency of a rhetorical flow, the spirit or style of a literary piece.

[2] The term for "genre" is *t'i*, which means body, substance, form, or genre in literary criticism. It is also used to mean style. This shows again that there is no consistent way of rendering Chinese literary terms. Their meaning has to be determined in context.

to these genres. By style is meant that rhetorical form most naturally suggested by a specific genre. It follows just as naturally as the straight course of an arrow shot from a bow, or the whirlpool at the bend of a rapid mountain stream. The round [heaven], because of its roundness, tends naturally to rotate; the square [earth], because of its squareness, tends naturally to remain at rest.[3] Literary genre and style likewise follow natural tendencies. Those who pattern their writing after the classical genre will achieve the excellent qualities of severe elegance and grace;[4] and those who pattern theirs after the *sao* genre will succeed in capturing the flowers of charm and high-mindedness. Superficial writings are as a rule shallow in style, and those which are clear-cut in language and logical and simple in ideas are generally devoid of embellishment. For it is the natural tendency [*shih*, or style] of rapid waters not to be rippled and of withered trees not to give shade.

In painting, it is colors which present the infinite possibilities of form; and in literature, it is literary phraseology which attempts the adequate expression of emotional moods. Different mixtures of colors produce the forms of dogs and of horses; different emotional moods produce the different styles, of which some are graceful and some vulgar. In this art of literary casting, each piece has its one specific principle, and even if it has no rigidly defined scope, its limits should not be trespassed. However, those who would be well versed in literary composition must comprehend all possible styles. For although the eccentric and the orthodox are opposed to each other, both should be mastered; and although the vigorous and the delicate are different, each should be used at the appropriate moment. If one loves the elegantly severe and dislikes the ornate, he will be one-sided when held up against the standard of comprehensive mastery. We are reminded of the two men of Hsia, one boasting about his bow and another about his arrow, [not knowing that] with neither alone would it be possible to shoot. If a writer allows himself to include both the graceful and the

---

[3] The round and square are symbols of heaven and earth, respectively.

[4] The *Book of History* is characterized by severe elegance and the *Book of Poetry* by grace.

vulgar in the same literary piece, he violates the principle of unity. This is like the man of Ch'u, who, while praising his shield [as impenetrable], hawked his spear [as irresistible, without realizing that] it would be difficult to sell both [on such recommendations].[5]

When a writer encompasses all genres within his scope, he must exercise discriminating judgment. Whether the mode of *kung* or the mode of *shang*[6] ought to be used, or whether the color red or the color purple should be applied, depends upon the circumstances.

In writing the *chang*, or memorial expressing thanks; *piao*, or memorial expressing feeling; *tsou*, or memorial to impeach; and *i*, or memorial to discuss,[7] one should aim at elegance and grace; for the writing of *fu*, or poetic narrative; *sung*, or ceremonial ode; *ke*, or song; and *shih*, or poetry,[8] purity and beauty are the standard; in the case of the *fu*, or tally; *hsi*, or proclamation; *shu*, or epistolary writing; and *i*, or despatch,[9] correctness of style demands lucidity and clear-cut judgment; in the case of the *shih*, or historical writing; *lun*, or essay; *hsü*, or preface; and *chu*, or commentary,[10] the stylistic features worthy of imitation are thoroughness and pertinence; in writing the *chen*, or admonition; *ming*, or inscription on articles; *pei*, or inscription on monuments; and *lei*, or elegy,[11] one's style should be comprehensive and deep; and finally, in writing *lien-chu*, or continuous string of pearls, and *ch'i-tz'u*, or poetry in the form of "seven,"[12] one should seek artistry and charm of style. In all these cases, one chooses a style in accord with a genre, adapting his style to the particular situation.

[5] For the men of Hsia with their bow and arrow, see *Yü-lan*, chüan 347; and for the man of Ch'u with his spear and shield, see *Han-fei-tzu*, chüan 15, Chapter 36, "Nan-i," p. 265. A man of Hsia said, "My bow is good, so I need no arrow." Another said, "My arrow is good, so I do not need a bow." The man of Ch'u was selling a shield and a spear. He first praised his shield: "My shield is so strong that nothing can pierce it." Then he praised his spear: "My spear is so sharp that it pierces anything."

[6] For the five whole-tone scale, of which *kung* and *shang* are two tones, see note 2, Chapter VII. Each of these tones may be used as a primary note, giving thus five modes.

[7] See Chapter XXII.　　　　　　　　　　[8] See Chapters VI, VII, VIII, and IX.

[9] See Chapters XX, XXIV, and XXV.　　[10] See Chapters VIII, XVI, and XVIII.

[11] See Chapters XI and XII.

[12] For *lien-chu* see note 4, Chapter XIV; and for *ch'i-tz'u*, see note 2, on *ch'i-fa* (seven shots), in the same chapter.

Although there may be an occasional blending of styles, creating a tapestry of diverse literary passages similar to a variegated brocade, such a "brocade" must of necessity have one fundamental color, the color of the basic fabric.

Huan T'an once said, "Writers have each his own love. Some love what is apparently dazzling, not knowing the value of what is solid and veritable; some love a great quantity of information, blind to the importance of what is essential and simple." Ch'en-ssu [or Ts'ao Chih] also said, "Among contemporary writers, some love verbosity and erudition, keeping their meaning deep and obscure; some love to analyze their terms and sentence structure into clear-cut distinctions to the point of hairsplitting. The difference in their taste is a natural consequence of the difference in their training." In other words, they differ in their natural bents or styles.

Liu Chen once said, "The essence of literature may be expressed in a variety of styles: the romantic, the realistic, the vigorous, and the delicate. Among all the contemporary writers there is only one of whose writing it may be said that even when he has said all there is to be said, his style is still unspent."[13] Kung-kan [or Liu Chen] here uses the word [*shih* or style] also in the sense of *ch'i*, or vitality or force. The force by which a literary piece is carried along may be either vigorous or weak, and used in this sense force need not necessarily mean only vigorous expression and heroic mood. Lu Yün said that, before he heard the literary opinion of Master Chang, he himself tended in his literary judgments to emphasize expressions rather than feeling, and to pay more attention to the force [in the sense of vigor] than to the beauty of a style, but that after hearing Chang's view, he preferred to accept it.[14] The content should of course be emphasized over literary expression, but it is just as necessary for the style to be beautiful as [to be forceful]. Although [Lu Yün] missed the truth at first, he was able later to follow good advice.

[13] The quotation is unidentifiable, and it is not known which writer he has in mind.
[14] Quoted from Lu Yün's letter to his elder brother Lu Chi, the author of the *Wen-fu*. Chang is not identifiable.

Recent poets, in most cases, have been attracted by sophistry and artistry. A study of their style reveals that it is the consequence of a tendency toward pretentiousness.[15] Bored by the old, they defy all reason in the creation of new forms. This pretentious style, although apparently difficult, is in fact nothing other than a confounding of normal word order. Confounding the normal order in an essay may result in impoverishment of content, but reversing the word order in a sentence introduces novelty. The way to achieve this element of surprise is to reverse the order of words in a sentence, to suppress the second element of a correlative term, and to place what is normally found in the middle of a sentence outside that sentence. New patterns are obtained by departing from the normal way, reversing the order and changing the positions of words.

Many people, despite the fact that highways level and well-paved exist, take to short cuts, because by these short cuts they can reach their goals sooner. Many writers, although they know that essays as normally written are simple and clear, often indulge in the abnormal, because they are catering to the taste of the vulgar. But those who have profound understanding achieve artistry by new conceptions and ideas; and not only do those whose desire is merely to be different lose their hold on the genre, but also their works become specimens of eccentricity. A well-trained talent holds on to the norm by which to harness the element of surprise; but a novice, whose courage is born of inexperience, rushes after the odd, and so loses touch with the norm. When this tendency is allowed to go on unchecked and unreversed, literary style begins to decline. For one who is concerned with the art of expression, no pains should be spared to think the whole thing through.

The Tsan:

When a thing takes form, its style is also defined.
The beginning and the end agree in perfect accord.
A rapid whirl spins as a compass does,

---

[15] This tendency toward pretentiousness was in vogue at the beginning of the Sung period. See Chapter XXIX for literary trends during various periods.

And an arrow travels in a straight line.

When galloping a charger,[16] follow its natural tendency.

Emotional moods and their literary expressions will blend in perfect
   harmony.

But if one goes out of his way to imitate the steps of others,

His efforts will have the same reward as those of Shou-ling.[17]

XXXI. Emotion and Literary Expression

The literary writings of the sages and worthy men are summed up
under the phrase *wen-chang*, or literary pattern. What is this, if it is
not literary decorativeness?

   Water by nature is plastic,[1] allowing the formation of ripples; and
it is of the essential nature of trees to be solid, supporting flowers on
their calyxes. The ornamental pattern of a thing is of necessity conditioned by its essential nature. On the other hand, tigers and leopards,
deprived of their patterns, would have the same kind of hide as dogs
and sheep; and rhinoceros skins require red varnish [when they are
made into armor]. The essential nature of a thing also depends on its
ornamental patterns.

   For the depiction of our inner spirits, or the description of physical
objects, the contents of the mind are inscribed in "the markings of
birds"[2] [that is, in writing] and in the literary expressions woven on

   16 "A charger" refers figuratively to a genre, the natural tendency of which is the
proper style.

   17 *Chuangtzu*, 45/17/79: "Have you not heard of Shou-ling yü-tzu's efforts to imitate
the steps of others at Han-tan? Not only did he fail to learn the [dance] steps of the
master, he also lost his native ability to walk. He had to crawl all the way home."

   1 The original term is *hsü*, meaning empty. The reason for rendering it as "plastic"
is that it is matched by the term *shih*, meaning solid, in the next line. Furthermore, the
term empty does not seem to express the right idea. Liu Hsieh seems to be trying to show
the flexibility of water, by which it may produce ripples. This flexibility I try to express
by the term plastic.

   2 See note 15, Chapter I.

"fish nets" [that is, paper].[3] Brilliance achieved in this way we call literary decorativeness. Three main patterns are involved in the creation of literature: the color pattern, made up of the five colors;[4] the sound pattern, made up of the five sounds;[5] and the emotional pattern, made up of the five emotions.[6] It is the mixing of the five basic colors which produces elegant embroidery; it is the harmonizing of the five basic sounds which creates the ancient music, such as the piece "Shao-hsia";[7] and it is the expression of the five emotions which gives us the essence of literature. All these processes are natural results of the operation of Divine Reason.

In the *Book of Filial Piety* a classical example illustrates the dictum that during the mourning period one's words ought not to be adorned; from this we may infer that during normal times the words of a man of virtue are not without adornment.[8] It is because Laotzu hates hypocrisy that he says, "Beautiful words are not trustworthy,"[9] although his own "five thousand words"[10] are refined and wonderful; he never sacrifices beauty. Chuang Chou speaks of "eloquence carving likenesses of the ten thousand things." This apparently refers to literary decorativeness.[11] And Han Fei speaks of "enchanting appeal in argument and discussion," meaning embroidered beauty.[12] But to achieve a merely embroidered beauty by grafting enchanting appeal upon one's argument, and to effect mere literary decorativeness by the image-carving of eloquence are examples of an extreme decline[13] in literary tendency. A careful study of the *Book of Filial Piety* and the

---

[3] Paper was first manufactured of bark, hemp, rags, and fish nets by Ts'ai Lun in A.D. 105.

[4] Five colors: green, yellow, red, white, and black. See "I-chi" in the *Book of History*, Ts'ai Shen's commentary.

[5] Five sounds: see note 2, Chapter VII.

[6] Five emotions: joy, anger, sadness, pleasure, and resentment.

[7] See note 19, Chapter VII.   [8] See "San-ch'ing" in the *Book of Filial Piety*.

[9] See *Laotzu*, Chapter 81.   [10] *Laotzu* contains roughly five thousand words.

[11] *Chuangtzu yin-te*, 34/13/21.

[12] *Han-fei-tzu*, chüan 11, Chapter 32, "Wai-ch'u shuo," tso, shang, p. 204.

[13] The term is *pien* or change. As used here, it definitely implies "decline," the sense in which it is used in connection with the *pien-feng* and *pien-ya*, the lyrics which have declined in moral tone.

Laotzu shows us that both their rhetoric and content are conditioned by inner feeling and emotion, while a study of the *Chuangtzu* and *Han-fei-tzu* reveals to us that they indulged in language far more flowery than necessary to express the facts.[14] If we choose carefully between the sources of the Ching River and the Wei;[15] and if we rein ourselves in before we decide between the right and the wrong course, we shall be able to harness literary decorativeness properly for our use. Cosmetics are used to beautify the complexion, but the enchanting appeal in the look is born of natural beauty; similarly the function of literary decorativeness is to adorn discourse, and beauty of eloquence is based on real emotion. Therefore, emotion is the warp of literary pattern, linguistic form the woof of ideas. Only when the warp is straight can the woof be rightly formed, and only when ideas are definite can linguistic form be meaningful. This is the fundamental principle in literary creation.

The Ancient Poets, in writing their poems, built their literary forms on emotion, while later poets, in writing their *fu* and *sung*, created emotion to fit literary forms. How do we know this is so? Because the rise of the *feng* and *ya* was due to the fact that the Ancient Poets, full of real emotions and opinions, sang of these emotions and opinions in satirical remonstrances against their superiors: this is what is meant by building literary forms on emotion. The philosophers, on the contrary, felt no real frustration, but indulged in exaggerated ornamentation merely for the sake of winning fame and fishing for worldly glory: this is what is meant by creating emotion to fit a literary form. A literary piece will be pertinent, simple, and realistic, if it is based on feeling; but if it aims merely at literary achievement, though it may have deceptively alluring charm, it will be prolix and diffuse.

14 This may seem to mean that both Chuangtzu and Han Fei should be criticized for their emphasis on literary adornment. As a matter of fact, literary adornment is exactly what the two philosophers were trying to censure. Liu Hsieh quotes the expressions out of context, creating thus a wrong impression in the mind of the reader. Liu's criticism of these philosophers is rather based on their writings as a whole than on these lines.

15 Rivers Ching and Wei come to form one body in Shensi. The Ching is muddy, while the Wei is clear; hence to distinguish between the Ching and the Wei means to distinguish between what is pure and what is muddy.

Later writers take to the diffuse and neglect the genuine, and forsake the style of the *feng* and ya for that of the *tz'u* and *fu*.[16] Works which are based on genuine feeling become more scarce every day, while those which aim at merely literary achievement become more and more abundant. People whose minds are completely dominated by worldly ambition[17] sing vaguely of the blissful state of retirement, while people whose hearts are wholly entangled in the business of the day purposelessly paint a life beyond this workaday world. These people have lost their souls, and live lives of contradiction. Peach and plum trees do not speak, and yet paths are formed beneath them;[18] even an orchid will not be fragrant[19] if it has been planted by a male, for he would lack true inner feeling. When even in the case of such insignificant things as these plants, the inner feeling involved and the fruit borne are of prime importance, how much more should this be the case with literary writing, whose main purpose is to express the inner feeling! If words contradict the inner feeling, how can we look to the literary expressions for truth?

We put sentences together to form beautiful patterns for the purpose of making our ideas clear. If the patterns become too florid and the rhetoric too eccentric, our ideas will be rendered vaguer than ever. We know very well that to fish with fancy kingfisher-feather line and

[16] Referring to the poetry of the state of Ch'u and the Han dynasty.

[17] This line can be rendered as "whose mind is completely dominated by a desire to seek carriage and cap," both symbols of officialdom.

[18] A paraphrase of a line in the *tsan* to the biography of Li Kuang, in the *Shih-chi*. The implied meaning: If you have anything real to offer, like the peach and plum trees, though you do not speak, people will gather about you, just as people come to the trees, forming paths under them. Ralph Waldo Emerson seems to be expressing the same thought when he writes: "If a man has good corn, or wood, or boards, or pigs to sell, or can make better chairs or knives, crucibles or church organs than anybody else, you will find a broad, hard-beaten road to his house, though it be in the woods" (*Journals*, ed. by Edward Waldo Emerson and Waldo Emerson Forbes [1912], VIII, 528). A better-known and frequently quoted variant is believed to have been first used by Emerson in one of a series of lectures given in California in 1871: "If a man can write a better book, preach a better sermon, or make a better mouse-trap than his neighbor, though he build his house in the woods, the world will make a beaten path to his door."

[19] A paraphrase of a line in the *Huai-nan-tzu* (Chu-tzu chi-ch'eng ed.), chüan 10, p. 158. Fragrance is by nature a feminine quality.

cassia bait is to lose the catch.[20] The saying, "Reason is covered up by flowery expressions"[21] probably means just this. "She is dressed in a brocade dress, over which is an unlined slipover robe": it is dislike of the gaudiness of the brocade dress that prompts the use of the slipover robe.[22] In the hexagram *pi* [of the *Book of Changes*], under "hsiang," the ultimate color is said to be white.[23] The important thing is to return to the fundamentals.[24] If a writer can work out a plan for expressing his ideas and formulate a basic outline for speaking his mind [then his ideas will be well organized and his mind will be at rest]. When his mind is at rest, he may then begin to formulate a sound pattern, and when his ideas are well ordered, he may then array them with literary decorativeness. In this manner, the substance will not be damaged by the literary adornment, and the mind will not be drowned in a mass of erudite information. The classic pattern will shine forth in vermilion and indigo, and the vulgar color scheme of blue and purple[25] will be supplanted. Only then may a writer be spoken of thus: "Carved and chiselled is his external pattern,"[26] and it will be said of him: "He is indeed a man of virtue, whose external form perfectly balances his inner substance."[27]

   The Tsan:
Words travel far because of their literary beauty:
This is very fully borne out by experience.
When the thought in the mind is well formed,
It blooms forth in glory.
The silk from Wu easily fades,
And the blooms of the *shun* tree are beautiful to no good purpose.[28]

20 Ma Kuo-han, *Yü-han shan-han chi-i shu*, chüan 72.
21 *Chuangtzu yin-te*, 4/2/25.   22 *Mao-shih yin-te*, 12/57/1.
23 *Chou-i yin-te*, 15/22/shang, hsiang. *Pi*, the name of the hexagram, means ornamental. The original line runs: "To use white as an ornament is free from misfortune."
24 In this case, white is the fundamental color for ornament.
25 For the connotation of purple, see note 19, Chapter IV. Like purple, blue is a secondary color, and hence has a similar connotation.
26 *Mao-shih yin-te*, 60/238/5.
27 A paraphrase of a line in the *Analects*. See *Lun-yü yin-te*, 10/6/18.
28 The flowers of the *shun* tree, also known as *chin*, fade in a day.

Flowery rhetoric, when lacking in genuine feeling,
Soon dulls our taste.

XXXII. *Casting and Cutting, or, On Editing of Ideas and Rhetoric (Jung-ts'ai)*

When emotions and ideas are in order, literary patterns become apparent. The nature of the ideas expressed in a literary piece—their vigor or their delicacy—determines the choice of a fundamental form for a piece; and the flexible adaptability to changing situations enables one to meet the varying needs of different times. In establishing fundamental form, there are definite genres to choose from, although one may err through personal bias. But there is no definite formula for meeting the needs of the time; hence rhetoric often suffers from verbosity and confusion. The important task for a writer, then, is to cast and to cut, that is, on the one hand to give form to his emotions and ideas, and on the other to polish his rhetoric. For *jung*, or casting, means to give form to fundamentals, and *ts'ai*, or cutting, means to shear away or delete superfluous words. The operation of cutting will prevent the growth of verbal weeds, and the process of casting will bring into relief the immanent logical order. The results may be compared to the clearly marked distinctions of a carpenter's line, and the relief cut out with the blade of an ax. A double toe or finger is a superfluous part one is born with, and a tumor or goiter is a superfluous part acquired by one's body. In literature repetition of an idea is an intellectual polydactyl; and the redundance of a phrase or sentence constitutes a tumor of the rhetoric.

During the first moments of our thinking, we are often vexed with a welter of linguistic choices. Lack of a standard in our minds will certainly lead to a misplacing of emphasis. For this reason, we establish three criteria to be considered when a literary piece is contemplated: a good beginning, consisting in choosing the correct genre as the appropriate medium for expressing the inner feeling; as the next proper step, the collection of material which is relevant to the theme; and as the final step, the creation of linguistic patterns forceful enough to raise the important points into relief. And then one may attend to the floral embellishment and the arrangement of facts to be treated; or he may decide what new passages to add or sentences to delete. Strict application of literary principles and selective "carving" of material with intrinsic excellence will naturally result in unity, coherence, and order. If a writer fails to master these criteria and allows his mind to go wherever rhetoric leads it, he will be overwhelmed by mistakes and burdened with literary double toes and tumors.

Now that we have established the three criteria, we may begin to consider the choice of words, or forming of sentences. If there is any sentence that can be deleted, we know the writing is loose. And when not a word can be removed, we know the writing is well-knit. Essential ideas and important statements give us a short, pithy form, and winding thought and running rhetoric are always lengthy and discursive. The choice of whether to be discursive or pithy depends on the writer's taste. One may elaborate two sentences into one chapter, or he may condense a chapter into two sentences. A resourceful thinker is usually a good elaborator, and a logical talent is usually a good condenser. A good condenser deletes words while he preserves the ideas, and a good elaborator uses a number of different expressions to make the ideas clear. If the clarity of the ideas suffers because of the reduction, the result will be poverty of ideas instead of logic; and if linguistic redundance results from the rhetorical embellishment, the result will be weedy and vague instead of resourceful.

Chang Chün[1] once said of Hsieh Ai and Wang Chi, both literary scholars of Hsi-ho,[2] "Ai's writing is lengthy, but no part of it can be deleted; while Chi's is short, but nothing can be added to it." These two

---

[1] See his biography in the *Chin-shu*.   [2] In present Shansi.

may be called experts in the art of casting and cutting; they had a thorough understanding of the discursive and pithy forms.

Shih-heng [or Lu Chi] was talented, but he was long-winded in his rhetoric; his brother Shih-lung [or Lu Yün] was slow in thought, but he loved purity and brevity. Yün, in evaluating Chi's work, often criticized his discursiveness, but he did not consider it a fault because of the freshness of his thought. This attitude is, in fact, the result of brotherly consideration.

When a dress is to be made, even though the material may be a beautifully embroidered silk, there are still measurements to follow. A tailor will not, because of the beautiful pattern of a material, throw into disorder the relative position of collar and sleeves. If it is difficult for a writer who is clever to succeed in a style which is lengthy and discursive, how much more difficult would it be for a clumsy writer? Of course, in the *Wen-fu* [Lu Chi] says, "Even thorns and brushwood, when allowed to flourish, [will share the reflected glory of the beautiful birds which gather there]" or "strike up vulgar notes to complete a tune."[3] It is not that his understanding is not penetrating, but that he is unwilling to cut the lengthy short.

The hundred segments form one body, and all depend on the spirit for their being; and not a single one of all the various items in literary composition can be divorced from rhetorical expression on the one hand and the writer's feeling on the other. Without casting and cutting, it would never be possible to be rich in opinions and emotions without being too lengthy, or to employ beautiful language without committing excesses.

The Tsan:
A literary composition has its doors and windows,
Whose positions express the architectural balance of the piece.
Language flows like a stream,
And will overflow its banks if it runs too full.
Weighing what to cut and what to add,

[3] See note 13, "Preface."

Considering what to enrich and what to thin,
Cutting short the lengthy and shearing away the weedy,
This is the way to avoid tedious burden.

XXXIII. *Musicalness*

The origin of music is found in the human voice, inherent in which
is the scale of *kung* and *shang*.[1] Musical quality of the human voice
is inherent in man's very heart blood and physical vitality. On this
basis, early kings created music and song. So we know that musical
instruments depict the human voice: the human voice does not imitate
the sounds of the instruments. Language may be the crux of literary
writing and the key to the divine intelligence [imagination], but the
musicalness of the voice is the result of the movements of the lips and
mouth only.

In antiquity, instruction in singing was preceded by a study of
musical laws, according to which quick notes were to accord with
kung and slow ones with *chih*.[2] *Kung* and *shang* are high notes, while
chih and *yü* are low notes.[3] From the difference in the movement of the
throat, tongue, lips, and teeth, it is possible to distinguish the different
tonal qualities clearly.

When one detects a discordant note while playing a lute, he is aware

[1] Two of the five notes, the others being *chüeh*, *chih*, and *yü*. *Kung* is C; *shang*, D;
chüeh, E; *chih*, G; and *yü*, A. The use of two notes to stand for the whole scale is a
synecdoche.

[2] See *Han-fei-tzu*, chüan 13, Chapter 34, "Wai-ch'u-shuo," yu, shang, p. 245.

[3] The original reading: "*Shang* and *chih* are high notes, while *kung* and *yü* are low
notes." According to Huang K'an, the line should run: "*Kung* and *shang* are high notes
and *chih* and *yü* are low notes." See his *Wen-hsin tiao-lung cha-chi* (Peiping, 1934),
p. 64. However, interpreting *Kung-shang* to be level tones, and *chüeh-yü* abrupt tones,
Wang Li-k'i, who edited *Le Wen Sin Tiao Long* (Peking, 1951), chooses the following
reading: "*Chih* and *yü* are high notes, and *kung* and *shang* low notes." Huang's reading
is adopted here, because it is more reasonable to think of level tones as high notes and
abrupt tones as low notes than the other way round.

of it and will retune the string. But if there is any fault in a literary composition, the writer seldom recognizes it and makes the necessary corrections. The musical note is produced on strings, and yet it is possible to achieve harmony; but one often fails to achieve concord with the sounds which are born in the mind. Why? Because it is easy to be clever when listening to notes from an external source but difficult to be understanding when listening to the inner voice. The reason for this is that, when we listen to instrumental notes, it is our hands which adjust the strings; but when we listen to the inner voice, we often confuse the sounds with other mental activities. Music may be governed by mathematical formulas, but these cannot be adapted for verbal expressions.

Tones are of two kinds: the flying, or *p'ing*, literally level, and the sinking, or *tse*, literally abrupt; and consonance is also of two varieties: a pair of alliterated words or a pair of rhymed words. Neither an alliterated nor a rhymed pair can be separated in a line or in a sentence without doing some harm to the prosody.[4] Furthermore, a sinking tone, when enunciated alone, sounds abrupt, as if cut short; and a flying tone alone has a tendency to fly away, never to return. All these elements must be interwoven to produce a tightly knit harmonious whole. Should any one element in the concatenation go amiss, a discord will result. It is a type of disease which may be called a stutter in literary writing.

The literary stutter results from a love of the odd. In chasing after the new and strange, the writer naturally embrangles his throat and lips. To get rid of this stuttering, he must be firm in attacking it. If obstructed on the left, he should try his fortune on the right; if hampered in the rear, he should seek a solution ahead. Only then will the tone ring like resonant jade and the language fill the ear with smoothness like that of a string of beads: the beauty or the ugliness of the

---

[4] Both paired alliteration and paired rhyme are considered a compound, always to be kept together. The *Book of Poetry* abounds in these compounds. *Ts'en-ts'i* is an alliterated pair and *yao-tiao* a rhymed pair. See poem no. 1. Transliteration is Karlgren's.

spoken sound and the graphic picture[5] appears in the metrical chanting of it. Literary taste is expressed in words and sentences; and
vitality finds its full manifestation in *ho*, or harmony, and *yün*, or
rhyme. By *ho* is meant the harmony of different sounds and tones, and
by *yün*, the consonant response of the same final vowel.[6] The *yün* has
a definite pattern, so it is comparatively easy to arrange the sounds to
fit the pattern; but the *ho* elements are sometimes low and sometimes
high, so it is rather difficult to harmonize all the tones. Although it
may be easy for a writer to be deft in wielding a pen, he will find it
difficult to select tones which will be harmonious; on the other hand, it
is difficult to achieve perfection in literary writing, although it is easy
to versify according to a rhyme scheme. However, although the subtle
and delicate nature of the employment of *yün* and *ho* is difficult to
describe, we have here touched upon the main principles involved.

Perfect accuracy in music is illustrated in the blowing of a flute.
The choice of notes to achieve harmony is illustrated in the playing
of a lute. In playing a lute, the musician must move the bridge constantly and may therefore occasionally make mistakes; but in flute
playing, since the notes are all of a fixed nature, it does not matter
how the musician plays, he will always produce the note intended. The
writing of Ch'en Ssu [or Ts'ao Chih] and P'an Yüeh is of the nature
of a flute-blowing melody, while that of Lu Chi and Tso Ssu is of the
nature of the bridge-moving harmony of the lute player. On the basis
of these examples one may draw many further inferences.

The Ancient Poets generally emphasize purity and conciseness in
their rhyme scheme. But the songs of Ch'u manifest Ch'u characteristics, and their pretentious rhyme scheme is very complicated indeed.
When Chang Hua treated of rhyme, he said that Shih-heng [or Lu
Chi] exhibits many Ch'u characteristics; and in the *Wen-fu*, Lu himself mentioned, "Keep the full details without change."[7] [Lu] may be

----

[5] "The sound and picture" is from a line of Yang Hsiung's *Fa-yen*, quoted in an
earlier chapter. See Chapter XXV, p. 144.

[6] Two or more lines ending in the same vowel.

[7] Lu Chi's *Wen-fu*, in *Wen-hsüan*, chüan 17, p. 174. Liu Hsieh quotes this line to
show Lu Chi's love of pretentious style.

said to have attached himself to the musical pattern of Ling-chün [or
Chü Yüan],[8] and to have lost sight of the classical tune based on the
huang-chung[9] [and the twelve-tone scale]. The organization of sounds
in a musical pattern should be smooth and round. A pretentious sound
pattern in a literary piece is generally hopelessly more impracticable
than the forcing of a square handle into a round socket. If one is able
to avoid this fault of the square handle, he will not commit any great
mistake.

A well-trained talent with a deep understanding is usually fastidious
about the choice of words and tones; but a less experienced person
perfunctorily takes the sounds as they come along. Sounds taken as they
come may be compared to those produced by a sweeping wind, or the
jarring notes from the *yü*[10] played by [the inept] Nan-kuo.[11] The
Ancients arranged their musical jade pendants by placing the *kung*
jade on the left and the *chih* jade on the right, for the purpose of giving
melody to their steps, so as to avoid confusion in the pattern of the
sounds.[12] The musical patterns are used to regulate the sound of a
literary piece. Can they be overlooked?

The Tsan:
In expressing emotion, one must go far for his standard,
But the musical patterns are near at hand.
The rhythm of flute blowing is based on that of our physical vitality,
And the tones of bells, on the sounds of our lips and mouth.
When sounds have their seasoning of salt and plum sourness,[13]
The music will be as smooth as *yü* and *chin*.[14]

[8] The chief poet of Ch'u. See Chapter V.
[9] The first note in the chromatic scale. See note 3, Chapter VII.
[10] A musical instrument consisting of thirty-six reed pipes.
[11] *Chin-shu,* in the biography of Liu Shih: "Mr. Nan-kuo does not [know how to]
play the *yü.*"
[12] See *Li-chi yin-te,* 13/17.
[13] Salt and plum, which are sour, are used to season food. See *Shang-shu t'ung-chien,*
17/0524-31.
[14] *Yü,* elm, whose seeds are edible, and *chin,* a kind of vegetable, are used as spices.
Chin tastes smooth.

When the errors in sound pattern are eliminated,[15]
It will be difficult to hide the musical quality of a piece.

XXXIV. Paragraph and Sentence

There is a definite order to be observed in the treatment of emotions
and ideas, and there is a definite position for each word. The ordering
of emotion and ideas is known as *chang*, or paragraphing; and the
placement of words is called *chü*, or constructing a sentence. *Chang*
means literally "to make clear," and *chü* "to define a position." To
define the positions of words is to string words together to form a distinct sentence; and to make clear emotion and ideas is to give unity
of thought complete form. Although they differ, the functions of
chang and *chü* cross each other like main roads and side streets, afford-
ing good conditions for communication.

In order to express what one has to say, one needs to form sentences
from words, to organize sentences into paragraphs, and to organize
paragraphs into completed compositions. The brilliance of a literary
piece depends on the faultlessness of each paragraph; the clarity of the
paragraph depends on the flawlessness of each sentence; and the purity
of the sentence depends on a happy choice of words. For when the
stem stands up, the branches naturally follow; and when one understands a unifying principle, he understands all about the ten thousand
[phenomena subsumed under that principle].

Literary compositions are sometimes long and sometimes short; and
the division into paragraphs and the construction of sentences conform
to different tempos at different times. For these differences there is no

---

[15] These errors refer to the eight faults in sound patterns, formulated by Shen Yüeh
and others. See Kō Bō Dai Shi's *Bun Kyō Hi Fu Ron*, where these faults are extensively
treated. *Kō Bō Dai Shi Zenshu* (Tokyo, 1910), Vol. VIII, chüan 5, pp. 138-73. In
addition to these eight, Kō Bō Dai Shi discussed twenty other faults. For these additional
faults, see especially pp. 151-62.

fixed rule, and one must adapt his methods to varying circumstances. A sentence is composed of several words, which must be grouped to make sense; and a paragraph comprehends all aspects of one idea, and all must be fully expressed before the paragraph may be considered a paragraph. The way emotions and ideas are introduced and expressed, at tempos varying with different situations, may be likened to the whirl and swirl of a dance, in which each dancer has his special position in the formation and a special limit within which he is constrained; it may also be likened to intonation in singing, with rising and falling cadence.

The Ancient Poets, in forging metaphors, often take ideas out of their context; however, in a composition one organizes paragraphs and constructs sentences in an orderly manner from beginning to end, just as one would pull a silk thread from a cocoon. The beginning lines should lead to the ideas to be embodied in the middle of the composition, and the concluding sentences should reiterate the thought expressed in what has gone before. Thus one may achieve literary beauty in form and organic unity in content, and the piece from beginning to end will be such a tightly knit composition that its different parts will be to each other like flower to calyx. For words, if they lost their appropriate companions, would be isolated without friends; and feelings and ideas, when set down out of order, would float around forever with no place to rest. Therefore, in constructing sentences, one must avoid reversing the proper order of words; and in forming paragraphs, one must pay attention to the order in which the ideas are treated. This is the principle in dealing with feelings and ideas, and the general rule governing rhetoric.

Neither a composition[1] nor the sentences it contains are a fixed length, but the number of words in a composition or in a sentence may be arbitrarily fixed. A four-word line is a close-knit but unhurried unit; a six-word line, though loose, is not slow; and sometimes the pattern is changed to three-word or five-word lines as an adjustment to meet

---

[1] Reading with Wang Li-k'i *"p'ien-chü"* (i.e., a composition and the sentences [it contains]), for *"pi-chü"* (i.e., brush and sentences).

an exigency. The form of the poems and of the *sung*, or sacrificial odes, in the *Book of Poetry*, is marked with a dignity whose proper pattern is the four-word line; exceptions are "Ch'i-fu" and Chao-yin,"[2] which are made up of two-word lines. As far as we can determine, the two-word line pattern began with the "Tuan-chu," a folk song accompanied by the bamboo flute, which was popular during the time of Emperor Huang;[3] the three-word line pattern first appeared in the "Ode to the Chief" composed during the Yü period;[4] the four-word line pattern flourished during the time of the Hsia, as is seen in the song of "Lo-jui" [that is, "Song on the Trend of the River Lo"];[5] the five-word line pattern made its appearance in the Chou dynasty, with the poem "Hsing-lu"[6] as one example; and the six-word and seven-word line patterns are found in both the *Book of Poetry* and the *Songs of Ch'u*. [The last two patterns] achieved perfection in the Western Han period.[7] The evolution of the patterns in expressing feeling has gone full circle, one form replacing another in accordance with the needs of each age.

While some writers vary their rhymes, others repeat the same tone, in order to give cadence and rhythm to their expression and breath. Chia I and Mei Sheng changed their rhymes every two lines, while Liu Hsin and Huan T'an stuck to the same one for a hundred lines. In cases like these, each is carrying out his own intention. Wei-wu,[8] in commenting on *fu*, or poetic prose,[9] expressed disgust with the repetition of rhymes and praised those who were good at changing their rhymes.[10] Lu Yün also said that in the case of the four-word line

[2] See nos. 185 and 268 in the *Book of Poetry*.
[3] See note 3, Chapter XXIX.   [4] See note 17, Chapter I.
[5] Could this be what is called the "Writing from the River Lo?" See note 12, Chapter I. According to the "Wu-hsing chih" in the *Han-shu*, the "Lo River Writing" was given to Yü, the creator of the Hsia dynasty, and is contained in Chapter 24 in the *Book of History*, entitled "Hung-fan." The part considered to be the "Lo River Writing" is written in a four-word line pattern, though it is not a song or a poem, as we would expect. See *Shang-shu t'ung-chien*, 24/0090-0155.
[6] No. 17 in the *Book of Poetry*.   [7] Also known as Former Han.
[8] Or Ts'ao Ts'ao, the father of Ts'ao P'ei and Ts'ao Chih.
[9] See Chapter VIII.   [10] This quotation is not identifiable.

pattern it is best to change the rhyme every four lines.[11] From these expressions it would seem that the opinion of these two men about rhyme is similar to that of Mei Sheng and Chia I. However, if we change the rhyme every two lines, we may find the tonal pattern a little too hasty; but on the other hand, not to change the rhyme for a hundred lines will tax the lips and mouth to the full. Although an exquisite talent with a passion for words may be able to achieve the best in whatever form he happens to apply his mind to, it is better to hold to the mean with the certainty that one will not plunge into a pitfall.

The Ancient Poets used the [purely metric particle] *hsi*[12] as an integral part of a sentence; but in the "Songs of Ch'u" it is used as an extra word. In fact, *hsi* in a sentence serves to assist the words by prolonging their sound. It was used long ago by Shun when he composed his "Nan-feng."[13] But Wei-wu did not like it, perhaps because it adds nothing to the meaning of a piece? *Fu, wei, ḳai*, and *ḳu* are particles to initiate a sentence;[14] *chih, erh, yü*, and *i* are particles used traditionally as conjunctions inserted in the middle of a sentence;[15] *hu, tsai, i*, and *yeh* are particles usually used to conclude a sentence.[16] These particles seem idle words with no factual content, but in use they have

---

[11] Quoted from his letter to his elder brother Lu Chi.

[12] A particle giving pause to a line without adding to it any new sense.

[13] See note 10, Chapter VI.

[14] When placed at the beginning of a sentence, the particle *ju* serves to initiate the ideas expressed; *wei*, to show a contrast to the idea in the previous sentence; *ḳai*, to introduce a fact or a general truth; *ḳu*, to show a causal relation between the sentence it introduces and the preceding one.

[15] *Chih*, when placed in the middle of a sentence, serves as a particle to show a relationship between what precedes and what follows it; *erh*, to show a transition or addition; *yü*, to express a relationship or comparison; *i*, to show instrumentality, reason, etc.

[16] When placed at the end of a sentence, the particle *hu* serves to express either a question or an exclamation; *tsai*, to express an exclamation; *i*, to indicate the completion of an idea; *yeh*, to indicate the conclusion of a sentence, serving as a full stop. In explaining these particles, I have stated that "when placed" at certain positions, they would mean such and such, because we do find them also placed at other places than those enumerated by Liu Hsieh. Obviously it was not his interest either to make an exhaustive study of all the functions of the particles mentioned, or to study all the particles exhaustively, though such a study could have been very interesting and important. At any rate, Liu Hsieh deserves commendation for being the first to direct attention to some of the particles and treat them as a group.

a real function to perform. Clever writers will use them dexterously to fill in whatever is lacking in the style, assisting the sentences with these extra words. If no mistake can be permitted in the use of extra words, how much less can it be allowed when one is engaged in forming paragraphs and constructing sentences!

   The Tsan:
There are rules about the organization of a paragraph,
Though sentence construction is without a definite pattern.
Ideas should be developed around a central theme,
And elements of rhetoric should never be without appropriate companions.
Define emotion by the choice of a proper tune,
So that they may encircle and respond to each other.
When to separate, when to merge, when to emphasize similarity and
   when to emphasize difference—
These decisions are worthy of one's utmost effort.

XXXV. Linguistic Parallelism

Nature, creating living beings, endows them with limbs in pairs. The divine reason operates in such a way that nothing stands alone. The mind creates literary language, and in doing this it organizes and shapes one hundred different thoughts, making what is high supplement what is low, and spontaneously producing linguistic parallelism.

   During the ages of the T'ang and the Yü,[1] when language was not adorned to any great extent, we already find Kao Yao using the following expression:

   tsui i wei ch'ing
   kung i wei chung

---

[1] Dynasties ruled by Yao and Shun, two ancient legendary kings.

[Crime: when in doubt, then deem it light;
Merit: when in doubt, then deem it heavy.][2]

and I [another minister of Shun] saying:

man chao sun
ch'ien shou i
[Fullness of self brings decrease;
Modesty receives increase.][3]

Without intending to produce couplets, they did so, spontaneously. The "Wen-yen" and "Hsi-tz'u" of the *Book of Changes* embody the profound thought of the Sage. In the narration of the four virtues of the hexagram *ch'ien*, the sentences are matched in couplets, and in the description of the kinds of responses evoked by the dragon and the tiger, the words are all paralleled in pairs. When describing the hexagrams of *ch'ien* and *k'un* as easy and simple respectively, the passage winds and turns, with lines smoothly woven into one another; and in depicting the going and coming of the sun and the moon, the alternate lines form couplets. Occasionally there may be some variation in the structure of a sentence, or some change in word order, but parallelism is always the aim.[4] As to the parallelism found in the work of the Ancient Poets or in the antiphonal lines of the Chou ministers,[5] both contain both single elements[6] and couplets, each appropriate for the situation at hand; and these come forth spontaneously with no trace of labor. In the hands of Yang [Hsiung], [Ssu-] Ma [Hsiang-ju], Chang [Heng] and Ts'ai [Yung], all of whom stressed linguistic parallelism particularly strongly, couplet writing flourished as spectacu-

---

[2] The *Book of History* (Shih-san-ching chu-shu ed.), 4/7a. Kao Yao was a minister of Shun. I have arranged the two lines in such a way as to show the parallel structure. More freely translated: "When we are in doubt about the crime committed, we would rather err on the side of lenience; and when we are in doubt about someone's merit, we would rather err in giving a heavier reward than is deserved."

[3] *Ibid.*, 4/14a.

[4] For the text of this passage, see *Chou-i yin-te*, 1/1/yen, 2/1/yen, 39/Hsi shang/1, 46 Hsi hsia/3.

[5] It was the general practice at that time for diplomatic envoys to sing their missions in verse, and to be answered in verse.

[6] I use "element," because it may refer to characters, phrases, or sentences.

larly as Sung painting[7] and Wu casting,[8] and in fact they too indulged
in a species of carving and engraving; as a result of it, we find their
coupled sentences developing side by side with colorful patterns, and
their parallelism bursting forth in conjunction with exquisite tonal
arrangement. The host of talented writers during the Wei and the
Chin analyzed sentence structure with scrupulous attention and coined
phrases in harmony with their thought; they even split hairs, and
scrutinized the infinitesimal. But only those who struck the mysterious
spring entered into the realm of art. The superficial and the sophisticated labored to no avail.

Of the forms of couplet there are four kinds: the verbal couplet, the
factual couplet, the couplet of contrast, and the couplet of agreement.
It is easy to compose a verbal couplet, but it is comparatively difficult
to make a factual one; a couplet of contrast is superb, but one of agreement is comparatively poor. In a verbal couplet, one matches mere
words; in a factual couplet, one must deal with what is actually experienced; a couplet of contrast is one in which different ways of reasoning
meet on common ground; and a couplet of agreement one in which
different facts illustrate a single idea.

For example:

The verbal couplet: "Labor to improve your demeanor in the garden
of rites; let yourself soar in the field of books." From the "Shang-lin fu"
by Ch'ang-ch'ing [or Ssu-ma Hsiang-ju].

The factual couplet: "[The ancient beauty] Mao-ch'iang, hiding
herself behind her lapel, may not be the standard to compare [the
goddess] with; [the ancient beauty] Hsi-shih, her face covered, lost
color before [the goddess]." From the "Shen-nü fu" by Sung Yü.

---

[7] *Chuangtzu yin-te*, 56/21/45: "The ruler of Sung was having paintings made. All
the painters gathered together and stood up ceremoniously after receiving their commissions and doing obeisance to the ruler. . . . One painter came late, walking un-
hurriedly, and when he received his commission he did not stand up. Instead, he went
to his quarters. The ruler sent someone to watch him. He found that the painter had
taken off his dress and sat naked with his two legs stretched out. The ruler said, 'This
is the right way to behave. He is indeed a true painter.' "

[8] The state of Wu is famous for casting swords. See the "Ho-lü nei-chuan" in the
Wu-yüeh ch'un-ch'iu.

The couplet of contrast: "Chung I, the humble, played the music of Ch'u; Chuang Hsi, the prominent, groaned in the manner of Yüeh."[9] From "Teng-lou fu" by Chung-hsüan [or Wang Ts'an].

The couplet of agreement: "Han-tsu thought of Fen-yü; Kuang-wu thought of Pai-shui." From "Ch'i-ai" by Meng-yang [or Chang Tsai].[10]

A verbal couplet can be forged in one's imagination—hence it is easy; a factual couplet must have an actual source in one's knowledge—hence it is difficult; the "humble" [i.e., Chung I] and the "prominent" [i.e., Chuang Hsi] contrast, but express the same nostalgia—hence the couplet is superb; in the example of the couplet of agreement, the two main characters are both rulers and have identical hopes—hence it is poor. Furthermore, of the factual couplets, some may be couplets of contrast and some of agreement. If one can infer on the basis of these principal categories, he will see the ten thousand branches lying revealed before him.

Chang Hua wrote in one of his poems:

Roaming geese soar together wing to wing;
Returning swans know enough to link their plumes.

And Liu K'un also wrote:

Hsüan-ni [or Confucius] lamented the capture of the unicorn;
During the hunt in the west K'ung Ch'iu [or Confucius] shed tears.[11]

---

[9] Chung I, a native of Ch'u, became a captive in Chin. When asked to play the lute, he played a southern tune, a spontaneous expression of a desire to go home. See *Ch'un-ch'iu ching-chuan yin-te*, 228/ch'eng 9/fu 2. Chung Hsi, a native of Yüeh, became a high official of Ch'u. When sick, he groaned in the manner of Yüeh, also a spontaneous expression of a nostalgia. See *Shih-chi* (1739), chüan 70, the biography of Ch'en Chen, p. 18b.

[10] The first three pieces cited here are found in the *Wen-hsüan*. The last one is not, though two other poems by Chang Tsai with the same title are included in the *Wen-hsüan*. Han-tsu (or Kao-tsu), the first emperor of the Han dynasty, sacrificed at the temple in the village of Fen-yü in his home district, with the hope that the deities might help him bring peace to the empire. See *Han-shu*, "Chiao-ssu chih." Kuang-wu, the first emperor of the Later Han, also hoping for peace, for he had had to fight his way to the top, thought of Pai-shui, a river, the theme of an ancient poem now lost. Among the lines which are preserved in Liu Hsiang's *Lieh-nü chuan* are these two lines: "The state has not been pacified; where shall I proceed?" See Liu Hsiang's *Lieh-nü chuan* (Ssu-k'u pei-yao ed.), chüan 6, p. 4.

[11] Both "wing to wing" and "to link plumes" mean companionship or love. And in

Such redundance makes these lines examples of polydactylism in parallel sentences.[12]

In a verbal couplet, the beauty lies in artistry and cleverness; but in a factual couplet, the important thing is appropriateness. When two verbal expressions of unequal quality are matched in a couplet, it is like harnessing to a two-horse carriage a thoroughbred on the left and a nag on the right. An isolated fact unmatched is like the one-legged monster *k'uei*, which hobbles and limps.[13] If a literary piece lacks wonderful spirit or vitality, or if its language is without extraordinary patterns, then even if it is full of beautiful parallel expressions, their mediocrity serves merely to make our ears and eyes drowsy and to put us to sleep. What is important here then is to make the reasoning coherent and the factual reference pertinent; to fill the paragraphs with dazzling jade in pairs, to use alternatingly single and coupled elements, and to moderate the brilliance of the effect through the variety of the pendants. If one generalizes on the basis of these observations, he will see the main principles unravel of themselves.

The Tsan:

A body requires its limbs to be in pairs;
A phrase, once forged, must have its counterpart.
With the left hand one lifts; and one holds with the right,
To attain both the essence and the flavor.
Parallelism gleams and dazzles like flowers which are entwined,
Reflecting without distortion like a calm mirror.
It flows in two streams, smooth as jade,
Giving rhythm as do the pendant jewels.[14]

Liu K'un's verse both lines have exactly the same theme, that is, that Confucius was sad on hearing of the capture of the unicorn during the hunt in the west.

[12] Chang Hua's poem is found in the *Yü-t'ai hsin-yung*, compiled by Hsü Ling, 507-583; Liu K'un's poem is found in *Wen-hsüan*.

[13] For the one-legged monster, see *Han-fei-tzu*, chüan 12, Chapter 33, "Wai-ch'u-shuo," tso, hsia, p. 222; and *Chuangtzu yin-te*, 44/17/53.

[14] See *Li-chi yin-te*, 13/17.

XXXVI. Metaphor[1] and Allegory (Pi and Hsing)

Broad and profound is the *Book of Poetry*, in which are contained the Six Elements.[2] Master Mao[3] in his commentary, however, drew particular attention to the *hsing*, or allegory, alone; was this not perhaps because the *feng*, or lyric, spontaneously stirs the emotions, the *fu*, or narrative, might affect them indifferently, and the *pi*, or metaphor, is obvious, but the *hsing* alone is obscure? *Pi* involves reasoning by analogy, and *hsing* response to a stimulus. When we reason by analogy, we group things by comparing their general characteristics; and when we respond to stimuli, we formulate our ideas according to the subtle influences we receive. The *hsing* is the result of our responding to a stimulus, and the *pi* a consequence of reasoning by analogy. Formally, the *pi* is a linguistic expression charged with accumulated indignation, and the *hsing* is an admonition expressed through an array of parables.[4] Since the Ancient Poets had to treat of a variety of situations with ever-changing significance, they needed these two devices to express their responses to them.

The parables employed in the *hsing* appear subtle, but they are so apparent! They may sound insignificant, but they are profound in their implications. For example, in the "Kuan-chü"[5] the fishhawks know a formal separation of the sexes, an oblique reference to the virtue of the queen; and the *shih-chiu* bird[6] [in another poem] is chaste, which is also symbolic of the character of the royal mate. Do

---

[1] *Metaphor* is used to cover both simile and metaphor.

[2] See note 2, Chapter V.   [3] See note 20, Chapter XVIII.

[4] Note the moralistic conception of poetry first propounded in the prefaces of the *Book of Poetry*: the "Main Preface" and the prefaces to individual poems, attributed to Wei Hung of the Later Han.

[5] The "Kuan-chü" is the first poem in the *Book of Poetry*, and seems to be a marriage song. But it is traditionally interpreted to be a poem celebrating the virtue of the bride of King Wen, father of King Wu, the founder of the Chou dynasty. *Chü-chiu*, fishhawks, are taken to be the symbol of virtue, because they are believed to practice a formal separation between the sexes, i.e., to have a sense of sexual honor. For this reason, the poem is thought to allude to the virtue of Queen Wen.

[6] The theme of another poem in the *Book of Poetry*, no. 12. *Shih-chiu*, thought to be doves or cuckoos, are believed to be loyal to their mates, hence, a symbol of chastity.

not conjecture about these birds, for what is intended to be emphasized to us is chastity; and do not let these birds of prey distract your mind, because the important thing is the virtue of sexual separation. Such parables are like the first rays of light before the break of dawn, still enveloped in ambiguity. This is the reason why commentaries are required to make the meaning clear.

What do we really mean by *pi*? A description of things used to stand for ideas, and the use of figures of speech to intimate the nature of certain facts. Thus gold and pewter are used to stand for illustrious virtue, a jade tally signifies an outstanding man,[7] a caterpillar means education,[8] cicadas and grasshoppers denote howling and shouting,[9] washing clothes symbolizes sadness of heart,[10] and the rolling up of a mat is used as a figure for firmness of will:[11] these illustrate the meaning of the *pi*. As to lines such as, "Your hemp robe is like snow,"[12] or "The two outside horses go as if they were dancing,"[13] they all belong to the *pi* category.

When King Hsiang of Ch'u trusted in the words of the sycophants, the San-lü,[14] filled with loyalty and moral indignation, created the *Sao* in the spirit of the *Book of Poetry*; the *Sao*, intended as a remonstrance, employs both the *pi* and the *hsing*.[15]

The Han dynasty may have prospered generally, but the poets were weak. The principle of remonstrance was forgotten, and the meaning of *hsing* lost. In their stead we find the *fu*, or narrative, and the *sung*, or sacrificial song, loud in chorus, and *pi* forged profusely as cloud patterns. Such confusion and haste went counter to the principles of old.

There is a variety of ways in which a *pi*, that is, a metaphor, may be

[7] See the *Book of Poetry*, poems nos. 55, 252.

[8] *Ibid.*, no. 96. "Ming-ling" is a caterpillar of an insect identified as *Heliothis armigera*.

[9] *Ibid.*, no. 255.   [10] *Ibid.*, no. 26.

[11] *Ibid.* Actually, the line runs: "My heart is not a mat, you cannot roll it." Rolling up a mat would seem to connote the opposite of firmness. But in classical allusions, Chinese scholars often quote out of context, and expect the reader to understand the meaning by referring in his own mind to the original context and the original meaning.

[12] *Ibid.*, no. 150.   [13] *Ibid.*, no. 78.

[14] The office Ch'ü Yüan occupied before he was alienated. The function of the office was to educate the young members of the three royal clans.

[15] For Ch'ü Yüan and his *Li-sao*, see Chapter V above.

made: it may employ similarity of sound, visual resemblance, comparability to a mental content, or capability of being illustrated by certain facts. Sung Yü, in his "Kao-T'ang fu," wrote: "The mourning of the branches sounds like a yü"; this is a *pi* comparing sounds.[16] Mei Sheng said in his "T'u-yüan," "Ablaze in confusion, [the birds] look like dust in the midst of white clouds";[17] this is a *pi* comparing appearances. Chia I, in his "Fu-niao fu," said, "Calamity and blessing are intertwined like the strands of a cord"; this is a *pi* comparing a physical pattern with a pattern of events. Wang Pao's "Tung-hsiao" contains, [The sound of a flute] "is soft and warm, like the voice of a loving father speaking to his son"; this is a *pi* comparing the sounds of an instrument with the feeling of the heart. Ma Yung's "Ch'ang-ti" has these lines: [The tune of the long horizontal flute] "is rich and continuous, like the eloquence of Fan [Chü] and Ts'ai [Tse]";[18] this is a *pi* comparing the wealth of a sound pattern with the eloquence of argument. And Chang Heng, in his "Nan-tu fu," said, "The dancers rose and danced a Cheng dance which was like the drawing of a silk thread from a cocoon";[19] this is a *pi* comparing the manners of things. Metaphors like these are the chief elements in *tz'u*[20] and *fu*.[21] But poets who employed this *pi* every day forgot the art of the *hsing*. They became versed in the insignificant and lost sight of the important. This is why their writing never equaled that of the Chou period.

As for Yang [Hsiung], Pan [Ku], Ts'ao [Chih], Liu [Chen], and their group, they described mountains and rivers, and the patterns of clouds and things. In these descriptions they wove metaphors into beautiful forms, capable of startling the ears and bewitching the eyes of the reader. This is their achievement. In An-jen's [or P'an Yüeh's]

---

[16] Sung Yü's *fu* is found in the *Wen-hsüan*. For *yü*, see note 10, Chapter XXXIII.

[17] Mei's poem, which is found in *Ku-wen-yüan*, has, instead of "Ablaze in confusion," "Swiftly and in confusion."

[18] Both Fan and Ts'ai were eloquent public speakers of the Warring States period.

[19] This piece and the previous one are both found in the *Wen-hsüan*. The line quoted here is an abbreviation. The original runs: "(They) sat singing the southern songs, and rose to dance the Cheng dance, which was like the soaring of white cranes and the drawing of a silk thread from a cocoon."

[20] See Chapter V above.   [21] See Chapter VIII above.

"Ying-fu," the line "Shooting gold in a sandy beach," and in Chi-ying's [or Chang Han's] miscellaneous poems, the line "Green branches look like a bundle of jade" are both in the true spirit of the *pi*.[22]

Throughout all the variety of the *pi*, the excellence lies in the aptness of the representation. A writer is valueless if, trying to carve a swan, he succeeds only in approximating a duck.

>   *The Tsan*:
> The *pi* and the *hsing* of the Ancient Poets
> Are perfect perceptions resulting from their responses to the stimuli
>   of facts.
> Things which are as far apart as *Hu* [in the north] and *Yüeh* [in the
>   south]
> May through their similarities be as close as the liver and the gall.[23]
> For a writer to be able to be faithful to the original in his representation
>   depends on the working of his mind;
> And in the forging of language he must be both firm and daring.
> In creating lyrics and poems, the mass of materials should be so organ-
>   ized as to flow as smoothly as a stream.

XXXVII. Embellishment as Description

"What is beyond shape is called *tao*, and what is within shape is called *ch'i*."[1] [*Ch'i* means literally instrument, the tangible, hence, the phe-nomenal.] It is difficult to depict the noumenal *tao*, for even words which have been refined cannot approximate it; but the phenomenal *ch'i* are easy to describe, for their forms can be accurately pictured

---

[22] Both P'an's and Chang's poems are found in the *Wen-hsüan*. The theme of P'an's *fu* is the fireflies, which appear like shooting gold in a sandy beach.

[23] *Chuangtzu yin-te*, 12/5/7: "From the point of view of difference, the liver and gall are as far apart as Ch'u and Yüeh." Liu Hsieh made use of this reference with some modifications.

[1] *Chou-i yin-te*, 44/hsi shang/12.

through vigorous language. Amount of talent, whether great or small, has no bearing on this; it is due to the nature of the *tao*, or principle, and the *ch'i*, or particular things, themselves. [In the phenomenal world] all things from heaven and earth downward partake of sound and shape. Whenever language is used to describe them, there is always embellishment in the description. Even in the *Book of Poetry* and the *Book of History*, whose language is marked with classic grace, and may serve as the standard for the whole world to look up to, we find exaggerated accounts of facts, expressed in highly ornamented language. For example: to describe height, we have: "Lofty is [the Sacred Mountain]; grandly it reaches to heaven";[2] to describe narrowness, we have: "[Who says the River is broad?] It is not even wide enough for a knifelike canoe."[3] Referring to a great number, we have: "His sons and grandsons will be a thousand, a hundred thousand";[4] and referring to a small number, we have: "Of the people [of Chou] there was not one body left undamaged."[5] In describing [how the great flood] inundated mountains, [the *Book of History*] talks about its "overflowing heaven";[6] and in speaking of the mutiny [of the Shang troops against their own ruler], it says that "pestles floated" in the bloodshed.[7] The language in all these cases is certainly exaggerated; but it does not do any violence to the ideas. The crying of an owl has always been ugly; could its cry become pleasant because it settled in the grove by the semicircular moat?[8] The *t'u* plants taste bitter; could their taste become sweet because they grew on the Chou plain?[9] Yes, for in these cases the real intention is to praise,[10] and the distortion of the ideas serves

---

[2] The *Book of Poetry*, no. 259. Karlgren's translation.   [3] *Ibid.*, no. 61.
[4] *Ibid.*, no. 249.   [5] *Ibid.*, no. 258.   [6] *Shang-shu t'ung-chien*, 1/0299-0302.
[7] *Ibid.*, 23/0343-0355. In the account of King Wu's campaign against the last ruler of the Shang dynasty, it is said that when the Shang troops revolted there was so much blood shed that pestles floated in it.
[8] The *Book of Poetry*, no. 299: "Fluttering are those flying owls, they settle in the grove by the semicircular moat; they eat the fruits of our mulberry trees, and comfort us with their fine note."
[9] *Ibid.*, no. 237: "The plain of Chou was rich and ample: even the *ch'in* and *t'u* were sweet like honey-cakes."
[10] Poem 299 is in praise of a marquis of Lu, celebrating his interest in the state college, symbolized by the semicircular moat. And poem 237 praises the ancestors of the Chou, who, through thick and thin, had made the plain of Chou inhabitable.

as a kind of ornament. The great Sage's recorded remarks may be treated as principles, expressed by Mencius in the following words: "Those who comment upon the *Book of Poetry* should not because of one term misconstrue the meaning of a sentence; and should not because of a sentence misconstrue the original idea."[11]

Lavish exaggeration in description was first employed in the works of Sung Yü and Ching Ch'a; and [Ssu-ma] Hsiang-ju, who gave [Emperor Wu himself] a sense of flying on the wind,[12] contributed to the ascendancy of literary oddities and excesses. In his "Shang-lin fu" he said that shooting stars and an arching rainbow entered the window of the Shang-lin palace; and elsewhere, in a description of a successful hunt, he wrote that *fei-lien*[13] and *chiao-ming*[14] were caught.[15] Yang Hsiung, following in his wake, spoke of the precious in his "Kan-ch'üan fu" by borrowing the gems of jade trees, and of height by referring to the fall of ghosts and deities.[16] As to [Pan Ku's mention of] the one-eyed fish swimming in pairs in his "Hsi-tu fu,"[17] and [Chang Heng's mention of] the sea deity,[18] in the light of reason there is no possible way to prove them, but as cases of exaggeration, they have not gone to extremes. When Tzu-yün [or Yang Hsiung], in his "Yü-lieh fu," flogged Fu-fei to feed Ch'ü Yüan,[19] or when Chang Heng, in his

[11] *Mengtzu yin-te*, 36/52/4.
[12] See note 2, Chapter XXVIII.
[13] *Fei-lien* is a mythological bird, with the body of a bird and the head of a deer, known as the dragon-sparrow.
[14] Another mythological bird, resembling a phoenix.
[15] "Shang-lin fu" is found in the *Wen-hsüan*.
[16] "Kan-ch'üan fu" is also found in the *Wen-hsüan*.
[17] Following Chi's emendation of reading "Hsi-tu" for "Tung-tu," which is apparently a mistake. See the *Wen-hsüan*.
[18] Also found in the *Wen-hsüan*.
[19] Fu-fei was said to be the daughter of Fu-hsi, a mythological character. She drowned in the Lo River, thus becoming Goddess of Lo. Ch'ü Yüan mentioned her as one of the beauties he wanted, but failed to get. In the original piece the line runs: [Emperor Wu's hunting party] "flogged Fu-fei and fed Ch'ü Yüan, P'eng, and Hsü." See *Wen-hsüan*, chüan 8. Yang Hsiung here tried to point out the extravagant scale of the emperor's hunting expedition. He disturbed the Lo River in the north, of which Fu-fei was the deity, and reached the banks of the rivers in the south where Ch'ü Yüan, P'eng Hsien, and Wu Tzu-hsü drowned. Flogging and feeding are figures for reaching these rivers. Liu Hsieh disregarded the original context and combined the two instances, the flogging and the feeding, as if the poet was flogging Fu-fei to feed Ch'ü Yüan, omitting, in the

"Yü-lieh fu," exiled the water deity to the desert in the north,[20] they were loose indeed in emptily using these excessive descriptions, for neither was the beautiful Goddess of Lo a spirit of the mountains and rivers, nor was the water deity the spirit of hills and marshes.[21] These are cases in which the effort to exaggerate the majestic air and adorn [. . . . .][22] has resulted in incongruity and inconsistent statements.

[There are writings which] describe the appearances of mountains and seas, or body forth the forms of palaces and temples; they make them stand in craggy height, some glimmering and some glowing; ablaze with brilliance, lofty in form, these almost come to life. Such extraordinary spectacles are achieved by exaggeration and adornment. Young talents, full of admiration for physical vitality and ambitious for fame, are thinking of real soaring when they think of flying, and feel ashamed of tolerating the least constraint in step when they think of galloping. When they describe something brilliant and dazzling, not even the colors of spring are good enough to present its beauty; and when they portray a state of blight and decay, not even a winter valley is adequate to indicate its desolation; when they speak of happiness, we hear laughter in the very midst of their words; and when they speak of sorrow, sound is mixed with tears. Writings like these can certainly unfold what is hidden and put to flight what has been earthbound; they open the eyes of the blind and startle the ears of the deaf.

But when adornment goes to extremes, sounds swarm disorderly in the mind; and when exaggeration exceeds what is appropriate, there is incongruity in both name and fact. If one can appreciate the degree of exaggeration employed in the *Poetry* and *History*, and stop short of the excessive elements in the writings of Yang [Hsiung] and [Ssu-]ma

---

process, the other two heroes who also drowned themselves in the water. Liu's chief purpose was, of course, to show the exaggerated embellishment of Yang Hsiung.

[20] Chang's *fu* is found in the *Ch'üan-hou-han wen* in fragments. The line cited here is not found there.

[21] The theme of these two *fu* is hunting, which is believed to be often obstructed by the spirits of mountains and rivers. Since neither the Goddess of Lo nor the water deity was such a spirit. they could do nothing about the hunting. Hence, Liu Hsieh speaks of their use as empty or purposeless.

[22] The text is corrupt here.

[Hsiang-ju], so that exaggeration is held within proper limits, and adornment does not involve falsehood, then he will certainly achieve true excellence.

The Tsan:
Exaggeration and adornment have their function:
When has literature ever followed a straitened path?
The sweep of words is always likened to the movement of a great roc
    [across the sky],[23]
And the expansion of vitality to the gradual rising of geese.
Pour out the sea to get the pearls,
And level Mount K'un for jade:[24]
These figures are exaggerations, but they are not excessive,
Extravagant they certainly are, but still faultless.

XXXVIII. Factual Allusion and Textual Reference

Factual allusion and textual reference are factors outside the realm of literary composition. In a factual allusion, one adduces a fact to support some generalization; and in a textual reference, one cites an ancient text to support a statement. When King Wen wrote propositions for the lines of the hexagrams which he had fixed, in his comment on the nine-in-the-third-place line in the hexagram *chi-chi* he alluded to the military expedition of Kao-tsung in the past;[1] and in his comment on the six-in-the-fifth-place line of hexagram *ming-i*, he mentioned the

[23] The roc is a fabulous bird of enormous size, flying at a height of 90,000 *li*. See *Chuangtzu yin-te*, 1/1/3.

[24] Mount K'un is famous for jade buried in it. Its full name is K'un-kang.

[1] A hexagram consists of six lines. The lines are of two kinds: the *yin*, i.e., a broken line like − −, and the *yang*, i.e., an unbroken line like — . These lines are numbered upward from the bottom. The *yin* lines are known as sixes and the *yang* as nines. The first *yang* line in a hexagram is called the "nine in the first place," and the first *yin* line, the "six in the first place," etc. Hexagram *chi-chi* is number 63 of the 64 hexagrams. "Kao-tsung" was one of the Yin rulers, generally known as Wu-ting, who reigned from 1324 to 1266 B.C. During his reign he led an expedition against the devil's

steadfastness of Prince Chi in recent times.[2] In these examples facts
are adduced to illustrate certain ideas. [In the *Book of History*], when
Lord Yin led his expedition against Hsi and Ho,[3] teachings from the
Cheng-tien were quoted [by Lord Yin];[4] and King P'an-keng repeated
to his people the sayings of Ch'ih-jen.[5] In these cases, maxims of antiquity are cited as general principles. It is then the rule of the Sages and
their general practice in the Classics to cite old maxims to clarify general
principles and to allude to sociohistorical facts to illustrate ideas.

The *Hsiang* commentary to hexagram *Ta-ch'u*[6] says: "The superior
man acquaints himself with many sayings of antiquity and many deeds
of the past," so it is possible that these might also be encompassed
within the scope of literary writing.[7] Ch'ü [Yüan] and Sung [Yü] are
known to have followed the example of the Ancient Poets in their
poetry; but on close examination we find that, although they cited the
Ancient Poems, they did not follow the original texts. However, Chia I,
in his "Fu[-niao] fu," pioneered with his direct quotation from the
Ho-kuan tzu;[8] and [Ssu-ma] Hsiang-ju, in his "Shang-lin fu," quoted

---

country, that is, the Huns, and conquered them. See *Chou-i yin-te*, 38/63/3.

[2] *Ming-i* is hexagram 36. Prince Chi, a relative of the evil tyrant Chou-hsin, the last
ruler of the Shang dynasty, maintained his firm conviction despite his cruel treatment
at the hands of the tyrant. *Ibid.*, 23/36/5 hsiang.

[3] See the "Yin-cheng" (The expedition of Yin), Chapter 9 in the *Book of History*.
Hsi and Ho failed in their duties as astronomers because of their indulgence in drinking.
Hence the punitive campaign.

[4] *Cheng-tien* is believed to be a work of government institutions in the Hsia dynasty.
The teachings cited: "When they anticipate the time, let them be put to death without
mercy; when they are behind the time, let them be put to death without mercy." James
Legge, *The Chinese Classics*, Vol. III, Part I, p. 166. *Shang-shu t'ung-chien*, 9/0162-0177.
"They" refers to astronomers. They were held responsible for the accurate calculation
of the appearance of the heavenly phenomena.

[5] P'an-keng was a ruler of the Yin. Ch'ih-jen's sayings: "In men, we seek individuals
of old families; in vessels, we do not seek old ones, but new." Legge, *The Chinese
Classics*, Vol. III, Part I, pp. 229-30. *Shang-shu t'ung-chien*, 16/0412-0426. For "individuals of old familiies" Legge also suggests "old, experienced men," which seems to
be a better rendering.

[6] *Ta-ch'u* is hexagram 26. For the quotation see *Chou-i yin-te*, 17/26/hsiang, and
also *I-ching*, I, 111.

[7] "These" refers to factual allusion and textual reference, which at the outset of the
chapter were considered as being outside of literary composition.

[8] By a Chou author, whose name is not known. The work is a mixture of Taoism
and legalism.

from a letter written by Li Ssu.[9] But these examples occur only once in ten thousand instances.

By the time Yang Hsiung quoted passages from the *Book of Poetry* and the *Book of History* in writing his "Pai-kuan chen," and Liu Hsin quoted from past histories in writing his "Sui-ch'u fu," writers had come gradually to employ such allusions and references fairly commonly. And when Ts'ui [Yin, ?-92], Pan [Ku], Chang [Heng], and Ts'ai [Yung] began to select passages from the Classics and histories, spreading their flowers and fruits far and wide, and established their reputations through writing, they became models who were imitated by later scholars.

Although ginger and cassia need soil to grow, their bitter taste comes from their nature; similarly, although literary composition requires hard study, real ability to compose comes out of one's natural endowment. Talent issues from within, and study is achieved by external effort. Sometimes one is erudite and yet lacking in talent, and sometimes one is talented and yet a pauper in learning. Poverty in learning makes a writer hesitant in alluding to facts to prove his ideas; while a lack of talent results in a laborious effort to coin phrases to express adequately the feelings. This illustrates the distinction between what proceeds from within and what is achieved by external effort.

Thus, in literary writing, the mind operates in harmony with the writing brush, with talent playing the part of leader, and learning the role of its assistant. When leader and assistant work in perfect harmony, vivid literary patterns will emerge; but if either talent or learning is one-sided or narrow, the result, although it may have artistry, will seldom be a work of high quality. Tzu-yün [or Yang Hsiung], with all his talent, said of himself in a memorial that he was a man deficient in learning, and that his literary achievement was the result of the study he did in the Stone Chamber.[10] That the inner and the

---

[9] Flourished in the latter part of the third century B.C. See D. Bodde's *China's First Unifier*.
[10] The Stone Chamber was built by Hsiao Ho, the first prime minister of the Han

outer must supplement each other is a rule that is true for all times. In speaking of the writing of Master Chang, Wei-wu [or Ts'ao Ts'ao] said that his work was poor; for Chang was superficial in his scholarship and limited in his literary experience, and his only specialty was plagiarizing the insignificant writings of Ts'ui and Tu. Not everything he wrote could be inquired into too closely, for if it were, he could not have identified its original source.[11] This is the result of the fault of being ill-informed.

The Classics and ancient historical records are deep and profound, and they are voluminous in quantity. They are the profound source of all writings, and the spiritual realm in which talent and imagination make their abode. Writers like Yang [Hsiung], Pan [Ku], and others all drew upon them as their sources. In them they tilled and farmed with all their might, and they fished and hunted as they wished. Anyone who is able to hold a knife and do some cutting will surely be among those who enjoy the riches of these sources. Therefore, the development of a writer's talent depends on the breadth of his literary experience. One piece of fur from under a fox's foreleg will not keep one warm, nor could one be satisfied until he had eaten thousands of chicken feet. So in acquiring learning the writer must read widely and in referring to facts he must be concise; in organization he must exercise his logical sense and in reasoning he must be clear and accurate. When all these good points meet in a writer, both his inner and his external potentialities will have been realized to the full. Liu Shao, in his "Chao-tu fu," said, "A retainer of Prince [P'ing-yüan] yelled at strong Ch'u and forced its king to take oath, dipping his finger in blood; and a subordinate official in the employ of a eunuch chided the powerful Ch'in and made its king play the earthen *fou*."[12] Such a use

---

dynasty, to house the maps, charts, and documents he collected from the Ch'in palace. The Chamber became an imperial library, where were deposited all literary works obtained in subsequent reigns. Yang Hsiung's statement is found in his letter to Liu Hsin, now preserved in the *Ku-wen-yüan*, chüan 10.

[11] Wei-wu's statements are not identifiable, and it is impossible to determine who Chang, Ts'ui, and Tu were.

[12] Fragments of "Chao-tu fu" are included in Yen Ko-chün's *Ch'üan san-kuo wen*, chüan 32. These historical facts are mentioned in the *Shih-chi*. See *Shih-chi chi chu-shih*

of historical facts is both entirely reasonable and very significant. For
when facts are adduced appropriately to make a point, these facts,
though not especially important in themselves, will yield real fruit.
Their function may be compared to that of the linchpin of a wheel
which, though only an inch in length, controls the whole wheel, or to
the bolt of a gate which, though only a foot in length, controls the gate.
When subtle words and fitting facts are misplaced so that their significance is lost, it is like using gold and jade to decorate one's legs or
applying cosmetics to one's chest. When a writer's allusions to past
events are appropriate to the situation in question, it is as if he himself
has created them. But if the facts alluded to are out of harmony with
the context, their use will always be a blemish.

Ch'en-ssu [or Ts'ao Chih] was the outstanding talent of them all.
But in his letter to K'ung Chang he said, "The song of Ke-tien was
sung by a thousand voices, and those who chimed in numbered ten
thousand; and for this reason, people did not value the ancient music
of *Shao-hsia*." This is a mistaken allusion, for the song of *Ke-tien* was
sung by a chorus of three men. And [Ssu-ma] Hsiang-ju, in his "Shang-
lin fu," said, "There was the dance of T'ao-t'ang and the song of
Ke-tien, which was sung by a thousand and chimed in with by ten
thousand." The "one thousand singers" and "ten thousand chimers-in"
are products of Hsiang-ju's own imagination, and a flight too far afield
of the original song of Ke-tien; to exaggerate three into ten thousand
is loose reporting and irresponsible rendering, clearly an absurdity.[18]

The "Yüan-k'uei," a poem on a garden sunflower, by Lu Chi, runs:

> [Things] *shelter* their *feet* by the same instinct,
> But each has a unique life pattern which differs from ten
> thousand others.

The sunflower's ability to *protect* its *feet* was cited [by Confucius] to

---

ts'ung-ho yin-te, 76/3b and 15/36b. The name of the retainer is Mao Sui, and the name
of the subordinate official is Lin Hsiang-ju. *Fou* is a musical instrument made of
earthenware. "Dipping a finger in blood" means taking oath at the signing of a treaty.

[18] Ssu-ma Hsiang-ju was the first one to make this exaggerated statement, which
was later quoted by Ts'ao Chih.

ridicule the artless Pao-chuang[-tzu],[14] and that creepers know how to *shelter* their *roots* was stated by Yüeh Yü.[15] So if [Lu Chi] meant to liken the sunflower to the creepers, his allusion is a mistake; and if he thought that *shelter* was a better term to use than *protect*, then he lost sight of the true nature of the original situations in his modification.[16] This is a case of very slovenly thinking. When men as brilliant and keen as Tzu-chien [or Ts'ao Chih] or as penetrating and meticulous as Shih-heng [or Lu Chi] could not avoid making mistakes of this kind, we may as well save our censure in a case like that of Ts'ao Jen, who made a mistake in alluding to Kao-t'ang.[17]

An artificer makes judgments about timber, and a literary man makes choices among the Classics. Good timber is transformed into definite form by the application of an ax; appropriate facts are turned into a part of a literary work through the exercise of knife and brush. May scholars, whose function it is to think, be worthy of their names in the face of the artificer!

The Tsan:

Profound and rich are the Classics and ancient texts,

Their language is exquisite and their ideas have far-reaching implications,

[14] *Ch'un-ch'iu ching-chuan yin-te*, 247/Ch'eng 17/5 Tso: "Confucius said, 'Pao-chuang-tzu did not have even the instinct of a sunflower, for even a sunflower is able to *protect* its *feet*.'" Confucius made this remark when he heard that Pao-chuang-tzu's legs had been cut off by the Duke of Ch'i because of a charge of implication in a certain court intrigue of which Pao was unable to clear himself. [Italics mine.—V.Y.S.]

[15] *Ch'un-ch'iu ching-chuan yin-te*, 155/Wen 7/5 Tso: "Duke Chao [of Sung] was about to dispose of the princes. Yüeh Yü said, 'This is not right. The royal clans are the branches and leaves of the royal house. Should they be disposed of, there would be nothing to *shelter* its *roots*. Even creepers know how to *shelter* their *trunks* and *roots*, . . . how much more do we expect a ruler of a state to be able to do so.'" [Italics mine.—V.Y.S.]

[16] To keep the allusion free from confusion, instead of "shelter their feet," Lu Chi should have said, "protect their feet," because "protect" was originally used with feet in a situation when the sunflower was cited as a comparison. Lu's modification serves only to confuse the picture.

[17] Ts'ao Jen should be Ts'ao Hung, who, in his letter to Wei Wen-ti, or Ts'ao P'ei, said, "It is said that people who pass by Kao-t'ang sing in the manner of Wang Pao." According to Mencius, it was Mien Chü, and not Wang Pao, who was a singer at Kao-t'ang, and whose song everyone wished to learn. See *Mengtzu yin-te*, 48/6B/6.

Their realm is vast as rivers and seas,
And fruitful as Mount K'un and Forest Teng;[18]
They are [filled with literary allusions and timber] for a literary
    carpenter to choose and take,
And jade and pearls in abundance as gifts.
To be able to use the words of others as if they were one's own creation
Is to have perfect understanding of the past.

XXXIX. Philology and Choice of Words[1]

When the array of written signs was complete, the practice of knot
tying was discontinued; it was the markings of birds which showed
the way toward the creation of characters. These signs and characters
make up the external appearances of our speech and are the dwelling
place of literary form. When Minister Ts'ang Chieh first devised them,
ghosts cried and heaven rained grain [as an omen of the power of the
characters].[2] The Yellow Emperor, through their use, made officials
fulfill their duties and chronicled the conditions of the people in bold
relief. According to the principles established by the early kings, all
characters ought to be written in the same style. And royal emissaries
were sent out to record opinions and usage among the people, for the
purpose of standardizing the script and pronunciation. In the *Chou-li*
(Book of Chou institutions) there is mentioned Pao-shih, whose duty

18 For Mount K'un, see note 24, Chapter XXXVII. Forest Teng is a legendary forest
mentioned in the *Huai-nan-tzu*, "Tsui-hsing": "K'ua-fu [a spiritual beast] threw away
his staff, which turned into Forest Teng."
1 The first part of this chapter is based on the "Epilogue" to the *Shuo-wen*, which
is a lexicon by a Han scholar named Hsü Shen. The book was completed in A.D. 100.
2 Ts'ang Chieh, a minister of the Yellow Emperor, was credited with the invention
of characters. In the "Pen-ching-hsün" of the *Huai-nan tzu* it is said that when Ts'ang
Chieh invented characters, heaven rained grains and ghosts cried at night. Wang Ch'ung,
a Han scholar and a naturalist, convincingly refuted this statement which suggested the
evil effect of the invention of characters. See his *Lun-heng*, "Kan-hsü p'ien" (Chu-tzu
chi-ch'eng ed.), p. 52.

it is to teach the six lexigraphic principles.[3] When the Ch'in[4] [autocrat] put the old texts to the fire,[5] it was the government officials who were made teachers instead.[6] Prime Minister Li Ssu created Ch'in's *chuan* or "seal style" by modifying the old script, which had been devised by Historian Chou [of King Hsüan of Chou, 827-782 B.C.]; later Ch'eng Miao created what is known as the *li* style.[7] Since that time the ancient script has been abandoned. In the code compiled during the first years of the Han, the rules governing character writing are clearly published. The grand historian, in his instruction of the pupils, taught them and examined them on the six styles.[8] And officials and others who made mistakes in writing characters in their memorials were customarily impeached and punished. For example, Shih Chien, missing a stroke in the character *ma* [horse, in his memorial to the throne], was afraid of the death penalty.[9] Although this was because he was a cautious man, it also indicated that the character writing was considered of great importance at the time. During the reign of Emperor Wu [140-87 B.C.], [Ssu-ma] Hsiang-ju composed the lexicon *Fan-chiang p'ien*. During the reigns of Emperors Hsüan [73-49 B.C.] and P'ing [A.D. 1-5],[10] attempts were made to collect philological works. Chang Ch'ang permanently standardized the correct pronunciation,

---

[3] These principles are: pictographs, simple ideographs, compound ideographs, loan characters, phonetic compounds, and derivative characters. See Y. R. Chao, *Mandarin Primer* (Harvard University Press, 1948), pp. 60-63.

[4] The first dynasty under which China was unified.

[5] This happened in the year 213 B.C. The first emperor of the Ch'in dynasty was intent on standardizing not only weights and measures and other more tangible aspects of the life of the people, but sought also to unify thought by doing away with all books which might for one reason or another challenge his authority.

[6] Not all books were burned. Books spared were housed in the imperial library. The people were forbidden to keep books in their homes, on pain of death. If they wished to learn, they had to go to the government. A neat method of thought control.

[7] A square type of script evolved by modifying the *chuan* style.

[8] According to the "I-wen-chih" in the *Han-shu*, the code was compiled by Hsiao Ho. The six styles are: *ku* or ancient; *ch'i* or strange (*ch'i* is a variety of *ku* style); *chuan* or seal; *li* or square; *miu-chuan* or winding seal; and *ch'ung* or worm style.

[9] *Shih-chi*, the biography of Wan-shih chün, chüan 103; *Han-shu*, the biography of Shih Fen, chüan 46.

[10] Instead of Emperor "P'ing," the text has Emperor "Ch'eng," which is apparently a mistake. See "Epilogue" to the *Shuo-wen*, and the "I-wen chih" in the *Han-shu*.

and Yang Hsiung wrote philological elucidations of strange characters.[11] Both [Chang and Yang] were versed in the lexicons [*Erh-*]*ya*[12]
and [*Ts'ang-*]*chieh p'ien*,[13] and made a comprehensive study of both
the pronunciation and the meaning of characters. These works came
to be thoroughly understood by all who were great writers. These
writers composed narrative *fu* on capital cities and gardens, employing
loan characters and phonetic compounds. For this reason, the philological studies of the Former Han were concerned mostly with re-
markably important characters. This was due not only to their unique
philological system, but also to the unusual fact that such a system
was common knowledge among all writers.

By the time of the Later Han, the study of philology went into
eclipse. Attention was directed to "double script" and "obscure commentary," of which half is good and half is poor.[14]

During the Wei dynasty, the emphasis was on literary patterns, and
there was a general rule governing the use of characters. When people
returned to the works of the Han, they found them difficult and deep.
Thus Ch'en Ssu [or Ts'ao Chih] spoke of the works of Yang [Hsiung]
and [Ssu-]ma [Hsiang-ju] as obscure in aim and deep in purpose, their
language incomprehensible in the absence of a teacher and their ideas
not understandable without broad scholarship. This was due not only
to the fact that Yang and Ssu-ma were outstanding talents, but also
to the fact that the characters which they used had become obscure.

Since the time of the Chin, writers in general have used simple and
easy characters. For if everybody is used to the easy, who will essay the
difficult? Now, one strange or unfamiliar character would arouse a
startled feeling about all of a writer's sentences, and would be described
as "impish" if unrecognized by three people. But what everybody
knows becomes easy, even though it was originally difficult, and what

---

[11] Yang's work is known as "Hsün-tsuan p'ien," also a lexicon. See the "I-wen chih"
in the *Han-shu*.

[12] A pre-Ch'in lexicon, treating of characters found in the Classics.

[13] Another lexicon, written by Li Ssu, the first prime minister of the Ch'in dynasty.
Li used the name of the first lexicographer as his title.

[14] Examples of "double script" and "obscure commentary" may be found in the
"Epilogue" to the *Shuo-wen*.

has been discarded by the age becomes difficult, even though it may have been easy originally. We should exercise the utmost discretion in our choice of words.

The *Erh-ya* was compiled by the disciples of Confucius, and is the lapel and sash of the *Poetry* and *History*. The lexicon *Ts'ang-chieh* was compiled by Li Ssu, and it is the remnant vestiges of Historian Chou's ancient script based on bird-markings. The lexicon *Erh-ya* is the prime source of philological elucidation; the *Ts'ang-chieh* a garden of wondrous literary forms. They differ from each other but supplement each other like the left and right limbs. Those who understand the new by inference from the old are savants in the art of writing.

The meaning of a character changes with the passing of time, as new senses are adopted and old ones are discarded. It also evolves from simple into complex forms, differing in their esthetic appeal. The sound of the mind is expressed in speech, and speech resides in characters: when reciting, we find beauty in *kung* and *shang*, that is, "the consonance of the speech"; and when we compose, our ability is made manifest by the forms of the characters which we choose.

In grouping words and composing a piece, a writer must be versed in the choice of words: first of all, he must avoid what is odd and strange; second, he must avoid characters with the same radical; third, he must weigh carefully his repetitions; and fourth, he must be balanced in the use of the simple and complex forms. By the odd and the strange is meant characters which are unusual. Ts'ao Chü, for instance, has a poem which runs:

> *ch'i pu yüan ssu yu*
> *pien hsin wu hsiung nu*
> [It is not that I do not wish to make this trip,
> But my narrowed mind hates brawling.]

Hsiung and *nu* are two odd and strange words, which spoil the beauty of the whole piece. There are other works using words even more odd and strange than these. How can they be looked upon without aversion?

By characters of the same radical is meant several characters in succession with one radical, that is, one half of each of their forms, in common.[15] In the description of mountains and rivers, such a device has been used in all ages.[16] But when applied to ordinary writing, the practice is a definite defect, because it offends our sensibilities. If it cannot be helped, it may be permissible for the number to grow to three in succession. Once it is allowed to go beyond three, is it not virtually a glossary?

By repetition is meant the conflict created by the appearance of the same character more than once in the same poem. Such occurrences in the *Poetry* and the *Li-sao* are spontaneous and accidental. But in recent times they are considered bad taste. However, if both positions require the same word, it is wiser to allow the second use than to weaken the composition by avoiding it. Therefore, good writers who have the wealth of ten thousand literary pieces to their credit may sometimes find themselves paupers with respect to the availability of one single word. For at times a single word looms large, because it is difficult to avoid repeating it.

Simple and complex forms refers to the plump or the bony appearance of the characters. If sentence after sentence contains a host of bony words, the lines will be thin and sparse, ugly to look at; if, on the other hand, a piece is filled with plump characters, the whole piece will be dark and blotted. One who can choose words well will use the simple and the complex in so harmonious a pattern that visually they will form a string of pearls.

The four points enumerated here, although not necessarily relevant to all writing, must be considered on general grounds. Should one happen to practice them without a conscious realization of their truth, he has not obtained the inner understanding of the art of writing.

---

[15] Note 3 above lists the six lexigraphic principles, of which one is phonetic compounds. A phonetic compound consists of two parts, one serving as the phonetic, and one serving as the signific. Characters constructed on this principle are always complete structures; each constituent may be a radical. In the Chinese language there are 214 radicals. It is possible to form a sentence of several words with the same radical.

[16] That is, it is logical to use characters with the mountain radical when describing mountains, and characters with the water radical when describing rivers.

Now Classics and old documents are often obscure and vague, and their wood and bamboo strips in confusion; the strips are often eaten by bookworms and the silk split to pieces; and many wrong characters creep in, in the course of three copyings.[17] Sometimes the mistake is in the pronunciation, sometimes in the text itself. The disciple of Tzu-ssu[18] [quoted from the *Chou-sung*]: *wu mu pu ssu* ("Oh, it is august and most similar") instead of *wu mu pu i* ("Oh, it is august and never-ending"). This is a mistake in pronunciation.[19] In the historical records of the Chin, there is a line: *san shih tu ho* ["three pigs cross the river"]. This is a mistake in the text,[20] which should run *chi-hai she ho* ["on the date of *chi-hai*, cross the river"]. In the *Shang-shu ta-chuan*,[21] there is a line: *pieh feng huai yü* ["strange wind and torrential rain"]; but in the *Ti-wang shih-chi*[22] we have instead: *lieh feng yin yü* ["strong wind and continuous rain"]. *Pieh* looks like *lieh*, and *huai* looks like *yin*; hence the shift from one to the other was made unknowingly. *Yin* [as used in *yin-yü*, "continuous rain"] and *lieh* [as used in *lieh feng*, "strong wind"] are perfectly appropriate words to use, and do not sound strange; but *huai* and *pieh* are contrary to normal usage and sound strange and odd. However, Fu I, in his "Elegy" [to Prince Ching of Pei-hai], had already used *huai yü* [torrential rain];[23] and Yüan-

---

[17] See Ke Hung's *Pao-p'u tzu*, "Hsia-lan p'ien," quoting a proverb: "When a book is copied three times, *yü* [fish] becomes *lu* [stupid]." These two characters look alike, and are easily mistaken by copyists, one for the other. *Pao-p'u tzu*, chüan 19, p. 97. Wood and bamboo strips and silk are all writing materials.

[18] Tzu-ssu was Confucius' grandson.

[19] The character originally pronounced *i* [ending] is mispronounced *ssu* (one of the twelve earthly branches) because it looks like the character which is pronounced *ssu*. Then this is again mistakenly changed to *ssu*, [similar] because of their being homophonous. The line is quoted from poem no. 267 in the *Book of Poetry*.

[20] *Tu* should be *she*, but since they have the same meaning, they are not what concerned the author. The point here is that *chi-hai*, a term for a specific date, is taken to be *san shih*, meaning three pigs; the mistake was made because *chi-hai*, when carelessly written, looks like *san shih*.

[21] Attributed to Fu Sheng of the Early Han.

[22] By Huang-fu Mi of the Chin, 215-282.

[23] Fragments of the elegy are found in the *Ku-wen yüan*, containing the line cited here. In his chapter on Elegy, Liu Hsieh quoted the same line. See Chapter XII above. But instead of *huai yü* (torrential rain), we find *fen wu* (mists and haze), showing that someone must have altered Liu's text.

chang [or Wang Yung, 467-493] in his "Preface" employed *pieh feng*.[24]
Thus we know that love for the strange is a weakness common to all
writers, both present and past. The textual lacuna has been treated
with caution by the Sage.[25] If one is able to give up what is strange
for what is in harmony with the normal sense, he will be in a better
position to discuss the problem of the right choice of words.

The Tsan:
Chuan, the seal script, and *li*, the square style, influence each other;
The lexicons *Ts'ang-chieh* and *Erh-ya* classify and elucidate.
The old script and the new differ in their forms.
They differ too in their esthetic appeal.
Characters easily become corrupt,
Making the free flow of literary writing difficult.
If both the pronunciation and the strokes of characters are clear and
    correct,
Literary patterns will dance with vigor and liveliness.

XL. The Recondite and the Conspicuous (Yin-hsiu)[1]

The movement of our thought reaches remote distances, and literary
feeling develops from deeply buried sources. A source which is profound permits growth in many directions, and vigorous roots foster
conspicuous branches. In the case of the beauty of a literary composition, it too has both conspicuous and recondite elements. The recondite
elements are the weighty ideas beyond the expressions, and the con-

[24] Yüan-chang's "Preface" has been identified as his "Ch'ü-shui shih-hsü."

[25] See *Lun-yü yin-te*, 3/2/18; 32/15/26.

[1] This chapter is only a fragment. Lines quoted in a work of the Southern Sung
period, 1127-1279, are not found here. An attempt was made to forge the missing
portion, but no scholar was deceived.

spicuous the startling excellencies in the piece. The beauty of the recondite lies in its mystery, and that of the conspicuous in its startling transcendency. It is these which are preeminently the exquisite qualities of the ancient literature, and form the happy conjunction of talent and feeling. The recondite, as a form, suggests ideas which are beyond linguistic expression and are comprehended indirectly through abstruse overtones, which unobtrusively reveal hidden beauty. This creation of meaning may be compared to the practice of forming a new hexagram by realigning the lines of another,[2] or recalling how rivers contain pearls and jade. The realignment of the lines of a hexagram gives birth to the "four images,"[3] and the pearls and jade in the depths of the water cause the formation of square and round waves.[4]

> North wind moves autumn grass;
> Horses at the border think of returning home.

These lines speak of cold weather and sad events, the lament of a man who finds himself exiled from home. Generally, in a volume of collected work, not one tenth may be considered good; and of this tenth scarcely two percent contains lines of startling excellence. The excellent and conspicuous come as the result of spontaneous thought; they are not to be sought by laborious effort. Furthermore, some writers try to appear deep by being obscure; their work may have profundity, but not the quality described as the recondite. Others painstakingly engrave and carve to attain artistry; their work may have beauty, but not startling excellence. Natural beauty is like that of plants lit up in the splendor of their blossoms, and colorful adornment may be compared to silk dyed red and green. The red and green of dyed silks are deep and, indeed, rich and fresh; and the blossoms that brighten the trees, whose beauty is completely exhibited on the surface, glow in blazing

---

[2] Take, for example, hexagram *k'uei*, no. 38: ䷥ ; one may form another hexagram by taking the second, third, and fourth lines, ☲, and the third, fourth, and fifth lines, ☲, to form hexagram *chi-chi*: ䷾, which is no. 63.

[3] See note 15, Chapter II.

[4] For this belief, see *Shih-tzu*, quoted in the *I-wen lei-chü*, chüan 8.

glory. In the same manner, outstanding lines glow in the garden of literature.

   The Tsan:
Profound literary writing contains hidden beauty
With a flavor that is rich and enduring.
The interlacing of the language
May be compared to the realigning of the lines in a hexagram.
An outstanding line
Is the hub where are gathered the ten thousand thoughts.
It moves the mind and startles the ears,
With the music of a *sheng* or a p'ao.[5]

XLI. Literary Flaws

Kuan Chung once said, "That which flies without wings is sound, and that which is firm without roots is feeling." Because sound does not depend on wings, it is very easy for it to fly; and because feeling does not depend on roots, it is not at all difficult for it to gain a firm footing. Since this applies particularly to literary writing, should one not compose with the utmost caution?[1]

Scholars have since earliest times been competitors, even though they may have lived in different ages. Some are endowed with outstanding talent, vigorous and quick; others are deeply contemplative, closely attentive to details. However, it is difficult to achieve perfection in thinking, and rarely indeed has thought ever been without flaws. The writing of Ch'en-ssu [or Ts'ao Chih] is the most talented of all, and

---

[5] *Sheng* is a musical instrument consisting of a number of pipes of different lengths. *P'ao* is also a musical instrument, made of a bottle gourd.

[1] The slightest mistake in literary writing would be broadcast without wings, and become firmly established in the minds of people, though without roots. Hence the necessity of extreme caution.

yet in his "Elegy for Emperor Wu," he said, "May his august spirit eternally hibernate."[2] And in his "Panegyric to Emperor Ming," he said, "His majesty's body flutters and is airy."[3] "Flutters" and "airy" connote qualities which characterize a butterfly, and "eternally hiber- said, "His majesty's body flutters and is airy."[3] "Flutters" and "airy" to apply these phrases to the most exalted of all men?

Tso Ssu, in his "Ch'i feng," speaks of filial piety, and yet does not follow through properly.[4] In the light of the violation of moral prin- ciples involved, there is no point in paying attention to the rest of the writing.

P'an Yüeh was particularly versed in lament. But in lamenting his brother-in-law, he said that he was moved by the remnant grace of the mouth; and in mourning the death of his son, he said that his heart was dazed as if in a state of doubt.[5] These phrases in the *Book of Rites* are meant for people higher in status, but were applied by P'an to those lower in status; although the writings express well his grief, they suffer by the misapplication of these phrases. [In the *Book of Rites* it is said] that a superior man compares people who are comparable.[6] And yet Ts'ui Yüan [77-142], in his "Elegy to Master Li," compared his conduct with that of the Yellow Emperor and Emperor Yü.[7] And Hsiang Hsiu [of the Chin], in his *fu* about Hsi [Kang, 223-262], compared Hsi's crime with that of Li Ssu. Although one ought rather to err in over- estimation than in overcondemnation,[8] if one must err at all, such com- parison is still like the songs which Kao Hou [of Ch'i during Chou

[2] Emperor Wu was Ts'ao Ts'ao, Ts'ao Chih's father, who, though powerful, never actually became emperor. The title was posthumously given him by his son Ts'ao P'ei, who usurped the Han throne in 221 and became the first ruler of the Wei dynasty.

[3] Emperor Ming was the second ruler of the Wei dynasty, Ts'ao P'ei's son and Ts'ao Chih's nephew. Both pieces are found in Ts'ao Chih's collected work: *Tz'ao Tzu-chien chi*.

[4] The work is lost. Liu Hsieh's text is so cryptic that without reference to the original work it is not possible to make it intelligible.

[5] "The remnant grace of the mouth" is used in connection with the mother (*Li-chi yin-te*, 13/24), and "as if in a state of doubt" is used in connection with the funeral of parents (*Li-chi yin-te*, 3/41; 35).

[6] *Ibid.*, 2/18.

[7] The work is not identifiable.

[8] A reference to a saying of Ts'ai Sheng-tzu of the Chou. See *Ch'un-ch'iu ching-chuan yin-te*, 312/Hsiang 26/fu 6.

times] sang, completely out of tune with the nature of the occasion.[9] Language used with artistry easily wins applause, but there is no way to cover up stupid expressions. For a flaw in language may lie even deeper than a flaw in white jade and still be seen.[10] As it is impossible to give examples of all kinds, only four kinds of flaws have been mentioned here.

The factors of prime importance in literary composition are the choice and the meanings of words. Correct choice of words results from a sound grounding in philology, and clarity of meaning comes from a process of careful reasoning. But at the end of the Chin dynasty, vagueness became the order of the day. At first the following words were in use: *shang*, "to appreciate"; *chi*, "to be in the midst of"; *ch'i*, "the strange or extraordinary"; and *chih*, "to arrive," or "the ultimate"; and then there came into vogue *fu*, "to touch"; *k'ou*, "to knock"; *ch'ou*, "to pledge with wine"; and *tso*, "to pledge a host in wine."[11] Often a single word was used to indicate a certain feeling. Now words like *shang*, "to appreciate," *hsün*, "to elucidate or admonish," *hsi*, "to confer," and *lai*, "to bestow," do not concern the understanding of the mind; neither do *fu*, "to touch," *hsün*, "to admonish," *chih*, "to grasp," and *wo*, "to hold," have anything to do with feeling and reason.[12] I have not heard of any reference to these words in the *ya* and the *sung*, nor have I seen them used in the Han and Wei writings. The topics of the writings taken by themselves seem to indicate clear ideas; but a close study of the content reveals that it is nonsense. This is the condition we find when writers become pretentious in expressing their feelings,

---

[9] *Ibid.*, 284/Hsiang 16/3 Tso. Kao Hou, a minister from Ch'i, sang a song at the diplomatic conference called by Chin. It was the general principle of the time to sing songs which were appropriate to the occasion. But Kao Hou selected songs which were not in harmony with the theme of the conference. This violation of the principle was taken by the Chin state to be an attempt on the part of Ch'i to challenge the leadership of Chin.

[10] A reference to the *Book of Poetry*. See *Mao-shih yin-te*, 68/256/5: "A flaw in a white jade can still be ground away; a flaw in language, for that nothing can be done."

[11] It is impossible to determine the specific cases to which these refer. Suffice it to say that these and many others were used during the Six Dynasties period in a way too vague to be considered "correct" or "clear."

[12] No specific cases offer themselves to illustrate the idea our author has in mind in citing the use of these words.

the result of a literary trend of increasing decadence. Writers since the Sung [420-479] have done nothing to alter the trend; it is a literary habit which results from the cumulative effect of constant practice, for such a trend is not the work of one day.

Recent poets are often suspicious. They are addicted to the habit of construing anything written to mean something obnoxious, either by homophonous reading or by a form of reverse spelling.[13] Such a practice, although it would never have been tolerated in the past, must be taken into consideration at the present time.[14]

When we find our writing similar to others' work, it would seem to be our obligation to delete it. Why plagiarize beautiful expressions as if they were our own creations? The precious ceremonial jade and grand bow of Lu will never belong to [the rebel minister Yang Hu].[15] Some indulge in wholesale plagiarism, "carrying away the trunk," and others in selected copying, "picking out of a satchel."[16] However, if one plagiarizes the Ancients, he will be regarded with small contempt, while if he plagiarizes his contemporaries, he is simply courting disaster.

In writing commentaries the purpose is to explain and emend facts and principles. But if the author makes a mistake in his effort to do so, his conclusions may be completely unfounded. In [Chang Heng's]

[13] For homophonous reading, an example of a later age is perhaps the best. Once the first emperor of the Ming dynasty was eulogized in the following words: *wei shih tso tse*, "to be the standard of the world." But, being suspicious in nature and thinking that the writer was ridiculing him because he rose from the lowest level of social hierarchy, he read this as *wei shih tso tse*, "to be the thief of the world." As an example of reverse spelling, let me cite the following case: Jen Fang (460-508) commented upon Ho Seng-chih's poetry as being *k̤ao-hou*, "lofty like heaven and thick or weighty like earth." Ho Seng-chih suddenly became enraged because, by spelling out the two words in reverse, instead of *k̤ao-hou* he got *k̤ou-hao*, "barking of a dog."

[14] Carelessness in this respect might involve one in painful experience, because of the suspicious nature of the writers of the time.

[15] A reference to *Ch'un-ch'iu ching-chuan yin-te*, 452/Ting 8/16. Yang Hu, a house minister of the House of Chi, the minister of the state of Lu. Having failed in a *coup d'état*, Yang Hu got hold of the precious jade and grand bow, insignia conferred upon the Duke of Chou by King Wu, the founder of the Chou dynasty. Literary plagiarism is here compared to the thieving of the state insignia by a rebel minister.

[16] "Carrying away the trunk" and "picking out of a satchel" are expressions describing the conduct of a thief, found in *Chuangtzu yin-te*, 23/10/1, 2.

"Hsi-ching fu," he mentions Chung-huang, Yü, and Huo. Hsieh Tsung, in his comment on them, said they were eunuchs. This proves that Hsieh Tsung had not heard of the man who captured [a monkey with his left hand], while [with his right] he was trying to hit a variegated tiger.[17] And in the *Chou-li,* or "Chou institutions," in connection with land tax, there is the first use of the term *p'i ma,* "one of a pair of horses."[18] Now Ying Shao[19] explained *p'i,* properly "one of a pair," as a suitable adjective to apply to head or hooves. Can we call this the proper way to explain the matter?[20] According to the proper use of terms in ancient times, the term *liang,* "a couple," is applied to carriages, and the term *p'i,* "a pair," to horses. Both *p'i* and *liang* are used to express parallelism. For in the case of carriages, there must be a secondary carriage supporting the main carriage. And in the case of the horses, there are two outside horses and two inner horses. Since neither carriages nor horses ever go alone, either may properly be modified by a term implying a pair. When this purpose of giving terms is properly understood, then even when there is only one horse, the term *p'i* is also applied. For when we speak of *p'i-fu,* "one husband," and *p'i-fu,* "one wife,"[21] the idea of "a pair" is implied.[22]

Now this matter of carriages and horses is certainly not of great profundity, yet it has been misunderstood for ages; and the art of

[17] Chung-huang [Hsia] Yü, and [Wu] Huo were men of strength and courage in ancient times. For Chung-huang, see Li Shang's note to Chang Heng's "Hsi-ching fu," and for Yü and Huo, see *Chan-kuo-ts'e* (Kuo-hsüeh chi-pen ts'ung-shu ed.), Vol. I, chüan 5, p. 40.

[18] Actually the expression occurs in Cheng Hsüan's commentary to "Hsiao-ssu t'u" in the *Chou-li,* and Cheng here was quoting from *Ssu-ma fa,* an ancient work on government and military institutions. See *Chou-li* (Shih-san-ching chu-shu ed., 1815), chüan 11, p. 6b.

[19] Flourishing in the latter part of the second century, author of *Feng-shu t'ung,* explanatory notes on different categories of things.

[20] Ying Shao's *Feng-shu t'ung,* as it exists today, is probably not complete, for it does not contain the cited explanation of the term *p'i.*

[21] These two expressions appear exactly the same in transliteration; therefore it may be puzzling to the uninitiated with regard to the Chinese language. In Chinese, they appear in different forms, and their pronunciation is also different. *Fu,* meaning "husband," is the first tone, and *fu,* meaning "wife," the fourth.

[22] For the very terms *fu* and *fu* mutually imply each other. They would never have been considered as standing alone.

poetry writing is of rather intimate concern to us, and yet it has been the subject of enormous misconceptions; how is it possible then to eliminate errors when one comes to the enquiry into classical texts? As it is palpably absurd to explain *p'i* in terms of counting heads and hooves, or to select men of courage by drafting eunuchs, I have chosen to present these examples here as a warning. Paintings may glow for a time after they are first created, but they will inevitably fade away; literary work, on the other hand, shines even brighter with the passage of time. And if for one morning a writer is able to correct himself according to the proper standard, he will have nothing to be ashamed of in the thousand years that follow.

The Tsan:

I [a most accurate archer] shot [his sparrow in] the wrong [eye],[23]
And [the great horseman] Tung-yeh [Chi] failed in his horsemanship;[24]
Excellent though a man's talent is,
He will fall if he takes an erroneous course.
If there is one flaw in the language of a piece,
Though one tried a thousand years, it could not be removed.
The nearest thing to perfection
Is for a piece to be [relatively] free from defect.

[23] I was the ruler of Yu-ch'iung tribe who usurped the throne of Hsia for a short time. Once, in the company of Wu Ho, he was asked to shoot the left eye of a sparrow. By mistake he shot its right eye. He never forgot this shame throughout his life. See *T'ai-p'ing yü-lan*, chüan 82.

[24] *Chuangtzu yin-te*, 50/19/59. Tung-yeh Chi came to see Duke Chuang [of Lu] on the recommendation of his art of driving. His movement back and forth was as straight as a carpenter's line, and his circle as round as a compass. Duke Chuang thought that not even embroidery could be more beautiful than his driving patterns. [Tung-yeh] was driving his horse to make a hundred turns, with the intention to come back to the original rut without deviation. Yen Ho met him and came in to see the duke and said Chi's horse would soon collapse. The duke kept silent and did not answer. In a short while, Chi's horse collapsed as foretold. The duke asked Yen Ho, "How did you know?" Yen replied, "His horse was exhausted, and yet he still drove it hard to get more out of it. Therefore I knew it would collapse."

XLII. The Nourishing of Vitality

Wang Ch'ung [of the Later Han] wrote a book on the theme of nourishing one's vitality;[1] it was based on his own personal experience, and not just on unfounded speculation. Ears, eyes, nose, and mouth are organs which serve our physical life; thinking, pondering, speech, and linguistic expression are functions of our spirit. When all these operate spontaneously, in accordance with our nature and in perfect harmony, the principles of things are revealed and feeling finds unobstructed expression. But if a man works too hard, he becomes weary in spirit and sapped in vitality. This is the law governing our nature and feeling.

During the time of the Three Sovereigns, the language was simple, and there was no desire to embellish it. The age of the [Five] Emperors first witnessed the emergence of linguistic adornment, and there was a general emphasis on arranging the words in artistic patterns. Although this tendency to embellishment gradually grew throughout the period of the Three Dynasties and the Spring and Autumn period, it remained always in perfect accord with the inner feeling of the writers, showing no sign of labor forcing the natural bounds of talent. But by the time of the Warring States period, the emphasis had been shifted to sophistry, and writers were laboring to be original and to be ornamental in their discourse. From Han times to the present, new elements in literary language have been added every day, competing in their brilliance and in their display of colorful patterns, and involving an exhausting waste of mental effort. The difference between a simple, sound language and a sophisticated, pretentious one is so apparent that it can still be recognized after a lapse of a thousand years. The one follows the nature of the mind, and the other exhausts the feelings; they are ten thousand miles apart, for one is spontaneous and the other

---

[1] Wang Ch'ung, A.D. 27-*c*. 100, wrote *Lun-heng* (Critical essays), the last chapter of which is autobiographical. In this chapter is mentioned his writing on the nourishing of vitality in sixteen chapters, based completely on his own personal experience. See *Lun-heng* (Chu-tzu chi-ch'eng ed.), p. 288.

laborious. In this we may see the reason why the Ancients were always leisurely and at ease, and later writers so hurried and hasty.

It is true in general that men in their tender years are inexperienced but extremely ambitious, while men of age have strong convictions but are weak in vitality. The ambitious are quick in thought, a habit which relieves them of laborious effort; but the weak in vitality are exhaustive in their thinking, a habit which depletes their vital spirit. These are the general characteristics of mediocre men, phenomena generally expected of people of different age.

Now a man's capacity and natural parts are limited, but he may work his mind without limit. There are men who are ashamed of their short "wild duck" legs and aspire to those of the crane:[2] they will force themselves to write and their minds to function. In so doing, they wear out the vitality within, which fades away like the feeble waves of a stream, or make themselves as gaunt and emaciated as the trees on Mount Niu.[3] In such a state of worry and anxiety, it is only natural for a man to soon fall victim to disease. Chung-jen [or Wang Ch'ung] placed [brushes and] inkstones [all over his house], so that he could write [his critical essays whenever he was inspired to do so]; and Shu-t'ung [or Ts'ao Pao] [went to sleep] with a brush in his bosom, in order to devote himself wholeheartedly to his work.[4] Year in and year out, through all seasons they were exposed to the heat of anxiety, and day in and day out, at all hours they were being roasted over the fire of anxiety. No wonder that Master Ts'ao should express the concern that literary composition tends to ruin a man's life, and Lu Yün should regret that over-thinking distresses the spirit: their opinions are by no means unfounded.

[2] The idea that man's capacity is limited but his desire to use his mind is without restraint is a modified version of Chuangtzu's idea that our life is limited, while the scope of knowledge is unbounded. See *Chuangtzu yin-te*, 7/3/1. The story of the wild duck's short legs and the crane's long ones is also from *Chuangtzu. Ibid.*, 21/8/9-10.

[3] The last reference is to *Mencius*, where moral depravity is compared to the sad condition of the trees on Mount Niu, for they are constantly at the mercy of the axes and bills, and the cattle and goats. See *Meng-tzu yin-te*, 44/6A/8.

[4] Ts'ao Pao devoted himself to the task of continuing what Shu-sun T'ung had started at the beginning of the Han dynasty in formulating ceremonial rituals. See his biography in the *Hou-han shu*.

Learning requires diligence; therefore [Su Ch'in] pricked his leg with an awl [to keep himself awake to study].[5] But in literary composition, the purpose is to express feeling which has been repressed; therefore, it is necessary that the writer be able to give free vent to his feelings in a happy and spontaneous manner. If in the process he has to burn up his inner force and dry up the harmonious natural flow of his vitality, his writing will only serve to shorten his years and do violence to his nature. Could this have been the conscious purpose of the sages and worthies, or indeed the reason for any literary writing?

Furthermore, sometimes we are sharp and sometimes dull in thinking; and there are moments when we are inspired and also moments when all our senses seem to be clogged. "When one is washing his hair, his heart [the seat of his reason] is out of position," and the result is abnormal thinking.[6] Similarly and with greater cogency, when one's spirit is overcome by darkness, the more it is spurred on, the more benighted it becomes. Therefore, in the art of literary writing, temperance and readiness for expression are of prime importance: that is, it is essential to keep the mind pure and tranquil so that its vitality may find spontaneous expression. As soon as one feels vexed, he should immediately give up thinking, so as not to let his mind become choked. When inspired, give vent to your heart and entrust it to the brush; but when ideas hide themselves, put the brush down and fold up your mind. A pleasant trip is a sure cure for weariness, and talk and laughter will bring restoration from fatigue. One should always try the sharpness of his talent in leisure, and spur on his literary courage

---

[5] I am adopting the reading of *Wen-hsin tiao-lung hsin-shu*, edited by Wang Li-ch'i (Peking, 1951), in omitting two lines, the forgery of one of which is apparent, because of the anachronism in its reference. Su Ch'in of the Warring States period drove himself to study and pricked himself with an awl to keep awake.

[6] *Ch'un-ch'iu ching-chuan yin-te*, 123/Hsi 24/Tso fu 1: "T'ou Hsü, a former attendant of the Duke of Chin, . . . requested an audience. The duke refused to see him because he was washing his hair. [T'ou-hsü] told his followers, 'When one is washing his hair, his heart is out of position, and this will make him think in a way contrary to the normal manner. It is natural that the duke will not see me.'" Note that ancient Chinese were good Aristotelian psychologists, for they also believed that the function of thinking belongs to the heart. Liu Hsieh cited the story to illustrate this point that there are moments when, due to circumstances such as this, the thinking may not be normal. In such moments, it is best not to force the heart to think.

when there is plenty of surplus energy, so that his knife may ever be as sharp as one newly honed,[7] and the circulation of the air [i.e., oxygen] through the veins to his muscles may be unobstructed.[8] Although this method of achieving refreshment may not achieve the results obtained by the art of breath control,[9] it is one way to protect our vitality.

The Tsan:
The world is filled with ten thousand things in confusion;
It is a very laborious task to think of even a thousand of them.
So it is imperative to preserve our inner spirit,
And nourish our native vitality.
Water shines because of its tranquility,
And fire brightens when it burns quietly.
Never overtax your literary thought,
But always keep the spirit fresh.

XLIII. Organization (Fu-hui)[1]

What is the meaning of *fu-hui*? It means a comprehensive view of a literary piece as a whole with respect to both its language and its ideas; it provides an underlying principle to unify all its parts, it defines the conditions governing what should be included and what excluded, and works elements from all the various fields into harmony; in short, it

[7] One's vitality is compared to the knife of the butcher in the *Chuangtzu*, and it may be kept ever sharp by not forcing it, just as the butcher kept his knife sharp by a perfect knowledge of the physiology of the bull, a knowledge which enabled him to send his knife through the body without encountering obstruction. See *Chuangtzu yin-te*, 7/5/8.

[8] See *Huangti nei-ching su-wen*, "Chü-t'ung lun."

[9] A Taoist method to achieve immortality by means of internal alchemy.

[1] *Fu-hui* is an abbreviation of *fu-tz'u hui-i*, to give order to linguistic elements and unity to ideas. Thus, the chapter deals with the organizational principles of a literary creation.

organizes the whole piece in such a way that, though composed of a variety of elements, it will not as a whole fall short of the proper standard. It may be compared to the role of the foundation in the building of a house and the tailor's pattern in the making of a dress, both necessary in their respective fields. When a child starts to learn the art of writing, he must first be taught correct organization: it consists of feeling and ideas as the soul, of facts and meaning as the bone and marrow, of linguistic patterns as the musculature and integument, and of *kung* and *shang*, that is, the resonance of the language, as its voice and breath. Only after he has learned this is he able to evaluate black and yellow,[2] to ring out the sonorous tones of metal and jade,[3] to offer what is appropriate and advise against what is not, and thus to reach what is considered the mean.[4] For it is in *fu-hui* that we find the lasting principle for the organization of thought.

In general, a literary composition has [like a tree] its branches and [like a stream] its forks. To arrange the forks and branches in order, one must follow the implications of the spring and the trunk. Similarly, in bringing order and unity into linguistic elements and ideas, one must have a comprehensive principle, by means of which he will be able to achieve his goal by ten thousand different routes, and give coherence to one hundred different kinds of ideas, so that, for all the variety of ideas, there will be no misplacement of emphasis and, for all the different linguistic elements, there will be no confusion; like a tree, he will be able to send out some shoots to meet the sunshine and keep in reserve others which remain in the shade. In this way he will achieve a close-knit organization from beginning to end, which manifests a unity of external and inner elements. These achievements constitute the art of *fu-hui*, or organization.

The painter who pays close attention to a hair misses the portrait,

[2] See note 2, Chapter I. In Chapter XXXI, this is called *hsing-wen*, the color pattern.
[3] The sound pattern, second of the three main patterns mentioned in Chapter XXXI.
[4] Liu Hsieh, in a pithy sentence, may have expressed the four main functions which a literary piece may serve: philosophical, ceremonial, as memorials, and as a necessary tool for the running of government.

and the archer who aims at the very small misses the wall.[5] Preoccupation with the fine and small naturally involves looseness in the general structure of the whole. Therefore, we should bend an inch to make
a foot straight, and bend a foot to straighten up eight;[6] in short, we
should give up the one-sided cleverness to gain the beauty that is
all-encompassing. This is the general principle governing the planning
of a literary composition.

There is no one definite way in which a composition may be developed, and opinions about development are rather confused. To be
too terse in treatment leaves the ideas isolated, but to attempt too
broad a treatment results in a verbal monstrosity; to be too straightforward will most certainly involve many mistakes, and yet to be too
consistently tentative will also do harm to the composition. Furthermore, people differ in their natural talents and gifts, and in their ways
of thinking. Some plan their compositions from beginning to end as
a whole, and some compose piecemeal, adding at one time a foot and at
another an inch. But there are few indeed who make over-all plans, in
comparison with the many who use the piecemeal method. Now if the
writer loses sight of the general principle, his language will become
confused; and if his ideas are not logically developed, his style will
seem dry and lifeless. Only on the basis of a transcendent knowledge
of the structural principle of the whole will he be able to achieve among
the different parts of his composition a harmonious cohesion as spontaneous as that of glue to wood, or stone to the jade which it contains.
Just as a team of four chargers may differ in their strength, while their
six reins operate like the strings of one lute and they proceed abreast
in a formation as perfect as that of the spokes gathering at one hub,
so in a literary composition a similar method of control must be exercised.
Whether to proceed or to stop is under the control of the mind, as
whether to loose the reins or tighten them is under the guidance of

[5] This is a quotation from the *Lü-shih ch'un-ch'iu* (Chu-tzu chi-ch'eng ed.), chüan
25, p. 324, with the order of the two lines reversed; the original being, "An archer who
aims at the minute misses the wall, and a painter who pays close attention to a hair
misses the portrait."

[6] See *Meng-tzu yin-te*, 22/3B/1. *Hsün* means eight feet.

the hands; for all that is necessary to insure the desired uniform pace is to control the reins.

Therefore, in the hands of those who are good at organization, even ideas which differ may be given as close a relationship as the liver and the gall; and in the hands of those who are poor at organization, even tones of the same quality will seem as vastly different as Hu and Yüeh.[7] It is more difficult to revise an existing composition than to write a new one, and it is more difficult to change already written words than to write a new sentence. This has been proved by the experience of writers of the past. Chang T'ang [of the Han] at one time had his memorial twice rejected, and Yü Sung [of the Wei] was repeatedly rebuked because of his; in each case, the reason for the writer's misfortune lies in the fact that his reasoning is not clear and he is confused in his language and ideas. However, after Ni K'uan had revised Chang T'ang's memorial and Chung Hui had changed a few words in Yü Sung's, Emperor Wu was amazed by the extraordinary quality of Chang's memorial, and Emperor Ching of the Chin[8] highly praised that of Yü. This was because the revised pieces are logical in reasoning and clear in presenting facts, and the revisers are quick-witted, and use appropriate language.[9] In these examples we see the vast difference between those writers who are clever at organization and those who are clumsy.

As to stopping the brush and bringing a passage to a close, it is like raising the oar while riding in a boat; and fitting expressions to ideas is like drawing on the reins while using the whip. A writer who can sustain the merits of his piece to the end achieves the expression of

[7] "Liver and gall" is a figure for intimate relationship and similarity, and "Hu and Yüeh" for great difference. Hu and Yüeh are two barbarian districts. These figures are taken from the *Chuangtzu*. See *Chuangtzu yin-te*, 12/5/7: "From the point of view of the different, even the liver and gall would be like Ch'u and Yüeh." Ch'u, a state which was as different from Yüeh as could be imagined, is changed to Hu by Liu Hsieh, with no appreciable difference in sense.

[8] Ssu-ma Shih, given the posthumous title of Emperor Ching when his nephew Ssu-ma Yen usurped the throne of the Wei in 265 and created the Chin dynasty.

[9] For Chang and Ni, see the biography of Ni K'uan in the *Han-shu*; for Yü and Chung, see commentary to the biography of Chung Hui in the *Wei-chih*.

profound ideas and a smooth-flowing, complete development of the style.[10] On the other hand, if a piece starts with a glorious tune and continues with weak and spiritless passages, it will tend to suffocate, unable to let its wind out fully. This is what the *Book of Changes* means by "There is no skin on his thighs, and walking comes hard."[11] If the beginning and end of a piece can complement each other fully, even the art of *fu-hui* cannot ask for anything more.

The Tsan:
If a general principle underlies the different parts of a piece,
And feeling is rich and ordered;
If it is well begun and well concluded,
The branches well laid out and the leaves spread well,
Then the piece will have an artistic harmony,
All the loose threads will be gathered up
And, like harmony in music,
The sounds of the mind will blend perfectly.

XLIV. Discussion on the Art of Writing (Tsung-shu)

We find current at present a statement to the effect that literary writings may be classified under two separate categories: *wen*, or patterned, and *pi*, or unpatterned prose, unrhymed writing being *pi* and rhymed writing *wen*.[1] Now pattern simply adds to the adequacy of *yen*, that is, plain words, and generally includes both the *Poetry* and the *History*. The effort to make them two different categories dates

---

[10] The text is somewhat corrupt. I follow Fan Wen-lan's reading, and accept at the same time suggestions from Wang's reading in my interpretation.

[11] *I-ching*, I, 180, 184. See also *Chou-i yin-te*, 27/43/4, 27/44/3.

[1] For the meaning of *wen*, see note 1, Chapter I. *Pi* means a brush, symbolic of a prosaic writing which is unrhymed. The term "rhyme" may mean only tonal arrangement in general, and need not be taken to mean a correspondence of sounds in the final syllable or syllables of two or more words.

back only a short time. For example, Yen Yen-nien [or Yen-chih, 384-456] believed that *pi* as a genre is *yen* with pattern,[2] that is, that all Classics are *yen* and not *pi*, while their commentaries are *pi* and not *yen*.[3] We may easily use Yen's own spear to pierce his shield.[4] How? Take the "Wen-yen"[5] in the *Book of Changes*, for example: is it not words with pattern? If, according to Yen, *pi* is really *yen* with pattern, then he has no right to say that the Classics are not *pi*. In making the above statements, Yen intends to establish a theory of his own; but I do not see how it can stand.

In my opinion, oral statements are plain words, and whenever these are committed to the brush, they are literary writings. And the Way which is constant is called a Classic, while that which elucidates the Classic is known as a commentary. The words [of the sages] committed to the brush form the Classics and their commentaries. The brush is at the service of the words, and may be either vigorous or weak. The eternal validity of the six Classics lies in their severe elegance and profundity, rather than in their literary qualities. The *Wen-fu* of Master Lu [Chi] has been known for its penetrating and exhaustive discussion of the art of writing but, in its superficial attention to details, it has not adequately dealt with the substance. For we know that if one is able to return to the constant Way in all his many[6] changing situations, he will never be exhausted; and it is difficult to be perfect in the choice of good words.[7]

Those who are intensely interested in literary composition often vie with one another in creating new and elegant phrases. Most of them

---

[2] Literally, *yen* with *wen*.

[3] Yen's statements are not found in his collected work. He is making a distinction between three categories: *yen*, plain words; *pi*, words with pattern but without rhyme; and *wen*, writing which is rhymed. In discussing the Classics and their commentaries, only the first two categories are relevant.

[4] For the use of "spear" and "shield" to mean contradiction, see note 5, Chapter XXX.

[5] See note 11, Chapter I.

[6] Literally, "nine changes," "nine" used to mean "many."

[7] This last statement is quoted from the "Wu-ti chi" in the *Han-shu*, which quotes it from "Poetry," presumably the *Book of Poetry*. According to Ying Shao, the commentator, this refers to a lost poem of the *Book of Poetry*. The latter part of the statement is aimed at the imperfect work of Lu Chi.

are obsessed with the desire to refine their linguistic expressions, but none wish to attend to the fundamentals of the art. As a result, brilliant jade is often lost in a pile of rocks, while common stones take on the appearance of jade. A penetrating mind is concise and brief, yet a mind that is lacking in scholarship is also parsimonious of words; the erudite mind is comprehensive in scope, but the confused mind is just as long-winded; the logical mind is clear and transparent, but the mind which is shallow may be just as unreserved; and the profound mind is rich in connotation and difficult to fathom, but the mind which is merely pretentious may also sound impressively archaic. Sometimes splendid ideas are expressed in sounds which are somber and feeble; sometimes unreasonable arguments are clothed in brilliant language. From such circumstances we know how difficult it is to make the tones of bells harmonious, and how far from easy it is to tune a lute. Now the sizes of the bells which musicians declare to be in harmony need not be absolutely exact; neither need the operation of the fan be of exactly the same pitch from beginning to end.[8] And Wei-wen [or Ts'ao P'ei], in his comparison of literary writing to music, is amply borne out. The point is that, as before applying the blade of a knife to knotted roots, we cannot prove the sharpness of the knife, likewise, before we make an effort to discover the secret of good literary composition, there is no way to determine whether a given talent is truly comprehensive. To be comprehensive, the writer must be versed in the art. If he lacks either a comprehensive view of his field or the penetration necessary to make its structure articulate, how can he possibly harness his inner feeling for the triumphant drive through the garden of literature?

Therefore, when one plies this art as the rein with which he guides his composition, he may be likened to a good chess player who knows his moves and the inevitable results of them. But the one who abandons the art for the whims of his own mind is like a gambler whose success is a matter of luck. The gambler's writing may be clever accidentally;

[8] The operation of the fan seems to refer to the tuning of a lute, the fan being some part of it. However, the meaning is not clear, and the allusion has not been identified.

but although his initial effort may be successful, it is difficult to count on his being able to continue with any consistent competency. He is unable to go on writing when he has little to write about; and he will also be baffled by the problem of selecting and omitting when he is confronted with too much material. If he is unable to overcome the difficulty of having either too much or too little material, how can he be expected to be able to distinguish between the beautiful and the ugly? The man who writes as a good chess player plays follows definite principles of the art. He moves in an orderly fashion according to certain patterns as he responds to emotions, making timely answers to varying circumstances; in a word, he moves in perfect harmony with the proper standard. If a writer's movement is perfectly matched to the exact requirements of each situation, his natural responsiveness to the working of the mysterious spring will find expression in the excellence of his work. In the work of such a writer we shall find galloping in parade like spirited chargers a host of brilliant ideas, and a clustering galaxy of exquisite expressions. To the eyes, it is brocade or painting; to the ears, sonorous music; it is sweet and mellow in taste, and fragrant as scented pendants.[9] In these achievements, one reaches the pinnacle of literary writing.

The legs of a thoroughbred may be strong, but it will not be able to cover one thousand *li* if the cords are too long. The length of the cords is only one factor among ten thousand, and yet it is enough to cause failure.[10] How much more surely will this principle operate in the case of the literary composition, where also many factors must work in perfect harmony; for here the slightest weakness in any one of them will most certainly cause the collapse of the whole. For this reason, I have given consideration to all these factors in this chapter, to prepare the student for all eventualities. This chapter is like the hub where the thirty spokes converge. The view given may not be worthy of attention, but it is my honest view.

[9] Referring to fragrant flowers used as pendants.

[10] *Chan-kuo ts'e* (Taipei, Kuo-hsüeh chi-pen ts'ung-shu ed.) Vol. 3, chüan 28, Han 3, p. 54.

The Tsan:

In the literary arena or the garden of brushes,
There are ways and gates.
First attention should be given to the fundamental thing,
And one's observation must penetrate to the source.
By the control of the first principle one controls the ten thousand,
And by harnessing the essential element one harnesses all the details.
Thinking may not have a fixed form,
But the reason is absolutely constant.

XLV. Literary Development and Time (Shih-hsü)[1]

As time has passed and as dynasties have risen and fallen, literature
has developed from the simple to the more ornate in form as well as
in content. It is possible to trace this development of feeling and ideas
from the earliest times to the present.

During the time of T'ao-t'ang, that is, the legendary ruler, whose
virtue was great and whose influence was wide, country elders spoke
of his effortless government and children sang of how his guiding
influence was not consciously felt by the people.[2] When Yu-yü Shun,
another legendary ruler who came after Yao, succeeded to the rule,

---

[1] In this chapter, Liu Hsieh treats of a literary principle which was first enunciated
in the "Great and Lesser Prefaces" to the *Book of Poetry*. In substance the theory is:
The literary forms and contents of each generation conform to the spirit of that generation and, when changes take place in the spirit of an age, the literary forms and
contents are modified accordingly. Liu Hsieh emphasizes particularly the moral and
political influence of an age on the character of literature.

[2] In Wang Ch'ung's *Lun-heng* (Critical essays), *Lun-heng t'ung-chien*, 8/13b, we
find the following quotation: "During the time of Yao, peace prevailed. Elders of fifty
years of age played games on the street. Spectators said, 'Great is the virtue of Yao.' The
elders said, 'We start working at sunrise and retire at sunset, dig wells to get our drink
and till land to get our food. What has the effort of Yao to do with us?'" In the
Lieh-tzu, chüan 4, Chapter 4, p. 49, we have the following children's song: "In establishing the people [he, the ruler] allows every one to develop to his full capacity.
Without consciousness and without knowledge, they spontaneously follow the law of
the lord."

the government was good and the people lived an easy life; the ruler composed the song "Hsün-feng,"[3] and the ministers the song "Lan-yün."[4] Both of these songs are extremely beautiful. Why? Because when one is happy at heart, his voice will be peaceful.

In the time of Great Yü, the land was divided so that the inundation might be easily controlled, and there were songs telling of his nine regulated accomplishments.[5]

Ch'eng-t'ang was sage and reverent, and his achievements were sung in the "I-yü" *sung*.[6] At the time of King Wen,[7] because of the great virtue of Chi,[8] the "Chou-nan" lyrics[9] expressed the hard-working spirit of the people without betraying any trace of complaint. And the influence of T'ai-wang[10] was so beneficial that the songs collected from Pin[11] show an enjoyment of life which does not indulge in excesses. But during the dark years of King Yu [781-771 B.C.] and King Li [879-842 B.C.] the poems "Pan"[12] and "Tang"[13] express the anger of the people. As King P'ing [770-720 B.C.] suffered a period of decline,[14] we have the poem "Shu-li,"[15] which expresses sadness [over the desolation of the old capital]. From these we know that folk songs and their contents change with the changing times and, when the wind moves on the surface, waves are whipped up down below.

[3] Also known as "Nan-feng." See note 10, Chapter VI.

[4] The song is given in *Shang-shu ta-chuan*. Modern scholars tend to question its authenticity.

[5] See note 18, Chapter I.

[6] No. 301 in the *Book of Poetry*. For *sung* as one of the six elements in *Poetry*, see note 2, Chapter V.

[7] Father of King Wu, who established the Chou dynasty.

[8] The surname of King Wen.

[9] The first eleven poems in the *Book of Poetry*, collected from a region south of Chou, where King Wen's influence was felt.

[10] Grandfather of King Wen.

[11] Pin was the place where T'ai-wang made his influence felt, and the collection includes poems 154 to 160 in the *Book of Poetry*.

[12] Poem no. 254, complaining about the misery under the rule of King Li.

[13] Poem no. 255, directing warnings to King Li concerning his corrupt rule. Both poems were directed toward King Li but, since Yu and Li had always been mentioned together, by force of habit Liu Hsieh strings them together.

[14] King P'ing was forced to move his capital to Lo-i, the present Lo-yang, under the pressure of the western tribes.

[15] Poem no. 65.

After the Spring and Autumn period, the states warred among themselves for distinction. The Six Classics hid themselves in the mud like dragons[16] and the hundred thinkers arose like gusts of wind. At this time, Han and Wei gave all their attention to strengthening their rule, Yen and Chao made expediency their principle, and the "Wu-tu" and "Liu-shih"[17] formed the content of the stringent code of Ch'in. Ch'i and Ch'u were the only states in which there was any emphasis on literature. In Ch'i residences were built along the main avenue to house scholars, and Ch'u enlarged the palace of Lan-t'ai to receive men of letters. Mencius was treated as a guest minister [in Ch'i] and Hsün-ch'ing [or Hsüntzu] was made the magistrate of a district [in Ch'u]. So it was at the Chi-hsia gate [in Ch'i, where scholars gathered] that this pure wind received its fanning, and in Lan-ling [the magistracy of Hsüntzu], that [this plant] enjoyed its luxuriant growth. [In Ch'i] Tsou-tzu [or Tsou Yen] became famous because of his discourse on heaven, and the name of Tsou Shih rang far and wide on account of his dragon carving. [In Ch'u] the poetry of Ch'ü P'ing [or Yüan] was as brilliant as the sun and the moon, and Sung Yü's writing was as colorful as the clouds before the wind. A study of their beautiful writing reveals that it has the grace of the *ya* and the *sung*. And the glow and dazzle of their extraordinary thought is thus the result of the impressive success won by the people in the political practice of vertical federation and horizontal alliance.[18]

The Han dynasty succeeded the [Ch'in], the latter being the dynasty during which books were consigned to the flames. Kao-tsu [the first emperor, 206-195 B.C.] stressed military affairs; he ridiculed scholars, and paid no attention to learning. Although the first step in the establishment of ritual and the codification of law was taken, no attempt was made to make the *Poetry* and *History* objects of serious study.

[16] Dragons are expected to be flying in the sky, their natural habitat. But there are times when, under adverse circumstances, they have to hide themselves in the mud. Pan Ku used the figure in his "Ta ping hsi." See *Wen-hsüan*, chüan 45, 11b.

[17] The "Wu-tu" is Chapter 49 in *Han-fei-tzu*, and the "Liu-shih" ("six lice," or six harmful things) are mentioned in Chapters 4 and 20 in *The Book of Lord Shang*. Since Han and Lord Shang are legalists, these two expressions are used to mean legalism.

[18] See note 26, Chapter XVIII.

However, Kao-tsu's songs, "Ta-feng" and "Hung-ku," may be considered the works of a genius.[19]

From Emperor Hui [194-188 B.C.] to Emperors Wen [179-157 B.C.] and Ching [156-141 B.C.], classical study was in the ascendant, and poets went into eclipse. This may be seen from the frustration of Chia I and the disappointment of Tsou [Yang] and Mei [Sheng].[20]

Emperor Wu [140-87 B.C.] showed great respect for scholars, and offered enthusiastic encouragement to the pursuit of learning. During his reign rites and music vied with each other in brilliance, and scholars competed in literary production. In the Tower of Po-liang, he initiated [the "round robin" type] of poetry with feasting as its theme;[21] at the break of the river dike, he expressed his concern about the people in a poem; he sent a carriage with rush-cushioned wheels for Mei Sheng, and allowed Chu-fu Yen to fulfil his ambition to eat from a tripod.[22] He elevated Kung-sun [Hung] to the top on account of his *tui-ts'e*,[23] and expressed admiration for the memorial drafted by Ni K'uan. [Chu] Mai-ch'en, a wood carrier, became a wearer of the brocaded robe of an official, and [Ssu-ma] Hsiang-ju, who washed dishes, was also clothed in embroidery. [Ssu-ma] Ch'ien, the historian, [Wu-ch'iu] Shou-wang, Yen [An], Chung [Chün], Mei Kao, and their group were not only not narrowly limited in their responses to the imperial questions, but were also ever resourceful in their strictly literary production. The strong literary enthusiasm and beauty of expression they manifested have never been equalled since their time.

Subsequently, Emperor Chao [86-74 B.C.] and Emperor Hsüan [73-49 B.C.] continued the trend which had been initiated by Emperor Wu. Scholars argued and discussed[24] [the problems of the Classics] in

---

[19] The "Ta-feng" song is found in his chronicle in *Shih-chi*, and the "Hung-ku" song in the biography of Liu-hou, i.e., Chang Liang.

[20] See their respective biographies in the *Han-shu*.

[21] See note 20, Chapter VI.

[22] For Mei and Chu-fu, see their respective biographies in the *Han-shu*. Eating from a tripod is a symbol of honored status in the officialdom.

[23] See Chapter XXIV above, "Discussion and Answer." Kung-sun's *tui-ts'e* is found in his biography in the *Han-shu*.

[24] Literally, "galloped."

the Shih-ch'ü palace [in 51 B.C.],[25] and met for literary purposes in their leisure time. Gathered together were the great talents of the time, forging striking metaphors in patterns of silk. At this time, Wang Pao and his group attained positions of honor as literary advisers to the imperial court. Emperor Yüan [48-33 B.C.] and Emperor Ch'eng [32-7 B.C.] paid great attention to charts and books, extolling learned talk about jade powder,[26] and clearing the way that led to the Chin-ma gate.[27] At that time Tzu-yün [or Yang Hsiung] won his reputation for perspicacity through his ability to recite one thousand *fu*, and Tzu-cheng [or Liu Hsiang] was given the charge of editing and collating the texts of the Six Classics—an achievement which may be considered a fit object of our admiration.

From the beginning of the Han dynasty to the reigns of Emperors Ch'eng and Ai [6-1 B.C.], although the world had seen the passing of over a hundred years,[28] and there had been many[29] developments in poetic style, the leading trend was to imitate the style of the *Ch'u-tz'u*. The lingering influence of Ling-chün [or Ch'ü Yüan] is still evident here.

From the decline during the reigns of Emperors Ai and P'ing [A.D. 1-5] to the restoration of Emperor Kuang-wu [A.D. 25-57], great attention was paid to the maps and apocrypha;[30] consequently, literature was more or less neglected. However, Tu Tu won pardon for himself with his *lei*,[31] and Pan Piao received appointment as a magistrate because of his memorials. So although [Kuang-wu] did not go out of the way to enlist scholars, neither did he completely for-

[25] See Chapter XVIII above.

[26] In Wang Ch'ung's *Lun-heng*, the term "yü-hsieh" (jade powder) is used to mean "miscellaneous literary bits, not worthy of attention." See *Lun-heng* (Chu-tzu chi-ch'eng ed.), p. 276. Here the term seems to mean just literary production.

[27] Where literary men were housed, ready to answer the imperial call.

[28] Actually, it was more than two hundred years. Chinese literary men have never been exact in figures.

[29] Literally, "nine changes." For the meaning of "nine," see note 6, Chapter XLIV.

[30] See Chapter IV above, "Emendation of Apocrypha."

[31] Tu Tu was thrown into prison on account of his bad conduct. Emperor Kuang-wu pardoned him when he submitted a brilliant elegy in memory of the great Ssu-ma Wu Han.

sake them. The twin luminaries, Emperor Ming [A.D. 58-75] and
Emperor Chang [A.D. 76-88] had great respect and love for scholars
and their learning. [Emperor Ming] discoursed on rites in Pi-t'ang[32]
[in A.D. 59] and [Emperor Chang] held discussions on the Classics in
Pai-hu hall [in A.D. 79]. Wearing his brush [in his cap], Meng-chien
[or Pan Ku, during the reign of Emperor Ming] took part in preparing the history of the dynasty;[33] and [during the reign of the same
emperor] Chia K'uei was given brush and paper to draft a *sung* on
the occasion of the auspicious appearance [of divine sparrows in the
palaces].[34] Prince Tung-p'ing [or Ts'ang] distinguished himself with
his elegant writing [on rites], and Prince P'ei [or Fu] made the general principles of the [Classics] the living issue of the day. The rituals
of the imperial court[35] and the protocol concerning the foreign tribes[36]
illumined each other with their respective brilliance.

During the period between Ho-An [Emperor Ho, A.D. 89-105, and
Emperor An, A.D. 107-125][37] and Shun-Huan [Emperor Shun, A.D.
126-144, and Emperor Huan, A.D. 147-167][38] there rose Pan [Ku],
Fu [I], the Three Ts'ui,[39] Wang [Ch'ung], Ma [Yung], Chang [Heng]
and Ts'ai [Yung], who may all be considered brilliant scholars; there
was no lack of talent. But as to literary pieces of high quality, we must
reserve our judgment. After the restoration [of the Han by Emperor
Kuang-wu], talented writers more or less modified the traditional
custom and, by emphasizing both the flower and the fruit, they resorted
to classical expressions. For after a number of classical discussions under
past reigns, a scholarly classical attitude gradually prevailed.

32 *Pi*, a round jade with a hole in the center, is a symbol of heaven. Pi-t'ang is a
heavenly hall, also known as Ming-t'ang, one of three halls completed in A.D. 59.
33 Wearing the brush in one's cap is a figure for a historian, who appeared in court
with a brush in his cap, ready to record happenings at court.
34 See the biography of Chia K'uei in the *Hou-han shu*.
35 This refers to the rituals discussed by Emperor Ming and those devised by Prince
Tung-P'ing. See Prince Tung-P'ing's biography in the *Hou-han shu*.
36 This refers to the ode written by Chia K'uei on the gathering of the divine sparrows, for the latter was considered an omen for the prevailing of China's influence abroad.
37 Omitting Emperor Shang, who ruled for a short time in A.D. 106.
38 Omitting Emperor Ch'ung, who ruled for a short time in A.D. 145, and Emperor
Chih, who ruled in A.D. 146.
39 Ts'ui Yin the father, Ts'ui Yüan the son, and Ts'ui Shih the grandson.

Emperor Ling [A.D. 168-219] occasionally indulged in literary creation. He wrote *Hsi-huang p'ien*, opening the way for scholars to gather together at the Hung-tu gate to write *fu*. Yüeh Sung and his group gathered together men of shallow learning and vulgar taste, whom Yang Ssu called Huan Tou[40] [after an upstart minister of that name], and Ts'ai Yung compared to actors and jesters.[41] The trend they created and the works they produced are not worthy of our attention.

During the reign of Emperor Hsien [A.D. 190-220], who was constantly forced to move from one place to another,[42] the fate of literary men was like that of dishevelled grasses tossed about by a furious wind. Only at the end of the Chien-an period [A.D. 196-220] was there any semblance of peace. Emperor Wu of the Wei,[43] who was then a prince and prime minister, had a deep love for poetry; Emperor Wen [or Ts'ao P'ei], who was then the heir apparent, was himself versed in *tz'u* and *fu*; and Ch'en-ssu [or Ts'ao Chih], who was the son of a prince, wielded a brush whose style was as brilliant as the sonorous jade. These three, important as their positions were, all showed great respect for others who had outstanding literary talent. Hence many talented writers gathered around them like vapors and clouds. Chung-hsüan [or Wang Ts'an] swore allegiance at Han-nan [in the present Hu-pei], K'ung-chang [or Ch'en Lin] submitted himself at Ho-pei, Wei-ch'ang [or Hsü Kan] joined the entourage at Ch'ing-t'u, and Kung Kan [or Liu Chen] enlisted for service at Hai-yü. And here Te-lien [or Ying Yang] organized his literary thought, and Yüan-yü [or Juan Yü] enjoyed his art of letter writing. Wen-wei [or Lu Ts'ui], Hsiu-po [or Po Ch'in], Tzu-shu [or Han-tan Ch'un], Te-tsu [or Yang Hsiu] and their group, goblets in hand, proudly showed their elegant style and, moving with leisurely grace while they feasted, formed songs with a

---

[40] See Yang's biography in the *Hou-han shu*. Huan Tou was one of the unruly ministers during the reign of Yao and Shun.

[41] *Hou-han shu*, biography of Ts'ai Yung.

[42] Between A.D. 190, when Emperor Hsien ascended to the throne, and A.D. 196, he was forced to move five times.

[43] See note 2, Chapter XLI.

swing of the brush, and out of the well-ground ink created witty pieces
which served as subjects of talk and laughter. An examination of their
writings reveals that most of them are full of feeling. This is because
they lived in a world marked by disorder and separation, and at a time
when morals declined and the people were complaining; they felt all
this deeply in their hearts, and this feeling was expressed in a style
which is moving. For this reason their works are full of feeling and life.

During the reign of Emperor Ming [227-239] the emperor himself
wrote poetry and composed musical scores. He collected writers and
housed them in the Ts'ung-wen kuan monastery. Here Ho [Yen],
Liu [Shao], and other literary men vied to outshine one another.
Among the young rulers who succeeded Ming, Kao-kuei [hsiang-kung,
or Mao, 254-260] alone was a man of refinement and grace; his very
glance conveyed an impression of literary elegance, and the words he
uttered formed perfect essays. The period was still under the lingering
influence of the Cheng-shih period, so that we find the works light and
detached.[44] In this period we find Hsi [K'ang], Juan [Chi], Ying
[Chü], and Miu [Hsi] galloping abreast on the thoroughfare of
literature.

During the Chin dynasty, Emperor Hsüan began to build the
foundation of the dynasty; Emperor Wen and Emperor Ching, who
followed, strengthened the structure.[45] During their times scholars and
poets were in eclipse, as the rulers were deeply interested in pursuing
political intrigues. When Emperor Wu [265-306] created the new
Chin dynasty, he received the mandate of heaven at a time of peace.
But he had never been concerned with literary creation. Later, both

[44] Cheng-shih, 240-248, is a period characterized by discussions of the *Tao* of Taoism,
under the impact of Buddhism. Metaphysics, which had not been the main interest of
Chinese scholars, became the central theme. This phenomenon may be explained by
the fact that the period was a period of disorder, and one had to watch what one said,
for one might be involved in political intrigue by as little as one inadvertent word.
Metaphysics, being a detached subject and not likely to involve anyone in trouble, came
to furnish a façade behind which to hide one's political allegiance.

[45] Similar to the case of Emperor Wu of the Wei, these Chin "emperors" never were
emperors. The title was given to them posthumously by Emperor Wu, who usurped the
throne from the Wei in a manner almost identical to that in which Wei-wen usurped it
from the Han. See note 20, Chapter XXIV.

Emperor Huai [307-312] and Emperor Min [313-316] lived in constant danger through years of great distress.[46]

However, although [the royal personages of the Chin] were not inclined toward literature, the period witnessed a large crop of literary talents. Mao-hsien [or Chang Hua] spread jewels with every stroke of his brush, and T'ai-ch'ung [or Tso Ssu] splashed ink which forms brocade; [P'an] Yüeh and [Hsia-hou] Chan bloomed like a pair of jades, and Lu Chi and [his brother] Yün, those two brilliant spirits, stood out in beautifully patterned relief; in addition, Ying Chen, Fu Hsüan, the three Changs,[47] Sun Ch'u, Chih Yü, Ch'eng-kung Sui, and their group all achieved distinction in literary beauty and refinement in style. Historians have consistently maintained that, as the Chin experienced the fate of a declining period, scholars living in that period were not able to develop their talents to the full. How true this judgment is! A fitting object for deep regret.

During his period of restoration [317-322], Emperor Yüan, an earnest student himself, enforced the traditional regulations concerning state examinations.[48] Liu Wei and Tiao Hsieh, because of their stringent application of rules, were held in great favor and honor by the emperor; Ching-ch'un [or Kuo P'u], because of his quick wit in literary creation, was promoted with special consideration. Emperor Ming [323-325], a prodigy [when a boy], loved to hold literary meetings. While on the throne, he devoted himself untiringly to literature. He refined his feeling through the writing of edicts and decrees, and exhibited his literary talent in *tz'u* and *fu*. Yü Liang was treated with something more than the consideration ordinarily shown to an intimate relation because of his literary ability; and Wen Ch'iao won the highest esteem with his literary thought. Devoted to promoting an interest in literature, Ming may be considered the Han Emperor Wu of the Chin dynasty.

[46] Both became captives of the Huns and died in their hands; Huai was captured in 311 and executed in 313, and Min was captured in 316 and executed in 317.

[47] For the three Changs, see note 40, Chapter VI.

[48] Previously, many students recommended to take the state examination had been given official appointment without the examination. See the biography of K'ung T'an, which is included in the biography of K'ung Yü, in the *Chin-shu*, chüan 78, pp. 5b-6a.

Emperor Ch'eng [326-342] and Emperor K'ang [343-344] both died young, and Emperor Mu [345-361] and Emperor Ai [362-365] ruled for only brief periods. But with the rise of Emperor Chien-wen [371-372], deep interest was shown in literary creation whose style was characterized by purity and loftiness. Subtle words and profound principles swarmed over the mats of the metaphysicians,[49] and speculative thinking couched in brocaded expressions sprinkled the garden of literature.

Emperor Hsiao-wu [373-395] had no successor;[50] and the reigns of Emperor An [396-418] and Emperor Kung [419-420] marked the end of the dynasty.[51] During this period Yüan [Hung], Yin [Chung-wen], Sun [Sheng], Kan [Pao], and their group distinguished themselves in literary and historical writing. They might not have been equally talented but, in view of their jadelike characters, they all served well in state functions.

Metaphysical discussion was emphasized during the early Chin, and reached its height in the Eastern Chin. Such discussions left their influence upon the literary trends of the time. For this reason, although the time was a time of turmoil, its literature is characterized by calm and serenity in both its language and its thought. In poetry, Laotzu's philosophy became the inevitable theme, and in *fu*, it was Chuangtzu's ideas that furnished the content. It illustrates for us how deeply literary development is influenced by the course of worldly events, and how directly the rise and fall of political powers bear on the trends of litera-

---

[49] The Chinese at that time, like the Japanese, who absorbed a great deal of Chinese culture, sat on mats when engaged in discussion.

[50] *Chin-shu*, "Hsiao-wu chi": "At first [before the birth of Emperor Hsiao-wu] Emperor Chien-wen saw an apocryphal statement which ran: 'The fate of the Chin ends with Ch'ang-ming.' At the time Emperor Hsiao-wu was conceived, Empress Li was told by a spiritual man in a dream that she would give birth to a boy and should name him Ch'ang-ming. When he was born, it began to dawn in the east. So the baby was named [Ch'ang-ming, meaning prosperous and bright]. When Emperor Chien-wen learned this, he sobbed." In the *Shih-shuo hsin-yü*, "Yü-yen p'ien," a commentator gives roughly the same anecdote, ending, however, in these words of Emperor Chien-wen, "I never anticipated that Ch'ang-ming would appear in my own family." Since, according to the apocryphal statement, the Chin dynasty was to end with "Ch'ang-ming," he is said to have no successor.

[51] Both were murdered by Liu Yü, who usurped the throne and established the dynasty known as Liu-sung. An was murdered in 418 and Kung in 420.

ture. If we adopt the method of determining a given outcome by establishing the source from which it developed, it is not difficult to tell what the development will be even in the distant future, one hundred generations hence.

During the [Liu] Sung [420-479], Emperor Wu [420-423] was devoted to literature, and Emperor Wen [424-453] achieved a literary style characterized by balance and grace.[52] They may both be said to have possessed high literary virtue. And Emperor Hsiao-wu [454-464], a man of great talent, created works of a beauty comparable to the patterns of clouds. But the years during and after the reign of Emperor Ming [465-471] witnessed the decline of both literary form and literary ideas.

However, among the gentry, writers rose like variegated clouds before a whirling wind. The Wangs and the Yüans were related by ties wrought in [literary forms as beautiful as] dragons' patterns;[53] and the Yens and the Hsiehs, generation after generation, produced works as wondrous as the colors of phoenixes.[54] And there were also the Hos [Ch'ang-yü, Ch'eng-t'ien, Shang-chih], the Fans [Fan T'ai and his son Yeh], the Changs [Fu and Yung], and the Shens [Yüeh, Huai-wen, and Huai-yüan], and their innumerable fellows. All these writers are well known, so I mention them in passing.

When our august Ch'i [479-502] came to rule, all good fortune descended upon the virtuous and enlightened.[55] T'ai-tsu [479-482],[56]

[52] By "balance" here is meant a sense of balance between content and form, or ideas and their linguistic expressions.

[53] "Dragons' patterns" means beautiful literary forms. According to the *Sung-shu*, in the Wang family were Tan, Shao-chih, Chun-chih, T'an-sheng, Seng-ta, Wei, etc.; and in the Yüan family were Shu and Ts'an.

[54] When Yen and Hsieh are mentioned together, they generally refer to Yen Yen-chih and Hsieh Lin-yün. Here Liu Hsieh must have in mind the literary members of the two families. In the Yen family we have Yen-chih himself and his two sons, Chün and Tz'e; and in the Hsieh family there were Lin-yün himself, the cousin of his father's generation named Hun, and his cousins Hui-lien and Chan.

[55] Although Liu Hsieh lived on into the Liang dynasty and is generally considered to belong to the Liang, his *Wen-hsin tiao-lung* was completed in the Ch'i dynasty. Hence his laudatory rhetoric with reference to the Ch'i rulers.

[56] T'ai-tsu, Hsiao Tao-ch'eng, was the first ruler of the Ch'i dynasty. He created the dynasty by usurpation in 479.

sage and martial, received the mandate of heaven; Kao-tsu,[57] a man of sagacity and literary quality, continued to further the dynastic fortune; Emperor Wen[58] was brilliant as the two celestial luminaries, and bountiful as the manifold forms of earth; and Chung-tsung,[59] endowed with the highest wisdom, made further advances to fulfil the dynastic destiny. All these rulers were gifted with literary talent and all were men of enlightenment; continuously brilliant, they have enjoyed great blessings.

Now His Majesty has just begun his sage reign, and the world is bathed in the light of his literary thought.[60] The deities of the seas and the mountains bestow upon him divine perception, causing his native talent to flower forth. He drives the flying dragons through the heavenly path, and harnesses the thoroughbreds for a ten-thousand-*li* trip. Works on the Classics and government institutions under his reign have surpassed those of the Chou and can look down upon those of the Han with contempt. They are comparable to those of the T'ang and the Yü; they are works which may be called truly great. Such great style and wondrous beauty I with my sluggish brush hardly dare try to depict. So I leave it to those who are better endowed with insight and wisdom to sing praise to the time.

The Tsan:

Against the background of ten dynasties,[61]
Literary trends have changed nine times.[62]
Once initiated at the central pivot,

---

[57] No Ch'i ruler was given the posthumous title of "Kao-tsu." The posthumous title of the second ruler is Shih-tsu. It is conceivable that Liu made a mistake here. The second ruler reigned from 483 to 493.

[58] He died as heir apparent and was posthumously given the title of Emperor Wen when his son, Yü-lin, succeeded to the throne.

[59] There was no ruler in the Ch'i dynasty who answers to this title. It could have been Emperor Ming (494-498), who was given the posthumous title of Kao-tsung, as Fan Wen-lan suggests.

[60] Presumably referring to the first years of Tung-hun hou, 499-501.

[61] The ten dynasties: T'ang, Yü, Hsia, Shang, Chou, Han, Wei, Chin, Sung, and Ch'i. Between the Chou and Han was a short dynasty, the Ch'in, which Liu Hsieh treats as part of the Chou.

[62] For the meaning of the term "nine," see note 6, Chapter XLIV.

The process of transformation circles endlessly.
Literary subject matter and the form in which it is treated are conditioned by the needs of the times,
But whether a certain subject matter or a certain form is emphasized or overlooked depends on the choice made by the writers.
Antiquity, however remote,
Can be made to display itself before us like a human face.

XLVI. The Physical World

Spring and autumn roll around, succeeding one another, and the *yin* and *yang* principles alternatingly darken and brighten.[1] When objects in the physical world change, our minds are also affected. When the *yang* principle begins to ascend, ants burrow, and when the *yin* principle congeals, the mantis begins to feed.[2] Insignificant as these insects are, even they are affected. Profoundly indeed are things moved by the four seasons. Excellent jade inspires the mind of the intelligent, and glorious flowers shower splendor upon the soul that is pure. All things exert influence on one another. Who is there that can rest unmoved?

Thus, as the new year is rung in and the spring begins to burgeon, we experience a joyous mood; as the luxuriant summer rolls by, our minds become filled with happy thoughts; as the sky heightens and the air becomes clear and brisk,[3] our hearts become darkened and heavy with distant thoughts; and when the ground is covered by

[1] "The spring and the autumn" represent the four seasons. The *yin* is the female principle and the *yang*, the male principle. According to the cosmology of the Yin-yang school, the universe with everything in it came into being with the interplay of these two principles. The most obvious examples of the manifestation of these principles are the successive movement of the seasons and the alternate lengthening of night and day.

[2] This is based on the *Ta-tai li-chi*, "Hsia shao-cheng p'ien." The *yang* principle begins to ascend in the twelfth moon, roughly at some time in January, and the *yin* principle begins to congeal in the eighth moon, roughly at some time in September.

[3] "Lofty sky and clear air" always means autumn in Chinese literature.

boundless sleet and snow, our souls become burdened with serious
and profound reflections. Many different things appear in the course
of the year, and each has a number of phases. One responds with
varying emotions to these varying phases, and the form of language
used depends on the emotion. One single leaf may suggest something
significant,[4] and the chirping of insects is often enough to induce an
inner mood. So how much greater an influence will be felt if we
experience a clear wind and a bright moon on the same night, or a
bright sun and a spring forest on the same morning!

In responding to things, the Ancient Poets operated on the principle
of endless association of ideas. They lost themselves in the myriads of
things, completely absorbed in the visual and auditory sensations. On
the one hand, they depicted the atmosphere and painted the appearances
of things in perfect harmony with their changing aspects; and on the
other, the linguistic and tonal patterns they used closely corresponded
with their perceptions. For example: *Shao-shao*, "brilliant," is used to
depict the brilliance of peach blossoms; *i-i*, "feeling of attachment," to
describe the sweeping willow trees; *kao-kao*, "brightly burning," to
describe the coming out of the sun; *piao-piao*, "fast and heavy," to suggest an image of rain and snow; *chieh-chieh*, "chirping," to imitate the
sound of orioles; *yao-yao*, "buzzing," to imitate the sound of insects.[5]
Then again in *chiao-jih*, "the bright sun," a reference to fidelity, or
hui-hsing, "little stars," a reference to humility, each only a simple
phrase, the Ancient Poets probe into the depth of the fundamental
nature of things;[6] and with *ts'an-tz'u* [describing the uneven lengths

---

[4] For example, the falling of the first leaf in the autumn.

[5] All these are taken from the *Book of Poetry*. For *shao-shao*, see *Mao shih yin-te*,
2/6/1; for *i-i*, 36/167/6; for *kao-kao*, 13/62/3; for *piao-piao*, 55/223/7; for *chieh-chieh*,
1/2/1; and for *yao-yao*, 3/14/1. *I-i* has also been translated as "luxuriant" (Karlgren),
"fresh and green" (Legge), and "spread their shade" (Waley). It seems to me that these
renderings lose the emotional mood of a departing traveler, who looks on the willow
trees fondly, reluctant to leave, and then projects his emotional state onto the trees and
attributes to them human feelings of attachment. For the traveler, these willow trees are
symbols of home, suggesting by their sweeping manner the sweet and gentle atmosphere
of home. *Chieh-chieh* and *yao-yao* seem to be cases of onomatopoeia.

[6] "Chiao-jih" is from the *Book of Poetry*, poem no. 73, a symbol of fidelity; "hui"
and "hsing" are not found in such a combination, although it is suggested by the
structure of the line in which "hui" and "hsing" occur separated by a particle (see

of water plants] and *wo-jo* [describing the glossiness of mulberry trees] each consisting of only two characters, the Ancient Poets have given us perfectly realistic descriptions of things.[7] In all these expressions, they have used a part to sum up the whole, leaving nothing whether in their feeling or in the appearance of things undescribed.[8] In spite of the thousand years of thought that have gone into this matter of poetic diction, no alteration can be made without difficulty.

By the time the *Li-sao* came upon the scene, types of description had multiplied, and it was practically impossible to depict all the aspects of things with faithfulness to their nature. For it had then been found necessary to describe the same things in a variety of forms. So various terms to describe craggy height, or to describe luxuriant growth, came to be collected. Ch'ang-ch'ing [or Ssu-ma Hsiang-ju] and his group adopted a pretentious style and extraordinary tonal patterns, and their descriptions of mountains and waters consist of strings of words in rows, like columns of fish. Such a state of things may illustrate the truth of the statement that the *fu* poetry of the Ancient Poets is beautiful and yet well balanced, and their language is terse and compact; while the poetry of the Tz'u writers is beautiful but excessive, and their lines are good examples of verbose diction.[9]

In the *ya* section [of the *Book of Poetry*] the blossoms of the *prunus japonica* are described as being "some yellow and some white";[10] and in the *Sao*, or *Ch'u-tz'u*, the autumn orchid is described as having "green leaves" and "purple stem."[11] In the application of the five colors, it is important to keep in mind the appropriateness of different colors seen at different times. If green and yellow are used routinely, they

---

poem no. 258), or by two words (see poem no. 21). Taken together, the phrase means "little stars," signifying a station of life that is humble and yet a necessary element in the harmony of the whole.

[7] For *ts'an-tz'u*, see the *Book of Poetry*, 1/1/2, 4, 5; and for *wo-jo*, see *ibid.*, 13/58/3.

[8] Liu Hsieh here gives the first clear statement of a synecdoche.

[9] These last clauses are a paraphrasing of a statement given in Yang Hsiung's *Fa-yen*, "Wu-tzu p'ien."

[10] "Some yellow and some white" is found in *Mao-shih yin-te*, 53/214/3. This phrase is meant to describe flowers in general, and not specifically the *prunus japonica*, as stated in Liu Hsieh's text.

[11] See *Ch'u-tz'u* (Ssu-k'u pei-yao ed.), chüan 2, p. 33.

merely add to the wordiness of the piece without accomplishing anything of value.

Recently, literary writers have emphasized realism in description.
They pierce through to the inner structure of a landscape and penetrate
the appearances of plants. Whatever their theme, they usually succeed
in expressing something deep and profound in their poetry. To achieve
perfection in the description of things depends on an intimate knowledge of the fitness of terms for certain specific descriptive purposes.
This perfect aptness of the happy expression to the form of things may
be likened to the relation between a seal and the seal ink paste, for
the impression made reproduces the seal exactly to the minutest detail
without further carving and cutting. Because of such skill, we are able
to see the appearances of things through the descriptive words, or to
experience the season through the diction.

Now the modes of physical things have a certain regularity, but our
thinking is more than a fixed routine. Sometimes we achieve perfection
through spontaneous thinking, and sometimes, for all our laborious
reasoning, our results are loose and unsystematic. Furthermore, what
is found in the *Book of Poetry* and the *Li-sao* seems to have covered
all the strategic ground, and this belief has made later writers afraid
to wield their own clever brushes in competition. They all seek to
obtain skill by following in the direction of the [*Book of Poetry* and the
Li-sao], and hope that in accepting these patterns they may perchance
achieve the extraordinary themselves. For if a writer is good at adapting
essentials to new situations, then, even if the essentials are old, his
writings will always seem fresh.

The four seasons repeat their cycle, proliferating forms in great confusion; but to use them as the elements of poetic allegories requires
measure and control. The physical world presents a variety of colorful
objects, but the language one uses to analyze them must be brief. Such
control of content and language makes the reader experience a sense
of exhilarating lightness, and puts him in an emotional mood ever
refreshingly new.

The poets from days of old have always followed in one another's steps from generation to generation. They refer to one another's experience and effect their own changes, and their success often comes from their being able to both accept and modify what has gone before. When one is able through his work to induce in the reader a mood that persists beyond the limit of the description of the physical things, he may be considered a man who completely understands the art of writing.

Mountains, forests, plateaus, and plains are certainly the ultimate source of literary thought. [But they are difficult to command.] For if described too briefly, the writing appears sketchy; and if described in too much detail, it sounds wordy. However, the reason why Ch'ü P'ing [or Ch'ü Yüan] was able to capture the spirit of *feng* and *sao* in the expression of feeling is that he was amply helped by his experience of the rivers and mountains.

> *The Tsan*:
> Mountains rise one behind another, and waters meander and circle;
> Trees interlace and clouds mingle.
> Such sights before the eyes
> Stir the mind to express itself.
> "Spring days pass slowly,"[12]
> And autumn wind "soughs mournfully."[13]
> The access of feeling for something is described as the giving of a gift,
> And the coming of inspiration as a response.

XLVII. Literary Talents

The literary output of the nine dynasties[1] is rich and glorious. In what

---

[12] See the *Book of Poetry*, poem no. 154.
[13] See *Ch'u-tz'u*, "Shan-kuei" and "Chiu-ke."
[1] In Chapter XLV are mentioned ten dynasties. As the last dynasty, during which

follows we shall discuss briefly the literary fashions and rhetorical style prevailing in those periods.

During the Yü and the Hsia we have Kao Yao[2] who dwelt on the "Six Virtues";[3] K'uei, who harmonized the eight timbres;[4] I, who wrote a [monitory] *tsan*;[5] and the five brothers[6] who composed a song [of complaint]. Both in language and in content, these works possess warmth and grace, and they constitute a veritable standard of literary excellence for all time.

During the period of the Shang and Chou, there were produced the [apologetic] "Kao" of Chung Hui,[7] the advice of I Yin,[8] and the poetry and *sung* of Yin Chi-fu and his group.[9] Their themes are, of course, classical and, in addition, their language furnishes models worthy of imitation.

During the Ch'un-ch'iu period, ministers paid particular attention to their language during their diplomatic missions. Their repartee scintillates like a garden of jade and jewels; it glistens and shines like brocade spread out in the market place. Wei Ao compiled laws and statutes for the state of Ch'u,[10] [Shih] Hui of Sui instituted rites for the state of Chin,[11] Chao Shuai's literary gift earned him a place at

---

this book was written—the Ch'i—is not included in this chapter, we have only nine dynasties.

[2] The *Book of History*, Chapter 2. Kao Yao was a minister of Shun, to whom he presented plans for the government in the "Kao-yao."

[3] These are given in the *Chou-li*: wisdom, benevolence, sageness, righteousness, loyalty, and harmony. See *Chou-li yin-te*, 3/19a.

[4] K'uei was another minister of Shun, and he was also a musician. The *Book of History*, Chapter 2. For the eight timbres, see note 40, Chapter VII.

[5] I was also a minister of Shun, whose *tsan* was an advice to Shun. It is given in Chapter 3 in the *Book of History*.

[6] See note 12, Chapter VI.

[7] The *Book of History*, Chapter 11, "Chung-hui chih-kao." Chung Hui was a minister of T'ang, who, after vanquishing the Hsia and putting Chieh, the last ruler of the Hsia, in exile, was smitten with remorse for his conduct against his former lord. Chung Hui, in this "Kao," tried to justify T'ang's conduct.

[8] Entitled "I-hsün," Chapter 13 of the *Book of History*.

[9] This *sung* simply means songs and should be distinguished from the *sung* which means sacrificial odes and is one of the six elements of the *Book of Poetry*. The term *sung* is used because Yin Chi-fu himself used this term to refer to the poem he wrote. See poems 259 and 260 in the *Book of Poetry*.

[10] *Ch'un-ch'iu ching-chuan yin-te*, 196/Hsüan 12/3 Tso.

[11] *Ibid.*, 206/Hsüan 16/Tso, fu.

the feast [given in Ch'ung-erh's honor by Duke Mu of Ch'in],[12] and Kuo-ch'iao [or Tzu-ch'uan] was enabled by means of his mastery of rhetoric to defend Cheng.[13]

[During the time when Tzu-ch'an was at the helm of the government of Cheng] Tzu-t'ai-shu [won honor] because he was graceful and gentle and gifted in literary art, and Kung-sun Hui because he was adept in diplomatic conversation.[14] These were the elite among the literary talents of the time.

During the Warring States period the emphasis was on the art of war; however, there was no dearth of men of letters. The speculative writers drew upon philosophical ideas as source material; Ch'ü Yüan and Sung Yü exhibited their literary talent in *Ch'u-tz'u*; Yüeh I's reply to [the king of Yen] is convincing and morally sound;[15] Fan Chü's memorial to [the king of Ch'in] is thorough and penetrating;[16] Su Ch'in's arguments to win over the rulers of the various states[17] are vigorous and to the point; and Li Ssu's memorial [arguing against getting rid of guest ministers] is beautiful and persuasive.[18] If these writers had lived at a time when interest in literature was great, they would certainly have been the equals of Yang [Hsiung] and Pan [Ku]. And Hsün K'uang [or Hsün-tzu], a literary lion, called his descriptions of things *fu*; in these *fu* he achieved a balance between substance

[12] Ch'ung-erh, the chief contender to the throne of Chin, fled his country and went to Ch'in on account of internal chaos. He returned to power with the blessing of Ch'in in 636 B.C. Chao Shuai, one of the followers who fled with Ch'ung-erh, was known for his literary ability. Literary ability at this time meant the ability to carry on a conversation properly during state functions, without violating any social or political taboo. One of the qualifications was to be able to recite appropriate poems to express delicate ideas.

[13] *Ch'un-ch'iu ching-chuan yin-te*, 307/Hsiang 25/7 Tso fu 2. See Chapter II, above.

[14] *Ch'un-ch'iu ching-chuan yin-te*, 336/Hsiang 31/Tso fu 6.

[15] Yüeh I, originally a general of Yen, was alienated from the King of Yen and fled to Chao, where he was enfeoffed Lord of Wang-shu. Then the King of Yen regretted it and sent a letter to Yüeh I, requesting him to return to Yen. In his reply, Yüeh I explained with a great deal of moral conviction why he could not return to Yen.

[16] See his biography in the *Shih-chi*.

[17] Before Su Ch'in was entrusted with the government of the six states in a vertical federation against the state of Ch'in, he had to travel from one state to another to convince their rulers of the serious consequences of not forming an alliance in the face of the ever-expanding Ch'in. *Shih-chi*, chüan 69.

[18] Li's memorial is in the *Wen-hsüan*.

and literary form which made him the finest of the Confucian writers.[19]

Under the House of Han, Lu Chia was the first to produce works of wondrous beauty. He wrote a *fu* on "Meng-ch'un,"[20] and produced the *Hsin-yü*.[21] In both he showed a wealth of argumentative talent. Chia I, an outstanding talent, was quicker of wit than a courser is fleet of foot. His reasoning is sound and his *fu* pure. He has not achieved his fame without merit. The "Ch'i-fa" of Mei Sheng[22] and the memorial to [Prince Hsiao of Liang] by Tsou Yang[23] are the work of brushes which are both brilliant and smooth; they express the souls of the writers in moving language. Tung Chung-shu was a devoted Confucian, and Tzu-ch'ang [or Ssu-ma Ch'ien] a perfect historian. Their works, as beautiful as embroidery, may be compared to the lamentations of the Ancient Poets.[24] [Ssu-ma] Hsiang-ju, an avid reader, modeled his writing on that of [Ch'ü] Yüan and [Sung] Yü. He has entered into the realm of beauty, and won the acclaim of a poet laureate. However, if one tries to analyze his ideas with any degree of thoroughness, one will find that his reasoning is too weak for his literary form. It is this which evoked from Yang [Hsiung] the statement, "Ch'ang-ch'ing [or Ssu-ma Hsiang-ju] is one whose writing, though beautiful, is of little use."[25] This judgment is sound indeed. Wang Pao's rhetoric is characterized by its tight structure and artful expressions. His intimate descriptions of sights and sounds make his works light and readable. Tzu-yün [or Yang Hsiung] may be considered the most

---

[19] Hsüntzu wrote "Fu-p'ien," in which he treats of "Li" [Rites], "Chih" [Knowledge], "Yün" [Clouds], "Ts'an" [Silkworm], etc. See Chapter 26 in the *Hsüntzu*, pp. 313-20.

[20] "The First Month in Spring," now lost.

[21] A work propounding mainly Confucian principles.

[22] See note 2, Chapter XIV.

[23] Tsou Yang was from Ch'i, in what is presently Shangtung. He came to Liang, in what is now Honan, with the purpose of getting an appointment from the prince. His literary talent aroused jealousy at the prince's court, and he was thrown into prison. The memorial to the prince written in prison not only saved his neck, but made him an honored guest of the prince. See his biography in the *Han-shu*.

[24] Both wrote *fu* on the theme of the frustration of scholars.

[25] This line is found in Yang Hsiung's *Fa-yen*, "Chün-tzu (chu-tzu chi-ch'eng ed.), p. 38. The idea may also be seen in the following quotation from "Wu-tzu p'ien": "If Confucius had included *fu* as one of the departments [of studies], Chia I may be considered as having ascended the hall, and Ssu-ma Hsiang-ju as having entered the chamber. However, their trouble is that their works are of little use." *Ibid.*, p. 4.

profound both in the language he employs and the themes he treats. His ability to couch his brilliant thought in firm language is due to his ideas, which are both sagacious and profound; to his relentless search for wondrous and beautiful expressions; and to his untiring effort to think things through. Huan T'an's works have been acclaimed as being as rich as I Tun,[26] and Sung Hung has compared him to [Ssu-ma] Hsiang-ju in his recommendation.[27] However, judged on the basis of his *fu* on the Palace of Chi-ling and other works, he is definitely shallow and lacking in talent. This proves that a writer who excels at satire and parable may not be able to write rhetorical pieces. Ching-t'ung [or Feng Yen] loved to write, and when he met with frustration in a time of prosperity, he wrote a *fu* to express his inner thoughts. Such a piece may be compared to a pearl, which is produced as the oyster becomes diseased. The two Pan [Piao and his son Ku] and the two Liu [Hsiang and his son Hsin] exhibited great literary talent in two successive generations. According to an old opinion, Ku was said to excel Piao in literary quality, and Hsin to excel Hsiang in scholarship. However, [Pan Piao's] "Wang-ming" is clear and convincing, and [Liu Hsiang's] "Hsin-hsü" comprehensive and well organized. A piece of jade, however exquisite, owes its origin to the jade-producing Mount K'un-kang, and as a product it would be rather difficult for it to excel its source. Fu I and Ts'ui Yin attained equal brilliance of style, and [Ts'ui Yin's son] Yüan and [his son] Shih ably continued the family tradition. Tu Tu and Chia K'uei both won fame in the literary world, but their works mark the beginning of the end of the trend that originated with Ts'ui [Yin] and Fu [I]. Li Yu aimed high in his writing of *fu* and *ming* but, lacking in talent and vigor, he finally folded his wings, unable to fly. Ma Yung, a great scholar of penetrating thought and wide learning, wrote in the tradition of the Classics, and in his work flowers and fruits support each other. Wang I was erudite

26 A Chinese Croesus, living in the state of Lu during the Chou time. He was originally a poor scholar, but later grew rich through his activity in selling salt and in other trade.

27 According to Sung Hung's biography in the *Hou-han shu*, he compared Huan T'an to Yang Hsiung and Liu Hsiang and his son Hsin, and not to Hsiang-ju.

and learned, and achieved beauty of pattern, but lacked strength. [His son] Yen-shou furthered his ambition, and achieved outstanding beauty in his work. His descriptive ability recalls the masterful hand of Mei Sheng. Chang Heng, learned and brilliant, and Ts'ai Yung, penetrating and graceful, two beacons in two generations, won equal distinction in both literary and historical writing. They may have differed in their hearts as the bamboo and cypress differ in their texture, but they are equally firm; and they may have differed in their substance as gold and jade differ in their nature, but they are both treasures. The *tsou* and *i* of Liu Hsiang convey an earnestness of purpose, although easy in tempo; the poetry of Chao I, however, overburdened with ideas, is incoherent and loose; K'ung Yung shows great vigor in the field of *pi*, and Ni Heng is adroit in the writing of *wen*. Each of these four writers has his own merit. P'an Hsü owes the ability he displays to the support of the Classics, and therefore his conferment edict is the outstanding specimen of its type;[28] Wang Lang, sensitive and articulate, did well for himself in the realm of *hsü* and *ming*. Writers before the time of Ch'ing [or Ssu-ma Hsiang-ju] and Yüan [or Wang Pao] mostly wrote out of their natural inclinations, and seldom took advantage of the experience of others; but after the time of [Yang] Hsiung and [Liu] Hsiang, many writers began to quote the works of past authors to help them in their own writing. It is at this point that we find the line drawn between those who take and those who give, a distinction which we should not allow to become blurred in our minds.

The writing of Wei-wen [or Ts'ao P'ei] is the work of a fine talent, and is distinguished by a style which is pure and beautiful. But he is depreciated by many writers, who believed that he is a thousand *li* behind [Ts'ao] Chih. It is true that Tzu-chien [or Ts'ao Chih], quick in thinking and outstanding in talent, writes beautiful poetry and fine memorials, and Tzu-huan [or Ts'ao P'ei], because he is thorough in deliberation and slow in execution, is unable to compete with him in speed. But Ts'ao P'ei's *yüeh-fu* songs are pure and exquisite, and his

28 See note 22, Chapter XIX.

Tien-lun [*lun-wen*] is logical and to the point; his critical judgment, furthermore, is certainly far from pointless.[29] Since people in general repeat the opinions of others in making their own judgments, it is probable that many have been influenced by those who depreciated the talent of Wen-ti [or Ts'ao P'ei] because he occupied the position of highest honor, and tended to overrate the talent of Prince Ssu [or Ts'ao Chih] because he was persecuted by his [emperor-brother].[30] Such judgment cannot be held to be valid.

Chung-hsüan [or Wang Ts'an], phenomenally talented, is both adroit and thorough; most of his works are good in every way, seldom marred by any rhetorical faults. Judging him on the basis of his poetry and *fu*, we must rank him at the top among the Seven Masters [of the Chien-an period]. [Ch'en] Lin and [Juan] Yü are known for their *fu* [or tally] and *hsi* [or proclamation]; Hsü Kan is praised for his *fu* and *lun*; Liu Chen couches his deep feeling in brocaded rhetoric; Ying Yang succeeds on the strength of his sound scholarship; Lu Ts'ui [?-214] and Yang Hsiu [173-219] are versed in the art of writing memoirs; Ting I [?-200] and Han-tan [Ch'un, 132-?] exhibit beauty in the writing of essays. All of these writers may be numbered among the best.

Liu Shao's "Chao-tu fu"[31] may be compared with the *fu* of earlier writers, and Ho Yen's "Ching-fu-tien fu"[32] is a beacon to young writers to come. Hsiu-lien [or Ying Chü], characterized by purity of style, pours forth his feelings in the "Po-i,"[33] and Chi-fu [or Ying Chen], well-versed in rhetoric, spreads out his variegated pattern in his "Lin-tan fu."[34] Hsi K'ang's essays express the mind of a master artist, and Juan Chi's poetry is permeated with his whole spirit and life. Together, these writers compose a symphony of different sounds and fly in perfect formation, although each has a unique pair of wings.

---

[29] The critical judgment mentioned here apparently refers to his critical remarks about the Seven Masters of the Chien-an period in his *Tien-lun lun-wen*.

[30] There was a great deal of undercurrent friction between the two brothers, Ts'ao Chih being the victim and Ts'ao P'ei the persecutor. Liu Hsieh is expressing an opinion common to many literary critics, that people's judgment about the literary quality of the two brothers is greatly influenced by their sympathy for the victim.

[31] See note 12, Chapter XXXVIII.   [32] See *Wen-hsüan*, chüan 11.

[33] See note 39, Chapter VI.   [34] See *I-wen lei-chü*, chüan 8.

The short pieces of Chang Hua sparkle brilliantly, pure and smooth. His "Chiao-liao fu"[35] is as great an allegorical piece as Han Fei's "Shuo-nan."[36] Tso Ssu, an extraordinary talent, is a man of profound thought. His whole life and spirit is spent without reserve in the writing of the "San-tu-fu,"[37] in which he distinguishes himself in his treatment of historical themes. P'an Yüeh, quick-witted, has a smooth, flowing style. He gives his best in the writing of the "Hsi-cheng fu,"[38] yet has energy to spare to devote to the writing of the *ai*, or lament, and *lei*, or elegy. His art [is the result of his native endowment and] is not due to external influences. Lu Chi has a natural tendency to probe deeply into the secret of things, and seeks in his language to adopt all available patterns. Therefore, he is able to couch his ideas in artistic form. However, he fails to check his inclination toward verbosity. Shih-lung [or Lu Yün] is lucid and well-disciplined, and manages to bring order out of confusion through a wide range of knowledge. So he is able to achieve freshness and purity of style. He is particularly keen in the art of writing short pieces. Sun Ch'u organizes his thoughts with direct relevance to the situation; and Chih Yü expresses his feelings with warmth and grace, always in conformity to the best literary standard. Yü's attempt to evaluate and classify literary works is systematic and sound. Fu Hsüan's writing is filled with exhortations; while the memorials of Ch'ang-yü [or Fu Hsien][39] are characterized by resolution and integrity. Both possess the character of [Liu] Chen and [Hsü] Kan, but neither may serve as brilliant stem and calyx for flowers. Ch'eng-kung Tzu-an [or Ch'eng-kung Sui] wrote the most beautiful *fu* of his time, and Hsia-hou Hsiao-ju [or Hsia-hou Chan] produced works which are all Classics in miniature. Ts'ao Shu is pure and beautiful in his long pieces, and Chi-ying [or Chang Han], clear-cut in his short rhymes. Each of these writers has his good point.

[35] *Chiao-liao* are tiny birds which, in spite of their size, are completely self-sufficient. As their small size renders them useless, they are spared as other more useful birds, such as peacocks, are not. Developing the idea of equality first propounded by Chuangtzu, Chang draws a lesson from the existence of the *chiao-liao*. For the *fu*, see *Wen-hsüan*, chüan 13.

[36] *Han-fei-tzu*, chüan 4, Chapter 13.

[37] See note 6, Chapter XXVI.

[38] *Wen-hsüan*, chüan 10.

[39] Fu Hsüan's son.

Meng-yang [or Chang Tsai] and Ching-yang [or Chang Hsieh] are equals in literary talent, comparable to the states of Lu and Wei, for theirs are the works of literary equals.[40] The works of Liu K'un [270-317] are characterized by grace and vigor, effervescing with spirit, and those of Lu Shen [284-350] are expressive in feeling and lucid in presentation of ideas. These qualities came as natural consequences of the conditions of the time. Ching-ch'un's [or Kuo P'u's] beautiful pieces crown the literary production of the period of restoration; his "Chiao-fu" is splendid and grand, and his poems on immortality invoke in the mind of the reader a feeling of lightness, as if he were floating and soaring—riding on the clouds.[41] Yü Yüan-kuei's [or Yü Liang's] memorials are neat and close-knit, written in a spirit calm and free; and Wen T'ai-chen's [or Wen Ch'iao's] memoir is reasonable and readable. Both are fine artists in writing. Sun Sheng and Kan Pao are at their best in historical works patterned after the classical *tien* and *hsün*. As literary architects they may have different ideas about the positions of doors and windows, but about the general artistic pattern they more or less agree.

Yüan Hung drives his chariot wildly, holding his head high in the air; hence his work is unique but rather lame; Sun Ch'o closely follows the trodden rut, producing works which are systematic but unexciting; Yin Chung-wen's "Ku-hsing" and Hsieh Shu-yüan's [or Hsieh Hun's] "Hsien-ch'ing" are examples which illustrate the decline of poetry into vain and disconnected sounds. Although they may exhibit a high degree of lyricism, they do violence to the principle of literature.

With respect to the talents of the [Liu] Sung dynasty, all we need say is that the literary production is profuse. As these works have been produced recently, they are easy to understand, and I shall not include them in my treatment.

The forest of talents of the Later Han is comparable to that of the

[40] Literally, "literary brothers." Lu and Wei were brother states; Lu was the fief of the Duke of Chou, and Wei that of K'ang-shu, both younger brothers of King Wu.
[41] Seven poems on immortality by Kuo P'u are included in *Wen-hsüan*, chüan 21.

Western Capital [i.e., the Former Han]; and the garden of literature of the Chin is equal in beauty to that of Yeh-tu.[42] However, during the Wei dynasty the literary world always referred to the Yüan-feng period [110-105 B.C.] as the period in which literary development reached its height; in the [Liu] Sung dynasty, it was the Chien-an period [A.D. 196-220] which was the subject of common admiration. Why? Because these were the golden ages when literature was respected, the periods of gracious patronage under which talented writers were gathered together. The Ancients did not, then, emphasize the spirit of time without reason.[43]

> *The Tsan*:
> Rare indeed is talent!
> Each individual is unique in his natural gift.
> If for once one succeeds in producing a talented piece,
> We have a brocaded work which will last a thousand years;
> The wonderful patterns he leaves behind will perpetuate themselves
> By profoundly influencing future styles.
> The work of the talented man will be free from admixture and
>   adulteration,
> Pure and bright, a fit object for an appreciative eye.

XLVIII. An Understanding Critic (Chih-Yin)[1]

It is indeed difficult to find an understanding critic of personal thought. It is true that personal thought is intrinsically difficult to understand; but what is still more difficult is to find someone who possesses real

---

[42] Capital of the Wei dynasty.

[43] The spirit of time is repeatedly emphasized in the *Book of Changes*. See *Chou-i yin-te*, 5/4/t'uan; 44/hsi, Shang/11; 45/hsi, hsia/1; and many others. And Mencius presented to Confucius the title of "The Sage of Timeliness." *Meng-tzu yin-te*, 39/5B/1.

[1] Literally, "Chih-yin" means one who understands music, that is, one who has a sympathetic ear. By extension, it comes to mean an understanding friend.

understanding. Hardly once in a thousand years do we happen upon an understanding critic. The [so-called] understanding critics have since time of old despised their contemporaries and devoted themselves to those who have passed into antiquity, just as it is said, "One disdains to harness the horses which are presented to him every day, but dreams of using those whose neighing he hears from a distance."[2]

When [Han Fei's] "Ch'u-shuo"[3] first appeared, the first emperor of the Ch'in expressed great regret for not being Han's contemporary;[4] and Emperor Wu of the Han felt the same way about [Ssu-ma Hsiang-ju] when he first read Hsiang-ju's "Tzu-hsü fu."[5] But once it was known that they were contemporaries, Han [Fei] was thrown into prison and Ssu-ma Hsiang-ju lightly regarded. Are these not clear examples of the contempt in which contemporaries are usually held?

Then there were Pan Ku and Fu I, whose achievements in literary writing are about equal, and yet Pan Ku ridiculed Fu I and said, "Once he starts, he does not know how to stop."[6] And Ch'en-ssu [or Ts'ao Chih], in his discussion of talent, also severely criticized K'ung-chang [or Ch'en Lin]. But to the request of Ching-li [or Ting I, ?-220][7] that Ts'ao Chih polish his writing, Ts'ao responded with a word of praise for him. Then there was [Liu] Chi-hsü, not a great writer himself, who loved to criticize, and was compared to T'ien Pa by Ts'ao Chih.[8]

---

[2] Quoted from the *Kuei-ku-tzu*. See T'ao Tsung-i, *Shuo-fu*, chüan 71, p. 16a.

[3] See *Han-fei-tzu*, Chapters 30-35.

[4] This was before the emperor knew that Han Fei was actually his contemporary. But when he found that out and succeeded in getting him to his court, he promptly threw him into prison on the advice of the jealous Li Ssu. By the time the emperor realized his mistake, Han Fei had already been poisoned by order of Li Ssu.

[5] See the biography of Ssu-ma Hsiang-ju in the *Shih-chi*, where the emperor is reported to have said, after reading the *fu*, "What a misfortune that I cannot live in the same period with this man!" *Shih-chi*, chüan 117, p. 3a-b.

[6] This case was first cited by Ts'ao P'ei in his *Tien-lun lun-wen*. See *Wen-hsüan*, chüan 52. As Pan Ku and Fu I were contemporaries, Pan's critical opinion of Fu is cited here to support Liu's statement that one despises his contemporaries.

[7] A younger brother of Ting I, whose *tzu* is *Cheng-li*. The elder brother is mentioned in the last chapter. Both died at approximately the same time.

[8] These were all Ts'ao Chih's contemporaries, mentioned in his letter to Yang Hsiu. See "Yü Yang Te-tsu shu," *Wen-hsüan*, chüan 42. Liu Hsieh here wrote laconically, assuming his reader's acquaintance with Ts'ao Chih's letter to Yang Hsiu. Ts'ao Chih's praise for Ting I was prompted by the latter's frank opinion of himself; and he com-

In these instances we have a glimpse of Ts'ao Chih's opinion. When Wei-wen [or Ts'ao P'ei] said, "Literary men despise each other,"[9] his statement was certainly not groundless.

Chün-ch'ing [or Lou Hu], a man of great eloquence, mistakenly estimated his own ability when he dabbled in literary discussion. He once made the statement, "The historian [Ssu-ma] Ch'ien, in the writing of his work, sought advice from Tung-fang So."[10] Huan T'an and his group noted this with sneering laughter. Now if [Lou Hu], who was only a gambler, was censured for passing judgment lightly, can one who considers himself a man of letters afford to make groundless remarks?

There are men of high intelligence and keen penetration who value the ancient and despise the modern, like the two rulers mentioned above. There are others, men of talent, who have a tendency to esteem themselves and look down upon others, like Pan Ku and Ts'ao Chih. There are still others who, although they are men of letters, lack scholarship, and are blind to truth and credulous of falsehood, like Lou Hu. [Liu Hsin's] expressed apprehension that [work of profundity] may be fated to cover pickle jars cannot be dismissed as a case of oversensitivity.[11]

Now the unicorn and phoenix are vastly different from a *chün*, or hornless deer, and a pheasant; and pearls and jade are immeasurably superior to gravel and stone; and yet in broad daylight and clearly presented before the eye, [these things have been mistaken for each

---

pared Liu Chi-hsü to T'ien Pa, a sophist in the Warring States period, because both Liu and T'ien were fond of criticizing others, although they themselves lacked talent.

[9] The opening sentence in his *Tien-lun lun-wen*.

[10] Quoted by Ssu-ma Chen of the T'ang dynasty in his commentary to the last chüan of the *Shih-chi*, chüan 130, p. 29b, as a remark made by Huan T'an. According to Liu Hsieh, the statement was made by Lou Hu, and Huan T'an was criticizing him for his audacity in making it.

[11] Pan Ku, in his *tsan* to the biography of Yang Hsiung, mentions that after Liu Hsin had read Yang's *T'ai-hsüan*, a work patterned after the *Book of Changes*, and *Fa-yen*, a work patterned after the *Analects*, he said to Yang Hsiung, "Your labor will all be in vain. At present, honor and wealth await scholars who understand the *Book of Changes*, and still there is no one who really understands it. How can they be expected to understand your *T'ai-hsüan*? I am afraid people who come after us will use it to cover their jars of pickles." See *Han-shu*, chüan 87, hsia, p. 17a.

other]. A minister of Lu took the unicorn to be a *chün*,[12] a man of Ch'u took a pheasant to be a phoenix,[13] a Wei rustic thought a jade [rule] which shone at night was a piece of an ominous stone,[14] and a fool of Sung treasured a fragment of gravel from Mount Yen as if it were a precious pearl.[15] If these, which are all physically tangible things, and easily distinguishable, have been so mistakenly perceived, how much harder it must be to judge accurately when we come to deal with literature, the nature of which is so difficult to understand!

Literary works are of all kinds, and their contents and forms are interlocked. Our knowledge tends to be one-sided; no one has been able to be perfectly comprehensive. Men of the heroic type[16] will [unsophisticatedly] beat time when they hear a tune; those who are reserved are often keenly perceptive, inclining to the lofty way of retirement; the superficially clever will look at ornate patterns with throbbing hearts, and those who love the extraordinary will listen to what is odd with ears pricked up. They all recite with admiration what suits their taste, but discard that which does not meet with their approval. Each holds fast to his bias, and wants it to be the measure of all changes. There is no wonder that he who looks to the east does not see the western wall. But one can be considered a good musician only after one has played a thousand tunes, and a collector of arms can be considered a connoisseur only after he has seen a thousand swords;[17] so broad experience and learning are the *sine qua non* of true wisdom. Only when experiences of large mountains and ocean waves form the background for a man's description of small mounds and ditches, can he be free from individual preconceived evaluations and prejudices. And only thus freed is he able, like a balance, to judge impartially, or like a mirror, to reflect without distortion.

[12] *Ch'un-ch'iu ching-chuan yin-te*, 487/A8 14/1 Kung-yang.
[13] *Yin-wen-tzu*, "Ta-tao," shang (Chu-tzu chi-ch'eng ed.), p. 6.
[14] *Ibid.*   [15] *I-wen lei-chü*, chüan 6.
[16] Literally, the term "K'ang-k'ai" means full of feelings. Men of genuine feelings are usually explosive in temperament. Hence the same term means also "heroic."
[17] Remarks attributed to Yang Hsiung and Wang Chün-ta, quoted in Huan T'an's *Hsin-lun*. See *I-lin*, a compilation by Ma Tsung of the T'ang dynasty of quotations from authors since the Chou and Ch'in.

Now before we begin to study a piece of literature, we should pay attention to six points: its genre and style, its rhetoric, its application of the principle of flexible adaptability, its conformity or nonconformity to orthodox principle, its factual and intellectual content, and its musical pattern. Once clear about these points, we shall be able to weigh its merits and its faults.

The writer's first experience is his inner feeling, which he then seeks to express in words. But the reader, on the other hand, experiences the words first, and then works himself into the feeling of the author. If he can trace the waves back to their source, there will be nothing, however dark and hidden, that will not be revealed to him. Although the life of an age may have passed beyond our view, we may often, through reading its literature, succeed in grasping the heart of it. We ought never to blame a work for being too profound, for our failure to understand it is often due to our own lack of experience and knowledge. If it is possible for a man's impressions of mountains and rivers to find expression in his lute playing,[18] how much easier it must be to depict physically tangible forms with a brush, from which no inner feeling or idea can be successfully hidden. Our mind reflects reason just as our eyes perceive physical forms; as long as our eyes are keen, there are no physical forms which cannot be distinguished, and as long as our mind is alert, there are no feelings or ideas which cannot be conveyed. However, because the popular taste is confused, profound writings have come to be discarded, and the superficial types have gained popularity. This is why Chang Chou ridiculed "Che-yang" music,[19] and Sung Yü was struck with melancholy at the [forlorn]

[18] Po Ya, an ancient musician, was playing a lute, and Chung Tzu-chi, a friend with an appreciative ear, was listening. While he was playing, Po Ya thought of Mount T'ai; Chung Tzu-chi said, "Exquisite, your music is just as majestic as Mount T'ai." In a little while, Po Ya thought of a river; Chung Tzu-chi again said, "Exquisite, your music rolls full like a flowing river." When Chung Tzu-chi died, Po Ya dashed his lute to pieces and never during his lifetime did he play again. For he believed that there was no one else understanding enough to make his playing worthwhile. See *Lü-shih ch'un-ch'iu*, chüan 14, p. 140. Chung Tzu-chi, also known as Chung Chi, has always been respected as the most understanding critic in China.

[19] See *Chuangtzu yin-te*, 32/12/91: "Great music fails to win popular ears, but when 'Che-yang' or 'Huang-hua' is played, they all start to laugh out loud." Both "Che-yang" and "Huang-hua" are ancient popular musical pieces.

fate of "Pai-hsüeh."[20] Long ago Ch'ü P'ing [or Ch'ü Yüan] said, "There is in my inner nature both form and substance, but the people do not know their wonderful patterns."[21] Indeed, an understanding critic alone is capable of seeing what is [inwardly] wonderful. Yang Hsiung once called himself a lover of literary works which are both profoundly erudite and beautiful. From this statement it is apparent that Yang did not indulge in the superficial and shallow.

Only those with deep knowledge and profound insight will [give the author an] experience of inner joy, which experience may be compared to the warmth people feel while ascending a terrace in the spring,[22] or to the feeling of a wayfarer halting his step for music and viands.[23] For it is said that the orchid, which is the most fragrant thing in the country, will give forth its full scent only when worn; and similarly, literary works, which too are national treasures, must be appreciated to display their beauty. May those who consider themselves understanding critics consider these words well.

The Tsan:
Grand bells of ten thousand weights
Need K'uei and K'uang to determine their tones.[24]
Books in the box may be of excellent quality,
But they depend on expert knowledge for an appraisal of their value.
The popular vulgar music drowns one's soul;
So do not let your hearing be misled by it.
Only the principles propounded here
Mark out the paths which are free from mistakes.

[20] "Pai-hsüeh" is classical music, not appreciated by people at large. See Sung Yü's "Tui Ch'u-wang wen," *Wen-hsüan*, chüan 45.
[21] *Ch'u-tzu*, chüan 4, "Huai-sha."
[22] *Laotzu pen-i* (Chu-tzu chi-ch'eng ed.), Chapter 17, p. 15.
[23] *Ibid.*, Chapter 30, p. 27.
[24] Both K'uei and K'uang were masters of music in ancient times.

XLIX. The Capacity of a Vessel (Ch'eng-ch'i)

Scholars, in the discussion in the "Book of Chou,"[1] are compared to the work of the carpenter,[2] because their value consists both in their practical ability and in the beautiful patterns in which that ability is expressed. In the same way, only after a block has been carved is vermilion applied, and only after the walls are up are carving and varnish put on.[3]

However, modern writers love the flowers and discard the fruits. This moved Wei-wen [or Ts'ao P'ei] to remark, "All writers, present and past alike, are generally careless in the small matters of their lives."[4] And Wei Tan, in his criticism, condemned a number of writers.[5] Later critics reiterate these opinions like thunder responding to thunder, tragically monotonous and repetitive.

The following are some of the faults of literary writers: [Ssu-ma] Hsiang-ju stole a wife and received bribes; Yang Hsiung loved to drink and was quite lost as to how to plan for his daily living; Ching-t'ung [or Feng Yen] was rather undisciplined;[6] Tu Tu was persistent in asking favors and was never satisfied; Pan Ku unashamedly flattered Tou [Hsien] to add to his own prestige; Ma Yung allied himself with Liang [Chi] and was insatiable in his thirst for bribes; Wen-chü [or K'ung Yung], haughty and conceited, hastened his own death; Cheng-p'ing [or Ni Heng], wild and naive, courted his own execution;[7] Chung-hsüan [or Wang Ts'an] was frivolous and hot-headed; K'ung-chang [or Ch'en Lin], was hasty and careless; Ting I was a greedy

---

[1] The Chou section of the *Book of History*.

[2] "Tzu-ts'ai," Chapter 31 in the *Book of History*. Actually, it is the scholar's ability to manage the affairs of the state which is compared to a carpenter's work.

[3] For the source of these figures, see Chapter 31, the *Book of History*. *Shang-shu t'ung-chien*, 31/0144-0170.

[4] See his second letter to Wu Chih, in *Wen-hsüan*, chüan 42.

[5] Included in the list criticized by Wei are: Wang Ts'an, Po Ch'in, Juan Yü, Ch'en Lin, and Lu Tz'ui. See the biography of Wang Ts'an in the "Wei-shu," in the *San-kuo-chih*, chüan 21, pp. 6b-7a.

[6] See their biographies in the *Han-shu*.

[7] See their biographies in the *Hou-han-shu*.

man, forever demanding gifts; Lu Ts'ui devoted his life to the problems of what to drink and what to eat, with no sense of shame; P'an Yüeh forged the prayer for the heir apparent, Min-huai;[8] Lu Chi attached himself to Chia [Mi] and Kuo [Chang];[9] Fu Hsüan, stubborn and narrow-minded, even scolded the prime minister; and Sun Ch'u, malicious and obstinate, engaged in a lawsuit against his superior.[10] All these are faults literary writers have committed.

Of course, literary writers are not the only ones who have faults; military generals are not free from them. We recall, for example, the following faults of generals and prime ministers of the past: Kuan Chung's petty thievery, Wu Ch'i's greed and debauchery, Ch'en P'ing's black character, the sycophancy of Chiang[-hou Chou Po] and Kuan [Yin], and numberless other faults of people who came after them.[11] If K'ung Kuang, a prime minister, had to flatter Tung Hsien,[12] how could we expect Pan [Ku], and Ma [Yung], who held petty official positions, or P'an Yüeh, who was a subordinate, to do otherwise? Wang Jung had a hand in the establishment of the [Chin] dynasty and occupied the highest official rank. If a man of his calibre vulgarly sold offices and haggled for bargains, what can be expected of [Ssu-]ma [Hsiang-ju] and Tu [Tu], who had to bend their backs like musical stones,[13] or Ting [I] and Lu [Ts'ui], who were almost paupers?

[8] Empress Chia was about to remove the heir apparent. On the pretext that the emperor was not feeling well, she sent for the heir and put him in a room, and forced him to drink until he was drunk. Then she told P'an Yüeh to write a prayer in the name of the heir apparent. The drunken heir was asked to copy it, and the empress presented it to the emperor. In the prayer, the emperor was told to dispose of himself, with the threat that if he did not do so, the heir would do it with his own hand. As a result, the heir was removed. See *Chin-shu*, chüan 53, the biography of Min-huai T'ai-tzu, pp. 4b-5a.

[9] Chia Mi was Empress Chia's nephew and Kuo Chang was her uncle.

[10] See their biographies in the *Chin-shu*.

[11] Kuan Chung was accused of being a petty thief from Ch'eng-yin. See Liu Hsiang's *Shuo-yüan*, chüan 8, p. 50, "Tsun-hsien p'ien." For Wu Ch'i's character, see his biography in the *Shih-chi*. For Ch'en P'ing, Chou Po, and Kuan Yin, see the biography of Prime Minister Ch'en, in the *Shih-chi*.

[12] K'ung Kuang had been a superior of Tung Hsien's father. But since Tung Hsien had become a favorite of the emperor, K'ung Kuang had to forget his dignity and treat him in a flattering way. See "Ning-hsing chuan," in the *Han-shu*.

[13] Symbolic of people occupying low positions and having to show respect by bowing to others all the time.

However, the fame of Tzu-hsia [or K'ung Kuang] as a great scholar did not suffer on account of his conduct, nor was Chün-ch'ung [or Wang Yung] excluded from the "Bamboo Grove"[14] because of his. This is because they had both achieved great names, and the criticisms levelled against them were somewhat moderated.

But [on the other side of the ledger] we have the loyalty of Ch'ü Yüan, the vigilance and alertness of Tsou [Yang] and Mei [Sheng],[15] the perfect filial piety of Huang Hsiang,[16] and the reticent and retiring nature of Hsü Kan. So who can say that all writers have stained characters?

Man is endowed with five elemental abilities.[17] Not all men are equal in these gifts, and they do not put them to the same uses. Short of a sage of the first order, there is rarely anyone who can be perfect. However, generals and great ministers, on account of their high station, usually enjoy great fame, while writers, being lowly and humble in their official positions, easily become the object of criticism. For similar reasons, rivers and streams roll majestically along, while brooks and creeks have to struggle for every inch they cover. Now, just as there is a reason why some people are famous and others unknown, so there is a reason why some people are prosperous and others frustrated. The reason for giving an appointment to a scholar lies in his usefulness in

[14] The names of the "Seven Worthies of the Bamboo Grove" are listed in Liu I-ch'ing's *Shih-shuo hsin-yü*, chüan 5, Chapter 23 (Chu-tzu chi-ch'eng ed.), p. 188: Juan Chi, Hsi K'ang, Shan T'ao, Liu Ling, Juan Hsien, Hsiang Hsiu, and Wang Yung. Imbued with the spirit of *Tao*, they were mostly at odds with the way of the world, and sought to live their lives spontaneously as their impulses and feelings directed them.

[15] Tsou and Mei were sent to serve at the court of Prince Wu. When they discovered that the prince was entertaining rebellious intentions and would not listen to their remonstrances, they left Wu and went to Liang. See Tsou Yang's biography in the *Shih-chi*.

[16] See his biography in the *Hou-han-shu*.

[17] There are three different definitions of "wu-ts'ai" (five kinds of materials or elements): the first—metal, wood, leather, jade, and earth—is given in Cheng Hsüan's commentary to "K'ao-kung chi," the last section of the *Chou-li*. The second—metal, wood, water, fire, and earth—is given in the commentary to a line in the *Tso-chuan: T'ien sheng wu-ts'ai* ["Heaven produces the five elements"]. See *Ch'un-ch'iu ching-chuan yin-te*, 318/Hsiang 27/fu 2. The third—bravery, wisdom, benevolence, trustworthiness, and loyalty—is given in the *Liu-t'ao*, where these were quoted as qualities a general must possess. Liu Hsieh, in using this term *wu-ts'ai*, seems to be merely referring to the abilities of a man in general.

practical affairs. [Chi] Ching-chiang of Lu was just a woman of intelligence, but she had sense enough to infer from her weaving principles applicable to the management of a state.[18] How then can it be explained when a man who has made achievements in literature yet knows nothing about government? The reason Yang [Hsiung] and [Ssu-]ma [Hsiang-ju], for example, remained humble in station throughout their lives is that, although they exhibited great literary excellence, they lacked real content. Yü Yüan-kuei [or Yü Liang] of the Chin was a man of brilliant talent; but because he had achieved renown as a military general, his literary fame was eclipsed. If he had not been a great minister and general, he would have been known as a talented writer. But both the art of literature and the art of war fit in wherever there is talent. Hsi Hu, just because he was versed in the Classics, was appointed a military commander-in-chief.[19] When did he neglect military affairs because he loved literature? Sun Wu[-tzu's] work on military science [*Sun-tzu*] is written in a language as beautiful as pearls and jade. But when did he, because he was skilled in military arts, ignore literary excellence?

A man of virtue keeps his ability hidden, and waits for the right moment to act. One who aims at achievement in affairs of state should on the one hand strive for perfection in cultivating the excellence of the inner man and on the other be able to express this inner excellence externally in beautiful patterns. In other words he should have a nature like cedar and a trunk like camphor-laurel. His purpose in writing will be to control affairs of state; and when he is asked to shoulder heavy responsibilities, he will be as dependable as a pillar or a beam. When frustrated, he will cultivate his inner excellence in retirement and immortalize it in words; when in office, he will take advantage of the opportunity to achieve worldly success. Such a writer will meet the requirements set up for scholars in the "Tzu-ts'ai."[20]

18 See Liu Hsiang's *Lieh-nü chuan*, chüan 1, p. 12.
19 *Ch'un-ch'iu ching-chuan yin-te*, 130/Hsi 27/5 Tso.
20 See note 2 above.

The Tsan:

Observe the writers of the past:

Some have achieved perfection in both literary quality and moral virtue!

The fame of some of them rings out in Ch'u in the South,[21]

And the literary excellence of others shakes Liang in the North.[22]

If a writer has no capacity for practical affairs then, despite his laborious carving,

What good will his excellence be to people?

Literature should not only be an ornament for its creator,

But should serve also to glorify the state.

[21] Referring to Ch'ü Yüan and Chia I, according to Fan Wen-lan.
[22] Referring to Tsou Yang and Mei Sheng, according to Fan.

GLOSSARY

ai	lamented, or to lament	哀
chan	divination	占
chan	to spy or watch	覘
chang	a chapter	章
ch'en	to exhibit	陳
chi	register	籍
ch'i	contract	契
chieh	all	皆
chieh	to borrow	借
chieh	to tie a knot	結
chieh	to untie, or a record of a settlement	解
chih	ordinance	制
chih	a particle placed in the middle of a sentence to show a relationship between what precedes and what follows it	之
chih	to arrive	至

chi-hai she-ho   cross the river on the date of   己亥涉河
                 chi-hai

ch'ü   a ditty   曲

chuan   commentary, or to comment   傳

chuan   notice, including obituary   狀

chuan   to transfer   轉

chüan   bond   券

chung   middle, or norm   中

erh   a mid-particle to show a transition   而
                 or addition

fa   regulation   法

fang   prescription   方

feng   a satirical writing   諷

fou-chia   superficiality and untruth   浮假

fu   authenticity   孚

fu   a particle to initiate the ideas   夫
                 expressed

fu   tally   符

hsiang	sign, or signal	象
hsieh	humor, or jest	諧
hsing	nature	性
hsing	surname	姓
hsü	empty	虛
hu	an end particle, to express either a question or an exclamation	乎
i	appropriate	宜
i	ending	巳
i	an end particle, to indicate the completion of an idea	矣
i	a mid-particle to show instrumentality, reason, etc.	以
i	to adhere	依
i	to discuss	議
kai	a particle to introduce a fact or a general truth	蓋
kao	to inform	誥

ku	a conjunction to show a causal relation between the sentence it introduces and the previous one	故
kuan	pass, or credentials	關
lan	to peruse	覽
lieh	narrative account	列
lieh-feng yin-yü	strong wind and continuous rain	列風淫雨
ling	order	令
ling	topic	領
lu	record	錄
lu	a road	路
lu	stupid	魯
lü	law, or pitch pipe	律
lüeh	a précis	略
lun	to discourse	論
lun	to set in order	倫
lung	a short song	弄
mao	description	貌

ming	mandate	命
pei	stone monument	碑
pei	walled terrace	埤
pi	to close	閉
pieh-feng huai-yü	strange wind and torrential rain	別風淮雨
p'ien	a literary composition, or a book	篇
p'i-fu	one husband	匹夫
p'i-fu	one wife	匹婦
pu	to spread out	布
pu	warrant	簿
p'u	chronicle	譜
p'u	comprehensive	普
p'u	vegetable garden	圃
san shih tu-ho	three pigs cross the river	三豕渡河
shen chih tiao i	the spirits have arrived	神之弔矣
shen-hsia	great defect	深瑕

shih	historian	史
shih	formula	式
shih	situation, or condition, or contour	勢
shih	solid	實
shih	to employ	使
shih	to resolve	釋
shih	to take an oath, or military proclamation	誓
shu	operation	術
shu	sales slip	疏
shu	to bind or control	束
shuo	to speak, or to discuss	說
ssu	one of the two earthly branches	巳
ssu	similar	似
ta	to convey	達
t'i	body, substance, form, or genre	體
tiao	to condole	弔
tieh	memorandum	牒

tien	important document	典
tsai	an end particle, to express an exclamation	哉
ts'ai	to cut or tailor	裁
ts'ao	a piece of instrumental music	操
tse	principle	則
tui	to please	兌
tz'u	to pierce	刺
tz'u	*viva voce*	辭
wei	a particle to show a contrast to the idea in the previous sentence	惟
wei shih tso tse	to be the standard of the world	為世作則
wei shih tso tse	to be the thief of the world	為世作賊
wen	to inquire	問
Wu-tzu	five persons	五子
yao	a folk song sung without instrumental accompaniment	謠
yeh	an end particle, to indicate the conclusion of a sentence	也

yeh	a leaf	葉
yen	condolence	唁
yen	proverb	諺
yen	to talk	言
yin	enigma	讔
yin	prelude	引
yin	a sad chanting	吟
yin	to hide	隱
yü	a corner	偶
yü	fish	魚
yü	a mid-particle to express a relationship or comparison	於
yüeh	to please	悅
yung	a song	詠

INDEX